THE CUSTOMER REVOLUTION

Also by Patricia B. Seybold

Customers.com:
How to Create a Profitable Business Strategy for the Internet and Beyond

THE CUSTOMER REVOLUTION

How to Thrive When Customers Are in Control

PATRICIA B. SEYBOLD

with RONNI T. MARSHAK and JEFFREY M. LEWIS

RANDOM HOUSE
BUSINESS BOOKS

First published in the UK in 2001 by Random House Business Books,
Random House, 20 Vauxhall Bridge Road, London SW1V 2SA

Random House Australia (Pty) Limited
20 Alfred Street, Milsons Point,
Sydney, New South Wales 2061, Australia

Random House New Zealand Limited
18 Poland Road, Glenfield,
Auckland 10, New Zealand

Random House (Pty) Limited
Endulini, 5a Jubilee Road, Parktown 2193, South Africa

The Random House Group Limited Reg. No. 954009

Papers used by Random House are natural, recyclable products made from wood grown in sustainable forests. The manufacturing processes conform to the environmental regulations of the country of origin.

ISBN 0 7126 6984 1

www.randomhouse.co.uk
businessbooks@randomhouse.co.uk

Printed and bound in Great Britain by
Biddles Ltd, Guildford and King's Lynn

Dedicated to:

My mother, Gertrude B. Seybold, whose energy, good humor, love, encouragement, and proactive helpfulness have set an example I'm still trying to live up to!

And to:

My exuberant, obnoxious, and much beloved dog, Sean, who understands that it takes a dog to write a book.

Acknowledgments

This book could never have been written without the major contributions of several people and the unstinting support of my entire company, the Patricia Seybold Group.

Special thanks go to:

- Manny Sodbinow, who is the architect and promulgator of our Customer Flight Deck℠ charting practice.
- Susan Lane, our company president, who gave me the freedom to research and write while keeping our customers' concerns front and center.
- Priscilla Chura, our EVP of finance and administration, who helped me refine the Customer Value discussion.
- Sue Aldrich, our Customers.com® consulting practice director, who contributed her expertise in monitoring the end-to-end quality of customer experience.
- Jayne Miller, my able Research Associate, who set up countless interviews, dug for details, spotted trends, and really "got it!"
- Laurinda O'Connor, who did all the illustrations, Fanny Wong and Jane Patrick, our able quality control team, and Jackie Duffy, who spent countless hours verifying facts and coordinating with the case study providers.
- Ronni Marshak and Jeff Lewis, my co-authors and cheerleaders, who supported me every step of the way.

Contents

Preface

Why does the customer revolution matter to you and your business? Every industry is under siege by its customers. The Napster phenomenon was not an isolated incident. Renegade customers in the music industry created demands that the major industry players couldn't ignore. The Napster revolt wasn't just about copyright infringement; it was about letting customers have it *their* way. All the music labels have now capitulated to making digital music available for electronic downloads. The producers and suppliers in the music industry spent all of 2000 scrambling to react to renegade customers' actions. The suppliers and retailers surrendered to customers' desires to have access to digital music files, and to be able to mix and match tracks of music and to manage their own music collections.

What happened in the music industry is happening in your industry. It may not be as dramatic or as obvious. But there's definitely a radical movement afoot. Customers are wresting control away from suppliers and dictating the new business practices for the digital age.

This book is your survival guide. By reading up on what to expect as customers demand unthinkable changes in your industry—changes that will radically transform the way your business operates—you'll be prepared. Not only that, but you'll be forewarned and forearmed with the best practices that will make it possible for your firm to surrender gracefully to its customers and to win their current and future loyalty.

In short, in these pages, you'll learn how to not only survive, but to thrive in the new customer-driven economy. In fact, you'll gain new insights into the mechanisms for value-creation in the customer economy.

How do you assess the current and future value of a company in today's turbulent economy? That's one of the questions that led me to research and write this book. As I watched NASDAQ stock prices plummet in March 2000, triggering a flight of capital away from Internet and technology companies, I sensed that investors wouldn't permanently abandon Internet, high tech, and telecommunications stocks. But what investors were doing was demanding an accounting for the unreasonably high valuations that had been promoted by the investment banking and venture capital communities. As the year 2000 drew to a close, economic growth in the U.S. economy had declined dramatically from its exuberant 5 percent level. Much of that decline was caused by a crisis in consumer confidence. When a portion of your retirement income is invested in equities whose value has diminished by 30 percent over the past nine months, of course you become wary about spending more money! Consumers stopped over-consuming and tightened their belts. Companies scaled back on their capital investments. They pared down inventory. They reprioritized projects.

I believe that the hype that led to the over-valuing of Internet and high tech companies came from a fundamental misunderstanding of the basis of value in the current economy. Companies are valued based on their future earnings potential. Where do companies' earnings come from? From customers. To increase your earnings potential, you need to focus on winning and retaining profitable customers whose needs you're serving. It's as simple as that.

In 2001, as investment analysts refocus on the fundamental drivers of value and begin to regain confidence in technology-leaders, I hope they'll add some new reality checks to their value assessments. I'm suggesting that we all begin valuing companies more explicitly on their customer franchise—the value of the earnings they'll receive from their current and future customers. This isn't just a "back to basics" suggestion. It's also a prediction: Your company's value will be determined by the strength of your customer franchise. Investors have a right to know how many customers you have, how much you're earning per customer, how well you're treating your customers, and how fast you're growing the value of your customer franchise.

What I discovered in researching and writing this book is that there are many companies in the world that have been single-mindedly focusing on customer value and on improving the total customer experience for a number of years. These are the companies that are well-positioned to thrive in the current customer economy. In the ensuing pages, you'll read in detail about the current best practices these firms employ to build, monitor, and sustain value.

Why are customers more important than ever? What's different today? Over the past four years, a subtle shift has been underway around the world. Economic power has shifted from suppliers to customers. Why? Thanks to the Internet, the Web, and to other ubiquitous technologies, customers now have access to information that lets them make much more informed decisions. They are no longer willing to be "locked in" to suppliers who don't value their time or their patronage. Customers are now in control. Customers' actions and their demands are profoundly impacting every industry.

What does the customer revolution mean to your business? Ignore it at your peril! Your customers and prospective customers will be more demanding than ever. In order to meet their needs, you're going to need to master a new set of competencies. You'll need to learn how to redesign your business based on customers' scenarios. You'll need to measure what matters to customers. You'll need to monitor, in near real-time, all of the business events that matter most to your customers through your entire value chain. And, you'll need to manage your company by and for customer value. That's a tall order. Let's get started!

January 2001

THE CUSTOMER REVOLUTION

1

EMBRACE THE CUSTOMER REVOLUTION AND THRIVE IN THE CUSTOMER ECONOMY

Fasten your seatbelts! The turbulence you've been experiencing in the stock market isn't over yet. In fact, it's probably going to get worse.

Why? Because we're in the midst of a profound revolution. And it's bigger than an Internet revolution or a mobile wireless revolution. It's a *customer* revolution.

Customers have taken control of our companies' destinies. Customers are transforming our industries. And customers' loyalty—or lack thereof—has become increasingly important to executives and investors alike. If you try to understand the ups and downs of the current economy by focusing on technology trends and investment fads, you're going to miss the true underlying shift that's underway. Customers are in control. They're changing the face of business as we know it. And your company's value is in their hands. Your customer franchise has suddenly become the scarcest and the most crucial resource for your business.

What's more, your company is probably at risk. Unless you act now to focus on the quality and consistency of the customer experience you offer, your firm will be hopelessly lost in the turbulence. Other companies—like the ones described in this book—have quietly reorganized themselves to manage by and for customer value. They measure and monitor what matters most to customers. If you continue to operate your business using the metrics of the old economy, you're going to be left standing on the ground as your competitors take off in the customer economy.

Listen to the Beat of the Customer Revolution

Over the past year, executives in a variety of industries have begun to feel the impact of the customer revolution. Let's listen to their stories:

- Arne Frager is the president of The Plant, a professional music recording studio in Sausalito, California. Arne's been in the music business for twenty-seven years and he's never seen the flow of new music dry up before:

> "My recording business is off 50 percent. The whole music recording business is off 50 percent this year (2000). About half the revenues in our industry come from new acts. But the big record labels are so paralyzed by the MP3/Napster/Gnutella/Freenet free distribution of digital music that they're not signing any new acts! Without the labels paying for the production of new albums, our studio isn't recording."

Customers, taking matters into their own hands, have profoundly altered the landscape of the music industry.

- Brennan Mulligan is president of Timbuk2 Designs, a U.S.-based manufacturer of backpacks and messenger bags:

> "Customers love the ability to custom-design their backpacks. But there's just no way to convince retailers to take custom orders in their stores. They can't handle one-off products. So we'll go direct to the customer and do it on the Internet. Customers can design their own backpacks, we'll ship them out the next day, and if the retailers want to participate we'll set up shop on their Web sites and put kiosks in their stores, too!"

Customers want capabilities that retailers haven't been able to offer. Now manufacturers are responding to customers' desires.

- Gideon Sasson, executive vice president of Electronic Brokerage, Charles Schwab & Co.:

> "Before the Internet, companies used to talk about how to lock the customer in. They thought about how to 'own' the customer. They incented customers. They brought them in, and then they worried about, 'How do I make a profit with these customers' and 'How do I get them to buy this product.' But companies can't afford to think that way any more. Even before the Internet, at Schwab we realized that if we do the right thing for our customers, they'll reward us. But other companies are facing a rude awakening. Before the Internet, companies could be customer-aware, but they didn't have to be customer-centric. Now they have no other choice. The Internet is forcing everyone to behave differently. What the Internet did was to move control to the customers' hands. People say, 'Your customers are only a mouse-click away from the competition.' Actually, the more important fact is that they're only a mouse-click away from other customers who will give them the real skinny!"

Customers are no longer willing to be locked in. They want great service, fair prices, and innovative offerings. If they don't get these, they'll go elsewhere, and they'll tell the world.

Sweet Surrender

You're no longer in control of your company's destiny. Your customers are. Thanks to the Internet and to mobile wireless devices, customers are now armed with new, more convenient tools with which to access our businesses (as well as those of our competitors) around the clock and around the globe. Business and consumer customers are challenging and disrupting the standard practices in virtually every industry. They're demanding that we change our pricing structures, our distribution channels, and the way we design and deliver our products and services to them. They won't be denied. They have the power and they know it. Companies that don't "get it" will be out of business soon.

Like most revolutions, this can't be stopped. We can't turn our backs on it. We have no choice but to surrender gracefully. Customers have always been the raison d'être for businesses. But now, for the first time in the history of modern business, we have the wherewithal to detect customers' needs in near-real time and to adapt quickly to their changing desires. Using the Internet, we can now reach out to new customer segments to test new offerings, innovate, and experiment more rapidly than ever before. Using the power of the 'Net, customers are inventing and refining new business models, including peer-to-peer file-sharing (Napster), open-source design communities (Linux), and self-policing marketplaces (eBay). Instead of resisting these customer-led business models, we need to embrace and extend them.

Surrendering to the customer revolution is a winning proposition. Our employees *want* to be customer-focused. Customer-centric companies have a much easier time attracting and retaining employees because companies that have a strong, unwavering customer-focused culture are much more fun to work in than those with warring, product-centric fiefdoms. It's much easier to make budget decisions based on customer priorities than it is to argue over product-centric goals and objectives. What's more, the companies that focus on building and sustaining relationships with customers are the most profitable companies in the world.

WELCOME TO THE CUSTOMER ECONOMY

This new customer economy is also spurring a new way of measuring company valuation. We have historically measured businesses on their use of investment capital, primarily through their return on fixed capital assets. High stock prices went to firms that extracted the most profit and growth from tangible assets or that owned the most valuable assets. Most general managers cut their teeth on such primary management indicators as profit and loss (P&L), return on assets (ROA), return on investment (ROI), return on capital employed (ROCE), and price-earnings (P/E) ratios. These performance disciplines are well established and important. Ignore them at your peril! Yet management is the art of the best use of scarce resources. Investment capital is no longer our scarcest resource.

In the customer economy, loyal customers have become the most precious commodity. Today the hardest thing for a company to acquire is not investment capital, products, employees, or even a brand. It's customer loyalty. Customer relationships are the fundamental source of value in the new customer economy. Customer capital is now at least as important as investment capital. And the value of your present and future customer relationships—your customer franchise—will determine the value of your company.

Managing By and For Customer Value

The seismic impact of this customer revolution is being registered by the world's stock markets. If you look below the surface to distinguish those stocks that are doing well from those that are languishing, you'll discover something important: the most highly valued companies are managing themselves by and for customer value.

Investors and financial analysts may not yet have articulated the importance of customer metrics for the companies they follow, but the executives who are running these companies know how important their customer relationships are to their future earnings.

It's customer metrics that matter to companies like Charles Schwab and Cisco Systems, not just P&L. Schwab and Cisco have consistently delivered revenue growth, after-tax profits, and return on equity year after year. They're examples of the many companies you'll be reading about in the following chapters that watch their bottom lines but run on customer metrics. In fact, that may be the most surprising finding in the research behind this book. The measurement systems that leading consumer-oriented and business-to-business companies are using to manage their businesses internally have shifted. If you ask them, you'll discover that the real leaders in today's economy run their businesses based on things like customer retention, customer satisfaction, growth in the number of customers, growth of customers' spending, and the predictors of customer defection. These metrics have become the major focus for weekly and monthly management meetings.

Look at Cisco's CEO, John Chambers. John spends 80 percent of his time in conversations with customers. Through speeches, visits, phone calls, executive briefings, and strategy sessions, he is taking the pulse of his customers constantly. He also personally reviews the interactions Cisco has had with its top customers every day. And he requires every Cisco executive to spend 50 percent of his or her time face-to-face with customers. Whether you're the CIO or the CFO, you aren't doing your job at Cisco if you aren't spending time talking with customers. Every Cisco employee knows what customer satisfaction goal she needs to beat in order to make her bonus—she walks around with that number in her head (and on her badge) every day. This approach really works. Every year Cisco's employees beat their customer satisfaction goal and set a higher goal for the next year.

The leaders in the customer economy understand that a laser-focused, customer-driven culture combined with a few key customer metrics are driving their revenues, their shareholder value, and their long-term profitability. Do you?

HOW TO SURVIVE THIS PROFOUND REVOLUTION

What should your company be doing to ensure that it will survive and even thrive in the customer revolution? How should you guide your business through the turbulence ahead? The first thing to recognize is that this revolution doesn't pertain only to e-businesses. Every business is now an e-business. Virtually every business on the planet now has ways for customers and suppliers to interact electronically. Second, you need to realize that there are no e-customers, only customers. At some point in time, every business or consumer customer may need to interact in different ways—by talking to knowledgeable people, interacting with your retailers, sending an email, picking up the phone, transacting via a hand-held device, or doing business online. Third, you need to be prepared to adopt new, dynamic partnering relationships as customers' needs present new challenges and priorities. Fourth, be prepared to participate in customer-led, self-organizing communities and to respond flexibly as customers' behaviors reshape the practices in your industry.

Master the Basics

In our last book, *Customers.com,* we introduced the mantra *"make it easy for customers to do business with you."* That phrase has become the rallying cry for businesses and organizations all over the world. Forward-thinking companies have been harnessing the Internet, the Web, and other customer-convenient technologies—like mobile phones and wireless hand-held electronic gadgets—to make it easier for customers to do business with them. These companies are the ones poised to thrive in the customer economy, not just because they've implemented customer self-service strategies but, more fundamentally, because their corporate strategies are now being driven by customers.

Companies that have already adopted the eight critical success factors outlined in *Customers.com* have an advantage over those that are just beginning their transition to a customer-centric business model. They're much further along on the customer technology learning curve. Their customers are more satisfied and more loyal, and they've continued to refine their ability to measure and enhance the things that matter to customers.

Focus on Customer Relationships

The mantra for this book is *"customer relationships count."* Customer relationships are going to start counting for your business in a way they never have before. Investors are going to start asking you to divulge your customer numbers such as how many customers you have, how long you've been in active relationship with each one, how you're growing earnings per customer, how much it costs you to acquire a new customer, and how well you're able to retain customers. In short, they're going to want to know how well you're growing the value of your customer franchise.

Product-centric companies are now scrambling to become customer-focused. Every company we've studied in researching this book either already has or is putting in place a comprehensive Customer Relationship Management (CRM) information system and strategy. Blue-chip, product-focused companies (such as IBM, General Electric, 3M, Royal Dutch Shell, Merck & Co., and Intel) that concentrated on R&D, innovation, growth, and operational excellence are now also wrapping their arms around their end customers, finding out who they are, and building relationships with them. Retailers such as Gap and Tesco—which always focused on increasing sales and profits per square foot—are now focused on increasing profits per customer. New Internet-enabled businesses—such as eBay, which began life as a consumer-to-consumer auction site, and Buzzsaw, a building construction management site—are intent on turning every supplier into a customer and every customer into a supplier and then leveraging the network effect to bring more customers-cum-suppliers into their folds.

Monitor and Improve Customers' Experiences (in Near-Real Time)

Eyeballs aren't the basis of currency in the customer economy; hearts and minds are. You build relationships through experiences. Customers have experiences—good or bad—with your brand. They may interact with your Web site, pick up the phone, see an ad, use one of your products, and interact with one of your dealers. Each time they do so, those customers or prospects are encountering the customer experience associated with your brand. Each of those experiences either cements or undermines customers' trust. Relationships are built on trust. The companies that will thrive in the customer economy understand how to build and maintain customers' trust by carefully managing customers' experiences with their brands.

For the first time in the history of modern business, it's now cost-effective for companies to establish relationships with each and every customer who wants us to know him. Thanks to the wealth of modern technologies that we can use to interact with customers and to capture information from those interactions, it's possible for us to avoid alienating customers by streamlining their dealings with us. By carefully monitoring the quality of customers' experiences as they attempt to interact with our firms and our partners, we can continuously improve those customers' experiences in dealing with our brands, our products, and our firms. The real masters of the customer experience game don't rely on monthly or even weekly reports to tell them how they're doing. They walk around with pagers that give them alerts when customers' needs aren't being met. They proactively monitor many of the processes that impact customers—delayed flights, low inventory, time-on-hold, and Web site performance.

Let Customers Dictate Your Business Direction

Customers will drive your business. It's time to embrace that fact, surrender to it, and get really good at anticipating both existing and new sets of customer needs. Customers will tell you how they want to interact with your company and its products. They'll tell you when you need to sell direct and when they want the convenience of using dealers, retailers, or independent agents. They'll insist that you have a Web site and that you answer the phone and talk to them. They'll demand that the employees in your stores be intimately familiar with the workings of your Web site. They'll urge you to offer mobile wireless access for the tasks they need to perform. They'll require that your products be sold through the e-markets they prefer to use. And they'll challenge any business policies or practices that they consider to be unfair.

Learn from the Veterans of the Customer Revolution

We've been studying some two dozen businesses around the world that clearly understand how to not only survive but thrive in the face of the customer revolution. Some are business-to-consumer companies; others are business-to-business players. They run the gamut of industries, including telecommunications, healthcare, retail, and manufacturing. Whether tiny company or massive conglomerate, they all have something in common: they've learned how to thrive in the customer economy by wholeheartedly embracing customers' needs and letting customers lead them toward a mutually profitable future. We'll tell you their stories and highlight the principles they've adopted. Whether your organization is a large existing company, a mid-sized bricks-and-mortar firm, a small conventional business, a dot-com subsidiary of a preexisting firm, or a struggling dot-com start-up, our goal is to prepare you for the revolution that's underway and to arm you with the tools you'll need to survive—and perhaps even lead—the transformation of your industry.

Whether you're a manager, executive, business professional, or information technology specialist, you'll gain valuable insights into where your world is going and why. You'll discover and/or reaffirm what you can do to ensure that your company will succeed. If you're an investor (and who isn't these days), you'll soon be able to spot the customer-led companies. They're the ones that will continue to lead the pack, to innovate by cannibalizing or challenging their existing business models, and to reinvent their industries.

MASTER THE THREE PRINCIPLES OF THE CUSTOMER ECONOMY

There are three principles underpinning the shift to the customer economy: 1) Customers are in control and they're reshaping businesses and transforming industries; 2) Customer relationships count, therefore the value of your present and future customer relationships—your customer franchise—will determine the value of your company; and 3) Customer experience matters, therefore the feelings customers have when they interact with your brand determines their loyalty. In the first three parts of this book, we elaborate on these three principles in detail and suggest ways that you can formulate strategies based on a deeper understanding of these underlying principles. In the fourth part, we introduce an operational framework you can use to ensure that your company will thrive in the customer economy, along with detailed case studies of a number of companies that are beginning to follow the steps we've outlined.

Here's a brief overview to whet your appetite.

Principle #1: Customers Are in Control—
They're Reshaping Businesses and Transforming Industries

Why are customers controlling our businesses now more than ever? Blame the Internet and the Web! Today's customers know they can go online and find out about our companies and our offerings. They expect to be able to do research, buy our products, and/or get service via the 'Net. They want to interact with our products and services—break them apart, recombine them, customize them, and deploy them—without expending much time or effort. And increasingly, customers are also being offered wireless data access to their account information and to a broad array of convenient services, from shipment tracking to online auctions. Customers interact with our businesses and organizations electronically, making demands and suggesting improvements twenty-four hours a day.

Customers—both consumers and business customers—are taking control. They're voting with their loyalty. They will no longer tolerate being treated as if they weren't important. They now know how much clout they have. They refuse to do business with companies that don't respect their time; time is the scarcest resource our customers have.

So what else is new? Haven't businesses always been customer-centric? Aren't there other, more fundamental principles that really drive major economic shifts? Won't dramatic breakthroughs in science and technology have a more profound impact on the future of business than the way we treat our customers? Maybe this customer revolution is akin to the total quality movement; being customer-centric is a necessary foundation for businesses to embrace, but it's not a profoundly revolutionary concept.

I beg to differ. Gone are the days:

- When you simply made and sold products. Now you need to attract and retain customers.
- When you grew revenues by adding more and more products and companies to your portfolio. Now you need to build flexible, dynamic capabilities for designing and delivering new value-added services to customers.
- When you were measured by year-over-year revenue growth and hefty profit margins. Now you *also* need to show growth in customer value and customer yield.
- When investors valued your ability to offer vertically integrated products with captive capacity and control over margins. Now you're rewarded on your ability to partner flexibly with others and jointly develop and produce products at competitive prices and with dependable quality.

Customers now expect us to harness information technology to make life more convenient for them. Yet once we've electronically linked our customers to the core of our businesses, something very profound happens: customers start to transform our businesses! Product pricing changes, development priorities shift, distribution models are altered, and business strategies are impacted. And once one business begins this customer-driven transformation, other businesses in the same industry have little choice but to join in. The result is that every industry is now in a state of customer-led transformation.

What's different now, in the twenty-first century, is that for the first time in the history of modern business, customers have the tools—the Internet, mobile networked devices, and flexible, dynamically interconnectable applications—to reconfigure their relationships with our businesses quickly and easily. Here's a quick litany of some of the ways that customers have taken control and are reshaping our businesses and transforming our industries:

- *In the past*. . . providers of intangible goods—information, software, music, entertainment, services—could reap high profit margins due to low cost of goods sold (after the creation of the first instance).

  - *Today* . . . customers demand to freely share and reuse digital goods, paying once (or not at all) and then altering, distributing, and repurposing the original material.

- *In the past* . . . banks, brokerages, and insurance companies counted on customers' inertia. The switching costs were high to move accounts from one firm to another.
  - *Today* . . . customers can easily move their financial records and their relationships.

- *In the past* . . . pricing for products and services could vary dramatically from one country to another, and pricing was so complex (particularly in the business-to-business realm) that it was difficult to compare the real costs of doing business with one firm over another.
  - *Today* . . . pricing is much more transparent; customers are demanding equal prices around the globe, and they now have much more information at their fingertips to allow them to compare prices. In many industries, customers are already dictating prices to their suppliers.

- *In the past* . . . manufacturers could give lip service to designing and configuring products for customers.
  - *Today* . . . manufacturers have the tools to make custom-manufacturing cost-effective and practical. Customers are voting with their feet and flocking to suppliers that offer them customized products and services.

- *In the past* . . . one could only imagine online marketplaces where buyers and sellers could efficiently find one another and transact business.
  - *Today* . . . those e-markets exist with customers' building projects, medical records, systems configurations, and/or inventory at their core. Customers' projects, processes, and supply needs are now the magnets that draw suppliers to compete and cooperate in dynamic e-market spaces.

You may believe that your industry is unlikely to be blown apart and reconstituted around customer drivers in the near future. Or maybe you believe that it has already happened. Your company has responded, and the danger is over. Of course, both points of view are dangerous. The leaders in the customer economy are constantly looking at other industries for examples of new, customer-driven practices they can adopt before someone else in their industry does.

Principle #2: Customer Relationships Count—

The Value of Your Present and Future Customer Relationships—Your Customer Franchise—Will Determine the Value of Your Company

What does the stock market care about? Investors are betting on your future earnings. Where do your future earnings come from? Your customers. Therefore in today's extremely volatile stock market, there are only two things that investors can count on: the breadth and depth of your relationships with your customers and your commitment to sustaining and growing those relationships for as long as possible. This is your customer capital. Customer capital is the sum of the value of all customer relationships—the number of customer relationships you have, the depth and quality of those relationships in terms of their capacity to generate current and future earnings, the duration of those relationships (your customer retention), and the profitability of those relationships.

Every company you'll find chronicled in this book has two sets of numbers: the set it reports to the financial community and the one it actually runs its business on. The standard financial indicators still matter. They're indicators of past performance, such as how fast did we grow, how much money did we make, and how much cash did we burn.

But all of these companies are also using other measures to drive their business. They monitor customer satisfaction very carefully. They look at customer retention rates, share of customers' wallets, and customer loyalty indicators, and they gather and analyze customer behavior information to understand which customers will be the most profitable ones over the long term. Even companies that are not in so-called customer-facing businesses, like pharmaceutical companies and oil and gas exploration companies, are discovering the importance of measuring customers' present and future patronage as a key indicator of their future health.

It all comes down to relationships. What's the quality of the relationships the company has with its customers? Are they deep or shallow? Will those customers remain loyal over time? Will they increase their dealings with the company or will they jump quickly to a competitive offering? Since customers now have more choice and more control, building deep relationships with customers is really the only guarantee of future earnings so long as you can maintain their trust and continue to deliver value through innovation.

After analyzing all the ways that today's leading companies are predicting and ensuring their earnings growth by focusing on the quality of their customer relationships, we suggest a new indicator that we'd like to see join Return on Equity and Return on Assets in investors' reports: a Customer Value Index. We believe that companies' earnings statements should provide investors with an average profit per customer as well as reporting the growth in the number of active customers, the current retention rate for customers, and the profits per customer from year to year. This additional financial reporting would enable investors to make their own judgments about what they think the future value of that company's customer franchise might be.

Principle #3: Customer Experience Matters—
The Feelings Customers Have When They Interact with Your Brand Determine Their Loyalty

Your customers are in the pilot's seat. They control the future of your business, both its course and its value. How do you ensure that your customers remain loyal, that you have a mutually profitable relationship, and that they don't lead your company in an unprofitable or nonviable direction? By establishing and sustaining a strong customer experience that your customers love.

Customer loyalty is rooted in experiences—the experiences that each customer has in learning about, acquiring, using, and sharing your products and services with others. Customer experience is the essence of any brand. There's a lot more to branding than a logo or a consistent graphical treatment. Your customer's experience with your brand includes how that customer *feels* when he is in your brand's presence, whether he's on the phone with you, in your physical storefront, on your Web site, reading an email you sent, or using your product.

Today's business leaders understand that a key to success is building and sustaining a brand presence that delivers consistent value, resonates with the customer, makes her want to come back for more, and prompts her to tell her friends and colleagues about it. A satisfying customer experience is one of the most important elements in building a loyal customer, a customer who is loath to change her habits. Yet customers have become much more demanding. They now expect us to deliver a consistent branded experience whether they are interacting with our company directly or through a distribution channel (i.e., via an independent retailer, reseller, dealer, or broker). Customers want a high-quality, predictable experience combined with high-value products and services.

Whenever we interact with a new client, we ask the question, "Who in this company owns the customer experience?" Usually we receive baffled looks. Sometimes the answer is, "That's Anne, the head of customer service." Sometimes the answer is, "We all do." Neither of those answers is the right one, in my opinion. Sometimes that's the best you can do. But it won't ensure that your flight will have a smooth landing in today's customer economy.

In our opinion there needs to be one high-level executive—at the EVP or GM level—who owns the total customer experience for your company across all interaction touchpoints, all distribution channels, all functions, and all products and services. At Hewlett-Packard, for example, there's a senior executive in charge of the total customer experience for each of the company's two customer-facing divisions—Consumer and Business. These EVPs report directly to the presidents of their respective divisions. This isn't a marketing or a customer service job; it's a rubber-meets-the-road customer metrics and continuous-improvement job.

Your Total Customer Experience EVP should discover what outcomes each customer segment considers successful for each of the key scenarios they're engaged in when dealing with your firm and its partners. For American Airlines' Executive Platinum members, success is measured by avoiding disruptions to their travel schedules. For Cisco's small business accounts, it's receiving the properly configured system from their distributor in a timely fashion. For HP's printer customers, it's never having to think about ordering supplies (the printer does it for you). For National Semiconductor's design engineer customers, it's the ability to design, simulate, test, and buy the circuitry for a complete power supply assembly online in three hours instead of three weeks. For each of these Customer Scenarios, you'll want to monitor in near-real time how your company, its systems, and its partners are doing in fulfilling customers' expectations.

Don't limit yourself to measuring conversion rates, click-throughs and orders on your Web site, and time-on-hold in your call centers. Worry, too, about things like "one-touch" problem resolution and accurate, real-time inventory availability. Start monitoring your customers' experience in interacting with your firm, its systems, and its partners. In short, don't be content to install a CRM system. That will help you identify and interact with your customers. Once that's in place, you need to keep them happy. The companies that are doing the best job of monitoring and proactively improving customers' experience are monitoring, measuring, and adjusting every day all day. Are you?

AN OPERATIONAL FRAMEWORK:

MEASURE CUSTOMER VALUE, MONITOR WHAT MATTERS TO CUSTOMERS, AND DELIVER A GREAT TOTAL CUSTOMER EXPERIENCE

How do you measure the right stuff? If you believe as we do that the value of your company is inextricably linked to the value of your customer relationships, you may want to improve the way you measure your progress in acquiring customers, retaining customers, building strong customer relationships, and improving long-term profitability per customer and account. And if you agree with us that customer experience has a great deal to do with customer loyalty, you're going to want to improve the accuracy with which you monitor the end-to-end customer experience across channels and touchpoints. We've taken the liberty of designing an instrument panel for you. We call it a "Customer Flight Deck."

Implement a Customer Flight Deck

Why the airplane metaphor? Many business leaders have told us that running a business in today's Internet-enabled era is like trying to fly a plane at the same time that you're replacing the engine. If you're flying a plane into the turbulent air of the customer economy, you'll need an appropriate flight deck.

What's the difference between a Customer Flight Deck and a Balanced Scorecard? For the sake of simplicity and focus, the Customer Flight Deck only measures the things that impact customer value and customer experience. It doesn't replace the need for a broader set of measures. It's simply an easy way to gain more visibility into the end-to-end business processes that cross organizational boundaries and impact customers' experience. We refer to these customer-driven business processes as Customer Scenarios and to the Internet-enabled ecosystem that supports them as Customer Scenario Nets.

Of course, there's no single flight deck for any company. Each employee, business partner, or supplier needs her own set of instruments linked to the overall customer value and experience goals. The things that matter to customers—such as on-time delivery, accurate bills, and proactive customer care—will ripple through your organization and through your Customer Scenario Nets. Each company's Flight Deck needs to monitor the customers' activities and outcomes across this network of interlinked players and services.

One of the most profound yet subtle transformations underway is the impact of near-real-time metrics on our businesses. As more and more companies shift to Internet-based infrastructures and link up electronically with their customers and their business partners, they gain the ability to monitor and measure their company's trajectories. Many of the companies chronicled in these pages have a set of core metrics they monitor on a weekly, daily, and sometimes even hourly basis.

But what should you be measuring? Which metrics make sense? Throughout this book you'll find our suggestions for what you should be monitoring based on the best practices we've observed to date. On the Web site that complements this book, http://www.customer-revolution.net, you'll find our latest thinking about creating Customer Flight Decks, the instrumentation you'll need to thrive in the customer economy.

Thirteen Case Studies

Of course, the devil's in the details. That's why we provide a set of case studies so that you can learn from what others are doing as they focus on delivering a great total customer experience and evolving their businesses to respond to customers. Most of the companies we selected are ones that already have brands with which you may be familiar, such as GM Vauxhall, Charles Schwab, W. W. Grainger, National Semiconductor, Hewlett-Packard, Snap-on, and Tesco. Others may be less familiar to you, such as Finland's largest native bank, Okobank Group; an apparel manufacturer, Timbuk2 Designs; a wireless services provider in Hong Kong, Sunday; a British financial services company, Egg; and two new digital marketplaces, one for building construction, Buzzsaw, and one for medical information and healthcare, Medscape. Throughout the book you'll also find lots of other anecdotal examples.

Eight Steps to Deliver a Great Total Customer Experience

What are these companies doing right? We've distilled the best practices we've found—from these cases and the many others we've researched over the past six years—into a new set of core competencies for you to understand and master. These are the eight key ingredients that seem to constitute the "secret sauce" for the companies that are doing a good job in navigating the customer economy. These eight steps don't replace the eight critical success factors introduced in our first book, *Customers.com.* Instead, they provide an additional drill-down and set of how-to's for those of you who are serious about delivering a great customer experience.

Develop Your Flight Plans for the Customer Economy

There's a lot of detailed information contained in these pages. You'll want to move fast. I've provided a set of brief guidelines to help you chart your journey. On our Web site you'll find more detailed flight planning information and some pre-flight checklists for business executives and technologists.

Finally, let us help you get started on designing your own Customer Flight Deck. You can start with the generic model we provide and customize it to suit your own business. Share your ideas with your colleagues. Invite them to build their own customized Customer Flight

Decks. If you decide you want to implement a Customer Flight Deck "for real," linked to your key operational systems, we'll be glad to help.[1]

Remember, our goal is to help you survive the customer revolution and to thrive in the customer economy. We care about your success in building and sustaining customer value. We care passionately about your customers' outcomes and the quality of the experience they have along the way.

Have a great flight!

---

[1] With your active participation in our Customer Flight Deck℠ Charting Session in conjunction with our Customer Scenarios℠ Mapping Sessions, we can help you take the strategic first steps that will let you "instrument" your business to measure customer value and monitor what matters to customers. We invite you to visit our Web site at http://www.customerrevolution.net for more information.

Principle #1

CUSTOMERS ARE IN CONTROL

They're Reshaping Businesses and Transforming Industries

2

WHAT HAPPENED IN THE MUSIC INDUSTRY WILL HAPPEN TO YOU

What happens when customers actually take control of an industry and reshape it? The recent transformation of the worldwide music industry provides a good example. What can we learn from the music industry that would apply to other industries coming under siege as customers take control? Here are some thoughts that may be useful for companies in any industry:

- Notice how customers use your products and services, then figure out how to make it easier for them to do so. Adjust your practices and pricing to support the ways in which customers want to use your products.
- Watch the renegades and early adopters carefully. They'll lead the way and show you how your business practices will be changing shortly.
- Once you discover what customers may be doing with your products and services in a clumsy or slightly difficult way, figure out how you can streamline that process for them, thus gaining their loyalty and allegiance in exchange for increased convenience.
- Customers want to take ownership and control over the products and services they purchase and use. By offering them services

that make it easy for them to better manage their assets, you'll build closer relationships with them.

- Many customers also want to "strut their stuff." Think about how your products and services can make your customers look good. Give them ways to amplify that experience.

Caught in the Crossfire

When Arne (pronounced Arnie) Frager was a teenager in the 1960s, he knew he wanted to be a professional musician. Being prudent, he got a degree in electrical engineering from Case Institute and went to work at Adage selling analog-to-digital converters. But his dream didn't fade. Arne got a band together and took the plunge. He left the world of high tech (for good, he thought) and made the transition back to his first love: the music business. To make ends meet, he rented space and built and ran a recording studio. Sadly, the band didn't make it. But Arne had parlayed his technical expertise and his ear for music into a new career; he became a recording engineer. Now he could at least hang out with musicians all night long. By the mid-1970s, Arne had launched one of the world's first digital recording studios in Venice, California. During the '70s and '80s, he was the recording engineer for a number of industry greats, including Paul McCartney and John Lee Hooker.

In 1988 Arne moved to Sausalito, California, and took ownership of The Plant, a legendary recording studio near San Francisco. Originally christened in 1972 by John Lennon and Yoko Ono (who arrived at the opening Halloween party dressed as trees), The Plant has given birth to major albums by artists such as the Rolling Stones; Aretha Franklin; Stevie Wonder; Crosby, Stills, and Nash; Fleetwood Mac; Jefferson Starship; Van Morrison; John Fogerty; and Prince. The Plant's more recent clients include Metallica, Chris Isaak, and the Dave Matthews Band.

The Plant is a rustic-looking, sky-lit, rambling, redwood building one block away from the waterfront in Sausalito—a short ferry ride from San Francisco. I walked down the maze of hallways, passing private lounge areas with kitchens and living rooms, and into the newest mixing room, dubbed the Garden, a state-of-the-art, elliptical surround-sound control room. The heavy metal band Metallica had been the Garden's most recent tenants. Serious musicians typically spend months working here and living on the houseboats anchored nearby.

THE DAY THE MUSIC DIED

I should have been feeling the energy pulsating from The Plant's four soundproofed digital studios. But many of the studios were silent for the first time in The Plant's illustrious twenty-eight-year history. "My business is off 50 percent," Arne bemoaned in July 2000. "The whole music recording business is off 50 percent this year. About 50 percent of the revenues in our industry each year come from new acts. But the big record labels are so paralyzed by this MP3/Napster/Gnutella/Freenet free distribution of digital music, they're not signing any new acts! Without the labels paying for the production of new albums, our studio isn't recording." Arne Frager has been in the music business for 27 years. And he's never seen the flow of new music dry up before.

MP3 Catalyzed a Shift in the Balance of Power

In 1998 a simple piece of technology turned into a strategic weapon that would revolutionize the music business. MP3 is a standard file format that lets you compress digital music files so they can be transmitted via the Internet in a reasonable amount of time and without losing too much audio quality. Music-loving techies got hold of this technology, began distributing it, and built software services that made it easy for consumers to copy songs and entire audio CDs onto the Net. There was only one problem: nobody was getting paid for the use of the music.

Understanding the Music Biz

The music industry is an interesting mix of creative, renegade talent and conservative business practices. It is also a deeply emotional industry. Music lovers care passionately about the music they choose to enrich their lives. Musicians care deeply about their creative freedom (and their creations). Between the musicians and the end consumers there's an ecosystem similar to that in most other industries. There are managers and independent producers, who turn the talent into a business proposition with marketing flair and business acumen. There are a few really large companies that fund and distribute most of the music that reaches the marketplace—the record labels (i.e., EMI, Sony, Time Warner, BMG, and Universal). Like the major players in many industries, these companies are in the process of consolidating.

There are also tens of thousands of small, independent producers who fund new bands and promote them. Many of these independent producers rely on the major labels for distribution (e.g., getting their CDs into stores). There are large retailers who "control" the distribution channel.

But now the technology of the Internet and portable digital devices allows music lovers to bypass everyone and everything between them and the musicians. Customers can find new and interesting music on the 'Net, sample it, and decide whether or not to buy it.

The Internet helps musicians reach a broader market, yet it still hasn't completely undermined the primacy of the major record labels. Even with widespread sharing of music via the Internet, most musicians still have difficulty reaching paying customers without funding from big labels. The Internet hasn't completely bypassed the major record labels, but it is transforming the way the labels need to do business.

THEN WHY DO THE RECORD LABELS CALL THE SHOTS?

"Most musicians don't have a prayer of making money on their CDs," Arne explained. The amount of money required to produce and launch a new act is about $1 million. That doesn't include the costs of manufacturing and distributing the CDs. Although there are the rare instant hits that sell in the millions, a popular CD typically sells 300,000 to 400,000 copies. Once the labels recoup their costs, there's little profit for the musicians' royalties to come out of. And since the $1 million up-front costs are deducted from the musicians' 12 to 16 percent royalties on profits, the artists wind up owing the record label money after their first albums. Using an industry-specific practice called cross-collateralization, the deficit from the first album is added to the deficit on the second album, and so it goes. Most musicians never manage to create the hit that frees them from being "owned" by a major label.

The power in the music industry is clearly not in the hands of the musicians, but in the hands of a few record labels.

Even if a band succeeds in recording and producing a CD on its own or through an independent label ("indie"), the album still needs to get promoted to gain a mass market audience. That means concert tours and radio airplay. Tours are expensive. The big record labels subsidize tours for new acts by guaranteeing sold-out crowds to the venues that agree to book these acts. (Now you know why radio stations always have free tickets to give away!) The cost of the tour, the music video, and the Web site for the album are deducted from the artists' share of the profits.

How do new bands get radio airplay? The major record labels influence airplay—many of them spend big bucks on promotion and advertising to the stations. In the United States, independently produced acts reach the radio stations through a small handful of indie promoters. These promoters' services are not inexpensive. And again, there's rapid consolidation taking place among radio stations. The result: radio stations are becoming more and more homogenized, so they are less interested in new or niche music. Therefore, a handful of indie agents call on an increasingly homogenized sets of mass-market radio stations.

THE MUSICIAN'S DILEMMA

Musicians all over the world were very conflicted by the MP3/Napster phenomenon. On the one hand, no one wants his intellectual property to be misappropriated. On the other hand, widespread sharing of music by fans might break the major record labels' stranglehold on the music industry. Musicians knew they were getting a bad deal. After all, most could barely make a living from their music. How could it get much worse, they wondered. Maybe fans distributing my music will result in greater exposure, higher CD sales, more demand for concerts and for additional music. Maybe more fans will mean more radio airplay.

Arne Frager is no stranger to high tech, and he was an early fan of MP3. "The ability for musicians and bands to market and distribute their own music via the Internet will begin to shift the balance of power in the music industry," Arne told me in early 1998. At the time, he was excited about the fact that new bands would be able to reach fans directly, bypassing the indentured servitude practices that had become commonplace in the music industry.

The music industry was clearly overdue for a shake-up.

Music Fans Took Control

Once music fans discovered that it was easy to make a copy of an audio CD and distribute it electronically, the rampant copying and sharing of music exploded. College campuses became hotbeds of music piracy. Students—armed with high-speed Internet access, almost limitless disk capacity, and help from innovative techies—managed to copy most of the world's most popular albums and make that music freely available online. Of course, they also discovered and shared music from lesser-known, "garage" bands.

▶ Napster Catalyzes Change

Empowering the Renegades

"Napster's import goes far beyond the balance of power in the music business. Napster represents a new idea, a different architecture for exchanging information. No one can say yet how important the idea will become or how it will change things. But people felt the same uncertainty seven years ago, when Marc Andreessen and some other University of Illinois students created an application called Mosaic—the browser that introduced the Web as an easy-to-use enclave within the Internet. Will Napster trigger a similar revolution? Who knows? The point is that it might, and the fact that it might is forcing people in a lot of different industries to rethink their *modus operandi*."[1]

Shawn Fanning may seem like an unlikely person to foment a revolution. This unassuming, easy-going, smart kid began playing around with his first computer that his Uncle John had given him on his sixteenth birthday. During his freshman year at Northeastern University in Boston, he took a computer science course and was learning how to write C++ programs. One evening as he was relaxing in his dorm room, his roommate began complaining about how hard it was to find and download the MP3 music files he wanted from the Internet. As Shawn listened to his buddy complain, he came up with a simple, compelling idea that quickly became an obsession.

He decided to write a program that would make it easy for people to share MP3-encoded files with one another. This would be Shawn's first programming project. He realized that if he combined the instant messaging feature of Internet Relay Chat, Microsoft Windows' file sharing, and some advanced searching and filtering capabilities from various Internet search engines he could make it easy for people to share files directly without having to go through a central server.

Shawn became so consumed with writing this program that he dropped out of school and took up residence in his Uncle John's office while he completed his self-appointed project. He called the program

[1]From "The Hot Idea of the Year" by Amy Kover, *Fortune* magazine, June 26, 2000.

Napster, after his nickname—for the tightly curled hair he hides under his ever-present Lids baseball cap. By January 1999 he had released his brainchild into the world.

It took off. The idea of making it easy for people to locate and share files from one another's disk drives quickly made the rounds of the college campuses in the United States and around the world. This was viral marketing at its best! Shawn had made the program available for free at download.com. When he hit 300,000 downloads, he realized that he had created a phenomenon.

That's when Bill Bales noticed the Napster phenomenon and contacted Shawn. Bill bankrolled the start-up company. They set up shop in San Mateo, California, in addition to Uncle John's office in Hull. Bill Bales had founded Quote.com. Now he was ready for something big, and Napster was big! Bill invested in and incubated Napster, serving as its original VP of Business Development. He quickly recruited Adrian Scott, a technological mastermind who earned his Ph.D. at Rensselaer Polytechnic Institute at the age of twenty and consulted for Charles Schwab, Hewlett-Packard, and Bank of America before becoming an angel investor and advisor to start-ups. Adrian was the first person Bill called to get involved with Napster's funding and technological development. "Bill and I had a tremendous experience helping Napster get off the ground," said Adrian Scott. "We recognized the unstoppable force of peer-to-peer networks."

Legal Battle Fans the Flames of a Revolution

Napster turns out to have been the first of many peer-to-peer file-sharing programs. And the company of the same name might not have made history, despite its wave of popularity, if it hadn't been sued in December 1999 by the Recording Industry Association of America for copyright violation. By the spring of 2000, Michael Robertson's MP3.com digital jukebox (myMP3.com) site had already settled out of court with four of the five big record labels. But Napster's executive team didn't believe that the U.S. courts had as clear a case against Napster. After all, MP3.com *had* copied CDs onto its file servers. (Note: This was a step designed to save customers' time. MP3.com's online jukebox service was only available to customers who already owned the physical CDs. By pre-copying the most popular songs onto its servers, MP3.com would save customers the time and effort of "ripping" the CDs themselves.)

By then, Napster had become a *cause celebre* and was attracting deep pockets. The venture capital firm, Hummer Winblad put $15 million into the fledgling company and moved its headquarters to Redwood, California. Hank Barry, Hummer Winblad's media and technology partner, took over as interim CEO of Napster and recruited the best-known intellectual property lawyer, David Boies, fresh from his victory against Microsoft (in the U.S. Dept. of Justice case). In a brief filed in the U.S. District Court's Northern District of California, Napster's lawyers cited the First Amendment, the Audio Home Recording Act, and the 1984 Betamax case in their rebuttal to the recording industry's request for a motion to shut Napster down. Boies argued that consumers have a "fair use" right to the service ("The use of the Napster service to sample a song is analogous to visiting a listening station or borrowing a CD from a friend, in order to decide whether to make a purchase").

The outcome is history. Judge Patel granted the injunction that the RIAA had sought against Napster and gave the company forty-eight hours to pull the plug on its service. Boies's team gained a counterruling from a higher court and won a stay of the injunction.

What was the effect of all this litigation on the fans? They flocked to the Napster site in unprecedented numbers. Napster outdid AOL, Yahoo!, MSN, and all the portal sites combined in traffic statistics as customers madly swapped music files. Saving Napster became a status symbol among music *aficionados*. It no longer mattered that there were many other, equally easy-to-use ways to locate and copy MP3 files. Napster had become the rallying point for the revolution in the music business. Shawn Fanning's picture appeared on the covers of magazines around the world. And traffic soared to 38 million visitors by the fall of 2000. Napster was no longer a teenage phenomenon. People of all ages discovered Napster's surprising simplicity and ease of use.

In fall 2000, Bertelsmann's BMG record label agreed to drop its lawsuit against Napster. Instead, BMG would invest in Napster and turn it into a legal purveyor of music. Instead of swapping files for free, customers would pay a low monthly subscription fee.

Technology Fueled the Revolution

The process of copying, posting, and sharing copyrighted music began using simple, brute-force technologies: the Internet for moving files around; MP3 as a format for storing and playing back compressed digital audio; and a few simple, mostly homegrown tools.

Next came wave after wave of innovative technology. Portable MP3 players, Web sites (e.g., MP3.com) that organized and listed music that was available for download, Web sites that organized music that fans had on their local PCs and servers (e.g., Napster), and peer-to-peer programs (e.g., Gnutella or Freeware) with no central servers made it relatively easy for fans to broadcast the files they had and to locate and copy the ones they wanted to have. What was fueling this illegal copying rampage?

Does Music "Want to Be Free?"

Of course, the technology makes it possible to post digital music on the Internet. But equally important are the feelings of power and creativity that are unleashed. Music fans can build their own custom collections of the music they love and share their tastes with others. It doesn't feel like stealing. It's liberating. It's a way for me, the consumer, to strut my stuff—to show others what great taste I have. And the nice thing about copying anything digital is that, even if I take it and use it, it isn't used up. In fact, the more people take it and use it, the more of it there is! This notion—that music and other forms of creative expression and intellectual property "want to be free" because they can be freely shared without being used up—has become a rallying cry for a vocal minority. Many musicians, frustrated by what they perceive as the unfair hold that the major labels have on their ability to reach prospective fans, tend to side with the "free music" advocates.

The counter-argument, promulgated by prominent musicians such as Metallica's Lars Ulrich, was that music and other forms of creative expression will die out if musicians can't get paid for their work as everyone else does. "Polarization is deep in the music industry," remarked music consultant Jim Griffin at an industry confab in late 1999. Jim explained that there's a split between dominant record labels that want to preserve their economic control of music distribution and "free music advocates" who look to digitization and the Internet to cut out the middlemen, the record companies, and producers. Chuck D, a musician who has been advocating free music downloads, predicted "a balancing out of distribution, not an eradication of the middleman."

Theoretically the music industry could be benefiting from this mass migration to digital distribution and widespread sharing. There are as many studies that show that audio CD sales are up as a result of music piracy as there are studies showing that people are no longer buying CDs.

But the major studios and independent producers look at the key demographic—college kids with high bandwidth Internet access—and there's no question that bricks-and-mortar retail sales of CDs are down for that demographic. In many college and university towns, music stores report that their sales are off 80 percent. The customers who used to buy a CD per week are now going into those same stores to buy rewritable CDs on which to record and conveniently carry their custom compilations of pirated music. However, in mid-2000 a study published by Webnoize Research reported that students buy 20 percent of their CDs online compared with the national average of 2.4 percent. The study estimated that CD purchases in the first quarter of 2000 were 30 percent higher than they were three years ago, despite the recent popularity of file-swapping among students. Despite the conflicting data points, the concern that at least one segment of the music-buying population was stealing music instead of purchasing it has changed the course of the music business.

Intertwined Issues: Intellectual Property and Renegade Customers

Let's be clear about the separate issues that seem to be at stake here. You're going to see similar issues crop up in your industry. Your industry may not be as involved with copyright as the music, publishing, software, or entertainment industries are. But your industry probably has middlemen, contractual relationships, business practices for marketing and distribution, and some ingrained assumptions about where the value resides in the products and services you offer.

The music industry has been the canary in the coal mine, both for intellectual property issues and for these other business practices as well.

INTELLECTUAL PROPERTY PROTECTION

Customers do not have the right to steal from companies—no matter what their rationale. The rampant copyright abuses that have taken place at the turn of the millenium are growing pains. As many of the world's most valuable assets have shifted from atoms to bits, society, the business community, and our legal institutions have all had difficulty adapting. This is an awkward and painful phase in the history of business. But it's a phase we'll outgrow.

Over the next several years we expect to see improvements, both in our abilities to protect digital assets and in our abilities to police those who continue to circumvent the law. This will be a painful and disruptive process. The perils are either that legal safeguards will become too cumbersome and constraining or that hackers will outwit all attempts to constrain their efforts.

Nevertheless, we remain optimistic that within the next few years only a minority of pirates will continue to practice piracy. Law-abiding citizens will be willing to pay a fair price for the goods and services they use. What's important to watch is what the hackers and renegades are doing. Just crying foul and turning to lawyers and governments for protection isn't going to make the behavior go away. Offering new legal services to replace the illegal ones renegades are promulgating is the most powerful offense. In other words, let the renegades (early-adopting customers) lead the way.

RENEGADE CUSTOMERS

What customers are demanding in the music industry is the ability to take full advantage of a new medium. Once music is in digital form, it can be easily moved around—from home to school to a friend's house or computer, to my car, my walkman, or my mobile phone. Music can be reorganized, recategorized, and recombined, and these new compilations and creations can be shared with others. Because digital music is now more malleable, customers want to shape it. They want to reuse it, repurpose it, and enjoy it in different ways—as ring tones on their cellular phones, as backdrops for their personal Web sites, or as part of their interactive gaming activities. But most of all, they want to share their enthusiasm with others.

In its simplest form, making custom compilations of your favorite music and then "republishing" or broadcasting that new creation is a natural human tendency. It's one that will clearly persist. The sharpest folks in the traditional music industry understand this. But they're in a quandary. "A record company can't make money selling music by the track. We need to sell entire albums to earn a reasonable profit," I was told. Even if that album only has three tracks of music the customer actually wants? "Yes, even then."

Customers will continue to insist on having the ability to mix, match, and share their favorite music electronically with others. The challenge for the music industry is to find ways to let customers have what they want and still find a profitable business model.

What Did the Renegades Do?

To understand how the Napster phenomenon might impact other industries, particularly those involved in the distribution of electronic goods, let's look more closely at the kinds of things customers were really doing when they shared these mostly bootleg music files.

FANS TRIED OUT NEW MUSIC

Many of the most active participants in the hyperactive days of rampant MP3 piracy reported that they liked being able to download lots of new music and then, at their leisure, listen to a few tunes to discover new bands and new styles.

FANS BUILT COLLECTIONS

Lots of people began creating their own private collections of all the music they enjoyed. They stored these collections on their own hard disks, on file servers on campus or at work, or on some of the jukeboxes that quickly began to emerge on commercial Web sites (e.g., MP3.com, Myplay.com, or Windows Media Player). Soon companies sprang into being that offered purpose-built home jukeboxes that would let you fast-copy your entire CD collection and store it (perfectly legally) on your home digital jukebox. One advantage to all of these solutions from the customer's standpoint was the ability to organize, catalog, and rearrange a digital music collection. Instead of dealing with piles of jewel cases and entire CDs, fans could use a computer or a TV screen to list all their music and sequence tracks to play.

FANS MADE THEIR OWN "MIXES"

Suddenly everyone could be a disc jockey. One of the most popular and seductive pastimes is creating your own compilations or "mixes" of tracks taken from a variety of CDs. These might be your current favorites, music for a particular mood, favorite tracks from several different CDs by the same band, or several different treatments of the same jazz tune played by different artists. The possibilities are endless. And so is the customer's imagination. These custom compilations found their way onto home-burned CDs so they could be handed out to friends. Custom mixes were posted on Web sites for friends to download and play.

FANS CREATED RADIO STATIONS

Soon these custom compilations showed up on the Internet on thousands of sites as "stations." If you went to most popular MP3 sites, you'd find that the most active areas were the "music wanted/music offered" sections. This is where radio-station producers, most of them hobbyists, looked for new music to fill out the play lists for their twenty-four-hour Internet radio stations. Musicians—both struggling professionals and undiscovered amateurs—posted their wares in the hopes that these niche stations would pick them up. By mid-2000 there were well over 10,000 of these niche Internet radio stations broadcasting simultaneously from a single website (Live365.com). Peter Rothman, Live365.com's chief technology officer crowed, "To put some perspective on this, the first commercial radio broadcaster, KDKA, launched in Pittsburgh in 1920. It has taken the broadcasting industry eighty years to build out the current radio broadcasting infrastructure. We have created an equivalent in nine months." These Internet radio stations were created by rabid music-lovers to broadcast custom programming—music compilations strung together by fans all over the world. Much of the music played on these stations had been freely offered by the musicians themselves. They were looking for airplay, even if it was only on an Internet station and heard by a handful of people around the world.

Within months the entire music industry was in turmoil. Customers—music fans—were finding more and more ingenious ways to make illegal copies of music and share them, not only with a small cadre of friends but with anyone in the world who wanted a free listen or a free copy. They were finding new ways to personalize and customize the music they enjoyed and share those creations with friends and strangers alike.

▶ Live365.com: Building Revolutionary New Business Models

Alex Sanford didn't set out to revolutionize the radio broadcasting industry. He simply wanted to "do something different." Alex had spent fourteen years in international law and business development, most recently stationed in Asia working for Freshfields, an international law firm. There he honed his skills in mergers, acquisitions, IPOs, licensing, and distribution. When Alex moved to California to embark on his entrepreneurial career in 1998, the opportunity that beckoned was the idea of building communities on the Internet for end users who would take advantage of high bandwidth multimedia combined with proprietary 3D streaming technology to create and disseminate content of their own. Alex formed a company called Nanocosm and recruited a set of top multimedia developers led by Peter Rothman, a pioneer in the development of 3D streaming technologies. Nanocosm's goal was to enable tech-savvy consumers to create 3D home pages with special effects that would be served off their Web hosting service.

By early 1999, as the company's proprietary 3D environment and downloadable design tools were set to go live at the nanohome.com Web site, the Nanocosm team noticed two things. First, broadband Internet access was not as readily available as their aggressive business plan had presumed. Second, there was a new nonproprietary technology that had been taking off among music fans: MP3. The Nanocosm team quickly regrouped and decided to take the company in a different direction. They watched what music fans were doing on the Internet and decided to run around to get in front of the parade.

Forget our fancy proprietary technology, they thought. We want to enable large communities of users to share their creative genius. Let's do it with MP3. These compressed audio files don't require high bandwidth. We can provide a platform that will enable music fans to produce custom "radio stations." We'll make it possible for anyone to become a DJ.

The Nanocosm team did a "soft launch" of Live365.com in June 1999. Their goal was to become the premier provider of Internet radio services for broadcasters and listeners. They succeeded.

The company began by targeting the existing community of some 600 Internet broadcasters that had already begun using a rival service called Shopcast. Shopcast was a streaming MP3 server created by a ten-person company called Nullsoft. Nullsoft's other product, WinAmp, became one of the most popular MP3 players (that is, software programs for downloading and decoding MP3 files). Nullsoft was acquired by AOL in 1999, and in 2000 the Nullsoft team was the renegade group behind the freeware Gnutella service, much to AOL's discomfiture.

Live365.com made its formal debut at Jupiter's "Plug In" conference in July 1999. Within three months, 300 Internet broadcasters were happily ensconced on the Live365.com service. By year's end more than 6,000 broadcasters were up and running. And by April 2000, nine months after its launch, Live365.com had surpassed the world's terrestrial radio broadcasting infrastructure, with more than 12,000 active broadcasters. By the company's first anniversary, more than 15,000 broadcasters were live and the listening audience had reached 1.4 million visitors per day from 75 countries (while continuing to grow). In twelve months, Live365.com had become the world's largest radio network (as measured by broadcasters and stations).

Becoming a Broadcaster in Cyberspace

There are three ways to broadcast through Live365.com. The first and most common approach is to use the company's easy-to-use tools to put together a playlist of songs and/or other recorded audio along with the MP3-encoded files and upload these to the site for rebroadcast. The second is to send a live feed directly from your computer over the Internet. This could be a selection of music played from the CD drive in your computer interspersed with your spoken commentary or your running commentary on your local high school basketball game uplinked via wireless modem. The third way is for an existing commercial or community radio station to provide a feed to be rebroadcast via the 'Net. Private broadcasters may broadcast free of charge, taking advantage of Live365.com's considerable investment in software and round-the-world Web hosting services. Commercial broadcasters and organizations pay a fee for the broadcast service.

Licensing and Legality. Like any regular radio broadcaster, Live365.com pays a negotiated license fee to the rights management organizations that monitor music airplay (ASCAP and RMI in the United States and their equivalent organizations abroad). Radio stations don't need to pay as much in royalty fees as those who sell music do because the music being broadcast doesn't "replace a sale." Instead, the musicians' interests are represented by organizations that negotiate and collect bulk licensing fees and apportion them back to the musicians and rights owners based on relative airplay.

The Revenue Model

For its first twelve months of existence Live365.com was largely advertising driven. In exchange for the ability to transmit their own programming across the globe, broadcasters agreed to host audio advertisements that would be interspersed within their playlists. Since many of the shows are highly niche-oriented—1930's jazz performed in Manhattan, or ragtime favorites, or Delta blues—the advertisers have the opportunity to "narrowcast" to a very dedicated audience. Next, Live365.com added electronic commerce. Advertisers could not only promote their wares but also sell them on the Web site. Live365.com received a commission from each transaction, which it split with the broadcaster. This additional revenue stream encouraged broadcasters to promote the products (CDs, t-shirts, or concert tickets) that their fans would be interested in.

In the fall of 2000, Live365.com began to pursue businesses, associations, and not-for-profits as broadcasters. What the team found was that many organizations had discovered the ease with which they could produce and disseminate custom programming to employees, shareholders, customers, and other constituents. First political organizations jumped on the bandwagon. Next came not-for-profits with a mission to educate and inform, such as Save the Whales. Soon businesses large and small discovered that they could produce and air a radio station with global reach for a closed or open community using Live365.com's tools and infrastructure. All they had to do was to communicate the station's URL to the targeted audience. Companies and associations were happy to pay the modest fees that Live365.com charged for one-time or ongoing broadcasts. By the end of 2000 the company's revenue model was 50 percent funded by businesses paying for the Internet broadcast service and 50 percent funded by advertising and transaction fees.

Interactive Radio

What's truly revolutionary about Internet radio is its interactivity. Here are just some of the things that are being done today. (Who knows what tomorrow will bring?)

- Listeners from around the world who are using their computers or wireless Internet devices to listen to a station can also join in a real-time chat session with other listeners, with the musician, and/or with the DJ at the same time that they're listening to the programming.
- Fans can select which stations they want to listen to at certain times of day and preprogram their radio preferences.
- Fans can listen to music from their Internetworked computers, mobile phones, and cars via satellite feeds.
- Listeners can download their own radio programming from the Internet, store the customized programs on their portable MP3 players, and listen from anywhere. They don't need to be tethered to a computer or pay for a live connection if they don't need real-time access.
- Listeners can specify the kinds of advertising they're interested in hearing or pay a fee to opt out of advertising all together.
- Listeners can respond to a broadcast via email or interactive chat in real time. They can purchase a song they just heard with a single click.
- Any fan can easily become a DJ, putting together her own programming from any assortment of published or previously unpublished content and making it available to the whole world.

- Any band can play its own music on an Internet radio station or produce a program of music they like for fans to listen to.
- Internet broadcasters and musicians can get into direct relationship with their fans. Instead of broadcasting to an anonymous audience, they can tailor their programming to the tastes of their listeners.

Customers have taken control of the radio airwaves—at least via the Internet.

How the Music Industry Reacted

The Recording Industry of America and a number of well-known bands, including Metallica, began suing the Web sites that acted as custodians and intermediaries for rampant music piracy. Many of the key digital music-sharing sites, such as MP3.com, agreed to out-of-court settlements for copyright infringement. And more and more "legitimate" music-sharing sites came on board, such as EMusic.com—sites that sell downloadable music by the track, by the album, and by subscription to a particular artist's music or a particular record label's music.

All of the major recording labels realized that customers were going to continue to vote with their ears. Customers wanted digital music to be readily available for them to access, recompile, and share. The big studios and the independent producers all struggled to find ways to follow customers' desires without losing their shirts. They all experimented with technologies that would allow the record companies to have tighter control over copyrighted material, digitally encrypting the music, and only unlocking that encryption once each listener had paid.

Large Record Labels Surrender to Customers

Sony Music was the first of the major record labels to capitulate. Sony quietly began offering commercial digital downloads in the spring of 2000. Despite its stealth approach, retailers complained vociferously. The large labels were placed on warning by the major retail chains: be careful not to disintermediate us! Behind closed doors, the executives from the major labels apparently agreed to coordinate their efforts. They didn't select the same technology platforms and approaches. But they did watch each other's movements carefully and tried to give customers what they wanted without ruffling the retailers' feathers.

EMI was next. EMI introduced its commercial download capability with a lot of fanfare during the summer of 2000 and did so in collaboration with a few online retailers. The hoopla was premature, however. The early incarnations of EMI's digital download capabilities at online retailers such as Virgin's Jamcast site, TWEC.com, and HMV.com were clumsy and hard to use.

In late July Columbia launched its own Internet radio stations. Next came Universal Music Group, with trials of limited downloads in August 2000. Also in August 2000, BMG Entertainment launched its own music download site—the first in Germany—featuring 300 titles from German-targeted acts. Then BMG opened up download sites in the rest of Europe, Asia, and the United States. By the autumn of 2000, the powers that be in the music industry had taken the plunge. They were offering rights-protected music for customers to purchase and download electronically.

The clicks-and-bricks integration began in 2000 and will continue throughout the next few years. One of the most insightful moves on the part of the record companies (this idea was pioneered by MP3.com) was the in-store digitizing option. This gives customers who are purchasing audio CDs the option of having the music on that CD "transferred" to an Internet-accessible electronic storage locker or jukebox. This transaction takes place at the cash register in the physical store or at the time of purchase if it's done online. (In practice, the digital albums are already stored on the 'Net, they simply need to be linked to each paying customer's virtual record collection.) The wonderful thing about this business model is that customers gain in convenience. They received the CD (which they could use to conveniently listen to a higher fidelity rendition). And they were spared the effort of having to make a digital copy.

Untold Story of the Digital Music Revolution

One aspect of this major industry transformation story that's not often discussed is the true revolution that's afoot. Certainly, we're witnessing a shift from atoms to bits, from analog to digital goods. And we're watching renegade customers experiment with entirely new ways to appreciate and to use these audio files. But there's something else happening. In the past the major record companies had no way to know who their customers were. They could do surveys and demographic studies. But they weren't in relationship with customers. Now customers are coming directly to the record labels and downloading tracks from new CDs. Or they're purchasing a CD at a retailer's Web site or in a store and gaining the ability to store and manipulate that information electronically. In exchange for this increased power and convenience, many customers are willing to let both the labels and the retailers—and certainly the musicians—know who they are. For the first time in the history of the music business, companies are beginning to get to know their end customers.

What We Can Learn from the Revolution in the Music Industry?

As I chronicled the story of the transformation of the music business, my heart leapt into my throat. After all, my company derives half its revenues from the sale of our intellectual property. We sell books like this one through retailers, we sell research reports online, and we license strategic planning services to corporate clients who receive our reports each week. Corporate clients aren't as likely as consumers to disregard copyright laws or to violate licensing agreements. Yet we've already experienced some of the cannibalization that has hit the music industry. And our clients are letting us know that they want to buy and use our material in ways that don't fit our current business model. We, like the rest of our industry, obviously need to change. It's terrifying, and it's inevitable. Here's what I learned. Hopefully these lessons will be of use to other companies that sell or leverage intellectual property.

TAKEAWAYS: HOW CUSTOMERS WILL RESHAPE SOFT GOODS INDUSTRIES

1. Customers Will Try Before They Buy.

When you sell hard goods, like cars or refrigerators, you expect customers to kick the tires before they make a commitment. When you sell software applications, molecular models, or other forms of information that customers will use again and again, you'll experience the same thing. Customers increasingly demand to download, install, and use your products before they're ready to pay for them. But what if yours is a product that is not likely to be used again and again? Perhaps it's a movie or a book. Chances are that most customers will only want or need to enjoy it once. The challenge in that case is to offer enough for free that customers can assess the value and applicability of your product for their particular needs.

2. Customers Will Buy by the Piece.

You need to offer your intellectual property in small, bite-sized chunks. If it's a software application, customers may only want a single, reusable component rather than the entire application. If it's a financial model, they may only value one particular formula. Novelist Stephen King sold his book online for $1 per chapter. He could afford to, since he has millions of fans. But what if you don't? What's the right price for a piece of a larger whole? Particularly if customers only buy one or two pieces? This is the track versus album dilemma. The music industry has already capitulated. So will the rest of us.

3. Customers Will Mix and Match.

You may believe that your products belong together or work best in the combinations that you've created and bundled and in the context of your brand. Customers, however, will want to combine pieces of your products with those of your competitors to create new hybrid entities. You need to design your goods so that they can be easily combined with your competitors' offerings. For example, Japanese consumers of NTT's DoCoMo i-mode mobile phones routinely design their own user interfaces, functions, and feature sets by combining ring tones from one supplier; cartoons and animation from others; electronic agents, information services, and software applications from a wide variety of suppliers. All of these "small footprint" applets were designed to coexist with one another.

4. Customers Will Want to Reshape and Repurpose Your Goods.

Once a customer has access to your digital information, she will want to be able to reuse it in ways that you never anticipated. You need to be prepared to see your products and information morph into new forms. In fact, you should anticipate and encourage this tendency. Getty Images' PhotoDisc subsidiary was one of the first companies to proactively support the repurposing of its stock photography. When you purchase an image from the PhotoDisc collection, you have the right to alter it in any way you choose.

5. Customers Will Want to Share with Others.

Once a customer has procured your product, he feels entitled to share it with others. You need to anticipate and allow for that natural tendency by making it as easy as possible for customers to pass your intellectual property around without violating your copyright. This may seem like piracy, but it's actually viral marketing. So you want to make it easy for customers to legally pass copies around.

6. Customers Will Want to Publish Their Own "Mixes."

You should assume that customers will want to repurpose your intellectual property, add value to it, and create a new hybrid form that they'll want to offer to others. The trick here is to maintain the brand and the cachet associated with your intellectual property so that customers who appreciate your contribution to the mix will recognize its provenance.

7. Customers Will Want to Co-Brand Your Material.

Even with the rampant illicit copying of music, there have been very few examples of customers passing someone else's music off as their own. In general, customers value the authority of the source. Having a mathematical formula or a research protocol that was created by an authority on the subject is a value that customers want to pass along to others, even as they add their own additional information, commentary, or derivative works.

3

A DOZEN CUSTOMER DEMANDS THAT WILL CHANGE YOUR BUSINESS

The turmoil in the music industry is a graphic example of what happens when customers, armed with fairly innocuous technology, begin to alter the long-standing practices and relationships in an industry. Every industry has a set of ingrained practices that are ripe for reexamination. If you think that your industry's traditional practices aren't likely to change in the next five years, we suggest that you retire right now! You're in for some unpleasant surprises. Customers, equipped with Internet and mobile technologies and seduced by new digital frontiers, are breaking down the status quo.

OUT IN THE OPEN

Nothing is hidden any more. You can't hide your prices, your inventory, your new product development, or your mistakes. Customers are demanding and receiving increased transparency with regard to price, inventory, logistics, business policy, and distribution channel partners. Customers now want to see into your business to make better decisions that affect their businesses and their lives. No matter what industry you're in, be prepared for any or all of these customer demands to hit you soon if they haven't already.

CUSTOMERS' DEMANDS: THE DIGITAL DOZEN

Often when we consult with a new client, he'll tell us how he wants to take advantage of new technologies and what he doesn't want to do. We've heard business owners say, "Only current customers should have access to our technical support knowledge-base; prospective customers don't need to see that information." "We need customers to tell us where they're located; we have different prices in different parts of the world." "We can't sell direct online; our dealers/retailers/channel partners will kill us!" "We can't tell customers if an item is in stock in the store nearest them; we have no way of knowing."

We always nod sympathetically but tell them the truth. You may want to draw the line where it's comfortable or practical for you to do so, but your customers are unlikely to let you get away with it for long. How do we know what customers will demand in an industry that's new to us? There seem to be some inexorable forces at play once you go digital. We've found at least a dozen of them to date.

The Digital Dozen: Customer Demands that Will Change Your Business

Today's customers are demanding:

1. Open, Equal Access
2. Real-Time Information
3. Specialist Information
4. Convenient Access
5. Information Portability
6. Process Transparency
7. Logistics Transparency
8. Pricing Transparency
9. Fair, Global Pricing
10. The Ability to Set Prices
11. Choice of Distribution Channels
12. Control over Their Information

As you think about each of these, try them on for size. How will each one play out in your industry?

The Digital Dozen: Customers' Demands in the Digital Age

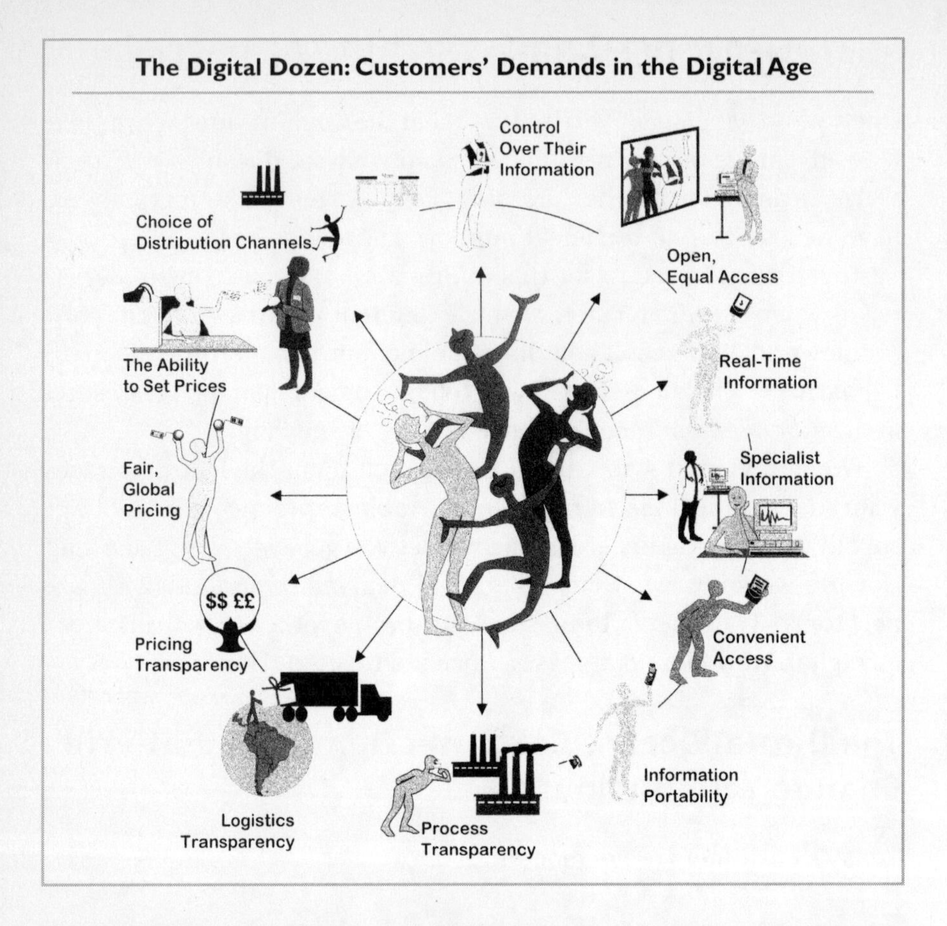

1. The Demand for Open, Equal Access

Have you noticed that the world's stock exchanges are under siege by customers? Two forces have combined to change the status quo. The first was online trading. The second was ECNs. ECNs (electronic communications networks) such as Archipelago and Instinet came into being in 1997 in response to customers' frustration. In the past, customers couldn't control the prices at which their stock buy-and-sell limit orders were being settled. (A limit order lets you specify the price at which you want to purchase or sell a stock.) Once the U.S. Securities and Exchange Commission (SEC) changed the limit order posting requirements in 1996, ECNs appeared on the scene and broker/dealers were required to post any limit orders they couldn't fill immediately onto an ECN. Automated trading software matched up buyers and sellers, bypassing the traditional market makers. Customers won.

Soon customers demanded after-hours trading. Next they demanded real-time feeds of information and access to the same analytical tools used by professionals. Today, amateur investors and day traders have access to the same tools and information that used to be available only to licensed brokers.

The rise of ECNs is also putting pressure on the world's stock exchanges. Customers are calling into question the role of market maker and the limits of trading hours. Soon traditional stock exchanges will give way to all-electronic exchanges. The market makers will be relegated to thinly traded stocks.

Customers' demands have altered the status quo in the U.S. investment community in other, equally dramatic ways. Patrick Garner, the CEO of the Motley Fool, which has developed a strong online investment community, remembers the day he received a phone call from Arthur Levitt, the chairman of the Securities and Exchange Commission. "Uh-oh," Pat remembers thinking. "What have we done wrong?" But Arthur wasn't calling to complain. He was calling to thank the folks at the Motley Fool. Over the summer the SEC had been collecting public comments on Regulation FD, the "selective disclosure" rule. (Under selective disclosure rules, publicly held corporations were permitted to release material information to institutional investors before making it available to individual investors.) The SEC received more than 6,000 letters and emails blasting this unfair practice, more than half of which came from "Fools" (individual investors from the Motley Fool's Community). In a passionate address to the Motley Fool employees after the vote was passed, Arthur Levitt said, "This is the only organization I've run into since being in Washington that has begun to mobilize the power of the people. Your efforts helped capture the vote I needed to make Fair Disclosure happen."

2. The Demand for Real-Time Information

Financial trading isn't the only arena in which customers are clamoring for equal access to information and for real-time or near-real-time information. Energy markets, agricultural markets, and airline reservation systems all offer real-time pricing.

Customers have also become increasingly demanding about inventory availability. They want to know what's available, where it's available, and how soon they can get it. If you don't provide that information in near-real time, they'll go elsewhere.

How do customers respond when something goes awry? Today's customers expect and demand full disclosure about any problem or defect the moment the supplier knows about it. Companies that attempt to cover up or delay reporting bad news and taking immediate corrective actions find that customers have very long memories.

3. The Demand for Specialist Information

What's the single most popular form of research on the Web? Health information. Customers are demanding access to detailed medical research, clinical trial information, and drug information—in fact, all the information that a trained doctor can read and interpret is now available online to any layperson. Customers now come to their doctors' offices armed with printouts and questions.

Customers are almost as greedy for highly technical information, details about genetic engineering, legal precedents, and raw weather data. Information that has always been filtered and interpreted by trained specialists is now available to the uninitiated. And increasingly, specialized Web sites provide the filtering, interpretation, and education that's needed to make sense of this domain-specific information.

4. The Demand for Convenient Access

Patients now want to be able to email their doctors with questions and updates. They want to be able to schedule appointments online and gain access to their test results and their medical records electronically (and securely).

E-health services are now appearing that cater to customers who want to avail themselves of online counseling, coaching, and monitoring by medical professionals. For example, Diet ReHab.com offers nutritional consultations via the Web. LifeChart helps patients with diabetes test their blood sugar and transmit the results over the phone to an online charting service that they and their doctor can monitor. Patients with asthma can breathe into a device and send the readings over the phone to the 'Net.

Mobile Wireless Access. In many parts of the world, customers expect to be able to use the wireless data features on their mobile phones or personal digital assistants to transfer funds, buy stock, book tickets, receive the latest news, check on the status of their orders, and make reservations. And with location-based services, they also expect to be able to quickly find the resources that are in closest proximity—for example, bathrooms, coffee shops, cash machines, gas stations, restaurants, taxis, or subway and bus stops. By the end of 2000, over 16 million Japanese already had convenient, mobile, wireless access to the Internet, using NTT DoCoMo's i-mode service.

5. The Demand for Information Portability

The days of lock-in are over. Banks, brokerages, and insurance companies are undergoing radical change around the world. Each one is vying with a slew of non-banks—such as Internet service providers, Web portals, grocery stores, and automobile companies—for the honor of handling your complete financial portfolio. It's true that consumers increasingly value one-stop investment and banking, competitive interest rates, the ability to control their investments directly, and the ability to manage the timing and allocation of their bill payments. But customers are no longer willing to be locked in to their financial services provider. They are demanding—and getting—increased ease of movement. With customer-driven portability standards in place, customers can easily pick up all their accounts with the associated account linkages and move them *en masse* to a competing financial services company.

The same is true with phone numbers. Phone number portability is now a legal requirement in most countries. Customers can no longer be locked in to a supplier simply because it would be inconvenient or cumbersome to switch. Switching costs are declining in every industry.

6. The Demand for Process Transparency

Customers are no longer willing to put up with invisible business processes and hand-offs. They expect to be able to see the status of any process they've set in motion or are depending on. The majority of manufacturers now subcontract the assembly and subassembly of much of their product lines. A new model mobile phone being launched by Nokia might easily involve 200 different subassembly contractors and component suppliers. Each of these parties is providing a small piece of the puzzle to others that are higher up in the value chain. Manufacturing is distributed around the globe to reduce risk and to optimize availability. In the past the product manager in charge of this product launch would have relied on the phone, email, and faxes to keep tabs on the status of what is obviously an interdependent set of manufacturing processes. Today she relies on electronic instrumentation. She insists that each player be electronically connected to its immediate supplier and customer and that she has visibility into the whole process.

The same requirement for process transparency holds true for construction projects, for product design, and for new drug trials. All of these are complex processes in which very small players—many of whom in the past have been technologically disadvantaged—are required and expected to link into the now-visible value chain via the Web.

7. The Demand for Logistics Transparency

Transparency is also the name of the game in the logistics business. Whether you ship products by truck, container, air, or camel, it is now a requirement that every party in the value chain know where each item being shipped is at any time. Recipients and shippers expect to be able to intercept an individual package en route and redirect it. Orient Overseas Container Lines (OOCL) is a good example of a logistics company that has completely redesigned itself from the outside in. The company's new information systems have customers and their freight consignments at their core. Every step of every shipment is logged and tracked as the item makes its way across land, sea, and air. Customers (shippers and recipients) and their designates can access the real-time status of any shipment in any part of the world at any time. And customers are in control. If items being shipped from Hong Kong to New York need to be rerouted to Kansas City, the customer can intervene directly, setting into motion changes in linked business processes such as customs clearance and duties as well as inventory replenishment.

Fulfillment companies that handle the distribution of goods for manufacturers and retailers also need to provide seamless customer service for each individual and customer. They typically receive orders; answer customers' inquiries about products; custom-configure products; pick, pack, and ship products; notify customers proactively at each step; and handle returns and refunds. At every step, both the customer and the supplier need to be able to examine the current state of affairs.

8. The Demand for Pricing Transparency

As soon as you begin selling your products and services via the Internet, your customers will force you to move to global pricing. Dell Computer discovered this in 1995. So did Getty Images and Cisco Systems. Before, these companies' different international operations had set "local prices," which meant the prices the local market would bear. But customers from other countries, from Afghanistan to Uruguay, could easily log onto these companies' U.S. Web sites and see the U.S. prices. International customers immediately reacted. Besides complaining vociferously about unfair pricing, they took action. They ordered their products from the U.S. version of the Web site, causing problems with shipping, customs, and local tariffs and taxes. The suppliers had no recourse; they had to adjust their prices to be commensurate with those around the world. That meant squeezing gross margins so that local distributors could still make money. It often required setting up local manufacturing operations in order to avoid import duties.

What happens to your business when you move to global pricing? The ripple effect is huge. As John Chambers, Cisco's CEO, explains, "Global pricing means tremendous cost pressure. It causes you to bring costs down across the board. Global pricing makes you focus on operational efficiencies really fast!"

Price comparison across products and manufacturers is now easier than ever before. Shoppers for products as varied as industrial plastic resins or microfleece slippers can easily compare pricing and availability of products within a few minutes on the 'Net. With a hand-held appliance—such as a Palm Pilot with a built-in modem or a mobile phone with Internet access—a shopper in a store in Sydney or Boston can scan the bar code of the latest model digital camera to get a real-time price check on that same model across online retailers and in the physical stores that are within a few blocks walking distance. Customers are now armed with up-to-the-minute pricing information.

9. The Demand for Fair, Global Pricing

Over the last couple of years, British consumers have been in revolt over unfair car prices. People who live and work in the U.K. can now easily compare local car prices with those in other European countries. It's true that consumers' car prices have been historically higher in Britain. There have been two reasons for this now-eroding price gap.

First, 60 percent of car sales in Britain are to businesses, which buy cars for their employees as part of their total compensation package. Car makers cater to their business customers, offering them good deals on bulk orders. Individual consumers—the spouse at home, the self-employed, the retired person—pay much higher prices.

Paul Confrey, Marketing Director for GM's Vauxhall division, explained the second reason for inflated car prices. "In the U.K., consumers have gotten used to a different approach to financing cars. They insist on very attractive financing deals. For example, there's a 0 percent finance option. You pay nothing down and get a no-interest car loan for 12, 24, or 36 months depending on the model. Then you pay the original car price. Or you select the 50/50 option. You pay 50 percent up front and then pay nothing for three years, at which time you can select a payment option for the remainder. The way this works, in Vauxhall's case, is that we buy the car loans from our sister GMAC credit division and then add that cost to the sticker price of the car."

Whatever the origins of these pricing disparities, the days of higher prices for consumers' cars are numbered in Britain. One of the favorite Internet pastimes in the U.K. has been to use popular sites such as Oneswoop.com or Virgincars.com to compare prices among the host of Scandinavian car dealers who will take your car order online and deliver your car to Britain. You pick the car up at the point of entry and pay the VAT, saving at least 30 percent on the price of your car. For consumers who can't be bothered to surf the 'Net, car brokers are happy to handle the entire transaction for you, delivering your registered car to your door (still at 20% under the price you'd pay if you went to your local car dealership).

Consumer backlash caused a major revamping of the car retailing practices and policies in the U.K. A government Competitive Commission was set up to investigate the trade practices in the retail car business. The Commission's findings and recommendations have dramatically changed the car buying landscape in the U.K.

Customers won!

10. The Demand to Set Prices

In the United States, Priceline.com pioneered the practice of letting customers explicitly set the prices they are willing to pay for products and services. Priceline began by selling distressed inventory of hotel rooms and airline seats.

In Singapore, where the price of your mortgage is likely to be $1 million or more even if your dwelling is modest, DollarDex.com pioneered the group buying of mortgages. Groups of consumers band together online to negotiate the best rates, terms, and conditions with a set of competing lenders. The lender that comes up with the most pleasing terms for the group as a whole wins their business.

Small U.S. businesses can join EqualFooting.com, a business-to-business e-market that lets small businesses aggregate their buying power to reduce prices for goods and services, from employee healthcare to office supplies. Auction sites around the world offer both consumer and business buyers the opportunity to bid the price up or down (in a reverse auction) for one-off or surplus goods.

The variations are endless, but the theme is the same. Customers increasingly get to choose what prices they're willing to pay, either individually or collectively.

11. The Demand for Choice in Distribution Channels

When companies first began selling direct via the Internet, most industry pundits assumed that distribution channels—such as car dealerships, insurance and travel agents, book retailers, and electronics distributors—would become outmoded. After all, if consumer and business customers could buy direct from the manufacturer or wholesaler at a lower price, wouldn't they all do so?

Manufacturer-Direct and Local Distribution Partners

Five years into the Internet era, customers have made their choices clear. They want both manufacturer-direct and distribution channel options. Manufacturers around the world have encountered customers' ire when they don't make all or most of their products available for sale directly from their own Web sites. Customers who have taken the time and trouble to research the right solution for their needs on the Web are upset when they discover that they can't place an order online if they choose to do so. It was this relentless customer demand that caused Keds and Hewlett-Packard to begin selling their products directly from their Web sites, although both companies rely heavily on retailers to move the majority of their products. HP's blended channel strategy offers customers a choice. Once a customer finds the product she's seeking, she can order from HP direct, order from one of the companies' online retailing partners, or locate the nearest retail outlet carrying the product in question.

The manufacturer-direct channel can also serve as a way to spawn a new business model. Snap-on Tools is a company that has traditionally sold to business customers—professional automotive technicians—only through its franchised dealer network. Yet hobbyists were constantly barraging Snap-on with demands to sell them its well-respected tools. The company finally capitulated.

What about industries in which strong dealer networks or retailers have reigned supreme? In the United States, automobile dealerships have a huge amount of clout. State laws protect these independent businesspeople from the manufacturers whose products they sell. In twenty-one of the fifty states, it's illegal for an automobile manufacturer to sell direct to either consumers or business customers. Yet customers have been flocking to the Internet to research their options online, compare prices, locate the cars they want, and make deals. Many consumers were hoping that the Internet would enable them to pay a fixed price rather than to haggle with a car salesman. Consumers were doing their research online at car shopping sites, such as Autobytel.com and Cars.com. They were happy to purchase online at the few sites that permitted it, such as Carsdirect.com. And customers flooded the car manufacturers' Web sites with complaints, making it clear that they didn't want to have to search across hundreds of dealers' individual websites; instead, they expected the manufacturers' websites (i.e., Ford or GM) to sell them the car they wanted at a competitive price. Finally during the summer of 2000, Ford and its U.S. car dealers joined together to offer customers the option to purchase their cars online yet have the cars delivered to them by a local dealer. Once the Ford dealers agreed, the other dealers and manufacturers followed.

In the music industry, the major record labels were initially intimidated by the large record stores, their largest and most powerful distribution channel. Yet once renegade customers had made it clear that they wanted online access to music, the record companies had no choice but to comply. Once-reluctant retailers embraced the inevitable outcome. Every industry will go the way of the music industry. Manufacturers will sell direct, and they'll also continue to sell through their distribution partners, offering customers choice and convenience.

The Role of Aggregators and Brokers

There are, of course, thousands of products that customers prefer to buy from aggregators or brokers. Imagine buying all of your office supplies from dozens of different manufacturers, booking travel reservations for a single trip from three different Web sites, or assembling a bill of materials for a new office building from hundreds of different Web sites! Distributors, brokers, and retailers make life more convenient for customers who want to aggregate products and services or who want an expert advisor to make selections and recommendations. Customers want and need the services of these middlemen. As the Internet era began to unfold, brand new middlemen sprang up in virtually every industry, competing with the existing "old economy" distributors. Online middlemen offered side-by-side comparisons and product finders, giving new transparency to product features, prices, and availability. New e-markets emerged, offering convenient one-stop shopping along with real-time exchanges for perishable commodities, streamlined procurement workflows, and logistics and risk management services.

What factors determined the winners and losers among middlemen? Customer convenience won out. Customers favored the aggregators that offered the best product availability, the smoothest business processes, and the most convenient and reliable delivery options. Customers flocked to aggregators (such as McMaster-Carr for industrial supplies or Alliant for food service supplies) because these companies combined state-of-the-art Internet capabilities with mature, phone-based order taking, account management, and customer service. This meant they could leverage their pre-existing warehouse and delivery capabilities to provide reliable same-day or next-day delivery for hundreds of thousands of needed products.

Customers Want Product Information Direct from the Manufacturer

Now that customers are in control, they're demanding more seamless relationships between the aggregator/retailer/broker/dealer and the manufacturer or supplier of the goods and services. Customers have made it abundantly clear that—when it comes to product information, specifications, and technical support—they are more likely to trust the information that's supplied by the manufacturer. What that means in practice is that manufacturers need to optimize their product information for customers to use for pre-sales customer support and decision-making and for after-sales usage, support, maintenance, and updates/upgrades. This information needs to be available both from the manufacturers' own online catalog or Web site and from those of any distributor, marketplace, retailer, dealer, or agent that offers the same product for sale.

Many Customers Want a Relationship with the Manufacturer

While many customers prefer to remain anonymous, a startlingly large number have also made it clear that they want the supplier to know who they are and which products they have purchased. In less than twelve months, Hewlett-Packard's consumer products division had built customer profiles for more than 20 million customers who had volunteered to be in relationship with HP after buying a printer, a scanner, a digital camera, or a PC from one of its many channel partners.

12. The Demand for Control over Their Information

If you think that customers are being vocal about privacy issues today, you haven't heard anything yet. Customers' insistence on the privacy and security of their (personal and corporate) information and interaction history is just beginning to gain momentum. Many companies, particularly American companies with a history of information sharing and invasive direct marketing techniques, will quickly fall out of favor.

There are two seemingly opposite forces at play when it comes to customer information.

On the one hand, customers demand that you keep track of every interaction and transaction they've had with you across all of your distribution channel partners and interaction touchpoints. A customer who has done business with you over the Web and in the store expects you to have a record of both transactions. A customer who has bought a computer from one of your dealers expects you, the manufacturer, to track the configuration he's bought and to alert him to necessary patches or upgrades he'll need.

On the other hand, customers want absolute control over every piece of information you collect or infer about them. And they certainly don't want you sharing any of that information in any form, even aggregated and anonymous, with other parties without their explicit consent.

The other tricky balancing act in dealing with customer information has to do with delivering personalized information, targeted offers, and special levels of service to specific customers or customer segments. Detailed customer segmentation is a powerful way to optimize your interactions with customers and to maximize customer value. But you need to be prepared to share your segmentation models and assumptions with your customers.

To effectively use customer segmentation models, you should:

- Gather as much information as possible, explicitly and directly from your customers.
- Have your customers verify the segmentation profile and categories that you've placed them into.
- Understand how your customer's behavior will change over time and how this will affect the segmentation models that you've created.

To make segmentation models useful, be explicit. Let your customers know what kinds of criteria you're using to create categories; let your customers contribute to and verify the kinds of information you've collected. Let them know how you intend to use the segmentation schema, and give them the opportunity to tell you how they think their information should be used. Sharing segmentation information gives you the opportunity to tell them how valuable you believe they are to your company, which is an important step in building strong relationships. Airline companies have set the standard here. They group us into frequent flyer categories based on the volume and value of the business we do with them. As consumers we know which category we're in, what the benefits are of being in that category, and what actions we can take to change the segment we're in.

A permission-marketing approach makes a lot of sense here. Why not send your customers a letter or an email describing the kind of segment and the characteristics that you've attributed to them? That way they can tell you whether they believe they fit into the schema or not. They can also tell you how they want you to manage this information and help you avoid violating their rights to privacy. And don't forget that circumstances and customers' tastes and needs change. The segmentation and targeting that's valid today may be irrelevant, insulting, or annoying in three months' time.

Next: Surviving the E-Market Revolution

In the previous chapter we talked about how the shift to digital information gives customers control over the way we shape, deliver, distribute, and price our digital products and services. In this chapter we've touched on many of the other forces at play in the e-world as customers' demands and desires shape the future of our businesses and transform our industries. In the next chapter we'll take a quick look at another factor that's contributing to the customer revolution: the rise of e-markets.

4

SURVIVING THE E-MARKET REVOLUTION

Think about the world before the advent of Internet-enabled electronic markets (e-markets). Both business customers and consumer customers only had access to goods and services they could easily locate and buy in their local markets. Comparison-shopping across products and manufacturers was tedious and difficult at best. Prices were localized and often varied widely from the prices for the same goods in other countries. In short, sellers had the advantage over customers.

WHY ARE E-MARKETS VALUABLE TO CUSTOMERS?

Customers' time is valuable. Sourcing products takes time. But now with the advent of Internet-enabled e-markets, it's suddenly becoming easier and more cost-effective to locate and procure everything from raw steel to ball bearings, from paper clips to computers, from contractors to consultants. Thanks to e-markets, customers can choose from a much broader array of products and suppliers from large and small companies around the world.

For business customers in particular, the cost of finding the right suppliers and products is a very large percentage of the total cost of procuring a product. Typically the expense (measured in people, time, and effort) involved in locating and sourcing products constitutes up to 30 percent of companies' total procurement costs. To reduce this sourcing cost companies will negotiate contracts with suppliers who do a good job and will stick with them as long as they can continue to meet the company's needs. These long-term contracts exist (and will continue to exist) for two reasons: 1) to guarantee pricing, quality, and availability of the needed supplies and 2) to lower the cost of sourcing products. Yet, eventually, every company needs to find new suppliers or to add suppliers for new products. That's where e-markets are most valuable.

For one-off products and services—things your company only needs to purchase from time to time—again, the cost of locating, selecting and procuring each item constitutes a large proportion of the total cost of procurement, each time you make a purchase. That's why business customers tend to buy from trusted aggregators of similar types of products—office supplies, industrial supplies, agricultural supplies, chemical distributors—to save time in locating and procuring these products. Yesterday's aggregators have now become today's e-markets. Many distributors and aggregators are now running e-markets.

E-MARKETS DESCRIBED

What are e-markets? They're electronic trading communities made up of buyers and sellers with common needs. There are e-markets for agricultural supplies and e-markets for steel, e-markets for industrial diamonds and e-markets for buying and selling electricity, e-markets for computers and e-markets for office supplies. There are e-markets springing up all over the world in every industry, addressing every conceivable need.

You'll find e-markets in which prices are dynamic and determined by auction (highest or lowest bidder wins) or exchange mechanisms (as soon as buyer's and seller's prices match a deal is struck).

Not all e-markets offer dynamic pricing. There are some e-markets that sell only fixed price goods, yet they offer a large variety of products from multiple suppliers. These fixed price e-markets provide one-stop shopping which saves valuable time. They only offer products that are currently available in inventory. And the e-market makers provide enough descriptive information, product comparisons, and decision-making tools so that buyers can easily find and purchase the products that meet their needs.

Many e-markets also let buyers issue Requests for Proposal (RFPs) and make it easy for prospective suppliers to submit bids. By moving the RFP process to an electronic market, companies are more likely to receive bids from smaller, specialist suppliers that they might never have found any other way.

E-markets typically offer a wide variety of ancillary services required by buyers and sellers, such as procurement approval workflows (the ability for an end-user to select a product, email a link to his manager for budget approval and to the purchasing department for final purchase), risk management (insuring the quality of the goods as well as the goods themselves as they move from seller to buyer), settlement services, conflict resolution services, and logistics services.

In late 1999 and 2000, literally hundreds of large-scale, well-funded, business-to-business (B2B) e-markets suddenly sprang into being around the world. This unprecedented rush to e-markets occurred in direct response to business customers' desires to take advantage of the Internet to streamline procurement. Customers jumped at the opportunity to lower the cost of finding and procuring products—both products they use all the time, and products and services they use infrequently.

HOW THE E-MARKET REVOLUTION WILL IMPACT YOUR COMPANY

Internet-enabled e-markets are here to stay. Business and consumer customers will continue to insist on having the ability to locate, compare, and procure goods and services from a wide variety of suppliers. Yet, the rise of e-markets won't obviate the need for suppliers of everything from children's shoes to gasoline pumps to offer customers a variety of ways to locate and procure their products. Customers will want to find your products in the e-markets they prefer. So, you'll need to be present in more than one e-market. And, prospects and customers will also insist that you continue to sell your products direct via the Internet. Large customers will continue to demand their own tailored extranet sites (sometime called Premier Pages, see below). Large customers will also require key suppliers to provide customized product and pricing information directly onto their Intranet sites, so that they won't have to log onto multiple suppliers' sites.

How will suppliers cost-effectively meet these varied, and seemingly competing, customer demands? They key to surviving the e-market revolution is to realize that e-markets are simply one of a number of avenues through which you'll be selling and procuring products and services. The other avenues don't go away. These are all additive business models. To succeed, suppliers will need to organize their product information and rules-based pricing using a single, flexible information architecture, so that all changes in products, descriptions, attributes, pricing, and availability are entered and managed in a single location. This centrally managed product information can then be used in a wide variety of Internet-enabled business models.

To understand all the different ways in which customers will want to locate and procure products, let's take a closer look at the evolution of e-markets. As you read through the chronology of events that led to today's e-market revolution, remember that none of these business models have been supplanted. They're all still viable. That means that your business strategy will need to incorporate several of them.

EBAY SPARKED THE E-MARKET REVOLUTION

While online auctions and exchanges existed pre-eBay, they didn't sow the seeds of the e-market revolution. EBay did. Before eBay, the world of retailing and b-tailing (selling to business customers through stores and catalogs) was a very different place. EBay began life as a consumer-to-consumer auction site, but it soon also became a business-to-consumer and even a business-to-business e-marketplace.

The eBay Phenomenon

EBay started out as a venue to auction off collectibles—baseball cards or Barbie dolls—or to get rid of that junk accumulating in your attic. But eBay's millions of customers also snapped up new digital cameras, new or recyled office furniture, and bulk lots of unsold inventory. Small businesses quickly discovered that this consumer-to-consumer online auction site had also become the world's largest and most cost-efficient marketplace to reach consumers and small businesses and to move virtually any kinds of new or used goods, from real estate to BMW parts. EBay still supports consumer-to-consumer transactions. But it also supports business-to-consumer transactions, and, increasingly, even business-to-business transactions. EBay is the premiere online trading community worldwide and the first mass market electronic marketplace.

By mid-2000, 16 million people were actively buying and selling on eBay—many of them, every day. Five million new items were being listed for sale each day—most of them by small businesses selling everything from jewelry to printer cartridges. Over $1 billion of new (not used) merchandise was sold each quarter in 2000 by small and large businesses using eBay as their marketing and sales channel. And over 63 million auctions were hosted each quarter. You don't even have to be at your computer to participate in an eBay auction. EBay Anywhere lets you bid in the back of a cab, using any wireless Internet device.

EBay has regional auction sites in 52 markets across the United States and country-specific sites in many countries, including Canada, the U.K., Germany, Japan, Korea, and Australia. In 2000, eBay acquired Half.com, which gave it the capability to offer fixed price goods in addition to auctions.

The eBay Experience

EBay has become the *de facto* arbiter of price. As a consumer or a small business person, if you want to know what the "going price" is for anything from a used car, to a copier, to a brand new digital camera, you check on eBay first.

And customer community is alive and well at eBay. EBay users form "neighborhood watch" groups to help guard against misuse or violations of site etiquette. Customers have also planned vacations together, hosted local picnics, and helped each other in tough times.

What made eBay so successful? One of the most important factors in eBay's success is customers' ability to rate the sellers. This gives customers much more control over the experience of buying online from an unknown party. Customers can choose to buy only from sellers who have received good reviews from other buyers. And if they have a bad experience, they can alert other customers. (Some customers have even been known to misuse this power by asking for discounts in return for posting favorable reviews.)

Why Businesses Flock to eBay

There are 25,000 businesses that account for the vast majority of eBay's sales. EBay calls these its "Power Sellers" and offers these high volume merchants the lowest transaction fees. To qualify as Power Sellers, merchants not only have to sell at least $25,000-worth of goods each month, they also must have received at least 100 ratings from customers, 98 percent of them positive.

GOOD MARGINS

The companies that are easy to do business with and whose products are high quality thrive on eBay. And for them, there's no more inexpensive form of sales and marketing. In exchange for listing fees and commissions ranging from 1 percent to 5 percent of the sale price, merchants can reach millions of customers each day. And most serious merchants selling on eBay report that their profit margins average 40 percent!

LOW CUSTOMER ACQUISITION COSTS

For consumer and business sellers alike, eBay's low listing prices and guaranteed high traffic are highly likely to deliver qualified buyers. eBay, the auction site, has been transformed into eBay, the retailing and b-tailing magnet. After all, if business and consumer customers are already flocking to eBay to look for goods and services, why should businesses spend hundreds of thousands of dollars advertising on Yahoo or AOL when they can list each of their products on eBay for a $2 insertion fee and reach millions of eager shoppers? And once shoppers buy from a company the first time on eBay, they usually go straight to the seller for their second and third orders, buy direct, and pay a standard price. EBay's e-market environment has turned out to be a cost-effective customer acquisition tool as well as an alternative distribution channel.

MARKET TESTING FOR PRODUCTS AND PRICING

What if you have a new product design whose consumer appeal and pricing you want to test market? What better venue than eBay to test out new product ideas?

What Did Businesses Learn from eBay?

At eBay:

- Pricing Is Transparent
- Product Availability Is Transparent
- Auctions Take Place in Real Time
- Customers Can Set the Price They're Willing to Pay
- Customers Are in Control—They Rate the Sellers and Those Ratings Matter
- Customers Can Become Sellers
- Sellers Can Become Customers

In short, customers are in control, yet sellers make good margins. Business people who had experienced eBay realized that Internet auctions, if done right, had the power to create new wealth and to shave procurement costs by offering convenient one-stop sourcing.

Why B2B E-Markets Emerged When They Did

EBay was the catalyst for the e-market revolution. Because of eBay, businesses got interested in the e-market phenomenon. But the eBay model wouldn't work for most large B2B transactions. There was a need for a new kind of e-market mechanism—e-markets designed from the ground up to meet the needs of large businesses as well as smaller ones. The business-to-business trading climate is much more complex than the eBay model. Business customers often don't pay with credit cards; they use purchase orders, open account billing, and other forms of payment. They expect to negotiate pricing and terms and conditions with the supplier and to have those negotiated prices apply for every subsequent purchase they make. Businesses have complex, formalized purchasing workflows. Large businesses have automated procurement and inventory management systems that need to be electronically linked to any e-market in which the business chooses to participate as a buyer, a seller, or both. (What would be the point of saving time in locating products using a one-stop-shopping e-market if you have to type in a purchase order at each e-market site and then re-enter that purchase order into your internal procurement and accounting systems?)

Let's take a look at the steps that led to the current B2B e-market frenzy. Then we'll make some predictions about how the e-market landscape will change in the next three years and what it will mean to your company.

Step 1: Business Customers Demand Their Own Customized Web Sites

By 1996 a number of companies—led by Dell Computer, Microsoft, and National Semiconductor—had acceded to customer demands to create account-specific Web sites (originally called Premier Pages) for key accounts. Each supplier tailored each customer's extranet to show only the products that the buyer wanted its employees to be able to purchase, in their preferred configurations, and with their company's preferred pricing. These customized Premier sites were popular for about twenty-four months.

But it didn't take long before savvy business customers began to tire of customized extranets. They realized that these customized Web

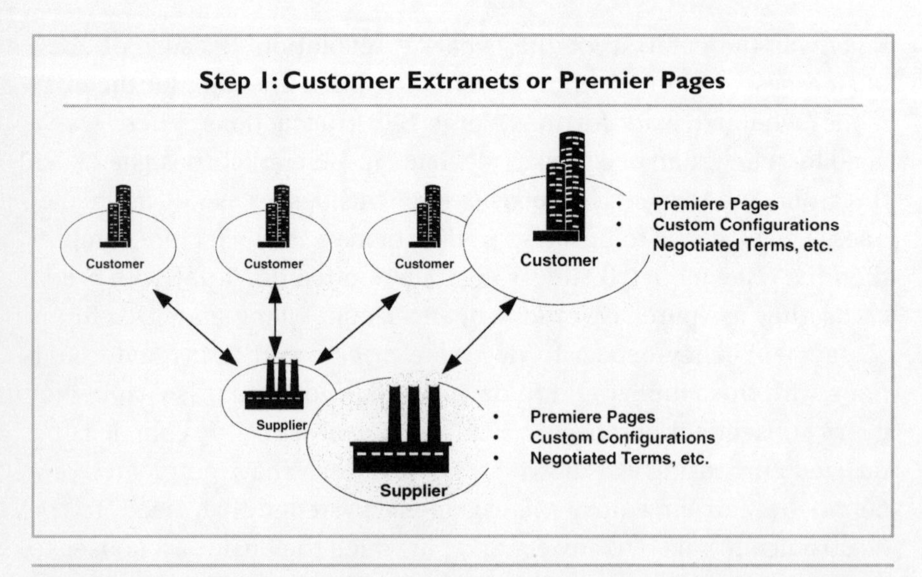

Dell Computer was one of the first B2B players to introduce the concept of Premier Pages, although many others quickly caught up. Customer extranets are dedicated, private Web sites that are set up by the supplier for each of its largest customers. These private Web sites typically offer one-stop shopping and support for prenegotiated configurations. Customer extranets are also used to preview new product ideas to selected customers and for suppliers and customers to co-design solutions.

sites caused three problems. Customized extranet sites required business customers to:

- **Log onto Multiple Sites.** Employees would have to log on to several different suppliers' extranet sites to do their jobs. That meant that these business customers had to remember a host of different logons and passwords.
- **Forgo One-Stop Shopping.** Since every supplier had a different extranet site, employees couldn't get everything they needed in one convenient, central purchasing location. Each time an employee wanted to research and/or purchase furniture or requisition a spare part, she would need to go somewhere different on the Web, log on with the company-approved password and ID, and hopefully see the products and pricing that had been preapproved by her purchasing department.
- **Bypass Corporate Procurement Workflows.** Even when employees did their research and procurement on a company-approved extranet site, many of these sites didn't link directly to their company's own approval workflows, budgeting applications, or corporate procurement and/or accounting systems. That made it difficult to track spending and manage and streamline the end-to-end customer experience.

Step 2: Large Customers Want Suppliers to Integrate into Their Procurement Systems

Between 1998 and 2000, large and powerful business customers began clamoring for suppliers to deliver their product information along with customized configurations and pricing inside their Internet firewalls. They wanted each supplier's product information to be provided in a format that could be integrated into their own intranet-based multi-supplier catalogs. These companies also wanted to be able to use their own internal purchasing approval workflows and to have orders placed directly into their own procurement applications.

Thus was born the notion of "punch-out" applications, as Ariba calls them (or "round trip" applications in the Commerce One lingo). Both of these e-commerce platform players provide mechanisms that interconnect a supplier's extranet site to a business customer's procurement or other enterprise applications. The employees who are

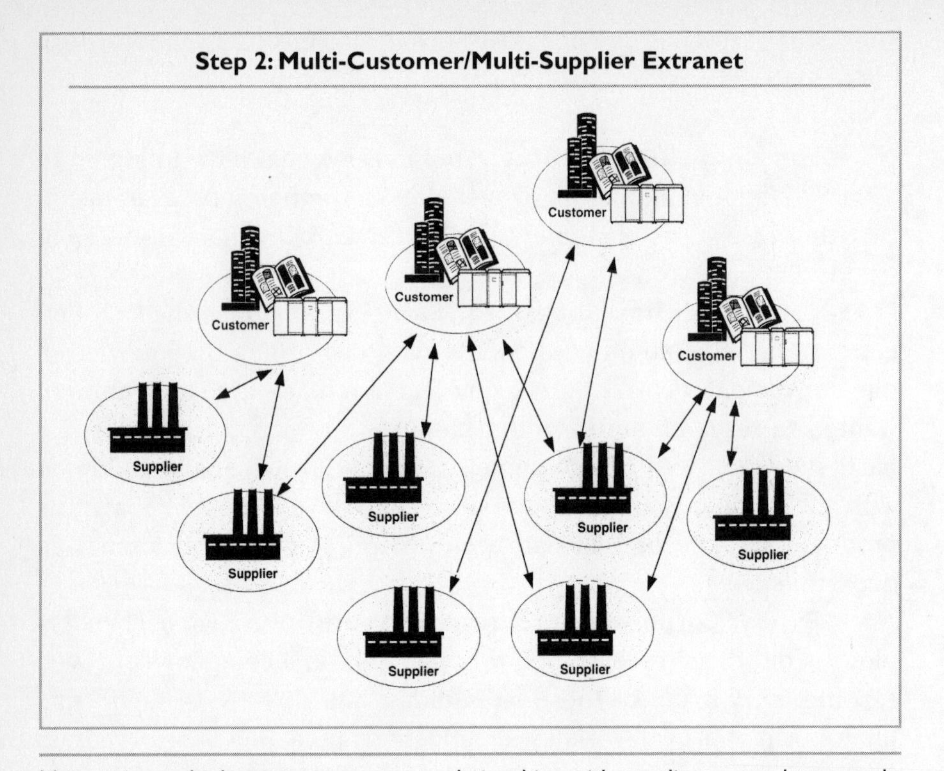

Maintaining multiple, separate extranet relationships with suppliers proved too costly. Buyers and sellers had to provide custom interfaces to each other's systems.

locating and ordering products aren't aware that they are leaving their intranet site and "punching through" to the supplier's extranet. They only know that they see the correct configurations, pricing, and inventory availability when they requisition or order the products.

The problem with this way of doing business for most large firms—customers and suppliers alike—was that it required too much work for each set of parties to interconnect to each other's systems. There had to be a better way, and there was.

Step 3: Exchanges and Auctions Spur Interest

The next driver of the e-market revolution was the emergence, also between 1998 and 1999, of Internet-based B2B exchanges and auctions. These Internet trading hubs sprang into being in a wide variety of industries.

Online exchanges turn out to be the perfect vehicle for turning

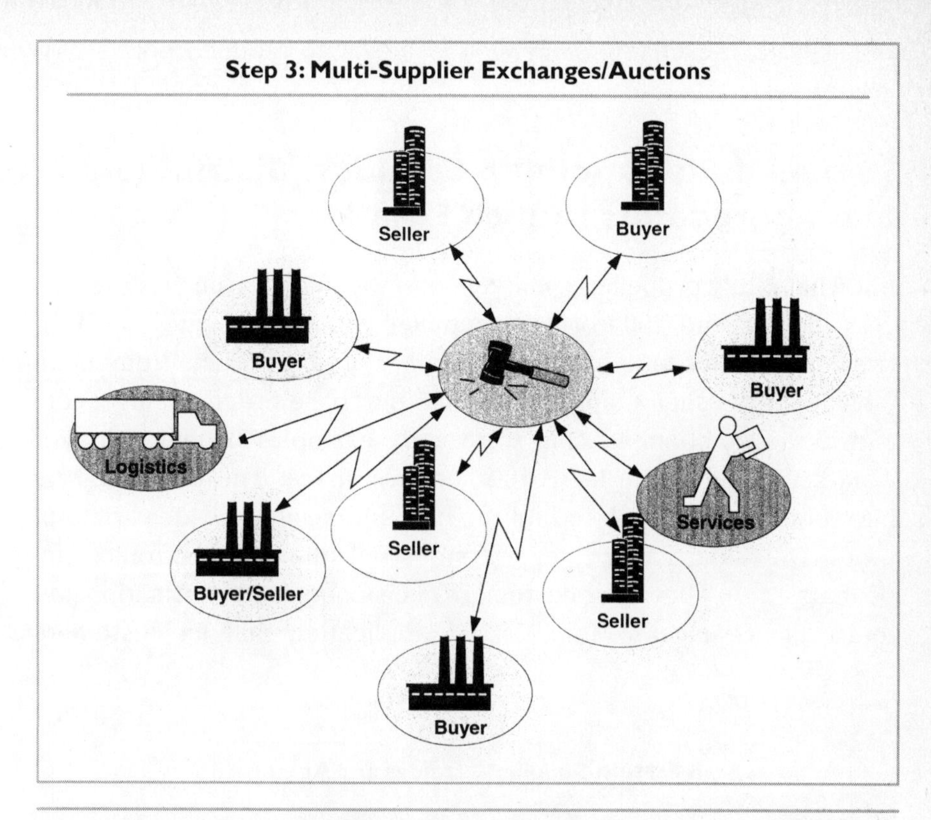

An electronic exchange automatically matches buyers and sellers of perishable commodities (like kilowatt-hours) using bid/ask prices, just like the stock market. In an auction, bidders vie against one another, often anonymously, either raising or lowering the price (in the case of a reverse auction) of the items on offer. Be aware that, in this business model, participants may be a buyer in one transaction and a seller in another. Suppliers may sell to other suppliers, customers may sell to suppliers, and suppliers may buy from their traditional customers.

highly perishable commodities and services into hard cash. Whether you're buying or selling kilowatt-hours, telecommunication minutes, lobsters, or capacity on a printing press, there's probably an Internet-based digital exchange that will automatically match buyers' and sellers' prices in your industry.

While exchanges are often used for commodities that are dynamic in price and perishable, auctions are well suited for buyers and sellers of less perishable items such as excess inventory or used equipment. If you're in the market for some refurbished manufacturing equipment, a batch of specialty chemicals, or a truckload of ladies' underwear, there's bound to be an Internet-based specialty auction site you could use to consummate a deal.

These B2B exchanges and auctions began to catch corporate buyers' interest.

Step 4: Multi-Supplier E-Catalogs, Distributors, and Aggregators Launch E-Markets

But what really propelled e-markets into the mainstream was the success in 1999 and 2000 of multi-supplier catalog or aggregator Web sites. These sites let a business customer order products from multiple suppliers using a single electronic purchase order. Grainger.com and Electrocomponents.com were early examples of multi-supplier e-marketplaces in the industrial supplies space. These aggregators have done the research to find the best sources for a wide variety of products in a particular category (industrial supplies, electronic components, etc.). They offer customers decision-making information and tools, like Grainger's MotorMatch® application that let customers

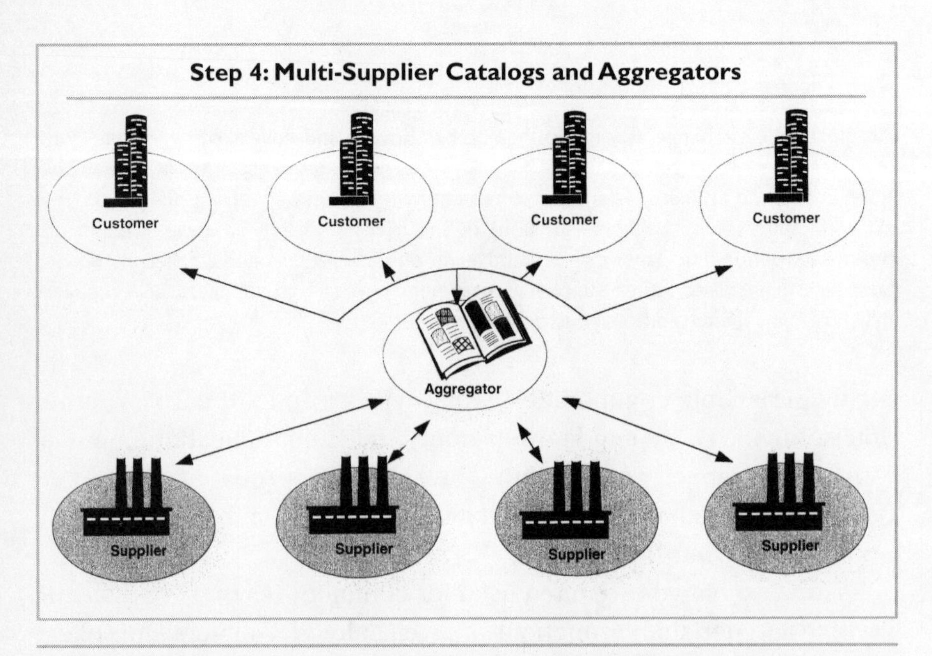

The earliest form of e-markets was embodied by the aggregators or catalog suppliers that offered multiple suppliers' fixed-price products. W. W. Grainger was one of the early leaders. Grainger.com is designed for corporate customers that need to make spot-buys of non–manufacturing-related supplies. Grainger.com offered one of the key criteria of a true e-market: the ability to buy products from multiple suppliers with a single purchase order.

locate the right product for the situation at hand. They save customers time by providing one-stop shopping.

Step 5: E-Markets Emerge in Every Industry

The result of this convergence of business models and customer demands was the rapid emergence of hundreds of B2B e-markets all over the world. Some catered to the needs of specific industries, such as hog farming, hospitals, hedge funds. Others addressed the requirements of all businesses, such as office supplies, employee benefits packages, computers, and telephones. Customers' demands quickly shaped these e-markets. Those that began as auction sites soon added fixed-price products. Those that began as listings of products and ser-

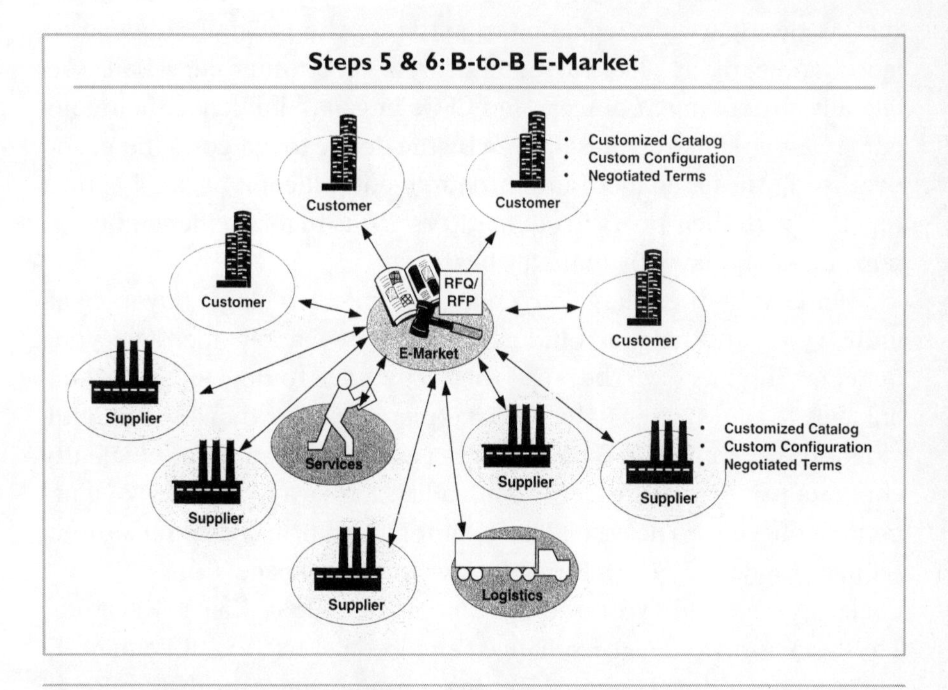

This is the form that many of today's e-markets have gravitated towards. E-markets tend to serve specific industries such as hotel chains, supermarkets, and automotive companies. They may start out as trading hubs for prepriced goods and later add auctions and exchanges. Still later, they typically add the ability for members of the e-market to issue Requests for Quotations (RFQs) and receive bids. Services providers (such as financial institutions and freight forwarders) are often active participants in these e-markets. This is the hottest area for B2B today. Companies that are not actively investing and participating in these industry-specific e-markets are afraid they'll be left out. Competitors in each industry are banding together to create industry-specific e-markets.

vices soon became multi-supplier catalogs. Today most B2B e-markets support the sale of fixed-price products and services as well as auctions and exchanges for variably priced unique or commodity products. They also support the ability for business customers to issue Requests for Quotations (RFQs) and Requests for Proposals (RFPs) to the e-market as a whole, or to specific players, and to receive bids and negotiate terms and conditions, all with electronic support. E-Markets typically also provide financing, risk management, conflict resolution, and all the other properties required by business-to-business players in each specific industry.

Step 6: Large Customers Form Their Own Buyer-Led, Industry-Specific E-Markets

Just as the dust was beginning to settle on the roiling B2B e-market landscape early in 2000, customers threw yet another curveball. Specifically, procurement officers and CFOs began to influence their companies' e-market strategies. Driven by the desire to cut costs, time, and overhead, these finance and procurement officers began banding together with their peers in competitors' firms to form efficient buying hubs on an industry-by-industry basis.

Here's what these large buyers realized: If all the large buyers in an industry create their own industry-specific e-market, then everyone benefits. Suppliers win because they only have to develop electronic linkages to one system—the e-marketplace—rather than to each individual buyer's system. Buyers win because they can more efficiently compare prices, features, and availability across a whole slew of competitive offerings. The result? Large automotive firms (General Motors, Daimler/Chrysler, Ford) formed Covisint; aerospace firms (Boeing, Lockheed), formed Exostar; metal companies (Alcoa, Kaiser, Reynolds, Thyssen) formed Mega-Exchange, and retailers (CVS, JCPenney, El Corte Ingles, Royal Ahold, Tesco) formed the Worldwide Retail Exchange. These are just a few examples of the scores of business-customer-led e-market consortia that have sprung into being since 1999. "Why let a third-party company create a new e-market to serve us? We know our industry better than anyone. Let's do it ourselves!" was the rallying cry from industry to industry. So competitors banned together, threw money into a large pot, and began the laborious process of building massive e-markets.

Step 7: Customer Scenario Nets: E-Markets with Customers' Scenarios at the Core

The next e-market variant on the horizon is what we're calling Customer Scenario Nets. These e-markets revolve around a customer's or a group of customers' specific projects, tasks, or processes. Each customer scenario begins with a task that a customer needs to perform,

Step 7: A Customer Scenario Net

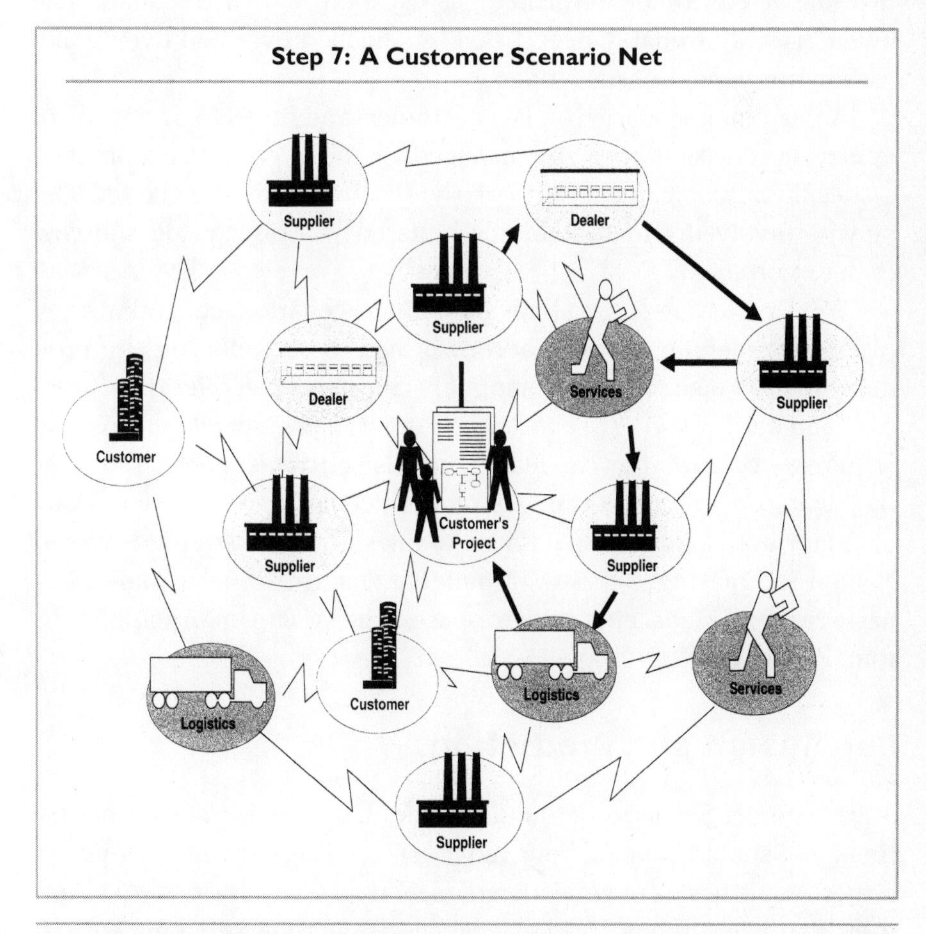

Customer Scenario Nets are e-markets with customers' projects, tasks, and business processes at the core. A Customer Scenario is a set of tasks that the customer needs or wants to have done in order to accomplish a particular outcome. For example, the customer may want to select and purchase new computers and have them installed and maintained. A Customer Scenario Net offers the customer one-stop shopping for all of the steps in his scenario. Different suppliers and partners may participate in providing needed products and services each time the customer returns to re-run the scenario or to launch a related scenario.

for example, manage a construction project or replenish inventory. Other players, partners, participants, and suppliers offer services that are tailored to the context of the task at hand. The state of the customer's project is carried along from player to player through the course of the scenario. The scenario ends with the customer's desired outcome, e.g., the building is completed or the inventory replenished. Note that the same e-market may support multiple interlinked customer scenarios. Once the construction project is concluded, the building needs to be furnished, landscaped, and maintained. The inventory will probably need to be replenished over and over again, with minor variations each time.

A Customer Scenario Net is a customer- and project-specific set of interrelated tasks that can be managed via the Internet to accomplish a specific outcome. It's a particularly dynamic form of e-market. The players involved and the services offered will depend on the customer's context.

What's exciting to us about Customer Scenario Nets is that they place customers in control. Yet they provide a very efficient and profitable market mechanism for suppliers. Suppliers can offer their products and services *in the context* of the customers' specific needs and requirements. And they can learn what else customers need and want by playing an integral part in customers' scenarios.

Later in this book, you'll find examples of two Customer Scenario Nets in the making: Buzzsaw, a building construction Customer Scenario Net, and Medscape, a doctor-patient healthcare information Customer Scenario Net.

Conclusion and Predictions

The Customer Scenario Net model is the B2B e-market model that we think you should have on your radar screen. There is a huge opportunity for some player or collection of players to offer a set of easy-to-use tools that will catapult this business model into market dominance. If you think you have some or all of the pieces needed to create a Customer Scenario Net in your industry, go for it! But be careful that you don't think of this as a customer lock-in or industry-domination play. Customers will demand to *own* and *control* their information. Customers will also require that all their profile or project-related information be easy to move to a competitive or cooperative e-market. And they will insist that e-market makers provide completely interchangeable information and tools.

HOW TO PROSPER IN THE MIDST OF THE E-MARKET REVOLUTION

How do you prepare your business to take advantage of the power of the e-market revolution that's underway? Here are the steps we recommend; most of these steps are useful for consumer as well as business e-markets:

1. Target the key customers with whom you're seeking to build relationships.
2. Find out which critical scenarios and projects these customers need to do and determine where your products and services fit in those scenarios.
3. Organize all the information about your products and services so that it's optimized for customers who need to make decisions and take action. You'll need to know what product attributes customers care about in different situations (e.g., pricing, availability, location, technical specifications, ingredients, and so on).
4. Create dynamic, rules-based pricing engines for all your products and services so that you'll be able to present each business customer with the accurate, negotiated, and customized pricing that's relevant for his company.
5. Organize your product information, pricing rules, and inventory information so that they can be leveraged across several of the different business models described above. The same product and pricing information should be re-usable in all of the seven different business models or steps we've described.
6. Participate in a variety of relevant vertical and horizontal e-markets—you want your products and services to be easy for customers to find in the e-markets they prefer.
7. Don't seek to be the exclusive product or service supplier to an e-market. Customers value choice.

8. Participate in e-markets that help to build your brand. If your brand will be marginalized in an e-market, then choose to play elsewhere.
9. Plan now to create or participate in relevant Customer Scenario Nets for your target customers. Find out what information customers will be willing to provide within the context of the tasks they're performing. Offer tools that let customers streamline their tasks. Make sure that any information you gather about customers and their projects is information to which they have access and information they can control.

Principle #2

CUSTOMER RELATIONSHIPS COUNT

The Value of Your Company
Is Based Upon the Value of
Your Present and Future
Customer Relationships—
Your Customer Franchise

5

IT'S THE CUSTOMER ECONOMY: LEVERAGE YOUR CUSTOMER CAPITAL AND GROW YOUR CUSTOMER FRANCHISE

There's another quiet revolution afoot. It has to do with a change in the way in which companies are valued. This is a subtle shift and one that will probably take at least five years to play out. We predict that by 2005 most companies will be reporting their customer numbers using a consistent reporting standard. We'll call it a Customer Value Index—an indicator of the future earnings potential of the company.

And by 2005 (if not before), investors will be actively assessing the quality of companies' customer relationships. Are these customers truly in relationship with the company or just visitors to its Web site? Do customers feel a connection and a sense of loyalty to the company? Are they currently spending money with the company and showing every sign that they'll continue their loyal patronage?

Investors in some industries already think in terms of customer value when they assess the value of companies. Newspapers, cable TV companies, wireless carriers, and Internet Service Providers are often valued on a per-customer basis. What's a mobile phone customer worth to Deutsche Telekom? What's a newspaper subscriber worth to the *Financial Times?* When investors calculate these numbers, they're checking to see whether the value of the company (its customer franchise) can be justified based on the discounted future earnings that are likely to be realized from its current customers and its likely future customers.

We believe that customer value is going to be an important measure for almost all companies in the not-too-distant future. And we believe that companies in many industries will soon begin reporting the number of their active customers and the growth in their earnings per customer. I mentioned this to Jeff Weitzen, Gateway's CEO, last October and he gave me the rundown on what his current customers were worth. Each Gateway customer, he explained, spends an average of $1,000 to $1,500 on a new computer, but over five years that same customer will spend on average a total of more than $5,000. The additional money is spent on software, Internet services, and education as well as upgrades and peripherals. Although he didn't volunteer the number of total active customers Gateway currently has, Jeff went on to mention that Gateway currently had 1.7 million online services customers who pay $19.95 per month.

Like Jeff Weitzen at Gateway, many of today's CEOs know what their customers are worth. They monitor that value carefully. Within a few years, as investors demand more detailed financial reporting—how many total active customers, what's the profit per customer, what's the customer retention rate, how do earnings per customer increase year-to-year, how does the number of net new customers increase year-to-year—we'll know the value of a company's customer franchise.

The day that I realized the basis of value in the economy had shifted was the day that AOL and Time Warner announced their intent to merge.

THE DAWN OF THE CUSTOMER ECONOMY

January 10, 2000. It was a cold Monday morning in Boston. As always, I opened the door to let the cat out and take in the morning papers. While impatiently waiting for my coffee to brew, I scanned the front page of the *New York Times.* The headline jumped out at me: *"America Online Agrees to Buy Time Warner for $165 Billion."*

As I read the details of the merger, I knew this was a watershed event. AOL, with $5 billion in revenues, could easily afford to buy Time Warner, with $28 billion in revenues. After all, AOL's stock was worth $164 billion while Time Warner's was valued at a measly $97 billion. A new economy company was buying an old economy company using its stock price premium to fund the deal. But what was behind that stock valuation? Was it simply the crazy hype of the Internet/high tech stock market—what Alan Greenspan had dubbed "irrational exuberance?" Or was there a more grounded explanation? I found my answer by reading further and thinking about the intrinsic differences between the two firms. As I did so, I silently thanked Saul Hansell, the *New York Times'* savvy Internet economy watcher. In the third paragraph of his analysis, he had included the numbers that mattered most to me: customer numbers. At the time of the proposed merger, AOL had 22 million subscribers to its online services. Time Warner had 27.75 million subscribers—13 million cable TV subscribers and 14.75 million magazine subscribers (of course, there was probably a considerable overlap—but I suspected that Time Warner had never merged these databases).

This meant that investors valued AOL's customers at $7,455 each, more than twice the $3,495 value of a Time Warner customer at the time of the proposed acquisition. Why did investors believe that AOL's customers were so much more valuable? Both companies derive their revenues from advertising, subscriptions, and content. Both companies are Internet pioneers. (Time Warner's Pathfinder site predated most publishers' online offerings.) Despite many similarities, there was a big difference in the value of the two companies' customer franchises.

Deep Customer Relationships Are Worth More Than Shallow Ones

AOL is in active relationship with its customers. AOL knows who its customers are. AOL's customers interact with the AOL-branded experience several times a week. For better or worse, AOL knows what its customers *do* online—what they look at, what they purchase, and, by inference, what they care about.

On the other hand, Time Warner has a passive relationship with its customers. In fact, it barely knows who they are. Time Warner may know that I'm a subscriber to *Fortune* magazine. It may know that my household subscribes to its cable services. But the chances are pretty good that the company hasn't even correlated those two bits of customer information. More important, Time Warner doesn't *care* about me as a customer. Its function is to send me bills and renewal notices. My brand loyalty is to *Fortune* magazine and to the programs I like on TV. I have no *relationship* with Time Warner. And I certainly don't think of myself as a Time Warner customer.

By contrast, AOL customers think of themselves as AOL customers. AOL has built more than a brand; AOL has built a branded experience. The experience of using AOL is what most customers talk about. Here are some typical examples:

- "I love AOL's Instant Messaging feature! Most of my friends use it, and I can set up a buddy list so that every time my friends log on I am notified (there is a little box in the corner of the screen that stays there unless I close it out, and when friends log on their names appear there)."
- "I've had AOL service for five years now. When I signed on, I found it sufficiently 'user friendly' (idiot-proof), and I made my way around both AOL and the Internet easily without any prior experience. I enjoy friends I've made in an occupation-specific chat room, and I also frequently 'speak' to friends (local and international) in Instant Messages. Using IMs [Instant Messages] has cut my long distance phone bill by two-thirds."
- "I have found AOL's technical support to be excellent. I am not computer savvy, and when I have had problems their techies have talked me through correcting problems without talking down to me or sounding patronizing. They have been very knowledgeable and friendly."
- "I like the AOL greeting screen. As someone who logs on perhaps as many as 15 times a day, the updated news headlines and weather are greatly appreciated when I'm working and have little time to watch TV or listen to the radio."

Fortune magazine (one of Time Warner's flagship magazines) is also a trusted brand. I may think of myself as a "*Fortune*-magazine kind of person." So I identify with the *Fortune* brand. But as an AOL user, I think of myself as a *member* of AOL. I have a *relationship* with the company and its brand. From the time I hear the cheery "you've got mail" announcement to the moment when I realize that Sarah and I are both online and we can chat using AOL's Instant Messaging about the upcoming baby shower, I'm having an "AOL experience." Also, the fact that my friends and family members are also AOL users is part of the AOL experience. It's because AOL's buddy lists and Instant Messaging feature are such a vital part of the AOL experience that the company fought hard for many years to keep competitors from linking their online chat capabilities directly into AOL's.

We believe that the AOL/Time Warner deal marked the dawn of the customer economy. While financial analysts certainly focused on the synergies that this deal would create, no analyst attributed the difference in the two companies' values to the depth of the relationships that AOL had built with its customers. But if you think carefully about why AOL's customers were worth almost twice what Time Warner's customers were worth, you'll come to the same conclusion that we did: customer relationships count! In fact, the quality of those customer relationships is what drives the value of your business.

The Customer Economy Is Easier to Understand

The "new economy" was confusing. Investors have been bewildered by Internet stocks, e-business plays, and high tech fads for the past three years. First they were entranced. Then they began to be skeptical. Venture capital funds, brimming with a continuous influx of pension funds seeking higher returns, flocked from fad to fad. First business-to-consumer e-tailers were hot, then clicks-and-mortar e-tailers and financial services institutions, then consumer-to-consumer auctions, then B2B plays and industry-specific e-markets. Then investors swarmed out of the overcrowded and underperforming B2B market space and flocked back to the safe bets—the "infrastructure" companies selling computers, networks, software, and services to keep the e-economy humming. After that investors migrated to mobile wireless technology plays, and then they fled the technology sector altogether. And on it goes to the next fad.

At the same time all this activity was taking place, a number of customer-focused companies in a variety of industries were hard at work building long-term value. They're now beginning to break out of the pack as investors grow weary of fads and return to fundamentals. The customer economy is already reflecting a revolutionary shift in everyone's thinking about what constitutes a company's value. As investors return to fundamentals—predictable profits and growth in earnings—they're becoming more interested in understanding the source and reliability of those profits and earnings: customers.

In the customer economy, the market value of your business is and will continue to be directly proportional to the value of your customer relationships. Here's why.

The Anatomy of Customer Value

How do investors determine the value of any business? They base it on an assessment of the value of the future earnings the business will generate. Where will those earnings come from? Customers.

Here's a concrete example. In mid-2000, Deutsche Telekom shocked the financial community by bidding $50.7 billion for VoiceStream, a U.S.-based wireless carrier. This valued each of VoiceStream's 2.29 million customers at a whopping $22,000 each. By contrast, another wireless carrier, Vodafone, had paid approximately $7,000 per subscriber when it acquired AirTouch Communications the previous year. What was the difference? These wireless deals are actually being based on the value of *potential* customers. With a coverage area and licenses capable of serving more than 220 million people, VoiceStream was valued at $265 per potential customer. Deutsche Telekom was paying not only for the projected earnings it believed it could generate from the current 2.29 million customers but also for the projected earnings it believed it could reasonably generate from some percentage of the available market of 220 million customers.

The value of any company is based on a combination of the projected earnings from its current customers (customer capital) and the projected earnings from its presumed future customers (customer momentum).

When investors were valuing AOL's customers at more than the twice the value of Time Warner's customers, they weren't saying that each of AOL's (at the time) 22 million subscribers would return a net present value[2] of $7,455 of future profits to the bottom line. They were betting on AOL's ability to retain a healthy percentage of its existing profitable customers as well as on its ability to continue to garner new profitable customers at a healthy rate of growth. And they were assuming that AOL would not only be increasing the number of its customers over time (as it had done in the past) but increasing the profits per customer (both old and new) year over year as well. In short, investors were placing a value on AOL's customer franchise—its ability to build and sustain strong, profitable relationships with current and future customers.

---

[2] Net present value (NPV) is defined as the value today of income to be received in the future. For example, $1,000 invested today at a rate of return of ten percent per

How should you think about your customer franchise? Here are some concepts we think you'll find useful. Start with your customer capital, the net present value (NPV) of the total lifetime value of your current customers. Add to that your customer momentum, the NPV of the lifetime earnings of your likely future customers. The resulting total will be your customer franchise, the total lifetime value of your current and expected future customers discounted back to the present. When investors evaluate your ability to deliver future earnings, they're really assessing your total customer franchise.

Does this way of thinking about company value make more sense than thinking about Price/Earnings multiples? Not necessarily. But it's a good way to test the validity of any company's P/E multiple. Is the company likely to grow the value of its customer franchise adequately to deliver the future earnings implied by the current P/E multiple? If so, how many years will it take to do so? If the time frame is too long or the discount rate you have to use is too low for comfort, then it's probably not a good investment.

You'll find it relatively easy to do these customer franchise calculations for your own company because you're likely to have the information you need at hand. Let's take a look.

Customer Capital

We define customer capital as the sum of the value of all your existing customer relationships. It's a measure of the number of customer relationships you have, the depth and quality of those relationships in terms of their capacity to generate current and future earnings, the duration of those customer relationships (your customer retention), and the profitability of those customer relationships.

Your marketing executives probably already live and breathe customer capital. They refer to it as the lifetime value of your current customers. Here are the elements that probably go into the way they measure and monitor the value of your customer capital. They look at:

---

annum would be worth $1,100 in one year; therefore, income of $1,100 projected to be received in one year would be discounted to yield a net present value of $1,000 today, assuming a rate of return, or discount rate, of ten percent. Similarly, a continuing income stream of $100 per year from now to the far future would have a net present value of $1000, assuming a discount rate of 10 percent, because an income stream of $100 per year is the yield on $1000 invested at a 10 percent rate of return.

- The number of active customers
- The different customer segments (based on demographics and how they behave) and/or cohorts (based on when they were acquired)
- The current average profit per customer in each segment
- The cost to acquire a customer in each segment
- The retention rate for customers in each segment
- The anticipated growth or decline of profits per customer in each segment (based on the recency, frequency, complexity, and value of their transactions)

Marketers have long used these elements to determine the profitability of different customer segments and the viability of their marketing campaigns. They usually calculate the customer lifetime value per customer segment. For each customer segment they know what it costs to acquire those customers, how much profit the company is earning per customer, what the current retention rate is, and (therefore) what the typical tenure or lifetime of a customer will be. And they know with a reasonable amount of certainty (based on past performance) how much the profits per customer are likely to increase over time as customers up-sell and cross-sell themselves and as the cost to serve those customers decreases over time.

Today knowing the lifetime value of your current customers is no longer an esoteric marketing exercise. It's a crucial management tool. In our research we've discovered that many of today's CEOs, CFOs, and other top executives are beginning to pore over customer lifetime value calculations as intently as their marketing executives do. Today's business executives realize that they need to focus on managing the company to maximize the value of their customer capital, their current customer relationships.

Your current customer capital is the net present value of the total customer lifetime value of your current customers. You should know this number for your firm.

Customer Momentum

We define customer momentum as the ability to attract and sustain new customers. Calculating the current lifetime value of your current customers alone won't tell you what your company's future earnings

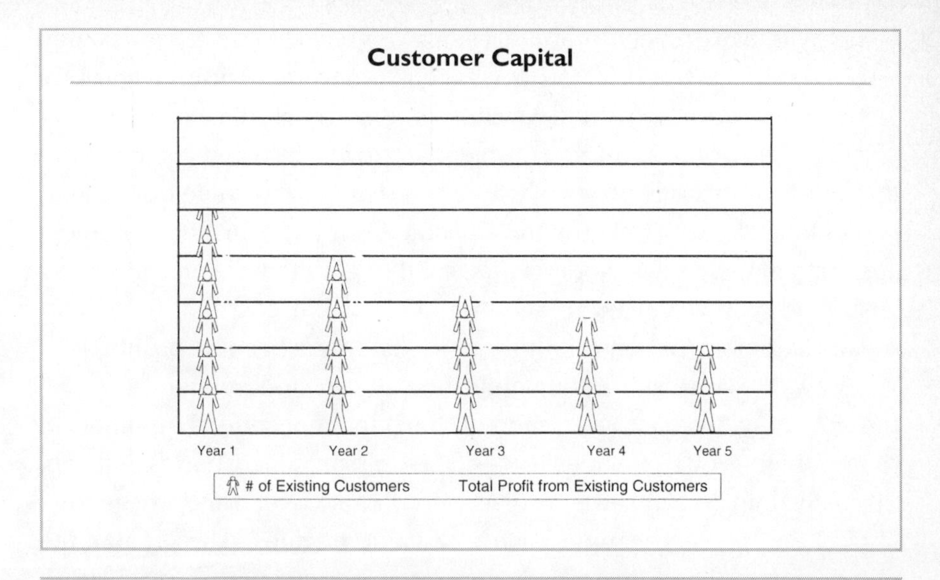

Here's a simple graph showing earnings from current customers. We assumed that the customer retention rate was 80 percent and that profits per customer increased 10 percent per year. Your total customer capital would be the Net Present Value of the sum of the total customer profits over the lifetime of these current customers. In other words, you'd add up the customer profits from each column and apply an appropriate discount rate.

will be. It will only tell you what you can expect to earn from your current customers over their lifetime if you manage those relationships as well or better than you're doing today. You also need to add in the value of the future earnings you expect to receive from new customers, the ones you have yet to acquire. To do this you'll need to make some assumptions:

- How much it will cost you to acquire each new customer in the future?
- What percentage of your marketing budget will you spend on customer acquisition?
- What will be the average profits per customer for each acquisition effort and/or time period?
- What will be the likely retention rate for each new group of customers you acquire?
- How fast will the earnings per customer grow in each segment?

The chances are that your marketing director has already done these calculations. All you need to do is get them and understand them. Every company makes revenues and earnings projections based on assumptions. We suggest you factor in your customer momentum when projecting your future growth in revenues and earnings. It's a useful sanity check. When you look at your projected growth in revenues and earnings over the next year or two, where will that growth come from? What percentage of projected growth will come from your current customers spending more? And what percentage of that growth will come from new customers you still need to acquire? What will it cost you to acquire those customers? When will those new customers become profitable?

Why do we refer to your ability to attract and sustain new customers as your customer momentum? In analyzing a number of today's high-growth businesses—AOL, Amazon.com, Charles Schwab, Cisco Systems, eBay—we've discovered that, over time, these successful companies become customer value engines. The greater the number of satisfied customers they have, the more they're likely to get. What's more, the cost of customer acquisition tends to go down, not up, over time. Why? Because loyal and satisfied customers recruit their friends, colleagues, and relatives. These referrals lower the cost of customer acquisition.

How far out should you project your customer momentum? If you're projecting for the purpose of forecasting your own revenues and earnings growth, you'll probably only want to go out a year or two and then make adjustments as you learn more. If you're projecting a future earnings stream for a company you're considering investing in or acquiring, you'll need to go out a number of years to capture the true value of the company's customer franchise. This, by the way, is no different than the kind of calculation that venture capitalists and investment analysts do to estimate the future value of a company. The major difference is that you're basing your projections on the growth in customer numbers as a basis for the overall revenue and earnings growth.[3]

---

[3] In calculating net present value (NPV) of future earnings from future customers, be prepared for surprises in situations where rapid growth in customer numbers and/or earnings per customer are projected. Once the rate of earnings growth exceeds the discount rate, the contribution to NPV of each future year's earnings keeps increasing the further out into the future you go. For example, if the company's customer franchise grows at 30 percent per year, and you use a discount rate of 10 percent, the value of the customer momentum increases exponentially year by year. Large variations in valuation result from rather small differences in how far into the future you project continued rapid growth. In other words, in rapid growth situations, the value

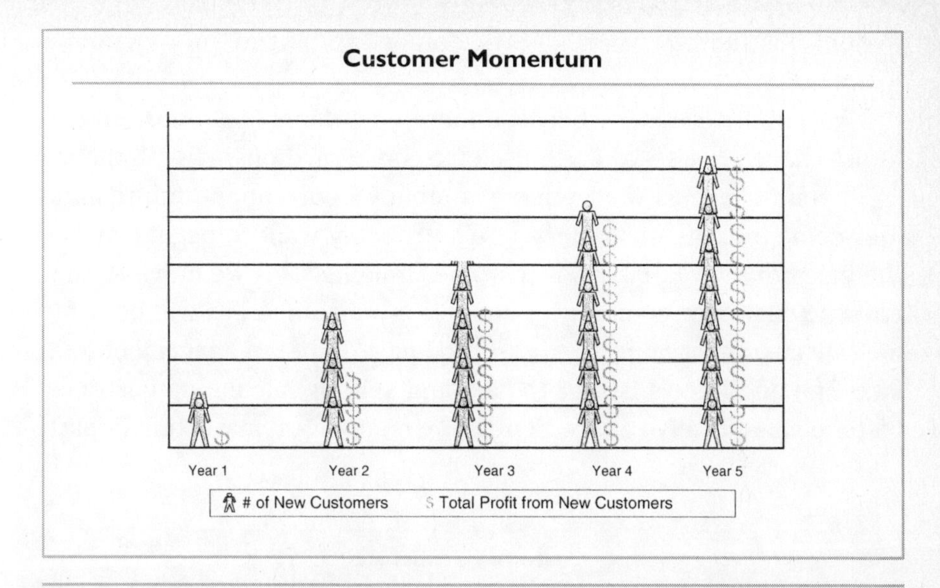

Here's a simplified graph showing the growth in earnings from future customers. We assumed that the company is adding new customers at a rate of 30 percent per year, and that the profits per customer are low for the first year for each new set of customers acquired in Year 1, 2, 3, and so on. This is due to the cost of customer acquisition. From the second year on, we assumed that the profits per customer increased at 10 percent per year. Again, we assumed a customer retention rate of 80 percent. To compute the value of your customer momentum, you'd add up the total profits anticipated from each set of future customers and then calculate the net present value of that total number.

Customer momentum becomes really interesting when your company grows by viral marketing—when customer referrals are so strong that they become the primary source of customer acquisition. Once customers begin recruiting multiple additional customers, as they do in an e-market like Buzzsaw or in an environment like Napster, the value of your customer momentum increases dramatically each year.

Customer Franchise

What investors really care about (and you should, too) is the value of your customer franchise. Your customer franchise is the total present value of the projected earnings from your current and future cus-

of customer momentum is strongly dependent on how far into the future you project that rapid growth will prevail. Assuming rapid growth for seven years, for example, yields a present value for customer momentum significantly greater than that resulting from assuming rapid growth ends in six years.

tomers. Just add together your customer capital and your customer momentum.

We call it a franchise because these customers (both current and future) have granted you permission to be in relationship with them.

If you believe as we do that a company's current and future earnings come from its customers, you'll probably want to begin tracking the value of your company's customer franchise. As we move further into the customer economy, more and more companies will be using lifetime customer value as an essential part of their management toolkits. The good news is that the art and skill of calculating customer lifetime value is alive and well in many companies' marketing depart-

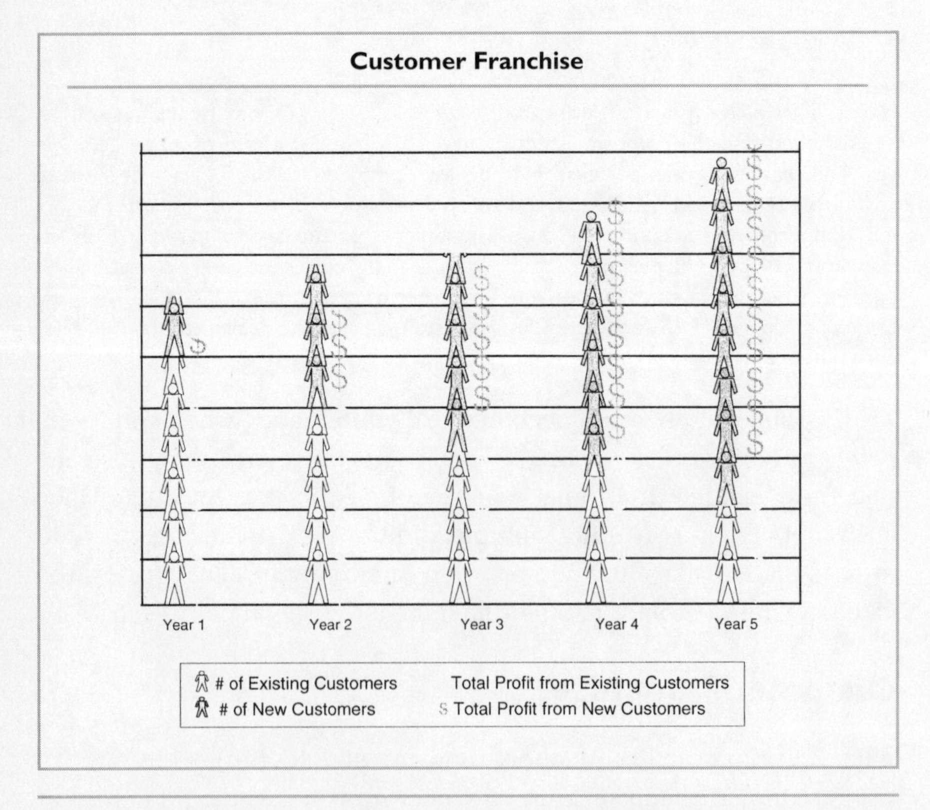

Here we've combined the customer capital and the customer momentum to depict the customer franchise—the total profits from current and future customers. To compute your customer franchise you'd add together your customer capital and your customer momentum totals. We believe that using a customer franchise as the basis for forecasting earnings from present and future customers is a useful approach for estimating a company's future earnings.

ments. What we're proposing is bringing that discipline out of the marketing department and into the boardroom.

USING CUSTOMER FRANCHISE AS A TOOL FOR INVESTORS

Calculating the value of your own customer franchise is definitely doable. However, calculating the value of some other company's customer franchise is difficult because you probably won't have enough information to do a very precise calculation. Calculating lifetime customer value is tricky when you only have average profits across aggregated customers as opposed to profits by actual customer or by customer segment. But as companies begin to disclose more complete customer information, we expect that someone in the financial community will come up with a clever "back of the envelope" formula that will help investors calculate customer value in a way that makes it easy to compare and contrast a customer value index to the current measures of P/E ratios and market capitalization. As soon as we discover one or more simple formulas that work reliably with the aggregate and average customer numbers that companies are likely to be reporting, we'll alert you on our Web site (www.customerrevolution.net).

Educate Investors on the Value of Your Customer Franchise

Charles Schwab was one of the first companies to begin educating investors about the value of its customer franchise. Chris Dodd, Schwab's CFO, stresses the importance of candor and transparency in dealing with the investor community by providing it with important customer metrics. These include total customer assets (broken out by investment category) and net new assets. In terms of customer numbers, Schwab reports its net new customer accounts and its active customer accounts each quarter. Schwab counts as "active" those accounts with balances or activity within the past twelve months and any online household that has had at least one online session within the last twelve months.

Many of the CEOs and top executives we interviewed are beginning the process of educating the investment community about the value of their customer franchise. Pradeep Jotwani, the president of Hewlett-Packard's Consumer Business organization, has been explaining to analysts the value of the consumer customers with whom HP now has active relationships. These 20 million customers are no longer anonymous. They are customers who have chosen to be in relationship with HP. Most of them buy an ongoing stream of supplies from the company. That recurring revenue stream is something that the financial community needs to understand, according to Pradeep.

Customer Relationships Are a Key Intangible Asset

The idea that customer relationships are assets may seem foreign in an accounting world that only knows how to value fixed assets like land and factories. We all know customers can't be owned. A company can't control its customers in the same way it controls fixed assets.

When companies are bought and sold, customer lists are counted as part of the "goodwill" in the transfer of intangible assets. Yet sometimes even a customer list can't be transferred. When Toysmart declared bankruptcy in June 2000, the U.S. District Court in Massachusetts blocked the sale of the company's customer list, ruling that Toysmart's customers hadn't given the now-defunct company permission to sell their names. That's probably why Amazon.com altered its privacy policy in September 2000, notifying customers that it does maintain the right to transfer customer lists when it sells off any of its "stores." We suspect that Amazon's privacy policy change may have been triggered by the deal that Amazon.com cut with Toys "R" Us in mid-2000. In this arrangement, Amazon.com stopped selling toys on its own Web site and replaced its online toy "store" with Toys "R" Us's online toy store. (Amazon.com also sold its toy inventory to Toys "R" Us.) Amazon.com now handles all of Toys "R" Us's online toy sales and fulfillment. Perhaps Amazon.com wanted to share or sell the customer information of Amazon.com's toy-buying customers with Toys "R" Us. If Amazon.com were to exit the auction business at some point in the future, it would want the right to sell that customer list to eBay. You can expect to see companies becoming much more explicit, both about their privacy policies and about their ownership and transfer rights with regard to their customer lists.

Customer lists have some value. What about customer accounts? If active customer accounts are transferred, as in the case of the sale of a bank with customers' money on deposit or the sale of a magazine with customers' subscriptions as a liability they have to fulfill against, these assets and liabilities are transferred from one company's balance sheet to another. But they're always heavily discounted, and rightly so. You can't actually transfer a customer relationship. The new owner can only hope to win the loyalty of a majority of the transferred accounts.

In other words, a customer list is nowhere near as valuable as a company's relationships with its customers. Unlike assets that can be sold or transferred, customer relationships are most valuable to the company that established them. They can rapidly diminish in value once that company is acquired or merged.

Yet customers—specifically, our relationships with customers—*are* an asset because they are the source of revenue in the same way a right-of-way is for a railroad, a coal mine is for a fuel company, or a network is for a telecommunications company. Without those customer relationships we have no hope of future revenue and earnings. We need to keep exploring more and better ways to get closer to our customers. Amazon.com's Jeff Bezos would be the first person to tell you that customer relationships must be earned and re-earned every day. You build deep customer relationships by knowing your customers as people—not just as a mailing list or an accounts receivable file—and by offering those customers an experience that they value. Are you ready for investors to begin monitoring the quality of your customers' experiences? You'd better get ready, because it's the quality of the total customer experience that will determine whether your company will retain its customers.

Companies Are Starting to Report Customer Numbers

Every company or industry uses different metrics for measuring success. Airlines measure revenue-passenger miles. Retailers measure revenues per square foot. Mail-order companies measure revenues per catalog page. Manufacturers measure revenues and profits by product line. Financial services companies measure assets under management. Yet all of these different kinds of companies have customers. And many are finally beginning to track how many actual end customers they have.

Today there are only a handful of companies that routinely report customer numbers. Charles Schwab and Amazon.com are much more upfront about their customer numbers than many other companies. Next come direct marketers such as Lands' End and retail financial services firms such as banks. Most telecommunications and cable companies also report customer numbers and churn rates. When cable or wireless companies are bought and sold, the deals are valued and reported in the press on the price per customer. The same measures are typically used for Internet Service Providers and magazine and newspaper publishers. In these subscriber industries, the financial community has decided that it makes sense to measure a firm's earnings potential by the size and value of its current and potential customer franchise. How many customers does the company have? How much can it earn per customer? How long will it be able to retain those customers? And how likely is the company to be able to acquire and retain new customers?

If yours isn't a subscriber-based business or a direct-to-consumer marketing business, chances are that financial analysts, investors, and shareholders aren't yet asking you, "How many customers do you have" or "What's the value of your customer franchise." Yet we predict that you're going to find more and more companies releasing these numbers as investors begin to demand them. Now that our customers are more than ever clearly controlling the fate of our businesses, growth in customer value matters. We think that, in addition to monitoring earnings per share, companies should also begin to routinely monitor their own customer value.

Obviously, the ultimate value of any company—its current and future earnings potential—is based on management's ability to deliver high-quality products and services and make sound decisions that will result in increased value by and for its customers. Remember, those earnings will come from customers. Once we get a handle on some key customer numbers and ascertain how well a company is doing in retaining and delighting its existing customers and in attracting new customers, we will be able to make a better-educated guess about its growth potential. Doesn't it make sense for investors to know how many customers the company is currently serving, how much it is earning per customer, how it intends to increase the number of customers, how much profit it derives from each customer, and how long they are likely to continue as loyal customers?

Who Counts as a Customer?

When I asked the management team at Snap-on Tools to give me the number of their customers, they were only able to give me the number of dealers and distributors they have as well as a "guesstimate" about how many end customers there were per dealer/distributor. This is not an uncommon state of affairs. Snap-on's management still thinks of its dealers as its customers in the same way that many consumer products companies think of retailers as their customers. Yet if there isn't someone who uses or consumes your products and services, you won't have any revenues or earnings down the road.

COUNT YOUR END CUSTOMERS

We encourage all companies to do the work required to find out who as many of their end customers are as possible. That's what Snap-on is doing as it evolves its direct-to-customer Web site at the same time it improves its dealer support services. It's a win-win situation when the dealer continues to manage the customer relationship, but the manufacturer acts as a not-so-silent partner in the relationship, standing by if need be to improve the quality of the customer relationship.

Charles Schwab has both a retail business, in which it has direct relationships with customers, and an investment advisor business, in which it provides services to independent investment advisors who manage individual client accounts. Although Schwab provides back-end brokerage services to the clients whose accounts are managed by advisors, Schwab doesn't interact directly with its advisors' clients, yet Schwab does know who those clients are. And Schwab does include these end-client accounts in its overall reporting of customer numbers and customer assets.

Business Customers: Accounts or Individuals?

Who are your customers when you sell to businesses—accounts or individuals? The answer is both. Most of the leading-edge businesses we interviewed are very clear about the fact that they need to know every individual who deals with them, whether that person is the purchasing agent who cuts the purchase order, the end user of the products, the decision-maker, or someone who influences the product selection decision. Why? Because these business leaders understand that you can't be in relationship with companies, only with people. And if a person leaves one company and joins another, you certainly want to be able to continue that relationship, gaining a new account in the process.

Remember that what matters is the depth of the relationships that have been built. Relationships are built between people. And no matter how strong the bond, customers will defect in a heartbeat if you violate their trust or disappoint them in some way.

Known Customers Versus Anonymous Customers

Companies that know who their customers are and have relationships with them are more valuable to investors than companies in the same industry that don't know who their customers are. There are some industries—oil and gas, pharmaceutical, building supplies, and so on—that will be slower than others to decide that customers count. But I believe that at least one company in every industry will begin to identify and build relationships with its end customers. Once one does, the rest will follow. Can you afford to be the company that doesn't?

Obviously, known customers—customers you can be in relationship with—are more valuable than anonymous customers. Yet there are many companies that have no idea who their end customers are. They can only tell you their estimated market share of a given demographic, product category, or geographic market.

Of course, many customers may choose to remain anonymous, yet they may be loyal to the company and its brand. How many avid drinkers of Coca-Cola are there who don't want Coca-Cola to know that they are customers? And what about occasional customers or customers who only buy your products by accident—do you need to know who they are? Probably not. In each industry there is likely to be a percentage of customers who will remain anonymous as market share statistics. That percentage will be higher in some industries than in others. In a few industries—financial services, airline travel, mail-order retail or business retail (b-tail)—it's not legally possible to remain anonymous. In others it's difficult but possible (electric utilities or telephone service). But in the bulk of business and consumer dealings, it is possible for customers to remain anonymous. If you want to build relationships with your anonymous customers, you start by gaining their trust and offering them a better customer experience each time they are willing to reveal more information about themselves.

Therefore we suggest that companies start reporting their known customers and their best guess about the number of anonymous customers they have (this is usually reported in terms of market share). We predict that it won't be long before the financial community will develop consistent customer-centric reporting standards as a requirement for all publicly held companies.

Start Tracking What You Know Today

Where should you start? Tracking your key customer metrics is a step in the right direction. There are already lots of customer economy companies out there. American Airlines, Charles Schwab, Cisco Systems, Dell Computer, Egg, Getty Images, W. W. Grainger, Hewlett-Packard, IBM, Lands' End, National Semiconductor, Snap-on Tools, and Wells Fargo are examples of companies we consider to be customer economy companies.

The difference between these companies and others is that they have been managing themselves by and for customer value for at least two years (many of them much longer than that). These are companies that know (or are beginning to find out):

- How many end customers they have
- Who their customers are
- What their profits per customer are
- How their profits per customer are growing
- What their customers care about
- How satisfied their customers are
- How loyal their customers are
- What actions are most likely to keep their customers loyal

Let's take a closer look at how today's leaders are managing by and for customer value.

6

MANAGING BY AND FOR CUSTOMER VALUE

As I entered Gideon's corner office, the purple and white football on the couch and the red Nerf® ball temporarily at rest on an armchair reinforced his unorthodox management style. I skipped the comfy couch and headed for the straight-backed chair across from his desk. I had something serious to discuss. I began, "What's the most dramatic change you've seen in the past three years?"

Gideon Sasson, who is the Enterprise President of Charles Schwab's $420 billion online brokerage business, replied, "Customers are now in control. And the competitive landscape is much more transparent. Before the Internet, customers had no real way to measure or compare the value of the exchange; they gave us money, we gave them something of value. A company could block you from knowing its profit margins, its costs, and so on. As a customer, you had no idea what it cost to do something, what the margins were."

"Of course, customers have always been critical for any business. Otherwise companies wouldn't be in business. But in the past, companies weren't forced to always start with customers. What the Internet did was to move control to the customer's hands. People say, 'your customers are only a mouse-click away from the competition.' Actually, the more important fact is that they're only a mouse-click away from other customers who will give them the real skinny."

"Before the Internet," Gideon continued, "Companies could be customer-aware, but they didn't have to be customer-centric. Now they have no other choice. The Internet is forcing everyone to behave differently. Companies used to talk about 'how do we lock the customer in?' They thought about how to own the customer. They incented customers, they brought them in, and then they worried about, 'how do I make profit with these customers' and 'how do I get them to buy this product.' But nobody can afford to think that way any more."

"Even before the Internet, at Schwab we've realized that if we do the right thing for our customers, they'll reward us. But other companies are facing a rude awakening."

Gideon talked a good game. But how could I tell if Schwab was leading the transformation of its industry, or will be one of the many companies that will fall victim to the customer revolution?

Not Just P&L

It was Gideon's next statement that clinched it for me. "The way we manage our organization is fundamentally very different from everyone else in our industry. For example, I'm an enterprise president of a $420 billion business. I sit on the management committee. And I don't have a P&L. I don't need to pay attention to profit and loss. At Schwab, operating P&L is handled by a small, central organization that manages the books in parallel with the *real* business."

Customer Metrics

"So," I asked, "how do you measure your *real* business?" His answer was music to my ears.

"We run our business through customer metrics!"

"What metrics," I asked. "Customer profitability? Lifetime value of a customer? Cost of customer acquisition?" He turned the tables on me. "You're a Schwab customer. What do you care about?" After a moment's reflection, I answered, "I care about having a great customer experience and having my money grow." "Exactly," Gideon replied. "And that's what we measure ourselves on: how satisfied our customers are and how fast their assets grow. The metrics for my business aren't P&L-related, they're based on total customers' asset accumulation, customer satisfaction, and customer retention. As head of Schwab's online retail business, I have to grow the number of online customers and their assets faster than my counterparts in the rest of the retail brokerage business. And to ensure customer satisfaction, I also need to have the fastest and most available online brokerage Web site."

In the old economy, Gideon went on to explain, companies grew by managing valuation. Companies' valuations were driven by P&L, P/E ratios, and managing the bottom line. While such metrics are still relevant, they're no longer the sole drivers of companies' behavior. "Our brokers have no idea what they're earning per customer. They're incented based on asset accumulation of customers' portfolios and on customer satisfaction. Our branch managers have no idea whether their branch is more profitable than another. A Schwab branch manager doesn't know how much the branch costs per square foot or the cost of electricity. She doesn't know how much her employees cost compared with those at other branches. What she *does* know is how many new customers she's acquired, how satisfied all of her customers are, and how their assets are growing."

Schwab Manages for Customer Experience and Customer Value

Chris Dodd, Schwab's CFO, explains, "We live our lives around the question, 'how can we make the customer experience a better one?' We don't focus on current trading volumes or even on new accounts. We aren't rewarding or pushing people to get more new accounts. We focus on providing the best customer experience and on growing our customers' assets."

How does this work in practice? Charles Schwab and David Pottruck function as the Co-CEOs at Schwab. They have a small executive management committee that meets once a month. Schwab is organized around five large "customer enterprises": U.S. Retail Broker/Dealer, International Retail, Investment Management (the independent financial advisor channel), Capital Markets, and Retirement Plan Services. "We do have P&Ls for each enterprise. We know their revenues and their direct costs," Chris explained, "but we spend most of our time focusing on maximizing the customer experience." Schwab doesn't worry about the contribution to profits of its online brokerage unit compared with the rest of its retail brokerage business. But the company does seek to grow online brokerage faster than the traditional retail brokerage. Why? Because Schwab's online brokerage customers are its most satisfied customers.

"I meet with the head of each enterprise each month and do a hard close on the fourth or fifth of each month. Then for each enterprise, we do a quarterly review. But when we meet, we only spend twenty minutes on the financial profile. The rest of the time is spent reviewing what we've done for our customers."

For each customer enterprise, Schwab tracks customer's asset accumulation, customer satisfaction, customer retention, and employee retention (the latter is important both for customer satisfaction and overall profitability). These are the measures on which managers and employees are incented. By focusing single-mindedly on customers' success, Schwab continues to grow the value of its customer franchise.

Managing P&L in Near-Real Time

Like most customer-economy companies, Schwab has learned how to deliver predictable earnings and revenue growth. Part of the secret of its success is the company's fanatical focus on increasing its customers' assets. Another factor is the eagle eye that Chris Dodd and his financial colleagues in each customer division keep on the revenue stream and the costs to serve. Although employees don't need to worry about P&L, they all know the correlation between high trading volumes and gross margins. What's the daily indicator that Schwab's employees pay most attention to? Trading volume. "We all watch the Daily Trading Revenues and adjust our spending programs appropriately," explains Janice Rudenauer, Schwab's VP of Relationship Marketing.

Schwab isn't unique in its ability to keep an eagle eye on the bottom line and adjust its spending levels on the fly. One of the advantages of running your business in near-real time is that "surprises"—from trading storms to chip shortages—are witnessed in near-real time and can be compensated for immediately.

Egg Manages for Customer Value

When asked what key metrics he and his top executives track closely, Richard Duvall, Managing Director of Customers and Portals for Egg (the U.K.-based financial services firm), reports that Egg runs the company based on the net present value of the lifetime value of its customers (in other words, its customer franchise). The most closely tracked metric is customer acquisition cost, and the second is the number of products each customer holds. Egg's financial models indicate that once customers are using 2.5 Egg products, they become profitable. "We've engineered our whole business for cross-sales." As of mid-2000, the Egg credit card, had proven to be the company's most cost-effective customer acquisition tool ("You'd be silly not to own one"). The Egg card offers low interest rates, exceptionally low interest on transferred balances, and cash back on purchases made with the card. "It's a marginally profitable product for us, but it works to bring customers in." Egg's branded experience and the allure of its other products then help to move each customer into the profitable zone as he adds additional products.

Cisco Manages for Customer Satisfaction

Cisco Systems is an acquisition machine. The company's phenomenal growth has been fueled by acquiring and integrating companies with a remarkable efficiency. Cisco's ability to close its books on the last day of each month ("zero close") has become legendary. The company is so Internet-enabled that it's possible for all employees to get a near-real time look at virtually every aspect of the business—orders placed, orders shipped, account activity, and so on. Where the rubber meets the road at Cisco is with customer satisfaction.

The two key customer metrics that Cisco tracks are the percentage of business customers who transact online and how satisfied customers are. Cisco measures the amount of business customers do online for two reasons. First, the Internet yields a lower cost to serve customers, and second, self-service customers are more satisfied customers. Cisco measures customer satisfaction with its Web site and its call centers every week. A small percentage of customers receive an email or phone survey after they've completed an interaction. "We look at these numbers on a weekly basis; they let us spot trends and deal with them quickly," reports Todd Elizalde, director of Internet Commerce and Customer Service. The ongoing surveys measure customers' satisfaction at the transaction level. Customer emails are tracked, responded to, and categorized.

Then every six months, Cisco has a relationship survey done. This survey targets the decision-makers as opposed to the people who have been transacting business with Cisco on a daily or weekly basis. The results of the relationship survey are built into Cisco's bonus plan. Each year the company sets a customer satisfaction goal. There's a significant upside for all employees if they exceed the goal. Hitting it isn't enough. There's also a multiplier in both directions. So if they miss the target, the results are punitive.

By tracking customer satisfaction on a fairly granular basis (at the transaction and interaction level), Cisco is able to pick up patterns that it might otherwise miss. For example, the company discovered that the customer satisfaction scores from customers who interact primarily with Cisco's channel partners were lower than the scores from Cisco's direct customers. As a result, the company is rolling out a Customer Relationship Management (CRM) system that will allow Cisco to track and interact with its all of its end customers (both direct and indirect). This will not cut channel partners out of the loop but back them up with additional service and support as customers' needs dictate. For Cisco, like others chronicled in these pages, managing the quality of customers' total experience is a high priority.

NCR Monitors Customer Loyalty

To keep on track, today's business must effectively turn information about its customers into intelligence that can guide the company's actions. No longer can this be offline market research conducted leisurely in some back room. The pace of business now requires that near-real-time information be analyzed and responded to quickly.

The technology for handling near-real-time customer information has kept up with the increased pace of business. NCR is one of many companies that have invested heavily in its own customer intelligence. Over the last 10 years, NCR has refined and sharpened its focus. What began as an internal method for monitoring customer satisfaction has become a robust loyalty management process driven by a commitment to customer value.

Based on interviews, surveys, and questionnaires, NCR's system measures both satisfaction and loyalty. The process has two primary outputs. One feeds senior managers satisfaction and loyalty measures that affect compensation and strategy, and the other directly routes specific account information to field managers for action. Of course, NCR's account teams visit these customers immediately. And in parallel, the customer satisfaction and loyalty scores are aggregated and reported to management. The aggregated customer satisfaction and loyalty metrics impact product development, pricing, and marketing—all aspects of the corporate strategy. NCR also ties satisfaction/loyalty results to compensation so that employees will see the effects of their work. This multifaceted statistical and operational system embodies the capabilities needed in the customer economy—customer intelligence based on thorough research, constant monitoring, and quick response to needs. This attention to customers has produced increasing customer loyalty numbers and consequently increasing customer value. Specifically, customers themselves report that they see the value of their relationship with NCR increasing. It is worth more to them to do business with NCR because of its customer sensitivity.

Next: Monitor the Customer Experience

Managing by and for customer value shows you the big picture of how you're doing. It's like the navigation controls on a flight deck. You can see you're on track. You know what altitude you're flying at and in what direction. But monitoring customer value doesn't give you the leverage to control your destiny. To do that you need to focus on the quality of your customer relationships, with both existing and new customers. That means focusing on the total customer experience—one of the key secrets to success in the customer economy.

Principle #3

CUSTOMER EXPERIENCE MATTERS

The Feelings Customers Have When They Interact with Your Brand Determine Their Loyalty

7

THE SAVING GRACE: DELIVER A GREAT TOTAL CUSTOMER EXPERIENCE

Customers are in control. And customer relationships count. How do you win the customer revolution and thrive in the customer economy? How can you manage customers' expectations, gain their loyalty, and let them influence your business direction? Deliver a great customer experience.

Customers are much more likely to become and remain loyal if they identify with your brand, if they have positive experiences every time they come into contact with it, and if they build positive relationships with those who represent your brand. And once customers develop a gut-level sense of what your brand stands for, they'll be your most loyal advocates (and your most vocal critics any time you violate the spirit of your brand identity).

WHAT'S A BRANDED EXPERIENCE?

Here's a personal example of what we mean by a branded experience. A few years ago, I flew out of London via Richard Branson's Virgin Atlantic Airways. I opted for the hotel pick-up service. My driver turned up on a Harley Davidson, with a full suit of leathers, a helmet for me, and a sidecar for my luggage. It was an unusually beautiful day and, as we wove our way out of London, I realized I was having the time of my life! This was a definitely a "Virgin experience."

Virgin's brand-image-makers want you to think of "value with quality, innovation, and fun." They also want the Virgin brand to be thought of as iconoclastic. But they don't stop with a logo or an advertising campaign. Companies like Virgin spend a lot of money building and reinforcing their brand through advertising. But they also focus fanatically on execution. They ensure that every time they touch the customer in any way, he has a "Virgin experience"—whether it's flying on Virgin Airways, purchasing a CD at Virgin Music, or finding a car through VirginCars.com. Customers have given Virgin permission to extend its brand into category after category. And they haven't been disappointed. Customers expect the Virgin approach to any new category to challenge the status quo and to provide a high quality, innovative and fun, customer experience.

We define the total customer experience as *a consistent representation and flawless execution, across distribution channels and interaction touchpoints, of the emotional connection and relationship you want your customers to have with your brand.* Think about this for a moment. What is the emotional connection you want customers to have with your brand? What feelings do you want your brand to evoke? What are you doing to ensure that no matter how customers interact with you—by phone or in person, on the Web or in a store, dealing with one of your employees or interacting with one of your partners—they're always going to feel exactly the way you want them to feel in the presence of your brand?

Why Is a Branded Experience Critical to Success in the Customer Economy?

When we began researching this book, we didn't expect to find that branding itself and the customer experience around a brand were essential ingredients for success. What we discovered, however, is that truly customer-centric companies offer customer experiences that customers value. They build their brand identities not just around products, but around the way they want customers to feel in interacting with their companies. As Charles Schwab's David Pottruck explains, "When a company is able to build [its] brand around its dedication to the customer rather than its dedication to its product, it [the brand] will last for a long time . . . The customer experience . . . is central."[4]

We introduced the notion of the branded experience in our last book, *Customers.com,* in 1998 as we explored and dissected the third critical success factor: Own the Total Customer Experience. Since that time, many businesses have taken the total customer experience challenge to heart. They've reorganized their management teams to place a high-level executive in charge of the total customer experience for the entire company or for key customer segments. They've realized that their e-business initiatives can't be run as separate fiefdoms. Customers have made it clear that they expect consistent, coherent treatment no matter how they choose to interact with your firm—electronically or otherwise.

By identifying and bonding with your branded experience, your customers give you permission to continue to evolve that brand and the value it represents into new areas. In fact, often customers are so clear about the principles surrounding your brand that they'll make it their business to police them. Take the online auction powerhouse, eBay, for example. eBay's customers hold each other to high ethical standards. They don't want the eBay brand to be tarnished by a few hucksters. Customers have taken ownership of eBay's branded experience. That's the ultimate in customer loyalty!

What's Involved in Designing a Branded Experience?

There's a real art to creating an alluring branded experience. And it involves much more than a branding or advertising campaign. This is one of the sobering lessons from the first six years of the e-business boom.

MUCH MORE THAN AN AD CAMPAIGN

From 1994 to 2000 investment capital poured into dot-com startups in both B2C and B2B Internet ventures, first in the United States and then throughout the rest of the world. Investors and venture capitalists were

---

[4] *Clicks and Mortar: Passion-Driven Growth in an Internet-Driven World,* David S. Pottruck, Terry Pearce; Jossey-Bass, San Francisco, 2000, p. 254.

pushing for big advertising and branding campaigns to provide the "first mover advantages" for the companies in which they invested. The VC investors urged the eager management teams of these start-up ventures to spend big on establishing a brand. Advertising spending soared.

But most investors neglected to consider the costs required to deliver a high quality customer experience. As customers made it clear that they expected to be treated well (both on the Web and on the phone) and to have their products and services backed up with flawless customer service, expert advice and guidance, easy decision-making tools, and reliable fulfillment, delivery, and support, investors got cold feet. It turned out that e-business wasn't going to be the easy road to riches that investors had expected. Instead an e-business, like any business, was going to have to win and sustain customers through excellent, personalized customer service, flawless execution backed up by operational efficiencies, and good old-fashioned attention to detail.

What brought about the dot-com crash in spring 2000? It was the sudden realization that companies had overspent on advertising and branding and underspent on execution and fulfillment. Management teams looked to their investors for the next infusion of capital required to deliver on the promises their companies had made to customers. But the investors put their hands back in their pockets and refused to continue to back their investments. We believe that the investment community made three serious mistakes that precipitated the dot-com bust of 2000:

1. They overspent on branding and advertising versus execution and operational efficiency.
2. They expected unreasonably fast returns. It takes at least three years to become profitable in most business ventures. For some reason, the investment community expected returns on their e-business investments in 18 to 24 months—some in less than 12 months.
3. Investors failed to realize that customers aren't loyal to a brand. They become loyal to a branded experience. It takes time to hone and refine a sustainable customer experience and money to continuously improve it.

TODAY'S CUSTOMERS PREFER MULTI-TOUCHPOINT, MULTI-CHANNEL EXPERIENCES

There are still a number of dot-com success stories around the globe. But the majority of successful e-businesses left standing today aren't e-businesses at all. They're businesses that have succeeded in embracing the Internet, the Web, and mobile wireless devices to serve customers and to streamline operations. At the same time, these established companies have learned the hard way that they can't separate their e-business channel from their other business activities. Today's customers have little patience for in-store employees who don't know about the products that are featured online. They want to be able to do their research on the Web and find out if the product they want is available at the local store. They want to touch and feel merchandise in the store and then order it online. In short, they prefer the comfort and convenience of a seamless total customer experience across distribution channels and interaction touchpoints.

The Anatomy of a Great Total Customer Experience

Let's dissect what's required to build a total customer experience to which customers will become and remain loyal. In the following illustration, we've laid out all the ingredients that seem to be required to win customers and build relationships with them. We'll begin our discussion from the bottom of this diagram and work our way to the top. Then we'll provide a concrete example—a case study of a British company, Egg, that set out to create a branded experience from scratch.

Create a Brand Identity that Customers Enjoy

Having just said that many dot-coms overspent on brand creation and underspent on building a sustainable customer experience, there is no question that establishing a strong brand identity is crucial to success. That's why businesses with strong existing brands are in enviable positions. They don't need to establish a brand presence; they already have one. Companies do, however, need to ensure that their brand is one to which customers can relate.

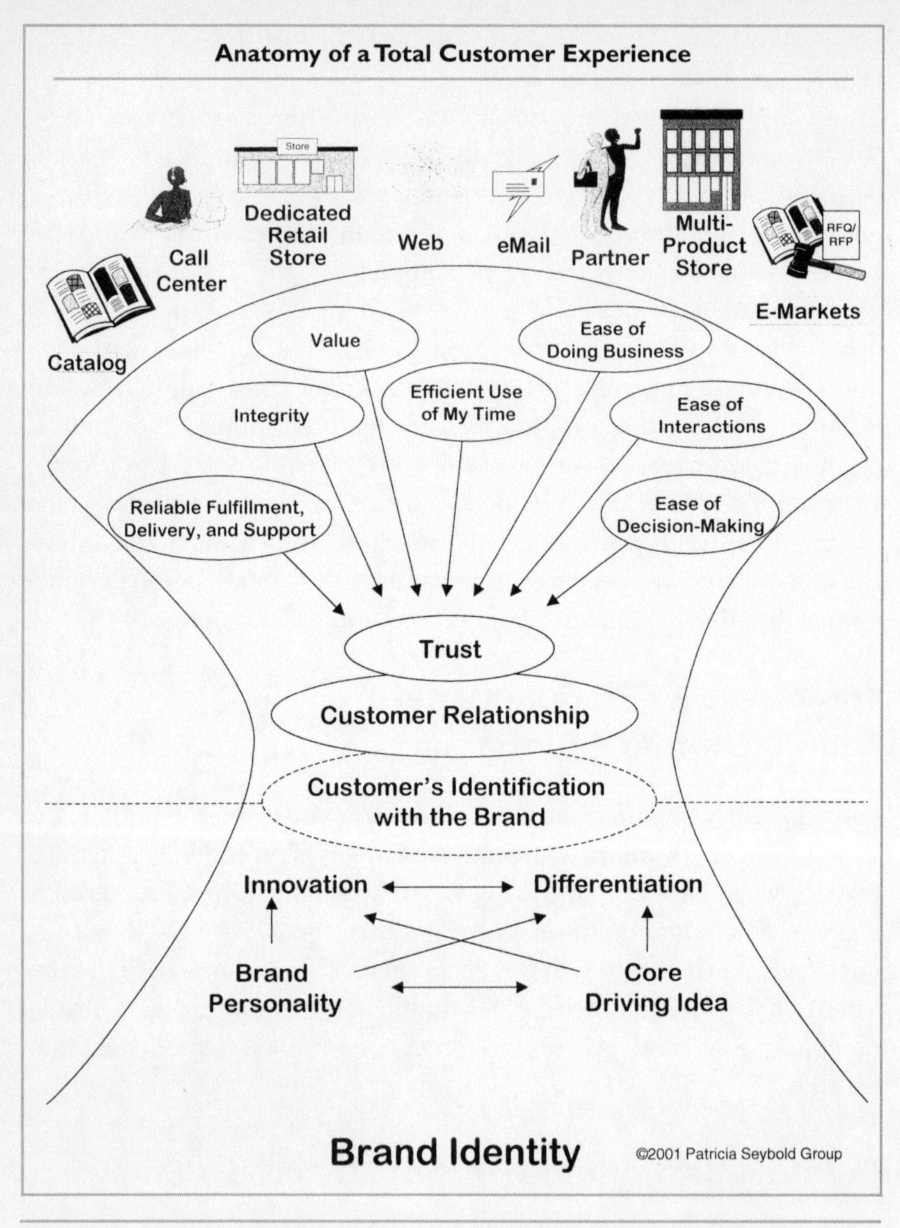

To succeed in the customer economy, you'll want to deliver a total customer experience that's consistent with your brand personality and brand image across all interaction touchpoints and distribution channels. Customer relationships are built on trust. You build trust with your brand by paying attention to the qualities that matter to customers, such as good value, reliable fulfillment, and ease-of-decision-making.

Begin by creating a strong brand identity including a brand personality, a core driving idea that customers relate to, differentiation from other brands, and innovation within the brand.

For the Virgin Group, the brand personality is Richard Branson, an underdog who challenges the status quo. The core driving idea is value with quality, innovation, and fun. How does Virgin differentiate? By making sure that each Virgin company offers a luxury customer experience at a price that most customers can afford. How do the Virgin companies innovate? By constantly finding new ways to deliver the unexpected—from selling cars online to offering massages on its airplanes.

Creating a total customer experience around your brand isn't a uniquely consumer phenomenon. It's equally important for B2B companies. Snap-on, based in Kenosha, Wisconsin, sells tools, technical information, and diagnostic systems and software to professional technicians in companies running the gamut from small auto repair shops to large organizations, like Ford Motor Company and the U.S. Navy. Snap-on's personality is professional excellence, and its core brand idea is high quality and performance. Snap-on differentiates itself from the competition by calling on each customer's place of business every week. And for more than eighty years Snap-on engineers have continued to obsess over functional innovations that keep the company in a leadership position.

You can even create a branded experience for commodities. Take rubber gloves. Dan Grinberg is the CEO of a forty-person, $40 million company that develops, manufactures, and sells rubber gloves to restaurants, hotels, and other institutions. Convinced that food safety was becoming a critical issue around the world and that his company was uniquely positioned to provide valuable services for food-handling professionals, Dan rebranded and renamed his company (from Island Poly to FoodHandler). He then proceeded to leverage that brand to make his product more valuable to corporate buyers. He offered food safety workshops and consulting services along with his products. His Web site, Foodhandler.com, became a trusted source of current information and industry regulations on food safety issues. Since FoodHandler's gloves are resold through distributors and electronic markets, Dan made sure that customers looking for rubber gloves saw all of FoodHandler's relevant food safety information so they could understand the key issues as they made their glove selections. Dan wants to be sure that, when restaurant managers buy gloves for their food-handling employees, they think of safety first. The brand personality of FoodHandler is attentive to the health and safety of food consumers. The brand's core driving idea is safe food preparation. Its differentiation is food safety information. And its innovations center around food safety services. Dan brings the FoodHandler brand to the fore with humorous advertisements. One example is an ad that featured a teenager with spiked hair and a pierced nose working in the kitchen of a restaurant. The copy read, "Thinks E. coli is the name of a Canadian rock band."

If your company and its offerings have a strong brand identity, customers will identify with your brand. They'll think of themselves as "Volvo people" or "Nordstrom shoppers," or "*Wall Street Journal* readers." That's what you want. Once the customer identifies with your brand, you have the makings of a stronger, more long-lasting relationship.

Build Strong Customer Relationships

As you roll out your brand identity, you begin creating relationships with individual customers. This is one of the things that's very different in today's customer economy. In the past, companies could create mass-market brands, relying on mass-market communication channels—television, print advertising, and radio—to establish their brand identities and attract customers to their products. But today you don't want to limit yourself to selling products and services to customers; you want to create relationships with them. That means that you want to be in dialogue with customers—on the phone, face-to-face, via the Internet—any way that customers choose to interact with you. Companies that understand the importance of creating relationships with customers (rather than just selling products) invest heavily in the customer support infrastructure required to build lasting relationships. That infrastructure typically requires having well-trained customer service representatives available by phone and email. It also requires having a customer database or CRM system capable of capturing all the information you glean about each customer through each successive interaction. You can't establish a strong total customer experience without investing in CRM.

Establish Trust

Relationships are built on trust. Customers learn to trust your firm over time as they interact with you and your representatives. Over the past four years we've monitored the practices of a number of businesses that have been successful in creating and sustaining trust with their end customers and distribution partners.

These companies deliver:

- **Integrity.** They set customers' expectations and deliver on promises.
- **Value.** Customers believe they are receiving good value.
- **Reliable Fulfillment, Delivery, and Support.** Customers can count on receiving the products they've ordered in the promised time frame. Customers can count on proactive and prompt service when and as they need it.

These companies make:

- **Efficient Use of Customers' Time.** Customers believe that the company respects their precious time.

These companies offer:

- **Ease of Interactions.** Customers don't need to make multiple phone calls and/or visits to accomplish their desired outcomes.
- **Ease of Doing Business.** Customers can do business with the firm in the ways they prefer, by visiting a physical outlet, going online, and/or picking up the phone.
- **Ease of Decision-Making.** They provide all the information and tools that customers need to help them make quick, informed decisions about which products and services to purchase or use.

Support the Customers' Preferred Modes of Interaction

Some customers like to pick up the phone. Others want to browse through a catalog. Others prefer to surf the Web. Still others want a person to call on them. If you want to win the hearts and minds of your customers, you need to invest in interacting with them in at least three or four different ways—by phone, Web site, and/or email; in-store, online, and/or catalog; through dealers, department stores, and/or direct. One thing the customer revolution has taught us is that customers get to decide how they want to interact with us. We can ignore their preferences at our peril. That's why traditional retailers now have Web sites you can order from. It's why manufacturers now sell direct as well as through dealers. It's why businesses sell to businesses through e-markets, through channel partners, and via direct sales.

How to Create a Branded Experience from Scratch

We've laid the groundwork. We've explained why having a branded experience is vital to your success in the customer economy. Now let's look closely at a company that built a branded experience from scratch. You'll see how a large, established British insurance company, Prudential, spawned a hot new brand to attract a fast-growing customer segment and then continued to evolve its business model on top of that customer experience.

Observations about the Egg Case Study

Egg's experience provides a number of lessons to the astute observer. Egg began by creating a brand identity that customers enjoyed and identified with. The company worked hard to establish personal relationships with each and every customer. Then Egg met and grappled with many of the challenges required to win and keep customers' trust. And like many modern businesses, Egg spawned a number of parallel business models within a relatively short time period (three years).

Flexibility is one of the characteristics of the modern customer-centric business. Once you build a strong branded experience as a foundation, it becomes relatively easy to change or add new business models on the fly.

EGG: CREATING A BRANDED EXPERIENCE FROM SCRATCH

British consumers used to be highly loyal retail banking customers. As in many countries, consumers placed their accounts with a bank in their neighborhood—one whose brand they trusted—and didn't think much about the fees for services nor the interest rates offered. But that picture has changed dramatically over the past five years. Today's consumers are demanding. They comparison shop. They're pressed for time. They want convenience and they want the best deals. When non-banks, like grocery retailers, began to offer banking services to British consumers in the late '90s, they found a ready market. Britain's time-pressed customers were happy to deposit their money with their supermarkets as long as they received a good interest rate. And they were happy to have easy access to credit cards they could use to buy groceries as well as goods and services at other stores. As a result of this competition in banking services, banking customers quickly became much more demanding.

Egg was born to serve this new breed of retail banking customers. Egg was created as a fresh new brand to offer a complete range of financial services to a new target customer base: customers who valued self-service, personalized attention, and value. Egg, plc. is a subsidiary of Prudential, plc., a large U.K.-based insurance company.

Egg did a great job of grabbing mindshare with its unique branded experience, its edgy marketing and personality, and its commitment to fair prices. Within six months, Egg had exceeded its initial targets in terms of number of customers and assets under management. Egg's current challenges have to do with retaining the customers it has, growing those customers' portfolios and product mix (share of wallet), and acquiring new customers in what has become an increasingly competitive and demanding marketplace.

Egg has staked its reputation on its customer experience, offering personalized, attentive service and fair deals. Over the course of its sometimes rocky existence, Egg has had difficulties delivering a consistently excellent customer experience. Yet even when Egg disappointed customers, it did a good job of managing customers' expectations by being honest and direct about problems.

Background: Prudential Expands from Insurance to Banking

In the mid-1990s, Prudential (no relation to the U.S. insurance company of the same name), Britain's largest life insurance company, was looking for ways to branch into new markets. The popularity of mutual funds and other nontraditional life insurance products was increasing competition. To make matters worse, in 1997 a pension scandal had rocked the industry. Insurance salesmen from a number of firms, including Prudential, were being accused of calling on blue-collar workers and wrongly advising them to opt out of their company's pension plans to buy retirement savings products. Prudential and other insurers had to replace customers' retirement savings. Prudential was also looking to modernize its distribution and it slashed its salesforce by 3,000. If it was going to maintain its leading position in the market, Prudential needed to take radical action.

In 1996 Prudential recruited Mike Harris to set up a Prudential Banking subsidiary. Mike had made his mark at Midlands Bank's First Direct in the '80s, setting up the first "bank by phone" call center operation in the U.K. Before he was lured to Prudential, Mike had also had a successful stint in the telecommunications industry.

Thanks to Mike Harris's leadership, Prudential Banking took off as expected. It quickly became the fastest growing direct bank (a bank with no physical branches) in the U.K.

The Birth of Egg

Although Prudential's traditional customers were being well served by this Prudential Banking subsidiary, Sir Peter Davis, Prudential Group's chief executive, was eager to do even more.

At the same time, Richard Duvall, a member of Mike Harris's management team, was troubled. Something was wrong. He saw other companies (such as the U.K.'s two largest supermarket chains, Tesco and J. Sainsbury) getting into the banking business. He also noticed that they were attracting a different customer set: younger people and two-career households who valued convenience. Richard described to Mike what he saw. While Prudential Banking was offering banking services to Prudential's traditional customers (the middle-aged, middle-market, advice-seeking, life insurance buyer), it wasn't attracting the younger, more self-directed crowd. They were going to go elsewhere, and Prudential's banking business wouldn't be able to continue to grow. With Sir Peter's drive and Mike and Richard's strong commitment to the same future, a prototype for a new Internet financial services company was created.

Spawning a Fresh, New Financial Services Company

Mike and Richard quickly gathered a small team together and launched the project to design a new direct banking business from scratch. They spent April through September doing customer research and coming up with a game plan.

On September 18, 1997, Mike and Richard met with Sir Peter Davis. Richard explained to Sir Peter that Prudential could offer a new value proposition to a new set of customers. It could create a fresh new brand and a fresh new financial services company, one that offered customers consistently good deals that were easy to understand. These services would be offered through the telephone first and on the Internet second. "At the time, banks were hated by customers," Richard explained. "We needed to fight the retailers (who were becoming our competitors) with retailers' tools, to build a strong branded value proposition that consistently puts great deals in front of customers the way Tesco's and Sainsbury's do."

Sir Peter's reaction was, "This is great work. Please carry on; how much do you need?" Richard and Mike asked for and received a budget to further develop the initial offering.

Customers Created a New Value Proposition

One of the first things they did was hire a branding consultancy. This firm launched the detailed consumer research that was required to test and refine the value proposition and to come up with a brand. They gathered input and feedback from 30,000 consumers as the project team honed its plans. The Egg banking experience was largely designed by its target customers. "Customers designed our value proposition, our customer experience, our company's values, and every single product we offer," Richard said.

Here's what consumers said they wanted:

- **Better Savings Accounts.** At that time, Richard explained, there were two kinds of savings accounts that were available in the U.K. market: a Notice Account ("This provided a half-decent interest rate, but you couldn't get your money out easily") and an Access Account ("You could get at your money, but the interest rates were lousy"). Consumers wanted to be able to access their money conveniently and earn higher returns on their money at rates that were guaranteed to remain above the norm. They also wanted simplicity. "Don't offer higher rates for higher balances," they said. "Give me a good interest rate even if I only put a few quid in the account; don't require a minimum deposit of £250 or more. Let me put money in a bit at a time."

- **Flexible Mortgages and Loans.** Consumers wanted more flexible loan and mortgage terms; ones they could tailor to suit their own individual circumstances. They wanted to be able to suspend payments for a few months if they were strapped for cash or to prepay with no prepayment penalties. They wanted to be able to change the duration of their mortgages in midstream, again without penalties or extra charges.
- **More Convenient Service.** Consumers wanted convenient, round-the-clock service. But they didn't want an indifferent, automated approach. They wanted to be treated as people, by people who care. Mike Harris summarized the research, "Customers want to be recognized as individuals—to be seen as a person, not a number. They want a relationship with someone who can help them to make the choices that affect their lives rather than being 'sold to.'"

Hatching a New Brand

The branding agency came up with the name Egg, working in conjunction with the company's in-house researchers. They tested the concept in focus groups, and when asked what came to mind when they thought of "Egg," consumers responded "fresh and new." The management team liked the new brand name too. To them it also evoked purity and 360-degrees—the view of each customer they planned to implement. As an added bonus, the name was very memorable. Consumers had no problem recalling it. And research showed that Egg would hold up as a global brand.

Planning the Customer Experience: Dancing with Customers

To convey the kind of customer service experience that would be associated with the Egg brand, Egg's customer service management team came up with the concept of "dancing with customers." "Every time they moved, we'd move with them. That way we could better meet their needs," they explained. "Dancing with customers" became the mantra as Egg's executives designed and staffed the company's new customer contact center in the spring and summer of 1998. To create a fresh, new experience, they set the facility up away from parent company's Prudential headquarters and created a purpose-built, 120,000-square foot communications center in Derby.

The communications center was designed as a state-of-the-art facility for handling customer calls and Internet correspondence. While many other firms have invested in Internet customer self-service to reduce call center costs, Egg invested heavily in its call center operations. After all, Egg's communications center was the primary vehicle through which Egg's customer experience would be experienced by customers, who had made it clear that they wanted a highly personal experience. Egg began life as a phone-based operation; support for Web and email interactions followed. Egg's customer service management team oversaw the design of the facility and the training programs for the nearly 1,000 associates who worked there. The design focused on employee comfort and morale. The workspace includes break rooms and exercise space for the associates to use before they hit the phones.

CUSTOMER DATABASE AT THE CORE

Egg also invested heavily in its CRM technology. The communications center is supported by a 360-degree customer database containing the customer's complete correspondence history as well as a marketing database. From the outset, the Egg team knew that it needed to provide customers with a seamless customer experience across products and interaction touchpoints and it invested in the technology foundation required to deliver that experience.

Egg's Rapid Rise and Evolution

While counting down to the launching of Egg (on October 11, 1998), the management team continued to do a lot of research. Before launch, a customer advisory board of 1,000 consumers began using and testing the system and its processes. This ongoing advisory panel was active in the design and redesign of the company's products, services, Web site, and overall customer experience from the outset.

Egg opened its virtual doors in October 1998. Six months later Egg had 500,000 customers with total assets of over £6 billion (equivalent to $9.5 billion). By August 1999, Egg had been dubbed the U.K.'s leading Internet bank and was the only U.K. institution rated in the top 10 worldwide Internet banking brands. But Egg didn't stop there. It went on to become a full-service financial services institution, an online shopping mall, a "help me manage my life" company, a provider of integrated financial services to retailers and their customers, and a powerful branded aggregator. It did this by reselling investments, insurance, and countless other products under the umbrella of the Egg branded experience.

Egg's Launch Created an Unexpected Surge of Demand

Despite its advertising and PR campaign in the fall of 1998, the Egg team had no idea what to expect. The heavy demand caught them by surprise. In the first week of business, there were 1.75 million hits on the Egg.com Web site, including thousands of applications for savings accounts each day. The call center was flooded with calls, with more than 100,000 inquiries within the first eight days. Richard Duvall recalls: "We had a huge response! It created a service crisis. Our call centers were flooded with call-waiting times going out many minutes and call-abandon rates going through the roof."

Egg quickly did an outsourcing deal with British Telecom to start taking the overflow phone calls.

Reset Customers' Expectations

Having set customers' expectations for a high level of personalized service, Egg was now in the position of having customers wait on hold for minutes at a time. At first customers called for information. Soon they began calling for reports on the status of their applications. "Our operations staff handled the crisis brilliantly," Richard recalls. They managed the pipeline coming in. Since they quickly became backlogged in processing applications and opening up accounts, they opened up the accounts first and then had the customers put the money in. By October 19, eight days after the floodgates opened, Egg's associates began advising customers that "they would be put in a short queue" until their account was opened. Although customers were being advised that they might have to wait up to a month before their account would be active, in practice, it was usually 48 hours. "To ensure that they don't lose interest on savings deposited elsewhere, customers are also being asked to delay sending in their checks until their accounts are opened," Egg's press release explained.

Kept Customers Fully Informed

By the end of its first month of operations, demand was still running very high for mortgages, loans, and savings accounts. Egg began posting the current processing time for each category of account on its Web site and in a recording on a toll-free phone line. These processing-time averages were updated daily.

Keeping customers informed every step of the way was one of the secrets to Egg's success. On the one hand, the company was completely overwhelmed. It received 335,000 inquiries in its first month of operation and received more than £100 million in deposits. On the other hand, Egg used this flood of interest to win customers' sympathy and patience. Prospective customers heard on the news that they should expect delays on the phone and that they shouldn't send their checks in until their accounts had been opened. When customers did get through on the phone, the associates handling their calls were personable, friendly, and informative.

By mid-November the crisis was over. Egg's operations staff had streamlined its processes and caught up with the influx of new business.

Kept Its Brand Commitments

During Egg's first month of operations, the Bank of England lowered its base interest rate to below 8 percent. Egg responded by keeping the interest on its savings accounts at 8 percent—above the base rate. Egg wanted its customers to be able to count on earning the interest it had promised. Of course, Egg lowered the interest rates on its loans and mortgages for both new and existing customers so they would benefit from the less expensive loans.

As Mike Harris explained, "We cut our mortgage and loan rates quickly in October but maintained the savings rate of 8 percent through three cuts to the base rate because we wanted our customers to enjoy as large a benefit as possible for as long a time as possible. In a time of falling interest rates, Egg's guarantee is now more than ever vital for its customers. The guarantee means that you know where you are with Egg. Equally important is Egg's principle of treating every customer fairly."

By December 16, 1998, ten weeks after it opened its doors, Egg had more than £1 billion of funds under deposit. Mike Harris thanked customers for their patience and recommitted the bank to excellence in customer service. "Due to the overwhelming response we've had from customers, we're aware that the quality of service provided by Egg has not always been as high as we would have liked. However, through acting quickly and increasing operational resources, we have ensured any delays have been dealt with as quickly as possible. Egg aims to make first-class customer service its priority in 1999."

Sustain the Customer Experience: Let Customers Complain in Public

Egg was the first financial services firm to solicit customer feedback on an open discussion forum on its Web site. This discussion area was launched in early 1999. Called the "Egg Free Zone," the name implied that Egg wasn't controlling customers' interactions or influencing the discussions. In fact, Egg bends over backwards not to intrude in customers' interactions.

Many of the customers' postings were irate complaints about poor customer service. Egg's own customer service personnel monitored this forum, but they didn't intervene other than to acknowledge the problems that customers raised. At first, Egg customer service's "non-responses" to the customers' concerns voiced in this open forum troubled many customers. Instead, other Egg customers began to come to Egg's rescue, countering the complainers' criticism with their own positive stories. After a few months, Egg added a feature that prompted customers to email customer service directly if they had a problem they wanted resolved rather than just sounding off.

Given Egg's focus on its branded experience of personalized service, why would the company amplify its customer service problems by letting customers complain on its public Web site? Here are three reasons why this was a great idea:

The fact that customers *could* complain publicly on the Egg site meant that they didn't have to go elsewhere to complain. In other words, although customers were in control—they had the power to badmouth Egg and to discourage newcomers from signing up—Egg could monitor customers' dissension and take action to solve individual customers' problems. If customers had gone elsewhere on the 'Net to sound off, Egg would have lost control completely.

Customers believed that they had more control over their experience in dealing with Egg precisely because they had an interested audience to whom they could complain about problems. Registering a complaint on Egg's Web site gave customers a satisfying recourse.

Many prospective customers were reassured by the open airing of Egg's customer service shortcomings. They believed that nothing was being hidden from them.

Egg Focuses on Becoming an "Internet Financial Brand"

Egg could have remained a direct call center operation with an ever-improving Web site. But given the demographics of the target market Egg wanted to continue to attract and the buzz surrounding the Internet, pursuing the Internet aggressively was consistent with the branded experience Egg wanted to deliver. As you'll soon see, Egg's Internet initiatives weren't particularly rapid or unusual. What was unusual was the buzz that Egg was able to build along with the public perception that Egg was an "Internet Bank," at a time when anything "'Net" was the next new thing.

Egg was actually late to the party as Internet banks go. In North America, Wells Fargo, Bank of Montreal, Bank of America, First Union, and others had been offering full-service online banking sites for a couple of years. In the U.K., Royal Bank of Scotland had been the first to offer Internet banking (via PCs) in June 1997, and Barclays launched Web-based Internet banking in April 1999. Yet by mid-1999, Egg had already managed to become "top of mind" among consumers and bankers alike as a premier Internet bank.

How did Egg manage to become one of the world's most respected Internet banks in six months?

Become an Internet Brand

At the time of its launch, Egg had been heralded as a modern-day bank, catering to the self-service, self-directed, technology-savvy customer. But the foundation of the direct banking experience was based on a heavily call center–oriented, hand-holding model. Egg's executives always intended for Egg to become an Internet and phone bank some day. They just weren't sure how quickly consumers would take to the 'Net.

The initial Egg.com Web site was essentially "brochureware." Customers could get information and fill in savings account applications. They could print out loan and mortgage application forms, fill them out, sign them, add the additional paperwork required to process the loans, and send the applications in. The initial site had also offered financial news, online rate quotes, a savings calculator, and a variety of guides—how to save money, draw up a will, plan for your children's education, or landscape your home. But now it was time to offer Egg customers the ability to service their own accounts.

Begin with Simple Functionality

In early 1999 Egg's technology team had launched a major upgrade of Egg's infrastructure, including plans for a more robust Web site. But it would take time to execute the revamp of the technology infrastructure to handle Egg's projected transaction volumes.

By February 1999, Egg's management team was fully committed to the Internet as a platform. Richard Duvall remembered, "We decided that by the end of 1999 we would have converted our business model to an online model and we'd take control of that sector."

On February 25, 1999, Egg rolled out the first in a series of upgrades to its Web site. These included:

- **Online Customer Service for Savings Account Customers.** Customers could access their balance information. They could transfer funds into and out of those accounts.

- **Online Financial Bookshop.** A Global Investor Online bookshop, Egg's first partnership with an online retailer.
- **Egg Free Zone.** The open discussion forum in which Egg customers could speak up about Egg and other related issues.

Help Customers Get Online

Once the Egg management team had made the commitment to become an Internet-only financial services firm, the first step was to make it easy for customers and prospects to become Internet-savvy. On March 24, 1999, Egg announced a package designed to help customers go online. Egg offered "free"[5] Internet access, low-cost PCs, and "white glove" free installation and training (someone would come to your home, set up your PC and Internet access, and show you how to use them). Richard described this as "one of the boldest initiatives we ever made."

Egg partnered with an Internet Service Provider and with the computer firm ICL to offer its customers free Internet access and email. The offer included MSN's (The Microsoft Network) information channels for news, computing, business, football, chat, shopping, and travel. Microsoft subsidized the ISP costs because it was eager to increase its MSN account penetration in the U.K.

The PC that was offered to Egg customers was a state-of-the art Pentium III multimedia computer from Fujitsu (ICL's parent company), complete with color printer and a full range of software including a personal financial management package (Microsoft Money).

The result of this ISP/PC offer was another marketing coup. The number of net new customers Egg managed to attract with the offer paled alongside the PR value Egg received as a leading Internet player. In truth, Egg was taking a page from Dixon's book. Dixon's Freeserve ISP had become one of the darlings of Great Britain by being the first "free" Internet Service Provider.

Set Public Goal to Become a Leading Internet Player

By the end of April 1999, Egg's revamped Web site was ready to handle higher traffic volumes and to deliver increased functionality. The

[5] Customers still need to pay for the cost of their phone calls.

processes were also in place to execute on the free ISP and PC offers. Mike Harris threw down the gauntlet. He announced that, having reached its initial five-year target of attracting 500,000 customers and assets of £5 billion in only six months, Egg was setting itself a new five-year target: two million Internet customers by 2004. "Two million Internet customers, each treated as an individual," became the external and internal mantra for Egg. Why was Egg anxious to become an Internet powerhouse? There were two reasons. First, it was obvious that letting customers serve themselves would be a much more profitable business model. Second, online banking fit the fresh, new, hip branded experience that the firm was committed to offer.

Accept Internet-Only Applications for Flagship Savings Accounts

To make good on his professed mission, Mike Harris announced the next phase of Egg's online banking strategy. As of April 1999, Egg would *only* accept online applications for its popular Egg savings accounts. Once a savings account had been opened, customers would still be able to interact with Egg by phone and mail as well as via the Internet. But Egg was making a commitment to servicing customers online. Accepting Internet-only account applications was the first step.

Richard reported that the number of new savings account openings immediately dropped from an average of 70,000 accounts per month to 20,000 new accounts per month.

Egg continued to serve its existing customers—those who preferred to interact solely by phone and "snail mail." Mike Harris reassured Egg's existing customers by stating, "We recognize some of our existing customers have no interest in going online. To them we offer a continuing commitment to provide a range of great value products available by post and telephone." Egg certainly didn't want to abandon its customer-base of 500,000 customers as it ramped up to attract two million Internet-only customers.

Lure Internet-Only Customers with Higher Rates

By June 1999 Egg was receiving 1,000 online applications per day for its signature savings accounts.

Today's customers are savvy. The Egg team quickly discovered that its Internet customers wanted to be *rewarded* for saving Egg money. If they were handling their own transactions via the 'Net, customers pointed out, shouldn't they benefit from the cost savings? These suggestions came pouring in via email and on the online forum.

The management team at Egg was also concerned about the relatively high per-customer cost of the level of telephone support it had promised. The company was looking for a way to decrease costs per customer, while at the same time, attracting and keeping the 'Net-savvy, self-directed investors it was seeking. It was time to shift the brand promise—to reward self-directed customers for being self-directed and to increase Egg's image as an "Internet financial services firm."

In July 1999 it pioneered a new concept in Internet banking. Egg announced an Internet-only savings account with an interest rate of 5.75 percent (0.75 percent over the then-base rate). The customers who sign up for this account would not only apply online, they could do all their servicing online as well (although telephone support is also available). The promise that Egg offered to these Internet-only account holders is that their interest rate would always remain higher than those of non–Internet-only customers.

Offer Online Mortgage Applications

In August 1999, Egg added the ability for customers to submit their mortgage applications online[6] and, at the same time, lowered the basic variable mortgage rate by 0.2 percent for both new borrowers and pre-existing variable rate mortgage holders. Egg's PR machine claimed that the lower-cost of processing online mortgage applications justified the lower interest rates. In reality, Egg would have probably lowered its rates anyway, as part of its continuing efforts to offer the most competitive prices. Linking the online application functionality with the new lower rates was simply a way to reinforce the branded experience of Egg as an "Internet lender."

There were two advantages for customers who used the online mortgage application process:

---

[6] Customers still had to send in all the accompanying paperwork by regular mail.

- Egg waived the application fee that it charges its phone and snail mail customers—a fee that is rebated once the mortgage has closed.
- Online customers gain a speedier "decision in principal"—once a customer completes the online form, he's immediately informed as to whether he qualifies for the mortgage he's seeking. He still has to send in all the paperwork to complete the application process and gain final acceptance. Customers who apply by phone typically have to wait 24 hours for a preliminary decision.

Launch an "Internet" Credit Card

Egg had a series of products it was planning to launch, based on its initial and ongoing consumer research. A better credit card offer was one of the cornerstone products that consumers had been requesting. By the time Egg was ready to do the credit card launch, the company had shifted its positioning to become a leading Internet brand.

Customers' Credit Card Wish List

What were consumers looking for in a credit card in 1999? At the time, there were two popular types of credit cards in the U.K. market. The first was a standard credit card with a low interest rate. The second was a credit card linked to a loyalty scheme—whereby the customer earns airline miles or points to be redeemed. Egg discovered that customers were looking for a combined card. They wanted a credit card with low interest rates. And they wanted to earn rebates every time they used the card. So Egg created the Egg Card—to meet customers' expressed requirements.

And because Egg was repositioning itself as an Internet financial services brand, the company, in consultation with its customer research group, decided that Egg's credit card should be an Internet card—one that's easy to apply for online; one you can service online; and one you can safely use for online as well as offline purchases.

The Egg Card Launch

Egg's Internet credit card, dubbed Egg Card, immediately captured customers' imagination and, as with the savings account launch, the flood of Egg Card requests caused customer service problems. This time, however, Egg's Web site was swamped rather than its call centers. Customers and prospects were unhappy with the poor performance. This led to more press coverage, which tended to fuel interest and demand.

Egg launched its "Internet credit card" on September 19, 1999 to considerable fanfare and hoopla. Egg was the first institution in the U.K. to offer a credit card designed to be used for online purchases. The company modeled its Egg Card initiative after NextCard which pioneered Internet-based credit cards in the United States in 1996.

What made this an "Internet" card? You could only apply for the credit card online. You could access your account and service it online. And customers received up to 2 percent cash back for online purchases they made at the new Egg shopping mall. What else did Egg's card offer?

- 9.9% interest rate—the lowest on the market, compared to around 20% offered by some of the leading High Street banks
- 4.5% interest on transferred balances for the first six months
- Cashback of up to 2% for Internet purchases at Egg's Shopping Zone
- Up to 1% cash back for all offline purchases
- No fee
- 24-hour online account servicing and payments
- An Internet fraud guarantee—designed to address customers' security concerns about shopping online

Swamped Again!

Egg's executives and operations personnel thought they were ready for the flood of customer activity they hoped that the Egg Card offer would bring. Pete Marsden and his IT crew had re-architected the underlying Web site and moved it onto more robust and scalable platforms. But they hadn't counted on the amount of performance tuning that would need to be done to the new systems as demand spiked. Pete and his team discovered that it's difficult to fine-tune new e-commerce systems during peak demand periods. Yet until you've experienced the demand, you don't know what to tune for. At the time of the Egg Card's launch, Egg was receiving millions of hits per day from between 30,000 and 40,000 unique visitors. Many of Egg's software suppliers had never seen that level of demand. This time the bottleneck only lasted a few weeks. By then the e-commerce systems had been tuned and the performance improved significantly.

Managing Customers' Expectations

As before, Egg's executives tried to reset customers' expectations, asking for their forbearance and blaming the slow response times on the popularity of the Egg Card offer. Apparently, this tactic worked. Within four months, Egg had signed up 175,000 Egg Card customers. Fifteen percent of these were existing Egg customers. But the rest of these customers were new to Egg. Within a year, Egg had gained 400,000 Egg Card customers.

Managing by Customer Value

Like most financial services institutions, Egg's management team focuses on lifetime customer value and share of customers' wallets as its key measures of success. Unlike other financial services companies, Egg has added a more complex mix of products and services to its quiver. Egg has three core lines of business: a retail banking business, an intermediation business for financial products, and a transaction portal for non-financial products and services. This makes it more of a challenge to assess the value of Egg's current and future customers and its services portfolio. However, we maintain that the game remains the same: acquire and retain customers, serve them profitably, and up-sell and cross-sell both financial and non-financial products and services to those customers. Each of the three businesses has the same goal: acquire customers, build relationships with them, and broaden those relationships.

Cashing In on the Value of Egg's Branded Experience

Egg's start-up costs and other related charges slashed Prudential's operating profit for the first six months of 1999. Yet Prudential continued to invest. Prudential reported that losses "from Egg and other banking activities came to £69 million for the first six months and would rise to about £150 million for the full year, compared to the £100 million the board had originally earmarked."

Egg's board was banking on three things: the success of the new brand, the eventual profits from the new direct banking model, and Egg's additional forays into new Internet-based business models.

On June 12, 2000, Egg sold a minority stake to the public. Egg's coveted shares were offered to Egg customers, to institutional investors, and to Egg and Prudential (Egg's parent company) employees at a price of £1.60 per share. This offering valued the company at £1.3 billion, or £1,300 per customer. As you may recall, this was just after stock prices around the world had dropped by about 30 percent, precipitated by a sell-off in Internet and high tech shares. Most companies had cancelled their IPOs. But Prudential and investment bankers were confident that Egg's branded experience still had value in the market. They were right. On the day of the offering, the stock soared to £1.90 per share, and closed at £1.775, valuing Egg at £1.46bn, and by extension, valuing Egg's one million customers at £1,460 each.

DESIGNED TO MORPH: EGG EXPERIMENTS WITH BUSINESS MODELS

MODEL 1: A TRANSACTION PORTAL TO INTERMEDIATE NON-FINANCIAL SERVICES

Combining Financial Services and Online Shopping

Egg executives had noticed a difference between the original Egg savings account customers and its Internet savings account customers. "Internet-only customers are very transactional," Richard Duvall explained. "These Internet savings customers often open several different accounts—earmarked for their kids, for vacations, for holiday spending—and they move money back and forth among them. They also transfer money from other banks into their online savings accounts." The highly transactional nature of the Internet saver gave Egg some important clues. Now the trick would be to lure even more online customers to Egg, by building on their propensity to transact business online.

Online Credit Cards Need Online Shops

In parallel with the credit card launch, the Egg team managed another huge initiative: the launch of an Egg-branded online shopping mall/portal site. By this point, the Egg management team was confident that the Egg brand and the momentum that they had built would be compelling to brand-name merchants. This was Egg's first of several forays into the "intermediation" business model.

Creating an Online Shopping Mall

Why did Egg become one of the first financial institutions to offer an online shopping mall? At first blush, this seems counter-intuitive. When customers want to manage their finances, they go to a financial services site. When they want to shop, they go to online stores. Richard explained, "It's hard to promote the advantages of an Internet credit card when there's nothing to buy online. We looked at the online shopping malls that were available at the time and were concerned that they weren't attractive enough."

The Egg team quickly put together a one-hundred-store shopping mall in time for the Egg Card launch. Called the Egg Shop, it was essentially a portal site that grouped online retailers together by category within the branded Egg Shop. Once the customer entered a store within the online mall, he or she was at the mercy of the store's own merchandising, navigation, ordering, and customer service processes. Once he or she placed an order online using the EggCard, Egg's 2 percent rebate would be automatically credited to the order.

Improving the Customer's Shopping Experience

Grouping online stores together under a common umbrella and giving customers cash back for shopping at stores in the Egg Shop was a good start. But it didn't really address online shoppers' needs to save time and save money by ensuring that they were getting the best deal on a book, a sweater, or a CD. By December 1999 Egg had implemented the first step in streamlining Egg customers' shopping experience: a "smart search" feature. With Egg's Smart Search, a query for "earrings" yielded close to 300 items across dozens of merchants, with the description and price for each. A search for "Robbie Williams" within the category "music" listed the albums and the prices from a handful of merchants.

There are two things that will vastly improve the online shopping experience for Egg customers:

1. The ability for the customer to have a single Egg shopping profile that could be used across all the retailers that participate in Egg Shop.

This would store the customer's credit card information as well as his or her list of shipping addresses. Each time the customer purchased from any of the Egg Shop stores, she could invoke the stored profile and re-use the relevant information without having to type it in over and over again at each merchant's site. Egg rolled-out an e-wallet capability in early 2001.

2. The ability for the customer to order items from multiple stores in a single order.

This is where an online department store, like Amazon.com, wins out over an online mall like Egg Shop. Being able to search across multiple stores is great. But being able to order conveniently across multiple stores and categories is even better.

Results from Egg Shop

During its first year of operation, Egg used a simple business model for Egg Shop. Merchants paid a small, per-transaction commission. "This didn't amount to much in the way of revenues," Richard reported. But he pointed out that online shopping results for the 1999 holiday season were disappointing, not just for Egg's merchants, but for most of the U.K.'s online merchants. By the fourth quarter of 1999, online retail sales in the U.K. were running 0.7 percent of total retail sales. Although Egg Shop ranked in the top ten retail sites visited, it didn't contribute a lot to Egg's bottom line.

Evolving the Business Model for Merchants

Despite the somewhat disappointing online sales history, Richard believes that the online shopping mall model will pay off. For one thing, with very good traffic to the Egg site, Egg has now cut better deals with merchants. Instead of settling for a simple transaction fee, Egg can easily justify a more complex business model to its merchants—one combining rent, click-through fees, and transaction fees. This hybrid business model is expected to significantly increase revenues. In fact, as soon as this new model went into effect, revenues quadrupled between the start and end of the third quarter in 2000. By November 2000, Egg Shop was earning £200,000 per month.

MODEL 2: AN INTERMEDIATION BUSINESS FOCUSING ON FINANCIAL PRODUCTS—BECOMING A FINANCIAL SERVICES INTERMEDIARY

First Step: An Investment Supermarket

In the United States, Charles Schwab was the early leader in offering *online* access to a broad range of mutual funds, starting in 1996. In the U.K., although other financial services firms were already luring online investors to their array of funds, Egg differentiated itself by becoming the first aggregator of popular funds that could be purchased and traded online in the U.K. market.

Egg Invest was launched on March 13, 2000, with 168 funds from twelve prominent U.K. funds providers. By November 2000 the selection had grown to over twenty-one fund providers and almost 300 funds. The funds on offer ranged from Index funds to generalist funds to industry sector to geographic funds. Customers could review each fund's performance, read prospectuses online, and buy into any of these funds directly from the Egg Invest Web site. In order to invest in any of the funds profiled, customers needed to be Egg Savings account customers.

There's obviously a two-pronged goal for Egg Invest:

- Gain a larger wallet/portfolio share for existing Egg customers;
- Attract new customers to Egg—customers who are more interested in investments than savings or credit cards.

Richard Duvall explained that in the U.K., taxes are due on April 5. The month before the tax deadline is when most people invest in the legal tax shelters that are available to them. These are known as individual savings accounts (or ISAs). The "ISA Centre" was the most prominent feature of the Egg Invest supermarket. Qualifying U.K. taxpayers could invest up to £7,000 in 1999–2000 and another £7,000 in 2000–2001.

Unfortunately, Egg missed a lot of the window for the lucrative ISA market in 2000. "We were so cautious about making sure that everything was perfect before we opened Egg Invest for business, we only caught two weeks of the hot ISA period," Richard noted.

What's the business model for the investment supermarket? Egg receives a commission on each customer's investments. If the customer invests up to £7,000, Egg receives a share of the annual management charge of the investment each year. Egg Invest has drastically reduced the cost of processing online investments—it is automated from front to back. Egg also uses its buying power to secure great deals from the fund providers. Egg passes this cost-saving back to the customer in the form of reduced up-front charges and reduced annual management charges—both of these are typically half the rate you would pay in the market. Egg is one of the pioneers in the U.K. of "no-load funds" with no up-front charges at all.

Second Step: Insurance Supermarket

The next financial services intermediation play on Egg's docket was an insurance supermarket. Richard Duvall believes that this is likely to be "a brilliant customer acquisition vehicle." After all, everyone needs basic car and home insurance, and most people also buy life insurance. What's more, unlike savings or investments, insurance policies need to be renewed each year. And the early indications are very good—in its first two months of operation, Egg Insure received over 300,000 individual expressions of interest.

Egg has taken what it has learned from Egg Invest and is applying that learning to the design of Egg Insure. Egg offers selected Prudential insurance products as well as competitors' offerings. And because Egg provides choice and side-by-side comparison of insurance packages, along with helpful advice, customers should believe that they're getting a fairer deal when purchasing or renewing their insurance policies through Egg.

What's the business model? Egg receives a sales commission for each insurance policy sold as well as a commission on renewals.

MODEL 3: AN OUTSOURCED PROVIDER OF BRANDED FINANCIAL SERVICES

Egg Leverages Its E-Jewels

Egg's executives would lump this next business model into the financial service aggregation bucket discussed above. But we see it as a very different kind of play. When you take one of your core business processes and offer it to a partner to use—that's called providing an e-service (product plus business processes, electronically supported). When you succeed in becoming an e-services provider and still maintain the branded experience that's associated with that service, rather than simply providing it as an anonymous, behind the scenes facility, then you've really played the game well. You've now gained new customers for your branded experience with whom you can build a lasting relationship. And you've done so by leveraging, not cannibalizing, one of your most valuable offerings.

Egg did this with its crown jewels: the Egg Card.

Egg and Boots: a Powerful Brand Combination

In fall 1999, a team of Egg executives approached executives from Boots—the U.K.'s largest chain of pharmacies (or chemists)—to sound them out about the possibility of creating a combined healthcare portal. Boots was intrigued but not ready to make a move. Then, in February 2000, Richard Duvall went back to Boots for a chat and discovered that they were in the midst of a major project to migrate their phenomenally successful loyalty card to a combined loyalty and credit card. "They were in the midst of selecting a credit card partner. We floated the idea of creating a co-branded loyalty credit card." Apparently, Boots liked the idea, because they added Egg to the list of potential partners. Within two months, the two companies announced their deal. Boots had signed up with Egg to turn its Boots/Advantage loyalty card into an Egg/Boots Advantage loyalty and credit card.

BOOTS' ADVANTAGE CARD

Boots has offered customers its Advantage loyalty club card since 1997. At the time of the Egg/Boots deal, there were 12 million cardholders; and 8.5 million active Advantage Club members. Boots Advantage customers get 4 pence of benefits for every pound they spend in Boots in the form of special offers that are targeted, based on the products they buy. The customer base for Boots' cards is overwhelmingly female. The customer experience Boots has established with its customers is one of pampering. Boots' stores offer "exclusive pampering days for Boots Advantage card holders." And the merchandise that customers buy for themselves with their accumulated Advantage points tends to be luxury items, like perfume and lotions, not necessities, like baby essentials.

EGG'S CONTRIBUTION

Egg developed the co-branded Advantage/Egg Card Web site and uses its infrastructure to handle the credit card application, administration and operations, as well as assuming the credit risk and liability. Egg is offering Boots the combination of its credit card handling infrastructure and online shopping mall as a ready-made utility. In return, Egg will be able to add millions of customers to its client list.

How does the business model work? "We pay them a bounty for each credit card customer acquired. The risk is shared. Some of it is paid upfront, and some of it is paid out over the lifetime of the customer's relationship."

Boots, meanwhile, gets an Internet-based credit card application. Boots customers who prefer to apply for the Boots credit card by phone can do so. As with regular Egg Card customers, Boots customers who apply for the Boots/Egg Card on the 'Net and receive and pay their bills electronically get the lowest interest rates. But if customers prefer to apply by phone and mail and to receive their bills in the mail, they can do so. Those phone/mail customers pay a slightly higher interest rate.

The benefit for Boots' customers are extra discounts: 4 points for shopping at Boots; 1 point for shopping anywhere else and an additional point if they shop online at the Egg Shop. These points can be redeemed at Advantage kiosks in Boots' stores, driving foot traffic into Boots' stores.

Results

The jury is still out on Egg as a success story. The company did a great job of capturing mindshare and marketshare at the outset. It has been aggressive in exploring and exploiting new business models. Of all the business models Egg has tried, the co-branded Boots deal is the most appealing one. It leverages Egg's customer experience as well as its existing core information technology and customer support infrastructures, while giving Egg an opportunity to attract a large customer-base of mostly women who are likely to prove to be profitable long-term customers for Egg, if it treats them well.

By the fall of 2000, Egg had responded to investor pressure to become profitable more quickly. Egg reduced its losses by 10 percent in the third quarter but did so at the peril of its brand promise to its customers. In October, Egg reported a hefty loss of deposits owing to less attractive interest rates. The company's move away from loss-leading interest rates prompted customers to withdraw £443 million in the three months ending in September. Net new customers dropped from 114,000 in the second quarter to 107,000 in the third. By year-end 2000, Egg had 1.33 million customers.

And by November 2000, Mike Harris began talking about adding physical branches to Egg's virtual operation. Customers were making it clear that they preferred the convenience and reassurance of being able to interact face-to-face as well as by phone and Internet. Luckily, Egg won't have to invest in real estate in order to offer physical branches. Parent company Prudential has physical branches. And it's possible that Egg will set up counters in selected Boots outlets, leveraging its co-branding.

Takeaways

Egg's experience teaches us a lot about how to build and sustain a customer experience. Both the successes and failures that Egg has had in setting and managing customers' expectations provide useful learnings. In fact, the job they had to do rearchitecting Egg's infrastructure, at least twice in the course of a year as the business model kept morphing, provides a great example of the unique e-business experience—flying the plane while you change out the engine.

Also, Egg doesn't seem to have organized itself properly to really own the customer experience it preaches. At first, there was initially no single high-level executive at Egg who is really responsible for the customer experience in a detailed way, across interaction touchpoints. Now there is. Liz Gratton is Director of Customer Experience. Liz runs

Egg's communications centres and is now also responsible for the overall customer experience on and offline.

Notice that Egg does run itself on customer value metrics. Its executives monitor these closely. However, unlike Schwab, Egg hasn't yet meshed compensation to closely match customers' outcomes and customer satisfaction.

AN OPERATIONAL FRAMEWORK

Measure Customer Value, Monitor Customer Experience, and Deliver a Great Total Customer Experience

8

IMPLEMENT A CUSTOMER FLIGHT DECK AND TAKE THE EIGHT STEPS TO A GREAT TOTAL CUSTOMER EXPERIENCE

With customers in control, transforming our businesses out from under us, they're more demanding than ever before. Thankfully, we now have the tools, the know-how, and the wherewithal to cost-effectively tune our businesses to meet customers' ever-changing needs. What's even more amazing is that we now have the ability to establish relationships with literally millions of customers. We can provide them the information they need in a timely fashion, serve them around the globe, and interact with them in the ways that they prefer to do business. And as we do so, we're now capable of monitoring how we're doing. Are we meeting customers' expectations? Are we delivering the quality of service they expected? Are we responsive enough? In short, are we monitoring customer value and measuring what matters to our customers?

The remainder of this book contains the "how to's" and practices involved in delivering the kind of total customer experience that will help you build and sustain customer loyalty and increase your customer franchise. First, we offer this instrument panel—our Customer Flight Deck—as a framework within which you can begin to think about what metrics and measurements your company should be tracking in the customer economy. Then, we offer a set of practices that other companies have found useful in delivering a great total customer experience. We tie each of these practices into the Customer Flight Deck so you can see how they relate.

TAKE OFF INTO THE CUSTOMER ECONOMY

I have a friend who was trained as a pilot and was an astronaut for twenty years. Joe Allen has been catapulted into outer space twice and has orbited the earth 208 times. Three or four of those orbits occurred while he was outside the shuttle holding a satellite above his head while engineers on earth tried to figure out how he could jury-rig some way to bring the satellite on board the shuttle (the tool that was supposed to do the job didn't fit). Today Joe is the chairman of Veridian, a global data security and testing firm. I asked him to describe a typical flight deck for me. What are the kinds of instruments that pilots use? He thought about it for a few minutes and then described four broad categories of instruments and controls: those used for navigation, those used to monitor performance, those used to make operational adjustments, and those used to monitor the environment (both outside and inside the plane). That's the framework we've used for our Customer Flight Deck.

Before we describe this metaphorical set of metrics you might want to use to monitor your company's own trajectory through space and time, I'd like to share one other insight from Joe. Today's pilots aren't limited to using the instruments that are built into the cockpit, he explained. Increasingly, pilots tend to also use portable devices. Thanks to the Global Positioning System (GPS) and sophisticated software, they can literally monitor the state of the plane and its flight path using a portable laptop computer. As you read on, don't think of your flight deck as a monolithic control panel on a computer screen. Think of it instead as a set of portable instruments you can carry around with you that will enable you to continuously monitor and even change your trajectory. And bear in mind that ideally each employee and business partner will have his or her own personalized view of your company's Customer Flight Deck.

View from the Flight Deck of the Customer Economy

Imagine yourself in the cockpit of an airplane (or a rocketship). You have customers on board. They trust you to get them to their destination in a timely fashion with the best experience you can deliver, despite a few factors that are completely out of your control, such as weather, other air traffic, and possible equipment malfunctions. What makes this challenge particularly exciting is that, as you're flying to your agreed-upon destination, your passengers are redesigning the plane around you. Yet you know that the ultimate outcome of your mission together depends on your ability to skillfully take off, navigate, and bring your craft in for a safe landing.

In the cockpit you sit in a cushioned seat that may or may not be comfortable; even if it isn't, you get used to it quickly enough because you know the flight ahead is going to be long. Before you is a vast array of instrumentation—dials, gauges, and LED readouts—each with its own meaning and purpose and each contributing to your understanding of the plane's operations. Ahead of you is the even vaster landscape, sometimes in daylight and thus illuminated, sometimes obscured by the dark or by clouds, and sometimes hiding peril in a sea of calm.

Your pre-flight preparations include, first and foremost, knowing the location of your destination and having a plan for getting there. You've already done all the pre-flight checks to ensure that everything is in good working order. Having gotten the tower's clearance, you take off and head into the wild new yonder. Before you get a chance to relax, thinking that the hard part is over, you take a long look at your flight deck, and you realize that the real work has only just begun—that work centers on the monitoring of your ***navigation*** to make sure you're headed in the right direction; your ***performance*** to make sure that all systems are functioning as they should; your ***operational controls*** to make sure you can make any adjustments you may need to make; and your ***environment*** to make sure the elements don't catch you unawares.

You've probably guessed that we think this is a useful metaphor for measuring your company's performance as regards its customers. The flight plan is, naturally, the company's strategy, and the navigation is its progress toward that plan. The performance and operational controls together represent end-of-process and in-process measures (not necessarily respectively), and the environment is the broad set of external factors that affect how and where the company does business.

What are these instruments measuring? They're designed to guide you smoothly so that you can maximize the value of your company's customer franchise by monitoring how you're doing with both existing and new customers. And most importantly, they tell you a lot about the quality of the total customer experience you're delivering to your customers while they're in your care.

You may think that what we're suggesting here is simply another variant on the balanced score card/control panel/dashboard mechanism that has been so popular in recent years. Certainly those tools have their benefits, and we have long believed that every company should have a coherent approach for assessing its performance on a regular (and highly visible) basis. But we see two key differences between those approaches and the Customer Flight Deck that we're describing here. First, the *customer* is the primary emphasis; company value derives from the lifetime value of your customer relationships, and the Flight Deck is designed to make sure nothing obscures that message. Second, the Flight Deck itself is directed toward helping companies monitor and manage the factors that will impact the quality of your customers' experience.

What kinds of customer metrics do we envision for our Customer Flight Deck? Before we think of them as navigation, performance, operational, and environmental metrics, let's first think about them in light of what we've learned in the previous chapters, namely that the primary factors to determining the depth of your customer relationships are:

- **The Number of Active Customers Your Company Has.** For the Navigational controls, this can be the known number of active accounts, individuals, or households, and guesses about the number of anonymous customers. Subsidiary measures for the Performance and Operational Controls might include the number of new customers generated by referral, growth in net new accounts, and any other measures indicating changes in the total number of customers.

- **The Number of Customers Who Remain Loyal to the Company over Time.** Classically, this is the retention rate (or, for pessimists, the attrition rate). The tenure of customers by segment is also useful to know.

- **How Positive Customers' Experiences with the Company Are.** These metrics are usually derived from customer satisfaction surveys. Companies for whom the Internet is an important touchpoint have begun developing other measures, such as shopping cart abandonment and purchases as a percentage of visits.

- **How Much Money Customers Spend on the Company's Products and Services.** Typical measures include dollars per purchase or transaction, total sales and earnings per customer, and share of wallet. Subsidiary measures might include revenues and earnings per account, individual, or household and growth in all of these measures.

Each of these customer-related factors lends itself to measurement and assessment of the sort described in our flight deck metaphor. For example, a company's strategic objective for customer penetration might be a 25 percent increase in the number of small-business customers over the next three years; this would be the flight plan for that particular factor. Assume that you have a set of four simple panels, each with a series of instruments that give you read-outs. And many of these instruments have accompanying controls that allow you to make adjustments as you fly. Here's what we'd be monitoring with regard to our objective of increasing the number of small business customers by 25 percent:

- **Navigation.** To make sure we're headed in the right direction with regard to this target, we would want a periodic review of how many customers we have, either in absolute terms or as a percentage increase since we set the 25% growth target. This navigation panel of the flight deck tells us where we are, how fast we're getting to our goal, and if we're heading in the right direction.

- **Performance.** The Performance panel is another set of results or effectiveness metrics and might be thought of as the answer to the question, "What caused the changes in the Navigation panel?"

For our example, those answers could include such measures as sales won and lost.

- **Operational Controls.** What caused the changes in the Performance panel? Why did we win some customers and not others? By the time we move to the Operational Controls, we're looking at the inner workings of our processes—our sales and marketing efforts, the availability of product and service features, overall time-to-market, and perhaps even the continued viability of a product line.
- **Environment.** Just as wind shear and snow are of concern to pilots, so should their analogues matter to company executives. Did we fail to win customers because some competitor had a better product or price? Is the overall market being affected by new or proposed legislation or regulation? Were we surprised by demographic changes?

Ideally, then, we should be able to develop a set of Customer Flight Deck metrics that looks something like the following example. Here's a sample flight deck for Egg, the U.K.-based Internet financial services company. For this example, we're assuming these long-term (2001–2004) strategic objectives:

- Two million total customers
- 75% of customers using products other than checking and savings
- £30 billion in assets
- Customer deposits growing 25% per year

Line of Sight and Internal Predictors

In the above example, we asked, "What caused that?" to determine how Performance affects Navigation and how Operational Controls affect Performance. The same question, when applied to the Operational Controls, often reveals another layer of controls; indeed, this is where the concepts of business process improvement come into play. Every externally measurable result can be linked, in one way or another, to one or more internal processes. This line-of-sight linkage is a powerful ally for us, since it reveals which internal processes most affect customer experience, satisfaction, retention, and spending. Looked at this

A Sample Flight Deck for Egg

	Navigation	Performance	Operations	Environment
Customer Numbers	Number of Internet customers Number of customers referred by other customers Number of products per customer	Number of active online customers Increase/decrease in customer referrals Increase/decrease in number of customers using two or more products	Number of unique Web site visitors Conversion rate Number of Web applications submitted Number of Web applications approved	Competitive rank in number of customers, assets, and products among: • banks • nonbanks
Customer Retention	Customer retention rate	Customer retention rate by product Customer retention rate by customer segment Customer retention rate by marketing campaign	Percentage of customers using new products or services Frequency of transactions by customer segment	Comparative metrics: Industry averages
Customer Experience	Customer satisfaction ratings Egg Free Zone customer complaint ratio	Task-specific customer satisfaction ratings by interaction touchpoint: • Web site • email • phone Product-specific customer satisfaction ratings Customer satisfaction with: • Rates and fees • Billing • Online and offline credit card usage • Product offerings	Time on hold Web site response times Time to complete most common customer scenarios Number of clicks in average Web transaction Percentage of customer support issues handled with one-time resolution	Comparative experience with competitors' service: • Time on hold • Web site response times • Percentage of task-specific customer scenarios completed • Time to complete most common customer scenarios • Number of clicks in average Web transaction
Customer Spending	Total assets under management Profits per customer segment Customer lifetime value	Increase/decrease in customer assets Acquisition and retention costs Walletshare by customer segment	Percentage of customers who upsell and cross-sell themselves: • online • offline Percentage of non-performing loans Customer-service and support costs by touchpoint	Competitors' fees and rate structures

way, the Operational Controls in our flight deck can be recognized as internal predictors of customer behavior. Just as in-process performance can predict end-of-process effectiveness, so can end-of-process performance foreshadow customer perception. If delivery time matters to a customer and if that delivery time includes your time to process his order and begin the fulfillment process, then your efforts to reduce that internal cycle time should make the customer happier with delivery time.

But the predictive nature of the flight deck metrics doesn't extend only in the horizontal direction (that is, from Operational Controls to Performance to Navigation.) The power of the flight deck will be more fully realized if we can identify the causalities connecting customer experience, retention, and spending. In other words, a rigorously developed flight deck will enable you to compute, at least approximately, the dollar benefit of a given service improvement or product upgrade.

Customers Only? An Aside

At this point, the operational and financial readers among you are starting to shake your heads because it's obvious that the flight deck model doesn't explicitly include such matters as expenses, assets, and liabilities. The human resource people among you are wringing your hands because the model also seems to ignore employee considerations. There are many other measurement and management tools and disciplines that will give you a balanced approach to measuring cash flow and monitoring employee satisfaction. The purpose of our focus on a Customer Flight Deck is to help businesses hone in on the key measures that matter most to customers—and the ones that will increase the value of their customer franchise.

Creating a Customer Flight Deck

There are three distinct ways to create your flight deck:

- Begin with your strategic objectives, define your key Navigation metrics based on them, and start defining the Performance and Operational metrics by asking yourself, "What causes that?" The key advantage here is that you're creating the Flight Deck from the outside in, that is, from the customer to the processes.

- Begin with an inventory of the measures you're already tracking and find where they fit by plugging them into a template and testing the implied relationships. The advantage to this approach is that you can leverage known and useful metrics (and along the way uncover metrics that probably should have been eliminated long ago).
- For process-centered companies, begin with a process hierarchy and use the known metrics to populate the Flight Deck template. This is especially beneficial (perhaps only so) to companies with a strong understanding of their processes and how they fit together.

However you do it, it's important not to go overboard. That's always useful advice, by the way, but it has special merit here. We want the Customer Flight Deck to be a useful analytical and diagnostic tool, but it will become overwhelming if we don't first take the time to limit it. The Flight Deck is supposed to present the metrics that have the most immediate or the most profound effects on your customer franchise objectives and on the quality of the customer experience.

What's the right number of metrics per Customer Flight Deck? Well, having cautioned you to be judicious, we now must confess that we don't know what the right number is. The Flight Deck template we presented a few pages ago has 16 cells; an average of three metrics in each cell means a total of forty-eight, which is already a big number. One more in each cell brings us to sixty-four, and this is before you plug in whatever partner and employee Flight Decks you decide to create.

This is not to say that you should track only forty-eight measures throughout the organization. You need many more than that. But remember that a Customer Flight Deck is emphatically not the complete record of organizational measures. It is the set of panels that all employees will review on a regular basis to get a true sense of where the company stands in its efforts to generate and sustain customer value and to deliver a great customer experience.

Will You Need More than One Flight Deck?

Absolutely! For the sake of clarity and focus, you may want to create a different Customer Flight Deck for each major set of customers—business customers vs. consumer customers, for example. Or you may want to create different Customer Flight Decks for different customer segments, for example, active traders versus delegators. Ideally, each group of employees will have their own personalized Flight Deck with which they can monitor both how the company is doing in meeting its overall customer value and customer loyalty goals, and how their team is doing in monitoring and improving the particular customer-impacting performance or operational issues over which they have purview.

Your company no doubt has many partners whose actions also impact the quality of the customer experience you jointly deliver. Each of these partners should have their own version of a Customer Flight Deck that is linked both to your company's strategic goals and to your customers' priorities.

Linking the Customer Flight Deck to the Practices and Case Studies

The companies whose case studies you're about to read haven't explicitly built the kind of Flight Deck we're describing here. Yet, as you'll see if you take a look at what they're currently monitoring and measuring, most of them are coming close. For each case study, we've taken the liberty of organizing the measures the company has told us that it uses (and there are probably some that each company doesn't want to share with the world) into our Flight Deck format. This way you can see the extent to which companies in a variety of industries are already managing by and for customer value and measuring what matters to customers. Finally, for each company, we've taken the liberty of proposing a few additional metrics that would help them monitor their progress in one particular practice area.

EIGHT STEPS TO A GREAT, TOTAL CUSTOMER EXPERIENCE

The best way to win the hearts and minds of customers is to offer a great customer experience and to listen carefully to what these (and other) customers tell you about where you need to take your business. In the ensuing chapters, we provide a number of case studies featuring companies from a variety of industries and continents. Each of these firms is well on its way towards offering a great total customer experience. Most are already beginning to reap rewards from the investments they've made in cultivating customer relationships and in delivering a great customer experience to keep customers coming back for more. All of them have met and surmounted numerous obstacles.

Why did we pick these particular companies? In a business climate in which customers are increasingly calling the shots, these firms are all doing what it takes to place customers at the core of their business strategies. And each of these companies has a number of lessons to teach us.

After monitoring these companies' efforts over the past couple of years, we stepped back and thought about what these firms were doing differently than the many companies that still seem to be fumbling in the midst of the customer revolution. Here's what we found. We noticed that these companies all seemed to be mastering the same key steps. These are the steps to success that today's businesses will need to take in order to thrive in the customer economy.[7]

Eight Steps to Deliver a Great Total Customer Experience

1. Create a Compelling Brand Personality
2. Deliver a Seamless Experience across Channels and Touchpoints
3. Care about Customers and Their Outcomes
4. Measure What Matters to Customers
5. Hone Operational Excellence
6. Value Customers' Time

---

[7] These Eight Steps required to deliver a great total customer experience don't replace the need to master the basics. You'll find those first eight critical success factors listed in our previous book, *Customers.com.* To refresh your memory, they are:

1. Target the right customer
2. Own the customer's total experience
3. Streamline business processes that impact the customer
4. Provide a 360-degree view of the customer relations
5. Let customers help themselves
6. Help customers do their jobs
7. Deliver personalized service
8. Foster community

7. Place Customers' "DNA" at the Core
8. Design to Morph

In the chapters that follow, we'll introduce each step, explain it so that you can begin to apply it to your own business, and then illustrate with examples from one or more case studies.

You'll notice that most of the companies we've chosen to profile have mastered at least five of the eight steps. And all of these companies are already measuring some of the key elements of customer value and customer experience. You'll find many of the metrics these firms use summarized in the Customer Flight Deck measurements we've included at the end of each case study.

As you read through these steps and the case studies to follow, ask yourself, how many of these steps has your company taken? How do your current customer metrics compare?

9

THE FIRST STEP: CREATE A COMPELLING BRAND PERSONALITY

Whether you're creating a brand identity from scratch or creating a customer experience to complement an existing brand, you need to start with a strong brand identity that customers can identify with. That means that your brand identity needs to have a personality as well as a core brand idea. Both of these need to appeal to customers. You've already read about Egg's brand personality. It's caring and fair-minded. Egg's core brand ideas are personalized service, "have it your way" product offerings, and fair deals. You'll find some interesting similarities between Egg's brand-building efforts and those of the case study you're about to read. Sunday is on the other side of the globe. Yet Hong Kong wireless carrier Sunday's brand personality is about being carefree on my time off and having things my way. One key difference is that Egg has established itself as the purveyor of "fair deals." Sunday is opting for a luxury image.

How did Egg differentiate? Egg always tried to be the first-to-market with a new, great deal for its customers. And Egg quickly established itself as an "Internet brand." By offering lower rates for customers who would serve themselves online, Egg caters to the self-directed, technology-savvy consumer. Sunday also caters to the hip, with-it crowd. It prides itself on being first-to-market with nifty new features. But it differentiates itself on the approachability and personality of its stores and its services. It innovated by providing services that support the personal lifestyles of its customers.

Let's take a look at how Sunday has built and sustained its brand in a commodity marketplace. Notice that the company didn't just build a brand. It built a branded experience.

SUNDAY COMMUNICATIONS LTD.: CREATING A BRAND AND A COMPELLING CONSISTENT CUSTOMER EXPERIENCE

Mobile phones and mobile phone service has become a commodity business around the world. Often the phone is given away to entice customers to sign up for phone service. Sunday is a good example of a company that is using a brand personality combined with a consistent customer experience to differentiate itself in a crowded, commodity market.

Hong Kong's consumer and business customers are among the most demanding in the world. Long accustomed to being at the hub of global commerce, business people in Hong Kong expect to be able to get virtually anything done in hours, if not minutes. Mobile phones are the lifeblood of the Hong Kong economy. They're also a status symbol and a lifestyle statement. Hong Kong's young people are just as busy as their parents. Whether they're in school, shopping, or playing, they stay in touch with their friends and relatives using their trusty mobile phones. In the past, mobile phone operators could "lock customers in," with prepaid non-refundable service plans. Customers were also loath to change mobile service providers because they didn't want to lose the phone number they had given out to hundreds, if not thousands of friends, relatives, and colleagues. In March 1999, Hong Kong regulators enacted "Mobile Number Portability." Now, customers can switch mobile providers without losing their phone numbers.

The Hong Kong mobile phone and data services market is as competitive as markets get. Hong Kong's customers are the world's most demanding. So why would you want to join an already crowded market to compete for mindshare with customers who are fashion-conscious and very demanding when it comes to quality, service levels, and price? Ask Craig Ehrlich and the Sunday team. They think they've found a way to win the hearts and minds of the world's most demanding customers. They're doing it by creating a strong, brand personality and customer experience.

The Genesis of Sunday

In Hong Kong there's a core group of telecom experts that have been together for more than fifteen years now, racking up success after success. They built Hutchison Telecom, the most successful mobile phone and paging company in Asia with profits of $150 million in its heyday. It was under this management team that Hutchison Telecom branched out into the European market to create the phenomenally successful "Orange" wireless operator in the U.K. (sold for $20 billion in 1999), the first truly branded wireless operator. The same team created AsiaSat, Asia's first private satellite company, in 1990, and Star TV, the first Pan-Asia satellite TV company, with Richard Li in 1991.

It was because of a disagreement over the vision for the growth of Hutchison Telecom with the chairman of the parent company, Hutchison Whampoa, that most of the management team left the company in 1993. In 1995, the same team banded together under the name Mandarin Communications and applied for a license to offer second-generation GSM services in the competitive Hong Kong market.

"We knew that the market was changing with so many new players. Mobile telephony was going to become a truly mass-market commodity play in Hong Kong," Craig Ehrlich, Group Managing Director of Sunday reported. "But we could see the convergence of wireless communications and the Internet. We knew that wireless voice was becoming a mass-market phenomenon, but we believed that there was a new upmarket opportunity for premium customers—the people who were already beginning to use the Internet to track their investments and the kids who would want to play games using wireless devices."

Creating the Brand Identity

"The success of Orange inspired us to go beyond the conventional to take a risk in coming up with the brand personality," said Craig. "We wanted to make a big splash in this crowded market so we intentionally kept a low profile when we got the license in 1996. . . . In 1997 we were ready for the launch and hired a famous graphic designer in Hong Kong, Alan Chan, to produce a logo and identity for the company."

There was only one problem. Mandarin Communications didn't give Alan a name for the new company. Up against the deadline, he had to produce a logo for a company that still hadn't been named. He was working on a Saturday and stewing about this problem when his wife, who was also his office manager, wanted him to go out shopping with her. He said, "I can't. I have to work." (Everyone in Hong Kong works six days a week; it's the norm.) He added, "Wait until Sunday and we can do whatever you want." As he sat there feeling frustrated that he couldn't go out and enjoy himself until the next day, the light bulb went on. The name of the company would be "Sunday." The brand image would be carefree. Thus the branding and ad campaign were set into motion. "We built the brand on an attitude and a personality," Craig explained. What's the brand personality of Sunday? Youthful, irreverent, and innovative. "Of course, we had to have good network coverage, competitive pricing, value for money. That's a given. But most of our competitors built their brands using a corporate positioning—very executive, very businesslike. We needed a point of differentiation. We wanted to challenge the status quo and be irreverent."

The ad campaign began two weeks before the official launch of the service with teaser ads in newspapers and in Hong Kong's transit system—subways and buses. The ads had an iridescent blue background with a bright orange typeface: "You look like you haven't had it in weeks," "How come you never get it on a Friday?", "The average man thinks about it twenty times a day," "How many of you are thinking about it right now?" Some people complained and the management of the Metropolitan Transit authority saw the ads and banned them. They thought the campaign was too suggestive. Sunday made use of this opportunity and ran a "banned ad" in the newspapers, saying that this campaign was banned by the Transit Authority and that people would have to wait until September 21st for the answer. This reaction further raised people's awareness and everyone wondered what the answer would be.

This was followed up by the "It feels like Sunday" ad campaign. This featured people of all walks of life doing the things they obviously most enjoyed doing—young children playing, a couple lazing about in bed on a sunny morning, a family celebrating, a man in a sweat suit doing Tai Chi in front of the Legislative Council building. He passes gas. You get the picture.

The secret about what Sunday was and what this new company was going to offer was so complete that most of the company's employees didn't even know. On the Friday before the commercial launch, Craig told the rest of the employees that their company was changing its name to Sunday. They were surprised and excited!

Creating the Customer Experience to Match the Brand

On Sunday, September 21, 1997, Sunday opened its doors for business offering a new style of mobile service—"A mobile phone network that's all about living." What were the differentiators? First, buying your phone was much easier, carefree, and fun. "If you go to a traditional network operator's storefront in Hong Kong, you'll see a very sober 'look.' The salespeople are dressed in business suits. They stand behind a counter. Customers wait their turn on benches. All of the mobile handsets are in showcases under glass," Craig explained. "Our stores are bright orange and blue. Our salespeople aren't behind any counters. They're approachable. They're dressed in fashionable, casual outfits, which change seasonally. The phones are out in plain view. You can pick them up and play with them." Sunday's shops are consumer-friendly. The services that Sunday is offering were designed to make your life easier. For example, Sunday was the first in Hong Kong to offer location-specific enquiry service, "Mobile Assist." At any time you can dial *66 and, based on where you're located at the time, learn the nearest gas station, restaurant, shoe repair location, ATM machine, and so on. A really popular feature among the cool, younger set that Sunday targeted is Mobile Cupid. This is a matchmaking service that notifies you when someone nearby meets your desired profile (including the right horoscope). Mobile Jukebox lets customers direct song dedications to any phone numbers in Hong Kong and download ring tones or pop music. Sunday's brand was quickly established as carefree, irreverent, convenient, and adding fun touches to my life.

Dealing with Price Wars in a Commodity Market

There is no more challenging marketplace for a mobile voice and data operator than Hong Kong. There are lots of competitors. And because customers have been guaranteed phone-number portability it's painless for consumer to switch carriers anytime they want. "One or two of our competitors want to buy marketshare and don't care about losses," Craig Ehrlich reports. "We strive for profitability. Saving face can play a major role in business decisions in Hong Kong. There's one company that believes it must be number one in terms of marketshare. Their prices are 40 to 50 percent cheaper than ours." This means huge market pressure.

Yet Hong Kong is a society based on aspirational characteristics. And that's what Sunday is banking on. "Our original target market—the eighteen- to thirty-five-year-old set—change their phones on average every nine months. You want to show off your phone, just the way you show off your clothes. This market is very brand conscious," explained Mah Bing Zet, Sunday's marketing maven.

In Hong Kong, customers typically prepay between $300 (HK) and $800 for a new mobile handset along with a twelve- to twenty-four-month commitment for phone service. If you walked away from your operator, you would lose the remaining prepayment. However, most of Sunday's targeted customers want to change their handsets for a newer, hipper model within six to nine months. Sunday offers more flexible service plans. Only the very lowest-cost bargain service requires a pre-payment (of $200 HK), which is rebated after twelve months. All of the higher value services don't require a pre-payment. And customers can change mobile handsets by walking into any of Sunday's convenient stores and upgrading their phone and their plan.

Measuring What Matters to Customers

Sunday's marketing team not only created and refined the Sunday brand, the chief marketing officer also owned customer service for the first two years of the company's existence. "Customers judge the quality of our service in two key areas: network performance (Sunday covers 99% of Hong Kong and has a 1% drop rate in a market that averages 3%) and the quality of our customer service. For customer service, we measure everything," Craig explained. "The two factors we track the most closely are the number of abandoned calls and how many seconds people wait before we answer."

On the direct sales front, Sunday uses a "mystery shopper" approach. Ten to twelve times per month, an unknown shopper appears at each store and plays the part of a customer. The sales staff is rated on factors like product knowledge and courtesy. The results of these surveys are shared with the employees and used to prioritize their training. If they surpass the benchmark, they get an extra bonus.

Actual customer surveys are conducted twice a year to measure customers' attitudes toward the company and the brand. And to monitor its brand awareness and mindshare, Sunday does fifty face-to-face surveys per week, forty-eight weeks a year, knocking on doors and asking people about their perceptions of Sunday and its competitors. The market researchers ask participants which company has the best roaming features, which offers the best value for the money, and which offers the most innovative services.

Competing on Innovation

Since innovation is key to Sunday's hip, with-it brand, the company has been aggressive in pioneering new services. For example, Sunday:

- Launched the world's first mobile "intelligent Network" with location-based services, in 1997.
- Launched the innovative "Enhanced Services": *28 Jetso, *66 Mobile Assist, *80 Mobile Reporter, and *88 Mobile Concierge.
- Completed worldwide roaming agreements so that Sunday customers have seamless global coverage with more than 130 providers around the world.
- Launched the first mobile banking and mobile commerce in Asia in partnership with CHASEinfinity Smart Credit Card at the end of 1998.
- Launched wireless Internet services in January 2000 under the rubric "So WAP," with 39 services providers (including banks, race tracks, and ticket agencies).
- Expanded its signature "Enhanced Services," including the 22 Mobile Cupid, 33 Mobile Jukebox, *88 Concierge, and *168 Mobile Racecourse to work as wireless data services as well as voice services.
- Launched Sunday.com, the Internet dial-up service and service portal.
- Launched a mobile wireless stock-trading application in partnership with boom.com, Asia's first Internet stock broker, in February 2000.

- Launched location-based advertising services (these are "opt in" services, in which customers can choose which brands or types of products they'd like to receive special promotions on. For example, Shumera cosmetics ads with coupons are sent to female customers who are in the vicinity of a store carrying the Shumera line. Because they're Sunday customers, they get a special offer, which drives traffic to the stores.).
- Partnered with Hewlett-Packard (Hong Kong division) to provide the first open WAP platform for e-trading in Hong Kong.

Results

Sunday continues to maintain a high quality of service, particularly in comparison to the marketshare leaders. In 1998 Sunday had a 35 percent churn rate, below the market average, which is 50 percent. In 1999 Sunday grew the number of its subscribers by 100,000 to a total of 300,000. As competition increased, so did the churn rate—to 45 percent. Yet by October 2000, Sunday had grown to approximately 400,000 subscribers. Sunday's most impressive accomplishment to date has been its ability to deliver a high-value, profitable mobile service while carefully growing its customer franchise. Sunday's management team isn't trying to compete on marketshare. It is intent on delivering high quality service and making money.

This positioning has appealed to investors. Sunday was listed on the stock exchange in Hong Kong and NASDAQ in March 2000, raising $380 million in new share capital.

Most impressive is the brand awareness Sunday has created and sustained. It was declared by Media Magazine, the authority in the Asian advertising industry, to be the number one consumer brand in Hong Kong in 1999. Sunday also won the Gold Prize as well at the Citation for Outstanding TV campaign of the HKMA/TVB Award for Marketing Excellence 2000 for its innovative marketing campaign (recognized as the most prestigious marketing award in Hong Kong).

Takeaways

The Sunday team knew that there was an opportunity to create a brand personality, a unique customer experience, and a lifestyle-based offering to compete in a commodity marketplace. While competitors were throwing money at acquiring new customers, Sunday's executives focused on brand-building, honing the customer experience, and operational excellence—in short on delivering the best customer experience they can. To date Sunday has managed to hold its own in marketshare yet grow its revenues per customer. The game plan is working.

Patty's Suggestions for Sunday

Sunday needs to be careful that it doesn't become marginalized in its market. Customers like to do business with a winner. Having a superb customer experience won't suffice if customers don't believe that you have mindshare and a reasonable marketshare. Sunday's executives plan to address the customer acquisition and marketshare problem by linking up with one of the more innovative players in the mobile wireless data market in the region. Sunday expects to combine forces with one of the players in the next generation of packet-switched wireless data services. Sunday plans to be around for the long haul, honing and refining its unique customer experience.

To hone and refine that brand, of course, Sunday needs to be absolutely certain that it is achieving its vision of a hip, with-it brand with attitude and personality. It needs to verify that its fashion-conscious customers are in fact keeping up with fashion, and that Sunday is helping them to do just that. And it needs to be sure that it does not fail on those aspects of product and service performance that have become "entitlements" among its customer base.

Attitude and personality arise in no small degree from the company's quirky, edgy advertising and publicity. There are at least two ways to determine if the advertising is having the desired effect: measure how the company ranks in *"unaided brand awareness,"* and take note of the *"age distribution of the customer base."* If people can recall the Sunday name and image without being prompted, the company can feel comfortable with its prominence in the public's eye. And if the average Sunday customer is youthful and affluent, that bodes well for its longer-term prospects with that group of customers.

But that group of customers is attracted at least in part by the stream of innovative services the company develops. Its product-development pipeline, therefore, needs to be kept fresh and vital, and that means Sunday must keep *time-to-market* low and *number of new services* high. It also means the company must have strong enough relationships with the mobile phone manufacturers that Sunday gets and markets *new products before any of its competitors.* One way to measure this is to track *how often customers change or upgrade* their phones. But this depends in turn on *how many upgrades* Sunday has available and *how frequently they become available.* And this depends, again in turn, on the *manufacturing-to-marketing availability* of its key phone suppliers.

Naturally, all of this breaks down if Sunday is unable to deliver on the entitlements, specifically *network performance* and *customer service.* The network state of the art is improving to such a degree that a 1 percent drop rate is likely to be a competitive advantage for only a short while. Today's watchword is "five nines," meaning 99.999 percent performance, and the company would do well to keep a target like that in mind.

Customer service expectations are likely to be just as dynamic. Today's customers have been weaned on an expectation of high levels of service, and Sunday's customers are no different. The other aspects of the company's brand may be strong enough to compensate for customer service that falls short of the five nines, but I'm pretty certain that won't be true for very long. The mystery shoppers are helping to keep service personnel on their toes, but they may soon have to raise the bar of customer service. The bonus benchmark may have to go up, but the company's personnel are probably up to the challenge.

If I were putting together a Customer Flight Deck for Sunday, then, an early draft of it would probably look like the following table. What I've included here are those metrics that will help the company track its brand personality. A full Flight Deck would need many more metrics, of course, but the remainder would have to derive from a full understanding of Sunday's overall strategic objectives for the long-term, as well as its overall vision and mission of what kind of company it wants to be.

Note that in the Customer Retention section, we felt it was important for Sunday to track the percentage of time the company is first-to-market with new mobile phones and new features. Since Sunday's target customers are very conscious of wanting to be the first to have new things, the company has to be vigilant that it always maintains that differentiation.

A Sample Flight Deck for Sunday

	Navigation	Performance	Operations	Environment
Customer Numbers	Number of customers Number of products and services per customer	Increase/decrease in number of customers by customer segment Increase/decrease in number of products/services per customer by segment	Number of new service sign-ups Number of service upgrades	Number of competitors' customers Number of non-customers (people who don't use wireless at all)
Customer Retention	Customer retention rate Upgrade frequency First availability percentage (has new phones and features before competition)	Customer retention rate by segment Frequency of new service offerings Popularity of new service offerings (percent uptake) Upgrade turnaround time New model availability	First-to-market ratio (how often are we first-to-market with a new service?) Manufacturing-to-market availability of new models of mobile phones	Competitive first-to-market percentage
Customer Experience	Unaided brand awareness rank Customer satisfaction rating Mystery shopper scores	Satisfaction with network qualtiy Satisfaction with service quality: • Phone support • Problem resolution • Accuracy of billing • In-store experience	Network uptime Service metrics (first-call resolution, courtesy, knowledge, flexibility, etc.)	Comparative satisfaction: • Wireless companies • All service companies
Customer Spending	Average spending per customer Profitability per customer Customer lifetime value	Percentage change in customer spending by customer segment Percentage change in profitability by customer segment	Effectiveness of advertising and marketing as measured in increased customer profitability Customer service and support costs	Total spending on wireless services Total spending on all communications services

Observations about Sunday

As you've just read, Sunday's position may be a bit precarious. It's not clear whether the company will be able to continue to grow its customer franchise quickly enough to satisfy its investors. Does that mean that it's not a good idea to devote the kind of attention to detail that Sunday did in creating and launching its brand? Does it mean that it costs so much to build a new brand identity that no one can afford to do it and still survive? I don't believe so.

I learned a lot from watching Sunday's brand-builder in action. Before we talked, I hadn't really appreciated the feelings and the subtleties that go into making a brand sing. Mah Bing Zet, the brand-image creator of Sunday, and her advertising team are world-class. They understand how to create a brand and a customer experience that customers identify with. They created a brand that makes you feel good about yourself and a little risqué. And they've remained focused on delivering higher, aspirational value.

Of course, this same brand personality and brand image approach won't work for all products and all brands. But Sunday's experience to date does serve to remind us that customers, even customers who are fomenting a customer revolution, care about qualities other than price.

What are the things you can take away from Sunday's experiences to apply to your own brand creation and amplification efforts? Whether you are creating, refining, or building on a consumer brand or a business brand, here are the steps I learned:

1. Customers appreciate a brand identity that makes them feel good about themselves as users of the product or services you offer. The brand identity should be based on the way the customer wants to see himself.

2. You *do* need buzz to launch a brand, but it can be created in a clever way, using PR as well as advertising.

3. The brand image and the buzz you create need to reinforce the customer experience. It's all about how you will feel using the product or service or coming into contact with it.

4. You need to carefully design every aspect of the customer experience, including the lighting in the stores, the way you

answer the phones, and the way you execute every customer-impacting move. This is not simply an advertising campaign, a set of uniforms, and a look. It's a way of being. It impacts the training your employees receive, the policies you put in place, and how your executives walk the talk.

5. Then you need to monitor the quality of your customer experience carefully. Sunday uses "mystery shoppers" to ensure that its in-store personnel and its customer service personnel are representing the brand appropriately.

6. Of course, your Web presence, your call center presence, and your in-store presence need to embody the complete customer experience and feeling you're creating. Again, we're not talking about the graphics you use on the Web site but about the site navigation, ease of use, and the extent to which you've correctly anticipated different customers' needs.

7. How you display and describe your merchandise is critical. Today's customers want and need to be able to touch, feel, and try out your products and services. And they need lots of information to make informed decisions. They need to feel empowered by having all the right information available in the right context.

10

THE SECOND STEP: DELIVER A SEAMLESS CUSTOMER EXPERIENCE ACROSS CHANNELS AND TOUCHPOINTS

Today's customers are increasingly demanding that companies offer them convenience and freedom of choice. Customers want the freedom to decide whether it's more convenient to call on the phone or to drop into a branch or store. And today's customers have absolutely no patience for the "seams" that occur between most companies' disparate customer support groups. Why should a customer call a different phone number for Web support than for phone support? If a customer walks into a bricks-and-mortar store, he expects to see the items that are featured on the company's Web site. If he shops on the Web, he expects to be able to go into a retail outlet and touch and feel the merchandise, or test drive the car before he makes a final decision. In short, today's demanding customers want a seamless customer experience, and a good one, no matter how they choose to interact with us.

Before we address the "how to's" and issues you're likely to encounter in executing this step, let's define our terms.

DEFINING TERMS: CHANNELS AND TOUCHPOINTS

TOUCHPOINTS

We use the term interaction "touchpoint" to describe the types of media through which customers interact with companies and their representatives. Touchpoints include stores, telephones, mail, fax, kiosks (and ATMs), and, of course, the Web.

Customers typically decide what touchpoint(s) they prefer. For example, you can transact business with your bank by walking in and talking to a teller, driving in and using an ATM, phoning the bank's call center, and logging on to the Web. Which touchpoint you choose is highly dependent on the context of your interaction. If you need cash you might interact differently than if you need to check your balance or pay a bill. It also might depend on the time of day, your location, or your preferences of the moment.

CHANNELS

We use the term "channel" or "distribution channel" to describe the business relationships set up by companies to make it easier to get products, services, and information to their customers. Channels can be defined as direct (the company deals directly with their customers) or indirect (the company has one or more sets of partners that deal with customers).

In the past, the choice of distribution channel strategy was made by the company rather than its customers. However, that's now changing as customers grab more and more control over our business practices. Many companies that have only sold through distributors and retailers to reach their end customers are now finding that customers are demanding ways to place orders direct.

Many companies have multi-channel strategies. Most companies that sell primarily to other businesses may have a small set of named accounts that they service directly and a large number of smaller accounts that are serviced through distributors. Business customers often find it more convenient to buy through distributors that can sell them products from multiple suppliers. For example, a restaurant chain may purchase pickles from Vlasic and sanitary gloves from FoodHandler as part of a single order to Sysco.

In the consumer space, multi-channel strategies include examples such as Bose (which enables customers to purchase directly from Bose stores or from consumer electronics chains) or your local dairy (which may deliver milk and cheese to your house as well as selling through the supermarket).

CHANNELS AND TOUCHPOINTS ARE COMPLEMENTARY

Channels and touchpoints can be used in almost any combination. Banking is an example of the customer dealing through a direct channel via multiple touchpoints. Conversely, my ability to order a Hewlett-Packard 970 printer from HP.com or Circuitcity.com constitutes a single touchpoint—the Web—with multiple channels—one direct and one indirect. Interestingly, if I order from Circuitcity.com I get my choice of touchpoints; I can have the printer shipped to my house or designate a local store to pick it up right away.

Many companies are now using the Web as the initial way to add a direct channel to their traditionally indirect channels. Compaq computers and Gibson guitars are two good examples. In other words, the customer may purchase direct from the manufacturer as well as through distribution channel partners.

Creating a Multi-Touchpoint Strategy: Bricks and Clicks Comes of Age

Many customers prefer to deal with businesses that they can touch and feel if they want to. They also generally prefer to deal with brands they recognize and appreciate. That's why 2000 became the year of the "clicks and bricks" business model. Traditional bricks-and-mortar retailers began blending their Web touchpoints more seamlessly into their conventional retail operations. And a few dot-com companies began opening physical retail branches. Clicks and bricks isn't just a consumer phenomenon. Companies like W. W. Grainger, an aggregator of industrial supplies, has long prided itself on its multi-touchpoint distribution strategy. Most businesses are within 30 minutes of a Grainger branch. But customers can also pick up the phone to place an order and/or go online.

Dealing with Channel Conflict

One of the thorniest areas of contention in evolving your business is what to do about your relationships with the partners that have traditionally sold and serviced your products. Customers have been, and will remain, unforgiving on this point. They expect you to make your products available through the distribution channels (e.g., retailers, dealers, and agents) that are most convenient for them. Yet they also expect you to sell your products direct (by Web and phone) whenever possible. They want, and increasingly demand, a seamless customer experience when it comes to pre-sales, sales, support, service, repairs, delivery, and ancillary products. And lo and behold, they expect the manufacturer of the product—the company with whom they associate the product brand name—to take ownership of their total end-to-end experience.

Manufacturers that are dependent on dealers and distributors to sell and support their products have been tiptoeing around their channel partners since the advent of the Internet. (Actually, they were tiptoeing before, but since the Internet the tiptoeing has become much louder!) The issue is one of profit margins and customer ownership. Dealers and retailers are intent on owning their relationships with the customers. They are paranoid about ceding any of that relationship—or the customer information—to the manufacturer for fear that the manufacturer will go direct to the customer, cutting the dealer or retailer out of the relationship and hence the profit margins.

However, it's the customer who owns the relationship. And it's the customer who gets to choose how she wants to do business. The good news is that customers still want to deal with most middlemen, including retailers and dealers. The other good news is that they also want to deal direct with the manufacturer. In fact, it has become increasingly clear that customers now get very annoyed when the manufacturer does not recognize the customer as a customer. Most customers want and expect the manufacturer to know what they've purchased, which model and/or configuration. And many customers would like that information to be kept on file by the manufacturer so that they don't have to worry about it.

Key Issues in Integrating (Channel) Partners

Before the Web we entrusted customer relationships to dealers, brokers, and agents because we honestly knew that they could do a better job of servicing our clients than we could. In general, that was true in the past. And it's still largely true today. What's different now is that customers have made it clear that they want a seamless, transparent relationship with us—the suppliers—*and* with our trusted channel partners. Customers don't want to think about whom they should call for what purpose. They simply want to pick up the phone or log onto the 'Net and get something taken care of. It's up to us, the supplier/dealer partnership, to sort out the business processes and the compensation structures and to deliver the very best possible and consistent experience to our mutual clients.

Channel partners are simply one kind of partner to consider. As you read through the case studies that follow, think about other partner relationships that you have today or may have in the future. Some of these will be long-term relationships; others may be ephemeral ones. But in each case, many of the same principles will apply. You might as well deal with them now.

TRUST

It's all about trust. And trust is best built between individuals, face to face and over time. As we move into this new, partnering era, we need to figure out how to establish and maintain trust quickly and cleanly. It's not a matter of legal contracts. It's a matter of values and ethics. People who are ethical and trustworthy will work for companies that share their values. Yet in spite of that, we've all had the experience of putting our trust in a person and being disappointed by their inability to deliver on behalf of themselves and their organization. Trust is built and sustained through clean, clear, heartfelt, and direct communications. The Internet doesn't change that, but it does require a change in our habits and practices.

The best tools that the Internet offers to support and sustain trust are transparency and visibility. Once a partnership is established and any activity takes place on behalf of a mutual customer, each of the parties involved (the client included) needs to have complete visibility into the status of the work in process.

CONTROL

What are we arguing about when we attempt to build and sustain a relationship but control? Who controls the customer relationship? Who controls the purse strings? Who calls the shots? Who controls the time line? The first thing to realize is that none of the partners controls the customer relationship. That's an outmoded concept; the customer revolution blew it away. Get used to it. You no longer have any control over the customer relationship.

However, there are lots of control issues remaining. They have to do with who performs which service(s), at what price, in what region, with how much exclusivity. What it boils down to in the end is that partners want to keep as much control as possible over the issues that will impact their future prosperity.

SHARING CUSTOMER INFORMATION

All customer information now needs to be shared. There's no other way to operate in the customer economy. The customer gets to decide which partners he will entrust with which kinds of information. And there are legal requirements that specify what customer information must be captured and how it is to be held in trust for the customer. Any partner who is providing a service to a customer, even if it's a behind-the-scenes service, needs to be explicitly identified to the customer. Also, there should be complete visibility of all customer-impacting information. All parties, including the customer, need to be able to access the up-to-date information about the customer and the status of his dealings with each party.

One way to think about structuring and sharing customer information is to put yourself in the customer's shoes and design your customer information systems for his use. In the past we've designed customer information systems to be used by our sales force, marketing departments, customer care center, or channel partners. Even as companies have begun to bring that customer information together into shared customer relationship management systems, they're still doing so from the inside out. In the General Motors Vauxhall case study, for example, you'll read about GM Custom, a customer database that was first developed in the U.K. and is now being used as a model for the rest of Europe. GM Custom started out as a marketing database but is now being enhanced to improve the customer experience. But it won't be until customers begin seeing their complete car service histories online that all of the parties—dealer, warranty company, customer care center, and manufacturer—will have a transparent view of this shared customer information. Furthermore, the information they'll see will be the information that matters to the customer.

COMMISSIONS AND LEADS

As you'll see in reading the Vauxhall and Snap-on case studies, the common approach to handling commissions for direct sales via the Internet is to make an accommodation with the partner whose pocketbook is at risk. W. W. Grainger compensates its sales force based on the profitability of each order. Lids makes sure that in-store sales associates get commissions on Web orders in their geography. Vauxhall pays its dealers a somewhat lower commission for Internet sales but still requires that the dealer do special things to earn that commission, like deliver the car to the customer's driveway.

Snap-on wasn't sure whether its consumer Web site would cannibalize dealer sales or whether any of the people who purchased online would do enough volume to warrant having a dealer relationship. Yet it established a structure that's working quite well. Customers who order three times online or who order above a certain threshold are assigned to a dealer's call list. And the dealer receives a commission on sales from any of his existing business customers. The one thing we didn't like about Snap-on's initial implementation of its consumer Web site was the fact that customers couldn't view prices until they had registered, and when they register they had to specify the dealer's number (if they have a dealer). This seemed too complicated and it was. Snap-on discovered that it had to make its list pricing visible on the Web, just like everyone else does. Customers shouldn't need to worry about which dealer calls on them. That reconciliation needed to be an easy behind-the-scenes function.

PRICING

Of course, there will continue to be a disparity in the price a customer pays and the price a dealer pays the manufacturer. That's the margin that makes it possible for the dealer to do his job. Generally speaking, customers buying online expect to see and pay the list price for the product or to receive a discount that has been prenegotiated for his account. What we do know from the first five years of experience in e-commerce is that customers will demand to see the list prices for all goods and services, and they will expect these to be the same all over the world (with the exception of local taxes and duties).

SHARING PRODUCT INFORMATION AND VALUE-ADDED TOOLS

It is the manufacturer's responsibility to provide accurate, actionable product information that is complete, up-to-date, and easy for both the partner and the customer to use to make configuration, selection, and purchasing decisions. But today's product information is no longer composed of Web pages or online catalog entries. Typically, product information is organized in a database with dynamically changing pricing, inventory, and specifications. Usually, the manufacturer maintains the product-specific information, including applications such as configurators, planning tools such as expert systems or CAD/CAM applications for architects and engineers, financial planning tools for investors, or software simulations for designers. The partner adds partner-specific information like pricing, availability, featured offers, or side-by-side product comparisons. The manufacturer can also provide pre-sales and post-sales customer support when appropriate.

Delivering a Great Customer Experience Seamlessly Across Channels: *Learning from Vauxhall and Snap-on*

General Motors' Vauxhall Division in the U.K. has been the most aggressive of GM's worldwide operations in listening to customers and stepping up to the plate in owning the customer relationship. Snap-on is a B2B player that has recently started using the Internet as a way to extend its customer experience online, hopefully in a way that will bring end customers into relationship with Snap-on while at the same time keeping its franchisees happy. And by the way, Snap-on has been successful in using the Internet to reach out to a new target market: consumers.

GENERAL MOTORS' VAUXHALL DIVISION: MANAGING THE CUSTOMER EXPERIENCE ACROSS CHANNELS AND TOUCHPOINTS

British consumers have been up in arms for several years. Their complaint: unfair pricing. They claim that prices in Britain are artificially higher than they are in other parts of Europe. And they blame this state of affairs on entrenched industry practices and lack of government attention to globally competitive pricing. Consumers are particularly annoyed about the relatively high prices for cars in the U.K. As we explained in Chapter 3 (How Customers' Demands Are Transforming Industries), part of the problem in Britain has to do with the fact that only 20 percent of cars are sold to consumers. The rest are bought by companies for their employees. The companies negotiate bulk contracts. Consumers pay higher prices and, of course, believe that they are getting the short end of the stick. And they are. That's about to end. In October 2000, a government commission called for substantial changes in the way cars are priced and sold to consumers in Britain.

At least one company was ready. Vauxhall (a division of General Motors) had already been working to change its pricing and policies for over a year. Vauxhall used the Internet as a medium through which it could give more power to customers. Vauxhall was the first automobile manufacturer in the world to sell new cars direct over the Internet. To do so, the manufacturer had to come to terms with its car dealerships—its only distribution channel. What happens to the dealer when customers want to buy direct via the Internet and manufacturers want to sell direct online? Vauxhall has paved the way. Its dealers support the Internet sales and have the opportunity to service the online customers.

Vauxhall's savvy management team also realized how critical it is to build a strong branded relationship with each customer and each household. But how *does* an automobile manufacturer with hundreds of independent and powerful exclusive dealerships build a closer relationship with its customers without taking dealers out of the loop? Vauxhall was the first of General Motors' business units to pioneer a new, closed-loop relationship management approach with the cooperation of its U.K. dealers and in cooperation with a variety of business partners. Here's the story of how Vauxhall has met and surmounted its customer relationship challenges.

Improving the Customer Experience

In mid-1998 Paul Confrey, a thirty-one-year-old marketing manager at GM's Vauxhall Motors, was tapped by Nick Reilly, the group's aggressive chairman, and Ian Coomber, its sales and marketing director, to head up a new Relationship Marketing division. Paul had spent ten years at Vauxhall in marketing, brand management, and direct sales in the United Kingdom and Germany. The goal of this new division was to build tighter relationships with Vauxhall's customers while at the same time offering its 450 dealers—which ranged from individual family businesses to large, multi-dealer groups—services that would increase their profitability. Vauxhall management knew that it was critical to increase customer loyalty in order to build marketshare and boost long-term profitability. Vauxhall's marketshare in the U.K. was averaging 13 percent. Vauxhall's loyalty rate—repeat purchases by the same individual household—was running at 50 percent per year, average for the U.K. new car market. Nick, Ian, and Paul knew that a good way to increase customer loyalty would be to improve customers' experiences in dealing with the different faces of Vauxhall. "We recognized that selling metal is not a great way to make money. We wanted to wrap the customer in the Vauxhall blanket—insurance, accessories, warranty, used cars, accident repair, etc. with a customer-centric, cross-selling approach that takes away as many of the hassles of running a car as possible."

The Vauxhall management team didn't think of its mandate as saving the customers time. They were focused on improving customers' relationships and increasing customer loyalty. Yet in tackling the issues that mattered most to customers, they wound up saving customers time and aggravation. They redesigned business processes across business partners to give customers a more seamless and streamlined experience. Vauxhall took on the responsibility of coordinating all customer-impacting business processes so that it could better control the quality of the customer experience. In short, Vauxhall took responsibility for the quality of the total customer experience that was being delivered to customers through a variety of partners.

Do Customers Want a Relationship with the Manufacturer?

THEY THINK THEY ALREADY HAVE ONE!

Like most manufacturers, Vauxhall was very nervous about supplanting the customers' relationships with its dealers. It was heavily reliant on this channel, since there is no other practical way to sell, service, and maintain customers' cars. Yet when the company asked customers whether they wanted a relationship with the manufacturer, customers claimed that they already had such a relationship. It just wasn't a very good one. Most dramatically, customers' concerns came through loud and clear. "You don't act as if you care about me. You're just trying to solicit my business. You call me several times about different, seemingly unrelated issues. You're wasting my time!" The moral of the story is that if you sell a branded product, customers have a relationship with you and your brand. If you don't control the quality of the customer's total experience with your brand, you're missing the boat. Customers will sense that you don't care about their experiences in doing business with you and they'll defect.

Vauxhall customers knowingly or unknowingly dealt with at least five different companies—each one providing a part of the Vauxhall experience. But Vauxhall wasn't contacting owners or prospects directly. The dealer was the first point of contact for purchasing and servicing the vehicle, and third parties were involved in warranty extension programs and car insurance. GM's subsidiary, GMAC, handled financing.

Building a Customer Relationship Management Foundation

In order to provide a much more seamless customer experience across these partners, Paul Confrey took over responsibility for upgrading Vauxhall's customer marketing database. He focused on delivering a unified customer relationship management system that would improve customers' experience of doing business with Vauxhall and all of its partners. Each of GM's business partners would continue performing its piece of the puzzle, but they would all be working from the same master CRM system and they would coordinate their efforts much more closely.

Although Vauxhall's marketing agency had been collecting basic customer information since the late '80s, Vauxhall wasn't really taking advantage of that information, except to execute direct mail campaigns. Vauxhall's CRM project had taken years to get off the ground. Suddenly it had a mission—to improve customers' experiences in dealing with Vauxhall—and some hard deadlines.

Within a year the new Oracle-based CRM database was fully operational, with 5.5 million current customers and hot prospects gleaned and updated from the old marketing database, car ownership records, and the results from recent lead-generation campaigns. All of Vauxhall's marketing partners—GMAC, GM Card, CGU Insurance, GGT (a direct marketing agency), Direct Dialog, and the SureGuard warranty program—were working off the same database and beginning to coordinate marketing efforts based on what customers wanted.

Vauxhall's customer relationship management program wasn't created in a vacuum. It will be the strategic beachhead for GM's European operations. The same customer database tools and the appropriate best practices are being adopted by the other GM divisions throughout Europe.

Getting the Dealers' Buy-In

The real trick, of course, was convincing Vauxhall's independent dealers that the manufacturer wouldn't be inserting itself between these retailers and their customers. In mid-1998 Paul met with Vauxhall's dealer council and explained the progress that had already been made. He told them that he could drive even more business their way by contacting customers on their behalf when it was time to bring their cars in for service and/or when their cars' financing programs were up for renegotiation. The dealer council approved Paul's plan to pilot this proactive CRM program for a year in the south of England involving twelve of Vauxhall's 450 dealers.

Piloting a Life Cycle Customer Relationship Management Program

For the customers in the twelve-dealer pilot area, the Vauxhall CRM team and its partners took a very proactive approach. They developed a set of key initiatives that were tightly coordinated and tracked. Here are some examples:

- When it's time for the first service on a new car (12,000 miles or 12 months), a telemarketer from Vauxhall's telemarketing agency, Direct Dialog, calls the customer to remind her that it's time for a service tune-up. The customer is asked if she'd like to have the dealer call to schedule an appointment and, if so, what days and times would be most convenient. This information is then passed directly to the dealer's service department along with the customer's preferred contact phone numbers. In that same call, the customer is reminded that her warranty will be expiring soon and asked if she'd like to extend the warranty.
- When a customer's financing deal has reached its "trigger point," i.e., the point at which the customer needs to make a decision about payment plans or refinancing (usually at the three-year anniversary), the telemarketing firm calls the customer and offers him a com-

plete "car valet" service along with a brand new loaner car. If the customer agrees, the dealer's representative brings the customer a brand new car of his choice to try out for two days, while his old car is thoroughly cleaned and its value is appraised. When the salesperson returns the spiffed up old car, he brings along a contract that shows the customer what it would cost him to simply keep driving the brand new car (e.g., "For only £45 more pounds per month, you can keep driving this wonderful new car").

The results from the first nine months of the pilot spoke for themselves. In the twelve-dealer area, cross-sells of warranties rose to 30 percent of customers from 11 percent. And dealers' service business increased a whopping 60 percent. But the real clincher was that 90 percent of the customers who took advantage of car valet service and free trial at the trigger point for their financing deals bought the new car! By October 2000 the pilot was extended to include one hundred dealers. By early 2001, Paul expected to have the entire U.K. covered.

Selling Direct via the Internet

Another part of Paul Confrey's mandate included all customer-facing points of contact: all direct marketing programs, all telemarketing programs, and of course, the Internet and the Web. At the time, Vauxhall already had a Web site.

In fact, Vauxhall was the first U.K. car manufacturer to have a Web site. Launched in 1996, it provided core information about Vauxhall's new and used cars, including pricing and financing options. During 1997 and 1998 a number of incremental enhancements made the site more sticky—encouraging customers to return over and over again; for example, a "TrafficMaster" section provided road traffic speeds for all the major highways. It was updated once a minute, so drivers could check traffic conditions before embarking on a trip. Another section was co-sponsored by the Ski Club of Great Britain and targeted customers (or prospects) for Vauxhall's four-wheel drive Frontera model.

Another Web application, Vauxhall BuyPower, was launched in the summer of 1999, enabling prospects to pre-configure their cars online, selecting options and pricing. These prequalified customers were then delivered as leads to the dealers. This game plan worked reasonably well—30,000 customers registered and 5,000 of them actually turned into leads for the dealers—but BuyPower made the dealers nervous about Vauxhall's plans for cutting them out of the loop altogether.

However, it wasn't until July 1999 that Nick Reilly got serious about selling cars online. "That's when Nick called me into his office for a chat," Paul recalls. "Nick is very Internet-literate and he's very aggressive in terms of being first." Nick gave Paul the opportunity to "set up some way for consumers to buy cars on the Internet from us. He didn't tell me how to do it. He just said, 'Figure it out.' Of course Nick realized that the dealers would be a big challenge. He said, 'See how you can get the retailers on your side.' "

Using the Project Team Approach

Paul quickly pulled together a team of about twenty people from a variety of internal and external groups.

The team quickly decided that the best way to sell Vauxhall cars online was to launch with specific, Internet-only car models. These dot-com cars would be configured and ordered via the 'Net but would be delivered and serviced by the closest dealer. Dealers would still receive a commission on the dot-com models. The team decided on three popular models for the initial launch, based on Vauxhall's current product lines: the Corsa.com, the Vectra.com, and the Astra.com. These were standard Vauxhall models that were available with the most commonly requested options. But these "special editions" were available at lower prices. They could only be ordered via the Internet. And each car had a distinctive chrome "dot-com" logo on the side. People would know that you were a dot-com kind of person.

Seducing the Dealers

At first the team had hoped to include a few dealers in its planning process. But they quickly realized that such inclusion would make it impossible to keep the project under wraps. It had to be done as a stealth project. Paul's team didn't want to leak the plan prematurely to the Vauxhall dealers. Paul, who had worked as a car salesman in the mid-1990s, played the role of dealer advocate on the team.

The game plan all along was to get the dealers' buy-in. Without it the project would be dead in the water. But the team had to aim for a November 1, 1999 launch date, knowing full well that the project might be killed at the last minute. "Anything that affects the retailers has to go before the Franchise Board for approval," Paul explained. "We scheduled ourselves onto the program for October 5th. We were planning to announce to the press on October 14th, a few days before the big Birmingham International Motor Show on October 19th."

At the meeting, Paul presented a marketing overview of the Internet landscape. His presentation included demographics—how many of Vauxhall's target customers were already online and would be going online—and the fact that the most profitable lifetime customers for the company were going to be Internet early adopters. Then he gave examples of what was happening in the United States, where intermediaries like Autobytel.com and CarsDirect.com were having a major impact on customers' car-buying practices. These "Yankee" practices were clearly about to hit the U.K. market.

The pitch Paul made was direct. He stated clearly that the customers now have options, and they could control whom they bought from. Thus, the company had to respond to this power. "We can sit back and let these intermediaries own some of the customer experience, or we can take control of the total customer experience. We can offer a car that's unique to Vauxhall on the 'Net. We aren't trying to cut you out of the deal. This isn't an experiment in selling direct and bypassing the retailer. We don't want WW III. We just want to keep this highly profitable customer segment happy. And we can only do it with your support."

The retailer gross margins were significantly reduced on the dot-com models by 3 percent, but the retailers were promised that they would retain at least as much profit as they did through their offline sales. Since the cars were priced at a good value-level and there would be no price haggling involved, the retailers would be getting pretty much the same commissions. They would simply be taking a different role to earn that commission. They would need to take a demo car to the customer's house for a test drive if required. They would still need to value and accept the customer's trade-in car. And they'd need to deliver the new car to the customer and take the old one away. The rest of the time-consuming sales process (interacting with customers about features and functions) would be taken care of through the Web site and by the call center specialists who would be supporting Internet customers.

"What if someone orders a car online and then changes his mind?" the dealers asked. "You're not going to lose money on this," Paul reassured the Board. "Whatever goes wrong, we'll make it good. We'll reimburse you for any costs. We'll do whatever it takes to make this initiative a success."

After three hours of active discussion, Paul's proposal got the green light to pilot the sale of these special-edition dot-com cars on the Web site for a year. The results would then be evaluated.

The Results

One of the early phone calls that Vauxhall's customer assistance center received as a result of the pre-launch publicity was from a sixty-year-old woman who wanted to be the first Internet customer. Mrs. Tavner wasn't particularly computer-savvy, but she loved the idea of being able to buy a car without the bother of going to a dealership and of having the car delivered to her door. Always embarrassed about having to drive an unfamiliar car home from the dealership where strangers may be watching, she wanted to be able to practice first in her driveway before venturing out on the public roads. Mrs. Tavner became the first dot-com car buyer when the new site went live at noon on November 1.

In nine months Vauxhall sold 1,000 dot-com cars, 2 percent of its retail sales volume in that period. "That's all we could handle without ramping up our four-person customer support center," Paul added. "Each of the four customer support representatives who are dedicated to the dot-com program can handle about fifty customers per month. And since we agreed to a one-year pilot program, we're not going to push more volume through the site until we've reached our one-year anniversary."

Changing the Rules of the Car-Buying Game

The automobile industry in the U.K. is under tremendous pressure from angry consumers. By fall 2000 the U.K.'s competitive commission was calling for major changes to be made in the way that cars were being priced and sold to consumers in Britain. Thanks to its dot-com initiative, Vauxhall was more ready than most of its competitors to deal with a new set of rules. As of October 2000, the Franchise Board approved opening up online sales to all Vauxhall model cars. "The key to this being able to happen is the spirit of partnership we have with our retailers. We're not cutting them out; we're changing the game together." This has meant a move to a different pricing structure with fewer "hidden costs" (e.g., financing charges bundled into the price) and a whole new ballgame in terms of Internet sales volumes. Vauxhall became the first automobile manufacturer in the world to offer all of its car models for sale on the 'Net.

Takeaways

What can we learn from Vauxhall's experience? Vauxhall dealt with channel conflict by soliciting and receiving buy-in from its dealer council. The company piloted direct sales via the Internet for a year. And they delivered results, both through online car sales and through the cross-selling and up-selling of services to all GM Vauxhall customers. Notice that customers want to be able to buy cars direct from the manufacturer via the Internet. Yet they are happy to have the dealers, as the manufacturer's representatives, deliver and service their cars. Customers appreciate the convenience of not leaving home to purchase a car. And customers are willing to pay a single, no-haggle price. Car dealers can make just as much money on commissions by letting manufacturers make the sale as long as they're willing to provide the pre- and post-sales service.

Vauxhall dealers benefit by letting the manufacturer solicit service business and warranty extensions. The customer benefits by having a seamless branded Vauxhall customer experience.

Vauxhall's coordinated customer initiatives should result in increased customer loyalty to the brand and to the dealer that provides the actual service.

Finally, note that GM Vauxhall used customer scenario-based design. Every offer is organized around a trigger event (e.g., warranty expiration or refinancing deadline) with the outcomes that matter to the customer (e.g., "Get my car serviced and my warranty extended quickly and easily" or "Give me a new car for the same price I'm paying for my current car").

Patty's Suggestions for Vauxhall

What's next for Vauxhall? Both the CRM initiative and the Internet sales began as pilot programs, the former within a limited geographic territory, and the latter with a few car models and offers. The careful groundwork that Paul and his team have done should pay off. It's unlikely that any of Vauxhall's U.K. competitors will be able to ramp up as quickly to sell cars direct via the Internet. Vauxhall is moving aggressively to cement its lead on the Internet and began selling all cars in November 2000.

It's also unlikely that competitors will be able to quickly replicate Vauxhall's ambitious, integrated CRM efforts. The power of the combined e-commerce initiative and the customer experience initiative will be hard to beat. Now it's time for Vauxhall to push full steam ahead on both the Internet and the CRM fronts.

GM's European operations, led by the German group, are planning to start their own CRM and Internet pilots. And GM's U.S. operation has a lot to learn from the accomplishments of Vauxhall in the smaller U.K. market. We hope that the GM organizations in other countries build on Vauxhall's learning and don't start off in a different direction. Although consumer behavior is very different in GM's various markets around the world, all customers will appreciate being treated better than they are now. And GM, like every car manufacturer, needs to figure out how to make cars easy for customers to buy online while at the same time keeping its dealers in the loop. Building on the learnings of the Vauxhall group and coordinating efforts around the globe may be an organizational challenge, but it's one well worth trying for.

There's a lesson here for every company that wants to use the Web as a touchpoint, but that has an entrenched retail base that could be affected by it. It's actually a simple one: There's no reason the two touchpoints can't coexist, if the company and the channels are really willing to work together. And the auto industry is actually showing the way, which can only be to the good, especially if, as Mark Hogan, president of e-GM unit predicts, one day all auto buyers will go to the Internet before making their buying decisions.

The Customer Flight Deck depicted here is actually a partial solution for Vauxhall and its peers. A similar one centered on the dealer network, along with appropriate lines of sight describing how the metrics in the one influence or are influenced by the metrics in the other, will go a long way toward giving the company a comprehensive understanding of how Vauxhall, its dealers, and its customers interrelate.

A Sample Flight Deck for Vauxhall

	Navigation	Performance	Operations	Environment
Customer Numbers	Number of customers and households with Vauxhall cars Number of customers and households with GM/Vauxhall: • Insurance • Warranties • Other services	Increase/decrease in number of Vauxhall customers and households Number of prospects with profiles online Number of registered Vauxhall.com users Number of customers who purchased online Number of customers who purchased offline	Number of unique visitors to the Web site Number of prospects who configured cars online Number of prospects who test drove a car Conversion rates: • Percentage of customers who buy online-configured cars • Percentage of test drivers who buy	Number of households without Vauxhall cars Number of households with more than one car, only one of which is Vauxhall
Customer Retention	Customer retention rate Household retention rate	Percentage of current owners who repurchased Percentage of purchasers who return for service Percentage of new purchasers within same household	Percentage of owners who purchased new cars at the financing trigger point Average duration of ownership	Percentage of Vauxhall buyers who traded in other models
Customer Experience	Customer satisfaction by touchpoint Customer satisfaction by channel	Changes in customer satisfaction by touchpoint and by channel Customer satisfaction with purchase (after 13 months and after 25 months)	Customer satisfaction scores per: • Scenario • Task • Touchpoint • Channel Total elapsed time per customer scenario	Comparative satisfaction: • Competitors • All cars • Other products and services
Customer Spending	Average spending per customer and household Profitability per customer and household Customer lifetime value	Percentage change in customer spending by customer segment Percentage change in profitability by customer segment Number of cross-sold warranties, insurance, service per customer	Effectiveness of cross-sell/up-sell campaigns by customer segment Customer service and support costs by touchpoint and by channel Commission paid by touchpoint	Comparative customer lifetime value

SNAP-ON, INCORPORATED: TAKING THE BRANDED EXPERIENCE ONLINE AND RETAINING DEALER LOYALTY

Wouldn't you like your company to have this problem: Would-be customers run into the street to flag down Snap-on's vans as they drive by. Drivers have to be careful that they don't run over prospective customers! This is a commonplace occurrence for Snap-on's dealers. Amateur automotive technicians love Snap-on's professional tools and diagnostic equipment so much that they're always trying to get a Snap-on van to stop so they can buy the company's products. Why? Because until mid-2000, consumers weren't permitted to buy products from Snap-on. The company only sold to business customers, not consumers. And it only sold through franchised dealers. In order to buy Snap-on's coveted tools, you had to be on a dealer's "call list." The transformation that's underway at Snap-on is end-customer driven, yet its dealers are intimately involved.

Let's take a look at how Snap-on has begun to accommodate consumers who want to buy its products, while at the same time keeping its franchise dealers happy. Let's also look at how Snap-on is beginning to forge relationships with its professional customers without taking those dealers out of the loop. Finally, we'll look at how Snap-on has managed to create a single technology infrastructure that delivers a consistent customer experience across touchpoints and channels. Snap-on leverages this environment as it moves into e-markets, hooks into corporate clients' intranets, streamlines its own dealer extranet, and provides a direct sales channel for consumers.

The Snap-on Brand

Snap-on is a brand name recognized by technicians around the world. The original Snap-on interchangeable socket wrenches were developed in 1919. "Five do the work of fifty" was the slogan that the company's original marketers used when selling their wrench sets direct to professional automobile technicians. As the company grew, so did its product line. Eighty-one years later, Snap-on's hand tools comprise about 40 percent of the company's product line. Snap-on also sells diagnostic systems, automotive lifts, alignment systems, diagnostic software, detailed vehicle service information, and training material and services to automotive technicians worldwide.

The Snap-on brand has very strong name recognition among technicians and tool lovers. Over the years the company has done a good job of keeping the brand alive and fresh. They understand how customers do their jobs and what they need. And they offer high-quality products.

Automotive technicians are busy people who are paid by the hour. They don't want to take time out of their workday to shop. The fact that a Snap-on dealer comes to them with the tools they need to do their jobs is an important part of the Snap-on value proposition. Snap-on's franchise dealers call on customers at their places of business every week in their fully-outfitted Snap-on vans. From the customer's standpoint, this weekly sales call has traditionally offered the ultimate in convenience. A subject matter expert comes to you, at your place of work. He understands what you need to do your job, and he can diagnose whatever problems you may be having and propose a solution. He brings his inventory with him so you can touch, feel, and try out the merchandise. Yet today's customers are even more demanding. Once a week may not be enough. What if I need something in between? What if I work the night shift, and the dealer comes during the day?

The Vision: Convenient, One-Stop Shopping for Technicians

The tradition of calling on customers in a logo-ed van that was stocked with the company's most popular products was part of the early Snap-on tradition. But in 1991 Snap-on switched from independent sales reps to a franchise dealer format. Most of Snap-on's dealers in North America at that time signed up for the new franchise program, giving the company the ability to standardize the customer experience. Each franchisee paid for and outfitted his own Snap-on van with the portable inventory appropriate to his routes. Snap-on provided a list of calls to each franchisee (these are the automotive repair facilities he was expected to call on each week), and Snap-on extended credit to both dealers and to customers who needed to pay for their tools over time. Snap-on uses this franchise dealer approach in the United States, Canada, the U.K., Australia, and Japan.

In the mid-1990s, Bob Cornog, Snap-on's CEO, had a vision. He wanted to expand Snap-on's presence from the individual repair technicians and their repair shops to industrial customers as well as the emerging market of skilled do-it-yourselfers. He wanted to increase the company's global reach, and he wanted to evolve its product line from tools alone to diagnostic systems and software as well as everything else technicians needed to do their jobs—from lubricant to paper towels. Bob christened this new concept the "store without walls." In 1995 he began promoting this vision and soliciting dealer input. How can we use technology to enhance our franchise and help our dealers grow our business? he asked. What other products should we be offering our customers? As tools and information become more and more electronic, what other services should we be offering our customers? And how can we make it possible for customers to interact with us around the clock?

Connecting the Dealers Online

The Snap-on management team consulted with its dealer advisory board to find out how to make it easier for them to do business with Snap-on. What resulted was an online sales system that franchise dealers could access from their laptop computers. At the end of each day in the van, the dealers could access Snap-on's real-time inventory database, upload their orders, generate quotes and invoices for their customers, and download updates to the product catalog and pricing.

Snap-on's technology team delivered the Snap-on catalog to dealers and their customers on CD-ROMs to make it easier for them to find the products they needed and to keep up-to-date.

Reaching out to Customers

By early 1998 Bob Cornog had realized that the Internet and e-commerce could move Snap-on further toward his "store without walls" vision. Al Biland joined Snap-on as VP and CIO, lured by Bob's vision of giving customers twenty-four-hour access to Snap-on products.

Al put together a cross-functional e-commerce strategy team with a representative from each of the company's business units. He decided to set up his Internet Commerce Center in the San Jose area where

Snap-on's diagnostics group was based. Al tapped Brad Lewis, a bright young technician from the engineering group, to lead the team. Brad was Internet-savvy but, more important, he had been a Honda mechanic, so he understood exactly how Snap-on's customers did their jobs. When Al discovered Brad in July 1998, Brad was using his spare time to design Web-based discussion groups for technicians. Al knew he had found his man.

Once the Internet Commerce Center had taken shape, Al Biland and Richard Caskey (Snap-on's VP of Marketing) hired Jim Stern, a well-known e-marketing consultant, to help Snap-on's executives wrap their minds around the impacts that e-commerce was likely to have on the company. Their strategic planning session in November '98 identified five key strategic imperatives for Snap-on to address. They were:

1. Use e-commerce to support the Dealer/Customer/Company relationship by developing dealer portals that would help dealers stay in touch with their customers in between van visits, let customers access Snap-on product information 24 hours per day, and enable both dealers and customers to better manage their orders and their relationships.
2. Use the Web to grow other distribution channels. Provide self-service for large industrial accounts. Reach out to consumers.
3. Web-enable Snap-on's software-based diagnostic products.
4. Use the Web to streamline all of Snap-on's internal processes.
5. Create a global Web council across geographies and product lines to oversee and coordinate our e-commerce initiatives.

It was agreed that Al Biland would continue to lead the charge in e-commerce.

Designing an Integrated E-Commerce Initiative

Once the e-commerce team had received its marching orders, Al Biland and Brad Lewis fleshed out their burgeoning strategy. Al decided to build a single e-commerce infrastructure to reach out to all of Snap-on's different customer sets and channel partners. He realized that Snap-on's product information would be a core asset that would need to be accessible across customer segments and channels. He also realized that, by linking customers and dealers directly into the company's new Baan ERP systems, he could give them real-time access to inventory and pricing, let them place orders online, and review the status of their orders.

Product Information at the Core

As Al and Brad began thinking about the kind of tools they'd need to house Snap-on's product information, they realized that they wanted this "store without walls" to come as close to the experience of buying from a dealer in a van as possible. When a customer meets with a dealer to discuss his needs, the dealer is always able to recommend the right tool for the job and to suggest other tools or materials the technician is probably also going to need to complement that particular tool. Brad, who had been a repair technician, absolutely understood this requirement. "If the customer wants to buy a socket wrench, you want to be able to offer him the whole set. If he wants a ratchet, you know he probably will also need a ratchet extension." The trick was to find a way to enter all of Snap-on's product information so that similar or complementary items could be linked together.

Brad found a brand new software application for this purpose from a company called OnLink Technologies (which has since been acquired by Siebel Systems). Snap-on became one of OnLink's first customers. And Brad's requirements drove much of OnLink's product development. "I was probably in their offices two to three days a week for several months, working with their developers to be sure that this tool would meet our needs," Brad reported. By the spring of '99, Brad was satisfied that the OnLink application could do the job. It was time to get started.

The first step was to download all the catalog information from RR Donnelley, the company that prints Snap-on's catalog and prepares its CD-ROM–based catalog. The second step was to reorganize the product information so that customers would see the right sets of related products as they shopped online. Brad hired subject-matter experts to do this content organization and linking task. He found two ex-automotive technicians, like himself, who had been Snap-on customers and who were eager to learn JavaScript, HTML, and the OnLink scripting language. These two subject-matter experts worked for three months, organizing the Snap-on product information for online access. This hard work has paid off. Now, as new products are added and updated, Brad's small team of subject-matter experts can update and relink the new product information.

Targeting Industrial Accounts

By September 1999 Snap-on's e-commerce system was ready for customer testing. Brad started with a nearby large account, the U.S. Navy's procurement office in San Diego, California. While the Navy buys tools from Snap-on, it uses its own part numbers and has its own prices and contracts. A simple table maps the Navy's part numbers to the Snap-on part numbers, and the pricing and availability is pulled dynamically out of Snap-on's Baan systems. Within two months, the purchasing agent at the San Diego shipyard had switched from placing phone orders to placing all of her orders online. Not only could she place orders online, she could see the status of her orders, review every order she had placed, and track the delivery of each order. After the successful Navy trial, Brad's team began rolling out the online ordering capability to other Snap-on industrial accounts. Within a year, more than 100 companies were ordering online.

Accommodating E-Markets through Manufacturers' Aisles

Just as Snap-on was playing catch-up by providing online sales and service to its largest industrial customers in the United States, the procurement climate was beginning to change. Once happy to log onto their suppliers' Web sites to place orders, corporate buyers were beginning to revolt. They now wanted one-stop shopping. They had begun to link their internal procurement systems into the new e-markets. Al saw this requirement coming. Even before Snap-on's corporate customers had begun requesting that the company provide an e-market linkage, Al had begun discussions with Ariba, a popular provider of e-procurement software and an e-market maker. Together the two companies realized that Snap-on could link its existing e-commerce infrastructure directly into Ariba's e-market environment. Here's how it works. A corporate customer uses his internal procurement system to access an e-marketplace to purchase a number of items from multiple manufacturers. As soon as the customer "enters" the Snap-on "aisle" of the e-marketplace, the market passes the customer's identification and authorization on to the Snap-on system and the customer "punches through" to Snap-on's online store. He can then browse the Snap-on catalog, select the tools he needs, see the pricing that is correct for his particular account, and complete the Snap-on portion of his order. The shopping cart containing the customer's Snap-on order is passed back to the e-market. Once the customer has completed his order and authorized the purchase from within his own procurement application, the final order is placed with Snap-on by the market. By spring 2000, just as the B2B e-market frenzy was reaching its peak, Snap-on and Ariba quietly completed their integration so that Snap-on's corporate customers could benefit.

Preparing Snap-on's Dealers for Consumer Sales

Naturally, Snap-on management wanted to be very careful about preparing its franchise dealers for the advent of direct sales online. Although the public Snap-on.com Web site would be designed for the amateur mechanic rather than the professional, there was certainly a good chance that Snap-on's traditional professional technician customers would log on to the Web site and begin buying online instead of through their own dealers. Nick Loffredo, VP of Dealer Sales, and Clark Jamison, Snap-on's Director of Business Development, began prepping the dealer channel. They talked to the dealer advisory council and presented their game plan to them. They promised the dealers that Snap-on would:

- Sell products at list price on the consumer Web site,
- Give dealers commissions on any products their customers bought on the site, and
- Refer appropriate customers—those who buy frequently (three times) or who spend a lot ($2,000) on the site—to the appropriate branch manager for possible inclusion on the dealer's list of calls. (First, the branch manager would call the customer to find out if he'd like a dealer to call on him!)

Nick, Clark, and Al described the Web site that they were designing for the dealers and their customers and solicited their input. The dealer advisory council approved the two-pronged game plan: 1) sell direct to consumers and pass the leads onto dealers, and 2) provide dealer-specific Web sites so that they and their customers could interact with Snap-on online as well.

Nick and Clark also met with each of the dealer branch managers and prepared them. They made a videotape describing both the consumer Web site and the dealer Web site and distributed it to all of the dealers before the consumer site went live. Then they held their breath! The careful preparation paid off. As the consumer site launched, Snap-on's dealers remained calm.

Selling to Consumers via the Web

By July 2000, Snap-on's e-commerce infrastructure was holding up well with the company's large corporate accounts. But these were accounts from which orders would be placed by a few individuals on behalf of a much larger company. Now it was time to see what would happen if Snap-on offered its tools to the public at large.

For years amateur technicians had been trying to buy Snap-on tools. In addition to following the Snap-on vans around, they would call the company's toll-free number and beg for a way to buy the company's products. Snap-on knew that there was a market of aficionados out there who were ready and waiting to buy direct. They weren't wrong.

On August 18, 2000, Snap-on did a "soft launch" (with no promotion or advertising) of a consumer-direct Web site. Snap-on's CIO, Al Biland, was excited by the immediate uptake. "Within 10 days over 2,000 people had registered and 127 had ordered, for a total of over $18,000 in sales. A physicist in Austin, Texas, purchased two items for over $3,000. A former BMW mechanic in the '70s, he understands the quality/value proposition of Snap-on products and wanted to get his son a very nice twentieth birthday present! This customer was essentially unreachable prior to the Web channel. Wow!"

Rolling Out the Snap-on Dealer Sites

In fall 2000 Snap-on began rolling out the first phase of its dealer Web sites: "My Snapon.com." The first release was essentially an extranet that was designed to support dealers in doing their jobs. It let dealers view and update the orders they placed using their own Dealer Support System, and let them add additional order information and/or make changes to orders already placed. Dealers could also get all the latest information about new products and promotions.

The next step was to provide private versions of the Snap-on public site to dealers to share with their customers. This is where the real benefit will be for both the dealers and for Snap-on. Dealers' customers will be able to place orders or to check on the status of orders twenty-four hours per day.

Results

Snap-on's approximately 3,700 U.S. dealers are in direct relationship with close to one million automotive service technicians each month. That's almost 80 percent of the market. In the U.K. and Canada, Snap-on has about 70 percent of the total market. In Australia and New Zealand, Snap-on has lower marketshare and penetration, but the company is serving over 50 percent of that market. And in Japan, Snap-on reaches about 25 percent of the total technicians through its dealers. To net it out, Snap-on is currently selling to 40 percent of the world's automotive technicians.

In its first three months of operation, 90,000 people took the trouble to register on Snap-on's consumer Web site, Snap-on.com. Al says that online sales have met his projections. The consumer Web site is also serving a clientele that Snap-on didn't anticipate: professional mechanics who work the night shift at many of the locations that are on dealers' call lists. They love the Web site because they can find the tools they need and order them right away. One of the busiest times on the Web site is 2 to 3 A.M. Of course, the dealers who serve these businesses earn a commission on the middle of the night sales. They love the idea that they can now sell twenty-four hours a day!

Takeaways

What has Snap-on done that's worthy of emulation? On the business strategy front, Snap-on has single-mindedly pursued its vision of offering a consistent branded experience to professional technicians around the world. Through acquisitions, the company is attempting both to increase its "share of wallet" in every mechanic's shop worldwide and also to reach global customers where its other brand names are better known.

As Snap-on has reached out to new markets, the company has done a good job of keeping its franchise dealers in the loop. Keeping dealers happy is vital to the continued success of Snap-on's total customer experience. To many customers, the dealer in the van *is* Snap-on. Having hundreds of experienced sales representatives calling on your customers each day may sound like an old-fashioned (and expensive) way of doing business, but it's a model that most companies would die for today. Snap-on now offers its customers the ultimate in convenience: shop online and have the product delivered to you by mail or by your friendly Snap-on dealer when he comes to your shop this week. Shop online and return products that don't meet your needs to the guy in the van. Shop in the van, touch and feel the products, and get advice. Email your dealer for advice in the middle of the night. Snap-on's total customer experience is strong because it's a multi-touchpoint, multi-channel experience with a strong human touch.

Snap-on has also done an excellent job of rolling out a single, integrated infrastructure for all channels and touchpoints. Today, Snap-on's online catalog includes the Snap-on products. Tomorrow, the Mitchell information services offerings will be integrated in. Next, the company's other product lines will be added. Snap-on's executive team was smart to use a single online product database with a rich capability to link products together for up-selling and cross-selling and to integrate that product database into the real-time inventory management system and order entry and pricing systems. As Snap-on has tackled channels—first its industrial customers, then the new consumer customer channel, then its dealers and their customers, emarket makers, and other channel partners—the company has kept life simple by using a single, unified product database. No matter who a customer is or what channel he comes through, he will have the identical customer experience with Snap-on's products and offerings, and he'll see the pricing that is appropriate for him.

Patty's Suggestions for Snap-on

What does Snap-on still need to do? The biggest issue we see with Snap-on's current strategy is the company's single-minded focus on its dealers. When you say the word "customer" to Snap-on employees, they think of their franchise dealers, not their end customers. Snap-on has done a great job of keeping its dealers in the loop. And its customers love the personal relationships they have. But customers also want to have a closer relationship with Snap-on. The company's current dealer-centric culture makes it difficult to move ahead aggressively to establish relationships with each and every end customer.

We think Snap-on should be building a robust end customer database starting with its national accounts, its line-of-credit customers, and the end-consumers from its e-commerce initiative. Then, as dealers' end customers come online, they could be added, along with their dealer relationships. Having a comprehensive customer database would help Snap-on and its business partners better manage their mutual relationships with customers and do a better job of delivering on the total customer experience. Al Biland agrees. And he now has a strategic initiative in place to roll out a Customer Relationship Management (CRM) system in 2001.

This CRM system will let Snap-on see: What products has the customer bought to date? What did he buy on credit? How much does he owe? What issues, if any, has the customer had with products and/or service? What's on his wish list? Although many customers pay cash, the dealer still has a record of those transactions. What incentives could Snap-on provide dealers to share that information? As dealers' customers begin to interact using their dealer-customized portals, Snap-on has a great opportunity to help customers keep track of their inventory of tools by building an online tool chest, for example, and logging everything the customer has bought to date (both Snap-on and non–Snap-on tools).

Snap-on can go much, much further with the infrastructure and team it now has in place. We think the company's end customers will lead the way. If they do, and if Snap-on lets them, the company may very well unearth a rich lode of customer and product information that it hadn't thought about before.

A Sample Flight Deck for Snap-on

	Navigation	Performance	Operations	Environment
Customer Numbers	Number of active end-user professional customers Number of active business accounts Number of active consumer customers	Number of active end-user customers per dealer and per establishment Percentage growth in active customers per establishment Number of end-user customers referred by Web site Number of customers who purchased online Number of customers who purchased offline	Number of unique visitors to the consumer Web site Conversion rates: • Percentage of customers who purchased online • Percentage of online customers who were added to a dealer's call list • Number of professional customers who purchased through their dealer's site	Number of total repair establishments Number of total technicians Number of auto mechanic hobbyists
Customer Retention	Customer retention rate Account retention rate Purchases per customer per month	New products purchased per customer per month Add-ons per customer per month Service sales per customer per month	Percentage of customers who are active users of the Web site Percentage of customers who interact with dealers via email	Competitors' products owned
Customer Experience	Customer satisfaction by touchpoint Customer satisfaction by channel Customer satisfaction with products and service	Changes in satisfaction by touchpoint and by channel Satisfaction with ability to find the right products for the job Increase/decrease in satisfaction with products	Customer satisfaction scores per service interaction Accuracy of Web search results Product returns and claims	Comparative satisfaction: Competitors: • In high-end segment • All tools • All products and services
Customer Spending	Average spending per end customer Profitability per end customer Customer lifetime value	Percentage of sales from new products Percentage of sales from new spending by current customers Commission paid	Percentage of Snap-on share of customers' toolboxes Customer service and support costs by touchpoint and by channel	Total spending in technicians' tools and services segment

DELIVER A SEAMLESS CUSTOMER EXPERIENCE ACROSS CHANNELS AND TOUCHPOINTS: OBSERVATIONS ABOUT THE CASE STUDIES

VAUXHALL AND SNAP-ON

Despite some apparent similarities—both companies are involved with automobiles and both have exclusive dealer relationships—these two case studies provide different perspectives. Snap-on's is primarily a B2B business with a high personal touch, and despite the fact that the company has international operations, most of the focus for the current e-business and customer outreach efforts have taken place in North America. The area of Vauxhall's business that we focused on is its consumer retail business (which is actually 20% of the total). And although parent General Motors is an American-based multinational, the Vauxhall U.K. group has been given the autonomy to pioneer in a number of areas under a loose liaison and oversight from the U.S.'s e-business strategic planners. GM's strategy team believed that many of its international divisions were going to be able to move forward faster than its North American operation. Therefore Vauxhall was given lots of freedom.

Notice that both companies took their work-in-progress before their dealer councils for approval. Each wooed the most influential dealers, gave them an opportunity to impact the direction it was going, and solicited their input. Yet neither company waited for the dealers to buy in before beginning work on projects. Each knew that this was something it needed to do. Each funded its projects and began working on them. Then each brought its dealers on board. To maintain trust, both companies needed to provide full disclosure early in the design cycle and to discuss all the issues that would arise such as commission structures, handling of leads, shifts in roles and responsibilities. In both companies' cases, a lot of thought was given to keeping dealers informed, engaged, and involved.

GM is clearly ahead of Snap-on in capturing information about its end customers and building an integrated customer relationship management system. Snap-on still has a way to go before it will have an equivalent customer information system. But since Snap-on got a late start, it may take the more prescient approach of designing its customer relationship system from the customer's point of view.

LOTS OF HARD WORK!

What stands out in both cases, however, is how focused the companies are on the need to provide a consistent total customer experience to their customers across channels and touchpoints. It's not easy. As you can see from the two case studies, there are a number of subtleties to get right. Yet both of these companies are well on their way toward achieving the goal of delivering a seamless customer experience across channels and touchpoints.

11

THE THIRD STEP: CARE ABOUT CUSTOMERS AND THEIR OUTCOMES

I would never invest in a company that didn't know who its customers are or one that didn't care deeply about them. Would you?

The companies with the "right stuff" to thrive in the customer economy have one key element in common: a corporate culture and a set of core values centered around caring about customers—not as revenue targets, profit contributors, or advertising magnets, but as people.

Customer loyalty and lifetime customer value are two of the key metrics that foreshadow success in the customer economy. You can't build either one if you don't truly care about your customers. Customers aren't just looking for a good deal or convenience. Both consumers and business customers choose to continue doing business with companies that actually care about them as people and as businesses.

Caring about and for your customers isn't the only requirement for success. It wasn't enough to keep Toysmart.com alive. Toysmart employees cared deeply about their customers and did everything in their power to make toy shopping a wonderful, rewarding experience for them. Yet Toysmart lost its financial backing from its parent, the Walt Disney Company, in May 2000. Disney didn't have the patience or the desire to continue funding a small e-tailer that sometimes refused to sell Disney products (because they featured weapons or had other characteristics that Toysmart's customers didn't care for). In hindsight, the Disney/Toysmart relationship was probably doomed from the start. The two companies' agendas evolved in different directions.

Thus we see that a customer-caring culture isn't sufficient to ensure success. A healthy cash flow and profits from operations are necessary prerequisites. Yet there are many companies with healthy balance sheets that won't make it in the customer economy. They don't actually care about their customers as people. They don't take the time to learn who they are; determine what they want and need; and make them feel special, valued, and welcome.

You probably believe that your company has a pretty solid, customer-driven culture. But we want to show you some best practices—what others firms are doing to instill those customer-centered values in their employees and channel partners as guidance systems. These values enable employees and partners to truly embrace their customers.

In a minute we'll take you behind the scenes to see what Schwab does to reinforce its customer-caring culture and to provide closed-loop feedback systems. But first, let's look at the basic principles involved in caring about customers and their outcomes.

DEEP COMMITMENT TO CUSTOMERS AND THEIR OUTCOMES

I was standing at the cash register in the Charles Schwab company cafeteria, juggling my tray as I tried to reach into one of the two bags slung over my shoulder to unearth my wallet. The cashier smiled at me, reached out with both hands to take my tray, and said, "Here, let me help." That's when it hit me: the people in this company really care about their customers. Never before in forty-five-plus years of standing in line to pay had anyone offered to assist me in that way. Everyone at Schwab—from the cashier in the cafeteria to the CEO of the company—is passionate about the company's customers and what the customer is trying to accomplish. Once I had this epiphany, I wasn't surprised when I learned that Schwab's technical support reps—the ones who sort out your computer problems over the phone—are also licensed brokers (that way they can explain the differences between puts and holds after they've handled your browser incompatibility issues).

Schwab's customer focus is legendary. And it's heartfelt. Fidelity Investments can play catch-up by revamping its CRM systems. Merrill Lynch and Company can give Schwab a scare by developing an easy-to-use online brokerage site. And E*TRADE Group can lure active traders with lower fees and better access to IPOs. But nobody will beat Schwab in caring about customers and their outcomes. Why? Because a passion for customers' success is deeply ingrained in the Schwab culture.

In his book, *Clicks and Mortar,* Schwab's CEO David Pottruck describes the process the company used to revitalize its customer-centric culture in 1995 (and again in 1999) after the Internet had profoundly changed the fabric of the company. There are rituals that Schwab uses to revitalize and reinforce its core values, from the VisionQuest facilitated workshops (that help employees internalize company vision and values) to the "market storm" emergencies (when everyone pitches in on the phones to handle a spike in trading volume). There are heroic stories and folklore about helping distressed widows and families who are in tight spots. Schwab only hires people who truly share its customer-centric values: fairness, responsiveness, and respect when dealing with customers.

Heart Share Versus Marketshare

As I was finishing the research for this book, I sat back and thought about what really differentiated the companies I had chosen to profile versus the ones that had fallen by the wayside. I realized that many product-centric companies make the transition to becoming customer-centric companies by focusing on increasing marketshare. Being fanatically focused on winning in the marketplace isn't the same thing as truly caring about customers. And in the long run, customers can tell the difference. In the high tech industry, for example, Oracle and Microsoft battle for marketshare. But neither company is really perceived as caring deeply about its customers. The companies that will survive in the customer economy will, by necessity, become customer caring. Arrogance and hubris won't hack it in the midst of a customer revolution.

Soul Connections

For a lesson in making soul connections with your customers, make a trek to Galway, Ireland, and visit with Maureen Kenny and her sons at Kenny's Bookshop and Art Galleries. Maureen and her husband, Des, built their family business on a strong foundation of deep customer connections. It's normal for a good bookshop to be appreciated in the local community it serves. What's unusual is for the bookstore's fan club to reach to all corners of the globe. The strong connection that Kenny's visitors and customers feel to the establishment is a deep, soul connection. It's a feeling that stems from mutual appreciation. But it's not enough to care about your customers; you need to meet their needs. The need Kenny's serves is to find a great new or used book of Irish literature, nonfiction, or poetry.

Maureen's son, Desi Kenny, has an uncanny ability to listen to or correspond with a potential customer and then come up with three or four books that that person will love to read. He has parlayed this knack into a profitable service. Here's how it came about. One rainy day in Galway, Desi recalls, an American visitor was browsing the shelves in the front room in Kenny's bookstore when all of a sudden he started to curse vehemently. Desi's mother (sitting at her usual perch in the center of the store) went into selective deafness. Desi asked the man if they had done something to offend him? "It's not you," he replied. "Jesus, I'm not a rich man. I can only come to Ireland once every couple of years. I walk into your shop, I see all these books, and I want to buy them all!" At that point Desi's mother piped up, "We'll send you a package every so often, if you'd like." "Would you really do that?" the man asked. "Sure," Desi replied, "I know what you like. I've watched you when you've been in here." And he proceeded to walk over to the shelves and pick out three books. "You like that and that." "Fantastic," the man replied. "Here's my credit card. Send me four books every three months. If I like them, I'll keep them. If not, I'll send them back." With that gesture, Kenny's Book Club was born. It now has more than 3,000 members around the world. Each of us receives our own handpicked selection of books "every so often."

How does Desi Kenny know what each customer would like—particularly those customers he's never met (the ones who turn up through his Web site)? "I start a conversation with them by phone and/or email, and I keep track of the dialogue. The minute I open the person's file, there's a conversation. I speak to the customer through the books. 'This is what I think you'd enjoy,' or 'This person has something to say that I think would be of interest for you.' Then I get feedback, and I juggle with it, change it until it's right. The books are sent on approval, which means they can come back. You give the client the choice. I send out 150 packages per week and get four or five books back. Through the medium of books, we start talking, we get to know each other. I get involved in my customers' births, deaths, and other family matters. One of my customers was buried with a copy of a book I had sent him."

Creating a Customer-Centric Culture

The values that make up a core customer-centric culture often stem from the leader of the company and are transmitted through stories, tradition, and folklore. The passion that John Chambers (Cisco Systems), Charles Schwab (Schwab), and Jeff Bezos (Amazon.com) feel for their customers is hard to match.

At W. W. Grainger and Lands' End, direct marketing companies with catalogs (now ecatalogs) at their cores, the original founders (William W. Grainger and Gary Comer) instilled a deep sense of customer responsiveness into their companies. Their successors have continued the customer-focused tradition as they've moved their companies into the age of the Internet. At both companies, employees are empowered and thrilled to do whatever it takes to delight customers, including calling proactively to alert the customer if there's an unexpected problem with an order, upgrading an order to priority shipping at the company's expense, and locating hard-to-find items that the company doesn't offer. This habit of always going the extra mile to achieve the customer's desired outcome is what will differentiate the winners from the losers in the customer economy.

How do you build a customer-centric culture from scratch? By instilling deep values in your employees from the outset. Egg is a great example of a company that was designed with a clear set of customer-centric values at its core—to give customers great service, to treat them with respect, to always offer customers a fair deal that is easy-to-understand, and to provide highly personalized service.

Moving from Product-Centric to Customer-Centric

When Carly Fiorina became CEO of Hewlett Packard in July 1999, she brought with her an unwavering and deep-rooted commitment to customers. HP was a company with a good reputation for products and service among its customers. But she quickly realized that its product silos were impeding the ability to deliver a seamless customer experience. By November Carly reorganized Hewlett-Packard into five business units—two customer-facing organizations (consumer and business customers), supported by three product-generation organizations.

From the outset, Carly made it clear that one of the ultimate goals of HP's reinvention was to make customer experience management a core business process and a strong source of competitive advantage for the company.

In the past, HP's upper-level managers had been measured and incented to achieve financial goals for the company. Carly made it clear that a new set of measures were going to be put in place alongside the financial and the marketshare goals. HP would be measuring, and top executives would be accountable for, goals in three more areas: customer satisfaction, customer experience, and customer loyalty.

Carly's approach was a top-down reorganization of the company with customers coming first and product-generation activities supporting and innovating to meet the goals and objectives of its two core customer sets: business and consumer customers. She changed the company's measurement systems to give equal value to customer metrics. And she added a strategic core business process—owning the total customer experience.

The Renegade Approach to Changing Company Culture

If yours is still a product-centric company culture or if you have a CEO who is still largely focused on product-line and overall profitability, one who hasn't yet become fanatical about building and measuring relationships with each individual customer, you're going to have a tougher time moving your company from a product- to a customer-focused culture. However, there is a way to begin to shift the company culture. You can use any new e-business initiatives and supporting processes to begin to transform your company from a product-centric to a customer-centric culture. Pradeep Jotwani at Hewlett-Packard embraced this approach. He used the Internet to catalyze his business transformation. So did Phil Gibson.

Phil is the vice president of Web Business and Sales Automation at National Semiconductor. He has been using his Internet activities to gradually shift National's culture for seven years now. Phil's tireless efforts in refining National's e-business applications to save customers' time have paid off in terms of customer loyalty and mindshare. However, "we're still a parts company that knows a lot about its customers," Phil explains. Phil and his small team have managed to capture and disseminate customer information across almost every stage in the customers' decision-making process. They track and report out how many customers search for information about each device, how many download the data sheets, how many order sample parts, how many run software simulations involving that part, what distributors' advanced order pipelines look like for each part, and what parts have been ordered in what quantities. This information is reported out on a product line basis every day. National Semiconductor's global product line managers use the daily product-oriented information to monitor the health of their product lines, and the four regional managers use it to see which products are hot or lagging in their regions. Giving employees access to daily status reports by product line has changed the metabolism at National, but it hasn't yet shifted the company from a product- to a customer-centric focus.

Offer Customer Information to Account Executives and Distributors

Yet by gathering and using customer information to improve customers' experiences, Phil's team is also impacting the company's sales activities and, eventually, its culture. Today National's direct and indirect sales organizations rely heavily on the customer information generated by Phil's team. Soon, we think the entire company will be as customer-focused as it is product-focused, due to the actionable customer information that Phil's group provides.

When customers interact with National Semiconductor, each interaction is logged into National's customer database. Customers identify themselves by registering at the Web site and performing a task, by sending an email query, by calling into National's technical support hotline, or by showing up in a distributor's pipeline report on the company's distributors' extranets.

Forty-five percent of National's sales come from about 100,000 customers who are served through distributors around the world. The District Sales Manager in each geographic territory offers customer-activity information as leads to the distributors in his territory. He sends each one a list of which customers looked at which products, downloaded which data sheets, and what interactions they had with the technical support hotline. "Distributors love to receive this level of detail about what current or potential customers are interested in. And this information gives our DSMs something valuable they can offer distributors," Phil explained.

For National's top accounts, the account executive receives a weekly summary of all Web traffic by his accounts. This includes what part(s) they looked at, what Web simulations they did, and what information they downloaded. This information is sent to the account executives with a strong caveat at the top of the email reminding them of National's privacy policy (to use this information only to improve the customer's experience and relationship with National and not to pass it on to a third party). Phil also adds some suggestions for the sales team about the kinds of follow-up behavior that might be appropriate, such as:

> If you choose to contact these customers, please consider looking for ways to add value to the interaction. We suggest that you do not simply contact the customer and ask "Did you get the part and what are you using it for." A much more valuable interaction would be to offer correlated devices that are likely to be used along with the requested device. You could also offer a development board or simulation software if it exists.

National Semiconductor does not, of course, want to violate customers' privacy. We particularly like the fact that customers can see what National knows about them and their activities on its Web site. National gives customers access to their activity logs. National Semiconductor is one of the few companies that shows customers the information that it knows about them. When you check your profile at the National Semiconductor site, you'll see all the activities that you've conducted at the Web site that the company has recorded for you.

National also lets customers opt out by asking not to have information tracked or shared with other National Semiconductor employees or its agents.

Do You Know Who Your Customers Are?

The biggest obstacle we've encountered in helping companies shift their corporate cultures is a deep-rooted confusion about who the customers are. Pharmaceutical firms focus on doctors, not on patients. Newspapers focus on advertisers, not on readers. Automobile manufacturers are obsessed with dealers, not with drivers. Here's the bottom line: your customer is the person who uses your product or service. If yours is a consumer product or service, your customer is the individual consumer who consumes or uses the service. If yours is a business product, your customer is the person inside the corporation who *selects* and *uses* your product or service. Until everyone in your company is in vigorous agreement about who your end-customers are and what matters most to them, you won't be able to make progress in building a great total customer experience.

We certainly don't mean to imply that doctors are unimportant to pharmaceutical firms, nor advertisers to newspapers, and so on. We are simply pointing out that, without satisfied patients and delighted readers, both types of firms will be out of business in the long run. The trick is to keep your eye on the real end-customer while at the same time streamlining operations for all the interdependent ancillary partners, stakeholders, and other kinds of "customers."

Now, let's take a closer look at how Charles Schwab manages its company by caring for customers and their outcomes.

CHARLES SCHWAB: SUSTAIN AND MANAGE A CUSTOMER-CENTRIC CULTURE

The customer self-service revolution has swept through the financial services industry. Charles Schwab was one of the instigators. Schwab launched its electronic brokerage service in 1996. Schwab's customers took to the Web in droves. These self-directed investors were eager to have round-the-clock access to their accounts and to the investment tools and research Schwab began to offer online. However, many customers made it clear that they didn't want different prices for online trades versus phone trades. And Schwab's customers demanded a seamless experience whether they walked into a retail office, talked to someone on the phone, or interacted via the Web or touchtone phone. So Schwab pioneered the concept of "clicks and mortar" financial services.

Charles Schwab is the undisputed leader in full service online brokerage, with 7.5 million active customer accounts, 4.3 million active online accounts, over $6 billion in revenues, 15 percent profits, and over $1 trillion of assets under management. Much has been written about Schwab's customer-centric culture and its aggressive move into online brokerage. The story that hasn't yet been told about Schwab is how the company manages by and for customer value, and why that gives Schwab a competitive edge in the customer economy—an advantage that will be hard to beat.

Schwab was also one of the first companies to understand the benefits of offering customers a seamless set of cross-touchpoint services. It was Schwab's president and co-CEO, David Pottruck, who in 1998 coined (and later trademarked) the term "clicks and mortar." By that time, Schwab had already pulled ahead of its online-only competitors, in part because customers liked the reassurance of being able to walk into physical branches.

Schwab has built its success on a strong foundation of core customer-centric values. Every employee cares deeply about how well each Schwab customer is doing. Without these strong values, no measurement system would be effective.

Of course, Schwab also uses its measurement and feedback systems to reinforce its customer-centric culture, monitoring and rewarding employees based on customer satisfaction, the quality of the customer experience, and the growth of customers' assets.

Do Schwab's customer values and its employees' passion for helping customers realize their dreams mean that Schwab will always outshine its competitors in functionality and customer service? Not necessarily. Over the years I've heard complaints from Schwab customers about areas they'd like to see improved. However, I believe that Schwab's core culture does mean that Schwab customers will be treated consistently better than those of competitors because Schwab's employees care deeply about customers' success. The company's mission statement, "to provide customers with the most useful and ethical financial services in the world," isn't just lip service; it's a way of life.

Constant Renewal of Customer-Centric Values

"We are the custodians of our customers' financial dreams" is the mantra at Schwab. Charles Schwab and David Pottruck, Schwab's co-CEO's, are the keepers and the disseminators of the company's core values. "Chuck's" personality is at the core of Schwab's customer experience. He takes a personal and passionate interest in helping the average person invest wisely for his or her family's future.

- **Cement the Culture with Stories.** Schwab is one of many companies that uses customer stories constantly to reinforce the company's core values. These stories are surfaced, captured, videotaped, and passed around as part of the culture-building process.

- **Reinforce the Values in Writing.** Schwab was founded in 1974. It wasn't until 1991 that Schwab's values were formalized in written form. This was a major step—the beginning of a formal culture-building process at Schwab.

- **Periodically Revitalize the Values.** Schwab revitalized its customer-centric culture in 1995. Eighty of Schwab's top executives were intimately involved in renewing the company's vision and values and setting a new mission: Serving 10 million investors and having $1 trillion in custody within ten years. (It looks like Schwab will complete its ten-year goal in six years! The company hit the $1 trillion mark in 2000.) This culture-revitalization process lasted ten months, cost $1 million, and included all 7,000 Schwab employees.

In 1997, David and Chuck led another culture-building ritual. The company was about to do something pretty scary—combine its e-schwab online brokerage entity with its traditional branch office and telephone brokerage entity, and lower prices to a flat $29.95 per trade. In other words, Schwab was going to extend the lower Web-based price per trade to all customers, even those who used more expensive interaction touchpoints, and who were accustomed to paying $69 per trade. This time, they ran day-long VisionQuest exercises for all Schwab employees around the world. Everyone needed to be on board and to understand how the new merged retail brokerage business would better serve customers' needs.

Focus on Customers' Outcomes

So Schwab's top executives have paid conscious attention to reinforcing and revitalizing the company's corporate culture and its caring for customers and their financial dreams. How has the firm actually wired itself to insure that everyone is delivering on this commitment?

The first, and most important, measure of success Schwab uses is the growth in the size of customers' accounts. Schwab's goal is to increase customers' assets by 20 percent per year. "If we wanted to increase customer assets by acquiring a bunch of affluent customers, we could hire a bunch of expensive brokers," explained Dan Leemon, EVP and Chief Strategy Officer. Instead, Schwab's business model is to build a broad customer-base and to grow that base both in size and in value over time. Dan said, "I went back ten years and plotted the growth of our customers' accounts. Ten years ago, they were averaging $9,000; today the average account is $109,000. We've been experiencing an average growth rate of 20 percent in account size." Today, Schwab's average new account starts with $20,000 to $25,000. But it also grows at a rate of 20 percent per year. Susanne Lyons, Schwab's Chief Marketing Officer, elaborates: "The traditional brokerage business is commission-based. How many trades does the customer make? We focus on how many clients do we have and how many assets they brought us." Gideon Sasson, Enterprise President of Electronic Brokerage, reinforces this: "Our brokers have no idea what they're earning per customer. They're incented based on asset accumulation of customers' portfolios and customer satisfaction." Each customer is "owned" by a team of employees. They're responsible for the growth of that customer's investment portfolio as well as her customer satisfaction.

Schwab measures several aspects of customers' asset growth—how much each customer's portfolio is growing in value, how much each customer is adding to his portfolio (presumably customers wouldn't keep investing if they weren't satisfied), and how many net new customers have joined Schwab's ranks. Susanne Lyons estimates that 70 percent of new customers are "referral-influenced." In other words, they have a friend, colleague, or relative who is a satisfied Schwab customer.

Measuring Customer Satisfaction

"We are constantly surveying customers to gauge their customer satisfaction with our different touchpoints, including every individual who interacts with customers," says Gideon Sasson. "If you interact with us on the phone, we'll call and ask you to rate that experience. If you interact with us on the Web, we'll email you and ask you to fill in a survey, if you interact with us in a branch, we'll call with a follow up." (This program is carefully monitored so that customers don't have to answer multiple surveys for multiple channels, and each customer only gets surveyed about once a year.) Schwab uses an outside firm to handle its customer satisfaction surveying. The results of the customer satisfaction surveys are fed back to the employees who serve that particular customer.

Understanding Different Customers' Needs

Like many companies, Schwab is aiming for the holy grail of a completely personalized experience for each individual. In the meantime, however, the company has found it useful to begin by segmenting customers into different clusters based on their behavior, in order to be able to monitor and improve the customer experience for each different type of customer. Schwab keeps track of the information that customers freely offer. It doesn't invade customers' privacy. However, by using sophisticated analytics to model different customer segments and behaviors, the company is better able to match its customers' needs.

There are several different aspects of customer behavior that Schwab mixes and matches in order to better understand customer segments. Of course, Schwab knows its customers' interaction and transaction histories as well as each customer's assets under management and whether those are being handled by an investment advisor.

Customers also give Schwab demographic information—age, sex, income, etc. And they tell Schwab their preferences—if they want to interact over the Internet, which stocks they want to be alerted about, and so on. Customers also characterize their investment styles (from risk-averse to aggressive).

Based on these explicit customer characteristics, Schwab currently groups customers into "investment style" segments:

- **Delegators**. These are the customers who work through an investment advisor.
- **Validators**. These are the customers who like to do their own research and leg work, but then want to have a conversation with someone to validate their hunches.
- **Self-Directed.** Customers who do their own research, most of it online, and prefer to use the automated channels, such as the Web and/or Schwab's voice response systems.

In addition, Schwab currently divides its customers into three large behavioral segments:

- **Classic Customers.** These are the customers who have less than $100,000 of assets with Schwab and who perform less than 12 trades per year.
- **Active Traders**. Customers who trade more than 24 times per year.
- **HyperActive Traders.** Customers who trade more than 48 times per year—many of them 100's of trades per year.

As you can see, there's nothing mysterious or shady in these distinctions. Customers know what they are. They know whether they prefer to have guidance, or to do it themselves. They know how much money they have invested through Schwab and whether they have delegated some or all of their investment decisions to an advisor.

Customers can also opt into Schwab's explicit customer segmentation by signing up for Schwab's Signature Services. This is a program designed to cater to the customers with the largest assets and the largest number of trades or a combination of both.

What does Schwab measure and monitor out of all this customer behavioral information? A lot, of course. There are specialists who are constantly mining Schwab's customer data looking for patterns and early warning signals. According to Janice Rudenauer, VP Database and Relationship Marketing, the most promising area of analytics has been to be able to detect patterns that lead to a customer leaving Schwab for another brokerage relationship. Over the past few years, Schwab has experienced some true attrition—situations where customers transferred assets to a competing firm. By tracing back through customers' behavior in the three years prior to the defection, Janice's team has begun to spot some interesting patterns in customers' assets and trading activity. Modeling this past behavior may prove useful in flagging customers who are beginning to exhibit similar behaviors, in order to be able to spot defections before they occur.

Managing the Customer Experience Across Touchpoints

Schwab launched its e-schwab online brokerage operation as a separate entrepreneurial business in 1996, under the leadership of EVP Beth Sawi. But it quickly became clear that many Schwab customers wanted to use the online channel as well as the other touchpoints Schwab provided. In 1997, the company integrated online brokerage into the fabric of the organization. By then, Gideon Sasson, who had overseen the design and implementation of the online brokerage systems, under Beth, had assumed responsibility for the online brokerage unit.

By mid-2000, 70 percent of Schwab's customers were trading online. Because online brokerage had begun life as a separate business, however, it wasn't tightly integrated into the rest of Schwab's telephone-based and branch-based operations. All customer transactions and customer account information were captured in the back-end transactional systems, but the interactions customers had on an hourly and daily basis in the branch, on the phone, or via the Web, were captured separately.

CLOSING THE LOOP

Gideon recognized that these separate interaction touchpoints were causing customers aggravation. So he put together a service integration team and commissioned a "fix" for the problem. Called "The Loop," it was a customer communication system that serves as a conduit between the electronic brokerage unit and the field organization. When customers have an issue that they bring up online, it's reported out to the field organization, along with the resolution. If the problem couldn't be resolved, they explain why not. That way, if a disgruntled customer strolls into the branch office, or calls one of the phone reps, they won't be caught off guard. They'll know what has transpired and why. Often, the field reps come up with a solution to the customer's problem which is then reported back to the online brokerage group. Sometimes they find a way to work around it, which then gets implemented as a tactical solution.

Schwab is still not where it wants to be in proactively managing the quality of customers' experience seamlessly across interaction touchpoints. But the company does offer a number of best practices in planning and monitoring customer experience.

USABILITY TESTING

Schwab tests out new prototypes, software releases, and ideas on actual customers and prospects on a daily basis. Whether it's new functionality for the Web site, a new script for the voice response system, or a new user interface for a wireless data access, Schwab brings customers and other people off the street into its usability lab in downtown San Francisco several times a week. Engineers, marketing executives, and customer support representatives watch as customers try to use the new features. The videos of these sessions are then used to understand and improve the proposed functionality.

USING CUSTOMER SCENARIO-BASED DESIGN

Schwab is one of the few companies that makes use of customer scenarios[8] in designing for different customer segments—e.g., prospective customers, affluent customers, and active traders all have completely different outcomes they want to accomplish when they come to Schwab's Web site. Schwab's customer experience planners know, for example, that new prospects want to compare commission rates among online brokerage firms, they want to see where the nearest branch is, and they want to be reassured about the quality and the sources of the investment research they can access.

MONITORING CUSTOMER EXPERIENCES

Then, Schwab does a very thorough job of monitoring and improving the usability of each separate interaction touchpoint. There are customer satisfaction surveys by touchpoint. There are also automated measures in place. Schwab monitors end-to-end performance on its Web site, using both external performance monitoring services and internal instrumentation. What that means is that if customers in a

---

[8] See Chapter 14 for a complete description of how Customer Scenarios work.

particular part of the country are experiencing slow response times, Schwab's online brokerage team will probably already be aware of the problem and working to fix it. Schwab's six large customer service centers also have lots of metrics in place to monitor and correct for the number of rings before a call is answered, the amount of time a customer is on hold, and the number of times customers hang up. And the automated voice response systems are similarly monitored.

Gideon's online brokerage team monitors customers' navigation paths through the Web site to spot areas that need to be streamlined. They monitor how quickly customers' emails are answered and how satisfied customers are with those responses.

But what's still missing today is a completely seamless and integrated customer relationship management system that would capture and gather customer behavior in real time across interaction touchpoints. That's coming. (Schwab is in the process of rolling out a large Siebel CRM system that will provide the glue across the different customer touchpoints). Today, Schwab can monitor my customer experience on the phone or on the Web. But it can't yet monitor the quality of my experience when I do research on the Web and then pick up the phone, or when I walk into a branch and go home and log onto the Web. That's soon to come.

Sensing and Responding to Customers' Needs

What are some of the explicit customer-driven initiatives that Schwab has undertaken in the past couple of years? Schwab was the first of the U.S.-based online brokers to cater to Chinese American investors. In 1998, Schwab launched a Chinese-language version of its Web site and has opened fourteen Chinese-language branches. The Chinese version of the Schwab site is more than a translated site; it also offers an online Chinese-language news service that lets customers track U.S. investment news, earnings estimates, and other breaking news in Chinese.

In August 1999, Schwab launched a downloadable software product called Velocity for Schwab Signature customers. These customers wanted faster access to the Web. They liked the self-service aspect of online trading, but they didn't have the patience to log onto the Web and wait for pages to appear. Velocity is a Java applet that customers load once onto their PC or laptop. It's a trader's desktop that combines static information with real-time information and news, and real-time account information—balances, positions, order status. Customers can work offline or online. As soon as they're online, the information is updated in real time. But because only certain bits of information need to be updated, and not the whole screen each time, it's a much faster and therefore more gratifying experience.

Velocity appealed to Schwab's active traders, but they still wanted more. "We've been focusing on the active trader market. That's where we were starting to lose ground," Gideon reported in the spring of 2000. "We acquired CyBerCorp because of the active trader market. A lot of our customers trade more than forty-eight times a year—many of them are trading ten times a month." These customers value a different kind of trading experience—one that's designed explicitly for the active, professional or near-professional investor. Yet "many active traders also prefer the multi-touchpoint experience that we offer."

Linking Compensation to Customers' Outcomes

Fifty percent of each of Schwab's executives' bonuses are tied to the company's overall performance: did the company as a whole exceed its revenue goals, its profit goals, its goals for growing each customer's assets, and its customer satisfaction goals? A similar formula is applied throughout the company. Everyone benefits when the company's overall goals are met and exceeded. And there are also channel-specific customer interaction goals. Gideon explains, "Our online business has to grow assets and accounts. We also need to have the fastest and most available brokerage Web site, and we are bonused based on customer satisfaction—how many customers give us a 5 out of 5." Gideon is also measured on employee satisfaction and employee retention.

Results

Schwab's results are stellar! The company has delivered a predictable 20 percent growth in revenues, an after tax profit margin of 12 percent, and a Return on Equity of 20 percent for seven years in a row. Most impressive is Schwab's growth in customer numbers and customer assets, despite downturns in the market. For example, Schwab clients' assets grew 45 percent in the twelve months ending August 2000. On the online brokerage front, Gideon's team grew online brokerage to 4.3 million accounts and $420 billion of assets.

Takeaways

Notice that Schwab was an early pioneer in forging what Dave Pottruck dubbed a true "Clicks and Mortar™" strategy. Schwab has 415 branches, six call centers, automated voice response systems, Web access, email access, and hand-held wireless data access. And if you prefer to have professional advice, you can go two ways. You can sign up for a branch consultation with one of Schwab's investment specialists. Or, if you have over $100,000 to manage, you can get a referral for a third-party investment advisor, financial planner, or tax advisor who is part of Schwab's AdvisorSource network. Every time Schwab opens a new physical branch, the number of online customers in the region grows as well. There's a clear correlation about customers' comfort factor in using the Web as a touchpoint when they know they can also walk into a branch and talk to someone who will get to know them and will care about their situation.

Schwab's story isn't a just a story about metrics. It's a story about caring deeply for customers and their results—in this case, helping them realize their financial dreams. But it's also a story about focus. Schwab is in a highly competitive market. It's a market that attracts hot new upstarts every day. And one in which large, incumbent players, like Merrill Lynch, seem to be able to make a comeback. One of the problems with doing business on the Web is that everything you do can be quickly copied. Therefore, the barriers to entry are low. And as Schwab has found in its own customer research, just because a customer has assets with Schwab doesn't mean that he necessarily manages his portfolio on Schwab, that he does most of his investment research and planning there, or that he'll put his next influx of funds to work for him at Schwab. He may decide to try out a different player. The people at Schwab spend as much time watching their radar as would any players in a competitive market. What's different about Schwab is that everyone is absolutely clear about what makes the company successful and their role in achieving that success. The formula is simple: we want our customers to have a great experience, and we want to provide them with the tools to help their money to grow!

As we've watched Schwab plot and execute its technology strategy and its acquisition activity over the past several years, what shines through most clearly is that all of the company's decisions are grounded in its desire to improve its customers' experience and their outcomes. There are certainly challenges along the way, and many more seams to stitch up, but I'd place my bets on a company with the kind of singular focus and dedication to customer outcomes that Schwab has, any day.

Patty's Suggestions for Schwab

Schwab is investing heavily in a new, integrated customer information system, based on Siebel's CRM system, and integrated into Schwab's other systems. This should help Schwab sew up the remaining seams between its Web, branch, and call center operations. Yet I suspect these systems are being designed more for Schwab employees than for customers. As a customer, I'd like to be able to go online to see not only a record of all my transactions, but also a log of any interactions I've had with any of the folks I interact with at Schwab either by phone or online. I'd also like Schwab to show me explicitly which customer segment profile I'm in. It would be nice to be able to validate that, rather than to have Schwab making inferences about the kind of investor I am based on the knowledge they've pieced together about me.

In terms of touchpoint integration, I'd like to see Schwab offer a much tighter integration between its Web and its call center operations. I'd like to be on the Web site, push a button for help, and get an online chat or phone session with a real person who could walk me through what I'm trying to accomplish, in the same way that I can today with Lands' End. The Schwab customer experience researchers tell me that they've observed that customers tend to do one kind of thing on the Web (research and trading), and another kind of thing on the phone (ask questions), but that the customer is in a different context and a different frame of mind on each medium. At the moment, they don't find that customers are looking for a more seamless customer experience. Perhaps I'm different, but I doubt it.

Each time I talk with the folks at Schwab I find that there's a Chinese Wall between the clients served by independent financial advisors who use Schwab as their broker and administrator, and retail clients. Yet I know that many of the clients who have delegated the management of their portfolios to a professional advisor also like to invest some of their money themselves. Why not give these hybrid investors the opportunity to view all of their accounts in one portfolio—the self-managed accounts and the investor-managed accounts, I ask. "We can't violate the fiduciary relationship we have with those investment managers," Schwab's executives invariably reply. "What if a customer wants to see the whole picture and authorizes you to break down those stovepipes, can you do it?" "Theoretically, we can," is the answer I usually get. Remember, customers are in control. They get to decide how they want to do business with Schwab, and with Schwab's other customer, their financial advisor.

Finally, I'd like to see Schwab do an even more proactive and aggressive job in monitoring the quality of its customer experiences. Right now, Schwab measures how it's doing by touchpoint and in aggregate. But Schwab isn't yet able to monitor *my* experience as a customer trying to change some account details or as a would-be investor trying to accomplish a particular task, other than by surveying me after the fact. There's just too much data being collected to make sense out of it at a personal level. Yet that's where I think Schwab needs to go next. Ideally, Schwab should be able to automatically instrument the most commonly performed customer scenarios. And when customer XYZ takes much longer to complete the scenario than the norm, it should be flagged. Maybe he took a coffee break, or maybe he keeps getting confused at the same point each time. Some proactive help might be in order.

One measure of a customer's happiness with an outcome is her willingness to tell others about the experience. It stands to reason that Schwab should use a common loyalty metric—willingness to refer or number of referrals provided—and take it a step further: How effective was that referral? Thus, I would like to see Schwab record how many *new customers* actually come *from referrals* (so that Susanne Lyons no longer needs to *estimate* that it is 70%), and how many *unsolicited referrals* customers make. This kind of information could be an effective supplement to the traditional metrics of retention rate by customer cohort and by customer segment. But given that Schwab cares about customers' outcomes to the degree that bonuses depend on it, the company needs to make sure it uses every bit of customer-satisfaction information it can get its hands on. More than that, however, it needs to make sure it understands how customer satisfaction, employee satisfaction, and channel partner satisfaction influence and are influenced by each other. This is a *pas de trois* that requires not only a Customer Flight Deck, but Employee and Channel Partner Flight Decks as well.

Observations about the Schwab Case Study

Of course, we've only told a small part of the Schwab story here. As with each of our case studies, we've chosen to focus not on how Schwab implemented its technology strategy or evolved its business strategy but on the "difference that makes the difference." In Schwab's case, the company has done a lot of things right. But the real difference in how Schwab operates isn't in the details, it's in the essence of the company. It's one of the few companies I've found in which every employee truly cares about customers' outcomes.

A Sample Flight Deck for Charles Schwab

	Navigation	Performance	Operations	Environment
Customer Numbers	Number of active customers Number of active online customers Number of active financial advisor customers Number of active customer households Number of active accounts per customer and per household	Number of new active customers Number of new customers by referral Number of unsolicited referrals Number of financial advisor customers with individual accounts	Number of unique visitors to the Web site Conversion rates: Percentage of customers who enrolled: • Online • In a branch • By phone/mail	Total number of individual investors Total number of brokerage customers Total number of online brokerage customers Competitive offerings
Customer Retention	Customer retention rate Household retention rate Average customer tenure	Retention rate by customer cohort Retention rate by customer segment Customer loyalty rating	Percentage of customers who are active Web users Percentage of customers who interact via email Decline in customer activity Propensity to defect	Competitors' offers Share of portfolio Comparative retention Comparative customer tenure
Customer Experience	Satisfaction by customer segment Satisfaction by cohort Satisfaction by customer scenario	Customer satisfaction by: • Task • Touchpoint • Channel partner End-to-end performance by scenario Customer satisfaction with quality of informaton provided	Elapsed time for commonly performed tasks Accuracy of Web search results Percentage of trades executed with price improvement Percentage of emails answered accurately in one hour	Comparative satisfaction: Competitors: • Other online brokers • Other financial service firms • All products and services
Customer Spending	Average revenue per customer Average profitability per customer Growth in customer assets Customer lifetime value	Revenues per customer segment Profits per customer segment Growth in customer assets per segment	Daily logins at market opening Revenue trades per day Percentage increase in customer assets Cost to serve by touchpoint	Total brokerage assets Growth in brokerage assets

Five Steps to Make Your Corporate Culture More Customer-Focused

What can you do to ensure that your company will survive the customer revolution and thrive in the customer economy? It's not enough to have a great customer experience, measure the right stuff, execute well, and be flexible and ready to morph. You also need to have a core, customer-caring corporate culture. Here are five important steps to help move your company from lip service to passionate, focused, execution:

1. Start at the Top with a Passion for Customers.

Your CEO needs to reinstill and/or reinforce a clear passion for end customers and their successful outcomes into the company at all levels. It must become clear to everyone in the company that this is the top priority. Everyone in the company is expected to do what it takes to satisfy customers. This passion needs to come from the heart, not from the battlefield. It's not about beating your competitors to a pulp. It's about loving your customers to death.

2. Focus on the Customer Experience.

Improving the quality of your customers' experiences in doing business with you needs to become the focus for everyone in the organization. This is accomplished by having top executive accountability for the total customer experience and by focusing on continuously improving that experience across every segment of your business. Every time there's a question about priorities or trade-offs, "Does this improve our customers' experience of doing business with us?" should become the tie-breaker.

3. Use Customer Measurements.

Begin or improve the way you measure customer satisfaction, customer loyalty, and the quality of the customer experience. Make these measurements meaningful and build them into the company's compensation structure at all levels. Give them at least as much weight as your financial and marketshare goals.

4. Measure Long-Term Customer Profitability.

Start measuring or refine your measurements of long-term customer profitability across product lines and touchpoints. Don't focus on monthly or quarterly profits; focus on customer profitability over two to three years. Don't spend so much time and effort focusing on profitability by product line or by interaction style (phone versus Web). Focus instead on improving your revenues and profits per customer and account.

5. Tell Customer Stories and Instill Values.

Revisit your company's values and mission. Make sure that all of your values are ones that resonate with customers. Values like teamwork, integrity, fun, and innovation are ones that customers will be able to sense and benefit from. Use customer service stories to cement and reinforce your core customer-centric values.

12

THE FOURTH STEP: MEASURE WHAT MATTERS TO CUSTOMERS

Most companies measure and monitor the significant factors affecting their businesses: sales and profits, customer growth and defection, support costs by product line, inventory turns, profit margins, and so forth. On your Web site you're probably measuring hits and clicks, traffic, page views, and unique visitor sessions. You're probably also monitoring click-throughs, conversion rates, navigation paths, and abandoned shopping carts. But none of these metrics matter to your customers. They can't help you improve your customer's experience in doing business with you.

The companies that will be pulling ahead of the pack over the next few years are those that take the quality of their customers' experience very seriously. To compete with them, you'll need to assess the entire quality of experience that your customers have whenever they interact with you either directly and/or through partners.

DETERMINE CUSTOMERS' OUTCOMES

Your business should be designed around the outcomes that your target customers are trying to achieve. One of the symptoms that surround many of today's ineffective e-business initiatives is role reversal. Instead of focusing on what the customer wants to accomplish (e.g., increase the value of my investments, select and purchase a digital camera before the weekend, or get my new printer to work with my old PC), most e-business designers focus on what they want from the customer. They design their business processes and scenarios to manipulate the customer into doing something (e.g., maintain their investment portfolio on my Web site, buy a PC and a digital camera, or sign up for premium customer support service). Notice the difference; there are things that customers want and need to do, and there are things that you'd like customers to do. And remember, customers are in control. You need to satisfy their needs and offer them additional, appropriate opportunities along the way. For example, if you make it really easy for me to select and buy a digital camera that will arrive at my home by Saturday and you also offer me a great deal on a PC with all the appropriate software installed, I might decide not to go through the hassle of hooking the new camera up to my old PC. But I'm not going to be interested in the up-sell unless and until you've given me an easy way to achieve the outcome I came for.

Tesco, the U.K. leader in the supermarket business (see Chapter 13), has learned that many of its online shopping customers like to place their orders in the evening and receive their groceries that same night or the next day just before the dinner hour.

National Semiconductor has learned that design engineers not only want to design and simulate the circuitry for the mobile phones they're designing, but that they need to test the thermal properties of those designs as well.

UNDERSTAND YOUR CUSTOMER'S CONTEXT

Schwab has learned that its active trading customers have a completely different set of expectations than do its affluent investors who are not active traders. Both customers want to make money. But the active trader wants unfettered access to the market and rapid, economical execution of trades. The less-frequent trader wants research, hand-holding, and reassurance before he executes each trade. A Schwab customer with a large holding in IBM stock on a day when the stock is plummeting is probably in a different frame of mind than the customer who is thinking about buying some IBM stock for his four-year-old's education fund.

HP has discovered that some of its business customers prefer a consultative approach to certain tasks, while they like a transactional approach to others.

Buzzsaw has discovered that its customers want the ability to manage their building projects online, but they don't want anyone to foist a particular project management style or approach on them.

DETERMINE WHAT TASKS MATTER MOST TO CUSTOMERS

No matter what eventual outcome the customer has in mind from each interaction with your company, there are likely to be certain tasks that most customers perform on the way to accomplishing their goal. Here are some simple examples:

- Locate your company's phone number
- Find the address of the nearest branch/store/outlet
- Find out if the product I want is in stock and where it is
- Download software or services from the Web
- Search for something on your Web site
- Get help from a customer service representative
- Get the status of my order
- Report a problem I need to get resolved

Your first step towards measuring what matters to customers is to make a list of the most common tasks your customers need to do. Try them yourself. Discover how easy or difficult they are to accomplish. Then set up a way to measure the effectiveness and performance for each of these common tasks. How long does it take on average to accomplish? How many steps does the customer need to take? What does he need to know to be successful (e.g., a special phone number to call or your product name or number)?

MONITOR IN NEAR-REAL TIME AND TAKE ACTION

What's truly amazing is the fact that we now have the wherewithal to monitor many of the things that matter to customers in *near-real time.* We can watch how long it takes prospects and customers to perform many tasks. We can monitor how many search terms a customer uses before he gets to a product description and requests a trial version of the product. We can pop up a customer satisfaction survey after a customer has downloaded a printer driver to see whether his experience in getting his product to work was satisfactory. And we can use this input to make changes in near-real time.

Phil Gibson at National Semiconductor monitors the top 200 search terms customers use on his Web site every day. He uses that information to make daily changes to refine the effectiveness of the search capability. Leslye Louie from Hewlett-Packard gets paged every time a customer reports that he would not recommend HP's services to a colleague, along with background information about the problem the customer was trying to solve. Of course, all dissatisfied customers are contacted for follow-up by her customer support SWAT team, but Leslye can also deal with issues as they arise by suggesting changes to phone-answering protocols, escalation processes, and/or Web site information and/or navigation.

INSTRUMENT AND MONITOR CUSTOMER SCENARIOS

For each customer segment your business serves, there will be several key customer scenarios that matter (a lot) to those customers. Once you've identified them, the next step is to instrument them. Place proactive probes in the systems and processes that execute these steps in your customers' scenarios so you'll know how you're doing in meeting the customers' needs. For example, if quick delivery is important to customers who order from you via the Web, you'll want to monitor the elapsed time between when the customer places his order and when the product is delivered. That's one of the things HP measures, achieving 98 percent of its goal (which is to deliver every single product within two business days).

HEWLETT-PACKARD COMPANY: MONITOR CUSTOMERS' EXPERIENCE ACROSS CHANNELS AND TOUCHPOINTS

By 1997, Hewlett-Packard's consumer customers began to insist that they be able to buy HP's consumer products—printers, PCs, scanners, supplies—direct from the manufacturer. They also pushed for a more seamless customer experience. Even if they opted to buy products from HP's retail distribution partners, they wanted to have a direct relationship with HP for customer support and service. HP responded to customers' requirements with an innovative blended channel strategy.

HP now knows more about who its end customers are in both its consumer and business-to-business markets. Through its direct-to-consumer online presence, both in customer support and in sales, HP has begun to build a core asset—a database of over 20 million active customers who choose to be in relationship with the firm. There's also a CRM effort underway to ensure the HP knows who all its business customers are—those in large direct accounts, and those in smaller businesses served through channel partners. We were delighted to discover that HP is linking its consumer customers and its business customers together with a single identifier. Thus, if an individual is a user of HP's products and services both at work as well as at home, HP will be able to manage its entire relationship with that individual more consistently.

HP is one of the first companies in the world to commit at the highest executive level to managing and improving the total customer experience across product lines, distribution channels, and interaction touchpoints. Let's take a look at how this came about and we'll delve into the specifics: How HP decides which parts of the customer experience to measure and monitor.

Shifting from a Product-Centric to a Customer-Centric Corporate Culture

HP has a well-deserved reputation for customer satisfaction with its products. But the company had traditionally been organized into dozens of product line fiefdoms. HP's direct sales organization focused on very large business accounts. The rest of the sales organization focused on channel and distribution partners—not end customers.

In the mid-1990s, Pradeep Jotwani, at that time the sales and marketing manager for HP's Inkjet Imaging organization, recognized that HP's technology would be moving more and more into the home and becoming a consumer phenomenon. In 1997 he articulated his vision for a new customer-centric consumer business organization that would be driven by customer-centric imperatives. He outlined an organizational structure, processes, and metrics for this new organization. He identified several common initiatives that could benefit all the consumer products groups—PCs, laser printers, inkjet printers, digital imaging, hand-held devices, and so on. They were 1) to create and build relationships with consumers that presented HP as a single, unified entity—e.g., provide a common, branded HP consumer experience; 2) to build a shared customer information system across consumer product lines; and 3) to design and offer consumer-tuned products and services through a single, efficient consumer delivery system.

These were pretty heretical ideas at the time. But nobody stood in Pradeep's way, so he began to build consensus and the organization required to build this common customer experience and a set of shared business processes. He tapped Leslye Louie to oversee the call center operations for all of HP's consumer products and services. And in response to consumer demands, Pradeep set up a team under Shen Li to develop a direct-to-consumer e-commerce site, hpshopping.com. Shen had been in charge of channel partner marketing for North America. So he was uniquely qualified to deal with any channel partner conflict issues that might arise.

Next, a cross-functional team defined a common architecture for customer relationship management for consumers, and, by 1999, Leslye Louie began operating as the general manager for customer relationship management across all the consumer products groups. Pradeep's vision and execution had paved the way for the next major cultural shift that was about to hit HP.

On the business customer side of HP, there was also lots of action, much of it driven by customer input. The enterprise customer support organization, under Dave Swanson's leadership, had embarked on a customer experience program. "Our business customers were quite explicit about what they expected from us," Dave reports. "They wanted to be able to start an interaction on the Web, call us on the phone, and go back to the Web." At the time, customer support via the call center and the Internet were managed separately. "We thought of the Web as a way to lower our support costs. Customers also told us that they wanted us to own their problems," Dave reported. "If the problem they're having is with a partner's application, they don't want to be told to 'call company XYZ.' They want us to stay on the phone with them and the partner until the issue is resolved."

Reinventing HP around Customers

When Carly Fiorina became CEO in July 1999, the transformation of HP's consumer products business was already underway, and the effort to drive toward a more seamless customer experience on the enterprise side of the house was also in full swing. Both efforts had been gaining momentum due to the impact of the Internet. But when Carly talked to customers, she heard one message loud and clear: HP's customers—both consumer and business customers—were tired of having to deal with multiple, disconnected organizations, touchpoints, and channels.

The problem was that HP was still a very product-centric company. No matter what it tried to do to paper over the seams between product divisions, customers still felt the pain. When Carly began "reinventing" HP in November 1999, she reorganized it into two customer-facing organizations and three product-generation organizations. Pradeep Jotwani was promoted to head up the entire Consumer Business organization. Ann Livermore was tapped to head up the Business Customer organization.

Each customer-facing business unit is organized by worldwide functions and by geographic region. The customer-facing organizations focus the majority of their resources on customer and channel relationship management as well as product and service sales, delivery, and support. The product-generation groups handle all R&D and other activities related to product creation with tight integration into the customer-facing units.

HP's New Organizational Structure Focuses on the Customer Experience

Carly is committed to making customer experience management a core business process and a strong source of competitive advantage for HP. As she reorganized the company, she recognized that she needed to have a high-level customer experience "owner" in each of the customer-facing business units. Leslye Louie was named VP of consumer relationship management across all geographies and touchpoints through which a consumer has contact with HP, including traditional customer support, e-support, e-marketing, and direct Web sales. Nanci Caldwell initially became Leslye's counterpart on the business customer side of the house as VP of Total Customer Experience reporting directly to Ann Livermore.

Both Nanci and Leslye work at the strategic level, defining the ideal customer experience across channel partners, products, services, and touchpoints. They are responsible for establishing customer experience goals, measuring and monitoring the customer experience, and continuously improving the customer experience by working with teams of senior executives in both the customer-facing and product-generation organizations. Leslye drives her team with a passionate focus on real-time metrics and continuous improvement. Nanci's team gains support from a Total Customer Experience Steering Board, made up of key representatives from the business units and chaired by Ann Livermore.

Nanci and Leslye coordinate their efforts across HP. Both have defined parallel customer life cycle models and customer scenarios. And they are leading the customer relationship management strategy for HP.

Transforming Consumers' Experiences with HP

As Carly's new organization structure and charter clicked into place, Leslye and Pradeep responded proactively. Leslye pulled her team together from the previously distinct e-commerce, e-marketing, and e-support groups. The organization retained control over HP's consumer call center operations, coordinated closely with the sales organization (which is responsible for sales to HP's retail channel partners), and interfaced with the consumer business product delivery organizations. Instead of offering eighty-three separate product lines, HP could now go to market with an "integrated, high-impact delivery model." In other words, HP's product development teams were all feeding into a single set of customer-facing business processes. One key task was to establish priorities for the services that customers needed (e.g., streamlined product delivery, online support, and a simple and efficient returns process).

Change Management with the Internet as a Catalyst

The relatively rapid progress that HP's consumer business has been able to make in shifting the organizational culture and execution is based on four critical success factors:

1. The initiative is truly led from the customer's point of view.
2. The initiative has very clear customer-focused objectives and strategies.
3. There's a very strong integrated change management program in place.
4. HP used the Internet and the Web as the transformational force in making the organizational and business process changes required.

HP's Blended Channel Strategy

HP has honed its distribution channel strategy for consumer products to be a profitable engine. The company wasn't driven to sell direct to increase its already healthy profit margins on consumer products. Rather, it was customers that drove HP into selling direct. "About three years ago customers began showing us that they wanted a blended channel strategy," Shen reports. "We have a two-pronged competitive strategy. Our channel partners are our first punch. (HP's consumer enterprise still sells 95 percent of its products through retailers and other distribution partners.) Our Web-direct channel is our second punch. Once customers have chosen our products, we want them to purchase in the way that's most convenient for them." On HP.com the customer will find links and referrals to other online retailers, to the nearest local retailer or reseller who has the product he wants in stock, and to bricks-and-clicks retailers such as Circuit City. This blended channel strategy has been implemented in Europe, in many countries in Latin America and in Japan, through a joint venture with Softbank.

Once the customer has made a purchase, no matter where he bought the product, he's encouraged to come to HP.com to register the product, to avail himself of additional services, and to get into relationship with HP directly. Customer support—both phone and Web—

are available for all consumer customers, no matter where they purchased the product.

Figuring Out What Matters to Customers

In honing the customer experience across product lines, channels, and touchpoints, the consumer business had a great deal of history from which to draw. Leslye had been overseeing the consumer call center operations since 1997, so she knew exactly where the areas of pain were for HP's consumer customers—they wanted a single point of resolution for any problem with any product or activity, no matter where they had purchased it; they wanted a much easier way to return and exchange products; they wanted it to be easy to locate and/or reorder supplies. These are all examples of key customer scenarios that the customer experience team began to focus on.

Consumer Product Life Cycle Stages

In order to organize and prioritize their efforts, the team took a customer relationship life cycle approach. What are the different stages that any consumer goes through in relation to any of our products and services? What's the typical consumer product life cycle? Here's the strategic framework they came up with to help in proactively managing the consumer experience:

1. Awareness of HP's products and services
2. Select and buy a product or service
3. First 30 days of ownership
4. Use of the product or service
5. Eventual repurchase or upgrade of an HP product or service

Identifying Key Customer Scenarios within Stages in the Life Cycle

Within each phase of the customer product life cycle, the consumer team focused on a set of key customer scenarios to track and refine across distribution channels and touchpoints. "We needed to make sure that the entire process was seamless from the customer's perspective," Leslye explained.

STREAMLINING THE SELECT AND BUY EXPERIENCE

For example, in the "select and buy" stage, the consumer may begin the process at hpshopping.com, then pick up the phone to call the call center for an explanation or clarification. If he does so, the call center agent needs to know what the consumer has looked at on the Web and how far he got in the process.

The team also discovered that convenience is the key motivating factor during the select-and-buy stage. "So, we honed our logistics capability so that we could ship any order received by 10 P.M. EST that same day," reported Shen Li. "Ninety-eight percent of all consumer orders are received within two business days."

Part of the select-and-buy experience is the returns-handling scenario (i.e., what happens when the customer isn't satisfied with what she's received for any reason). The team refined the returns process for all consumer products purchased from hpshopping.com so that a customer could arrange for the product to be picked up at a convenient time and location at no charge.

FIRST 30 DAYS

In the first 30 days of ownership, the customer experience is important. "If they aren't confident getting up and running with the product they've just bought, we have a problem," Leslye reports. HP monitors and surveys customers on factors such as whether the support materials meet the customer's needs and whether the customer registers online within the first 30 days of use. "We focus on making the product registration process quick, painless, and rewarding."

STREAMLINING USE OF THE PRODUCT

Among the customer scenarios that the team developed to support customers' use of its products and services is a customizable online printing supply store. When a customer receives a product—for example, an ink-jet printer—she's offered the opportunity to set up an online store for accessories and supplies. She can specify the products she currently owns and the store will be automatically populated with the correct accessories and supplies. In fact, for some of HP's newest printers, the customer can authorize the printer itself to automatically reorder ink cartridges as it begins to run low.

The results thus far? According to Leslye, "The revenue growth for our Web site has increased on average 500 percent from year to year. Customers now come back twice as often as before."

REPURCHASE

We've already described the ease with which customers can purchase supplies online. Pradeep points out that HP has also spent a lot of time and effort re-engineering the supplies procurement process in the physical world as well. "Customers told us that it was too hard to find the printing supplies they needed. We realized they were right. Think about film. You can buy film in a camera store, but you can also find it at any drugstore, grocery store, convenience store, or discount outlet. We needed to make printing supplies available in almost as ubiquitous a fashion. So we added many more retailers to our distribution channel strategy." Once HP had solved the supplies availability problem, it discovered another customer issue. Customers couldn't figure out which cartridges they needed for their particular model. "Our packaging and numbering schemes were too confusing. We watched people in stores. They couldn't figure out which package to buy. So, we redesigned our packaging, color-coded everything, and simplified our product naming and numbering."

Measuring What Matters to Customers

How does the consumer team turn these product life cycle stages and customer scenarios into key metrics? Leslye reports, "We measure customer response at critical touchpoints and use the results to drive our decisions. We measure customer satisfaction on a task, an interaction, and a product basis." HP uses a five-point customer satisfaction and loyalty rating system. The questions include:

1. Were you satisfied with this interaction?
2. Did you get the outcome you wanted?
3. Would you do this again?
4. Would you recommend this to a friend or colleague?
5. Would you repurchase with us?

MONITORING CUSTOMER SATISFACTION IN NEAR-REAL TIME

One of the biggest advances in monitoring customer satisfaction and customer loyalty was integrating Web, email, and phone-based customer satisfaction surveys into a single closed-loop feedback system. "The Web and email customer feedback loop is immediate," Leslye reports. "Conventional ways of gathering customer satisfaction information have a six- to twelve-week delay. With Web and email-based customer satisfaction monitoring, we can respond in days, even in hours. I see emails and comments in real time. This is a powerful tool to be able to redirect your priorities, programs, and strategies."

"We also measure our costs-to-serve on both a task and a product level," Leslye adds. "We know what it costs to repair a DeskJet printer versus a PC. We know how much money we've saved by letting the customer download software for his PC or his printer. We know and track what it costs every minute we're on the phone with a customer. We know what it costs to pick and pack each product."

Using Customer Life Cycles and Scenarios on the Business Side of the House

While the consumer organization worries about five stages in the consumer life cycle, HP's business customer organization has identified eight key stages:

- Awareness
- Choosing
- Ordering
- Installing and delivering
- Learning
- Using
- Supporting
- Growing and/or upgrading

In addition, for each stage in his product or services life cycle, Nanci Caldwell explains, the customer may want one of two very different kinds of relationships with HP—a consultative relationship or a transactional relationship. Of course, a given customer may want handholding for one stage and just be able to perform a simple self-service transaction at a different stage. These stages and relationships are further broken down into actual customer scenarios. These are then implemented and tracked across channels and touchpoints.

Having this total customer experience focus and framework makes a difference as new products are brought to market. HP's high-end UNIX computing solution, SuperDome, was designed from the ground up to offer the best customer experience in its class at every touchpoint on the consultative customer life cycle. Each customer is appointed a dedicated solutions manager who is his interface to HP and has responsibility for ensuring that his experience is optimized throughout the product life cycle. To help achieve this, HP measures itself on customer-valued items such as the time taken to prepare quotes and response times to support calls. Most importantly, HP tracks not only how long it takes to install a system but how long it takes to have it operating at the customer's desired performance level.

Let's look at the "supporting" stage in the customer life cycle. The Total Customer Experience team discovered that one of the key issues with its enterprise customers had to do with the critical shortages of skilled IT professionals. HP's enterprise customers typically expect their own internal IT professionals to provide the first line of support. Yet these folks are often understaffed and over-taxed. HP developed an extensive, online service tuned for the IT professional called the IT Resource Center (ITRC). By studying and working closely with targeted IT professional customers, HP created detailed "personas" to drive its development of a tailored, task-based set of customer scenarios to support the IT professional across the entire product life cycle. New features that customers required include "push" communications to mobile hand-held devices like pagers and mobile phones for urgent alerts on security and critical patches, and the ability to "tag" experts in HP's own IT community to enable real-time customer collaboration with thousands of HP and peer experts in a 24 × 7 knowledge collective. This adds an extra element of confidence and collective wisdom to the IT Pro's real-time decisions. Customer feedback is extremely positive, and the ITRC has won two industry awards: the Association of Support Professionals "year's ten best support Web sites" and CIO Magazine's "Web business 50/50 winner."

Cementing Customer Relationships

One of the most encouraging signs that HP's business customer organization really understands the complexity of the challenge ahead is the fact that HP's CRM system is organized around individual end users as well as business accounts. It's vitally important for HP's total customer experience focus to include all the individuals in each account, including purchaser or IT director, installer, and user, whether these individuals are in the accounts HP services directly or those served by its channel partners.

Instilling Customer Experience Metrics into HP's Compensation

HP is in the process of revising its employee rewards and recognition system to closely align with the customer voice. Leslye and her counterpart in the business customer organization are leading cross-functional management teams whose goal is to set customer experience goals that will become part of HP's compensation plan in 2001. During 2000 the teams were setting benchmarks, monitoring results, and understanding what could be measured. Now those measurements and associated stretch goals will become part of the HP way of doing business. For the first year of the new customer-loyalty–based metrics, only the top executives—from Carly down to Leslye Louie—will be bonused on the customer experience scores. "We knew we needed to put our money where our mouths were," Pradeep explained. After the top execs have piloted the new compensation program on themselves in the first year, it will roll out to the rest of HP's employees.

Results

HP's revenue growth has improved under Carly's tenure. Profit growth in 2000 was still below where she (and the market) would like it to be. But having a clear focus on the customer is bound to increase HP's customer loyalty and long-term profitability. In fact, Pradeep Jotwani has already begun educating financial analysts about the value of HP's customer franchise. There were over 20 million active registered customers in relationship with HP by mid-2000. And two million customers were connecting to hpshopping.com each month.

HP wants to build a critical competitive advantage around its focus on the total customer experience. But the company still has a long way to go. And its competitors are all implementing similar customer satisfaction and relationship management programs. HP has made the deepest corporate commitment to the total customer experience of any of its competitors. By measuring the outcomes, tasks, and scenarios that matter most to its customers, HP has a shot at regaining some of its lost walletshare.

HP already has a strong position in the consumer market for its printers, scanners, and consumer PCs. It's pushing hard into digital cameras and digital appliances, like digital music players. Pradeep Jotwani is hoping that consumers who begin an HP relationship with printers and PCs, will continue to think of HP when they buy and use digital cameras and information appliances.

Takeaways

The most important thing I've learned from watching HP's consumer business organization in action is how important it is to measure everything that matters to customers' experiences, customers' outcomes, and to your costs to serve customers effectively. Leslye Louie has a rare ability to both act as a visionary business leader and pay attention to the details that she needs to on the fly.

Another takeaway from the HP experience to date is the migration from reporting and assimilating customer metrics on a monthly basis to monitoring them and taking action on them in near-real time.

Patty's Suggestions for HP

HP's focus and commitment are admirable. But the scope and scale of what the company needs to do is daunting. I've talked to a number of customers whose experiences in interacting with HP still don't measure up.

On the consumer business side, HP needs to roll this same seamless, blended channel strategy and total customer experience focus out around the world.

HP has an even bigger challenge on the business customer side. HP's move to e-services has yet to really gain traction. The total customer experience focus may serve as a real differentiator for HP. The company has a slight lead on its competitors in focusing on and executing owning and managing the customer experience. I hope it can keep that slight lead and leverage its learning to sprint out in front.

And what learning will HP be leveraging? First and foremost, the company needs to make sure it has a clear sense of *customer satisfaction* by relationship-cycle stage (that is, the five consumer product life-cycle stages and the eight business life-cycle stages). Within each of these stages are several product and service attributes that the company could evaluate. The purchase stage (selecting and buying for consumers; choosing and ordering for businesses), for example, gives customers an opportunity to rate HP's performance along such attributes as choice of channel or touchpoint, availability and configurability, quality of knowledge or information, price, ease of ordering, and overall speed of transaction.

But if HP truly wants to measure what matters to customers, it needs to know in exquisite detail what matters to customers, and it needs to know this on a scenario-specific basis. After all, not only do consumers, Small Office/Home Office (SOHO) buyers, small businesses, and enterprises all have different priorities. But those priorities are likely to change from one scenario to another—enough so that the same service attribute might matter to a greater or lesser degree during, say, the purchasing process than during the returns or servicing process.

Consequently, HP should consider context- and scenario-driven customer priorities as vital as data on performance in its overall measurement scheme. Getting this kind of data might require an analysis of the end-to-end scenario-specific customer experience. And a generalized custom Flight Deck designed from that analysis might start out looking like the one we've created.

A Sample Flight Deck for HP

	Navigation	Performance	Operations	Environment
Customer Numbers	Number of active known customers Number of active online customers Number of active known customers per account Number of active, known customers per household	Number of new active customers Number of new active online customers Number of new customers who defected from other vendors Number of customers who have opted into a relationship	Number of unique visitors to Web site Percentage of web visitors who purchased: • online (through HP) • through an e-tailer • through an offline channel partner Number of customers with active recurring services/supplies contracts	Total market size for consumer products and services in HP's segments Total market size for enterprise products and services
Customer Retention	Customer retention rate Household retention rate Account penetration	Retention rate by customer segment Customer loyalty rating	Percentage of customers who are active Web users Percentage of customers who interact via email Decline in customer activity	Competitors' offers Comparative retention rate Share of wallet
Customer Experience	Satisfaction by customer segment Satisfaction by product lifecycle stage Importance ratings by product lifecycle stage Satisfaction by customer scenario	Customer satisfaction by: • lifecycle stage • task • touchpoint • channel partner Customer importance by • lifecycle stage • task End-to-end performance by scenario	Customer satisfaction with and importance of: • Choice of touchpoint • Product variety • Availability • Information • Configurability • Price • Ease of ordering Accuracy of Web search results Percentage of emails answered accurately in one hour	Comparative satisfaction with: • Competitors' offers • Competitors' service
Customer Spending	Average revenue per customer Average profitability per customer Customer lifetime value	Revenues per customer segment Profits per customer segment Number of products/services held by customer	Recency/frequency of purchase Cost to serve by touchpoint Customer acquisition cost Customer retention cost	Competitive walletshare

WHAT AND HOW SHOULD YOU BE MEASURING

In the HP case study we saw a few of the steps that a company, committed to measuring the quality of experience, is taking. What else should you bear in mind as you begin to devote more attention to this crucial area?

Measuring the Customer's Quality of Experience

Remember that customers care about saving time, achieving their desired outcome, and about the quality of the experience they have while they're interacting with your firm or your representatives.

How do you measure and monitor the quality of customers' experiences besides polling them each time they interact with you?

The quality of a customer's experience with your business is dependent on streamlined business processes that are designed to make the customer's job easier, carefully respected policies, good customer service, thoughtful design of your Web site, and excellent operational execution. The customer's experience should be consistent with the expectation established by your brand.

The net results of excellent Quality of Experience are repeat business, higher revenues, and loyal customers, all of which generate rapid profit growth. What things should you measure to determine the effectiveness of your company's Quality of Experience? You need to monitor:

- **Customer Scenarios.** Measure elements such as how much time it takes to reach the first step; and abandonment due to confusion, slow response, or inability to connect to the desired scenario.

- **Customer Support.** Have the service levels you've established satisfied customer requirements? Did the customer get the needed guidance? Is he happy with your company? Track the average number of calls per customer, per order, and per customer incident. How much time does the customer spend waiting for help?

- **Web Site Experience.** It is easy to measure response time for top customers, but it's probably more practical to measure response time of a representative transaction that is reported every hour of every day. Make sure that this measurement is from the customer's perspective. Automated Web site measurement services will answer questions such as does the site offer consistent response time throughout the day and from page to page? Measure these by running test transactions based on scenarios. You also want to measure from machines at several points on the Internet backbone and around the globe to reflect customers' locations and connection speeds. Some automated measurements that you should monitor include the elapsed time for common scenarios and average download time.

- **Quality of Experience Dealing with Your Channels.** One way of testing the quality of your customer experience in interacting in the physical world—in retail stores, for example—is to use the "mystery shopper" approach. Send anonymous shoppers into your retail outlets or those of your distribution partners and have them rate the quality of the customer experience.

13

THE FIFTH STEP: HONE OPERATIONAL EXCELLENCE

Customers really notice consistent execution. We've already talked a lot about delivering a consistent branded experience across interaction touchpoints and distribution channels. Now let's talk about what's required to execute that in delivering products and services.

START DESIGNING CUSTOMER-FACING PROCESSES FROM THE BACK END

For the past couple of years, we've observed that new businesses have been designing themselves from the back end forwards. In other words, before they worried about designing their Web pages they hired logisticians and worked out the details around fulfillment, shipping, and transportation. They hired and trained their customer support personnel six to nine months before they opened their doors for business. They used the latest technologies to ensure that they would have the lowest possible costs-to-serve while delivering exquisite service. And as they outsourced and partnered for pieces of the business processes they used, they instrumented these processes so that they (and their customers) would have complete visibility into each business process.

We recommend that you think carefully about what matters to customers and then begin your design efforts by focusing first on nailing operational excellence. Then worry about the pretty Web pages and other touchpoints.

Avoid Black Holes

You and your customers need to be able to see and interact with every step of every customer-impacting process. Here's an example. Cisco Systems lets customers configure their complex networking systems using Cisco's configurator and either Cisco's order entry system or the customer's own procurement system. The systems are actually manufactured, not by Cisco Systems but by a variety of contractors and subcontractors in a well-oiled electronic supply chain. This automated process worked pretty well. But Cisco and its customers weren't completely satisfied with the accuracy and efficiency of the manufacturing process, so Cisco did a couple of things to increase operational effectiveness and increase the customers' visibility and control into the manufacturing process.

First, Cisco developed quality-testing software that tested each configuration at the subcontractor's site against the customer's specifications. The objective was to ensure that each component and system configured met Cisco's exacting specs and the customer's requirements. That way, the system could be shipped directly from the contractor without going through an additional quality control and testing phase at a Cisco location.

Second, by 1999, Cisco's customer advocacy team had realized that more than 90 percent of the change orders the company received from its customers were occurring within twenty-four hours of the time the original order was placed. Customers would place the order and then change their minds or add to the order. Did Cisco delay all orders for twenty-four hours to reduce the complication and expense of change orders? No, Cisco's director of Internet Commerce, Sue Stemel, and her customer-facing applications team developed a module for the order entry system that allowed customers to revisit their orders and make changes to them as the parts were being manufactured. Customers loved this capability, and, sure enough, most of the changes requested were made within the first twenty-four hours as the parts were being assembled and the order processed through the supply chain. This increased flexibility was a huge win in operational effectiveness. It cut the time and expense associated with handling change orders dramatically.

Execute and Monitor End-to-End Performance

How will you know whether you're executing consistently and efficiently? Customer satisfaction surveys, gathered after the fact, are too late. Monitoring customer satisfaction in near-real time on an incident-by-incident basis is one early warning system. The best way to ensure that you're executing well is to proactively monitor the end-to-end performance (as perceived by the customer). We've discussed the idea of monitoring key customer scenarios in an earlier chapter (see Chapter 12). But the key services that will eventually impact customers also need to be proactively monitored. For example, even before it ventured into e-business, the Tesco supermarket chain had identified inventory replenishment as a key performance indicator it needed to monitor constantly at the individual store level. Keeping the shelves stocked is a key service that impacts lots of customers. Tesco tracks every step of its replenishment process, not just to increase inventory turns but also to keep operational efficiency humming. The goal is for customers to have a consistently good experience shopping at Tesco. Tesco's balanced score card—a wheel with green, yellow, and red lights for each indicator—is on the wall of each store where all employees can see it. One of the key indicators that Tesco's in-store personnel monitor is when an item is close to being out of stock on the shelves. Then the light goes yellow.

Tesco is one of many modern e-businesses that also proactively monitors end-to-end performance on the Internet "on ramps" (points of presence and Internet Service Providers) and browsers its customers are using. Each time a new release of software is ready to be delivered, it's tested with every conceivable device and browser combination that customers are currently using to see if it performs up to standards. On a daily basis, Tesco runs online shopping scripts from a variety of points around the U.K. to monitor the quality of service its customers are receiving from different Internet Service Providers at different times of day. Wells Fargo, Cisco Systems, National Semiconductor, and American Airlines are just a few of the hundreds of companies that do the same kind of end-to-end proactive performance monitoring.

WHAT'S END-TO-END?

The important thing to understand here is that it's not sufficient to monitor your system's responsiveness from inside your own firewalls. You need to monitor performance from the devices your customers are using, whether those are hand-held wireless devices or Internet-connected browsers, in different parts of the world. Here's a good example. When Intel began offering e-commerce functionality to its customers in the Asian Pacific region, the company noticed that these customers were experiencing very slow response times. Intel spent six months working with its customers, fine-tuning their internal networks and systems to resolve performance problems. However, in Taiwan Intel's technologists discovered that the problem wasn't just with these customers' firewalls and internal systems. There was a bigger issue—the government-sponsored Internet backbone slowed to a crawl when customers tried to use Intel's highly secure applications. The Internet infrastructure in the country couldn't support this level of security encryption. Intel's executives took the initiative, meeting with the government and its technical advisors. They worked with the local ISPs. They documented and demonstrated the problems. And they offered to fix it for the country. The offer was accepted, keeping Taiwan's high tech chip manufacturers humming, which was a high priority for the government. The result? Intel's Taiwanese customers now have the performance they need to get their jobs done.

TESCO: USING OPERATIONAL EXCELLENCE AS A COMPETITIVE ADVANTAGE

Time-pressed customers have made it clear that they want the convenience of having groceries delivered to their homes. But many of the attempts to develop successful online grocery businesses have failed. How do you win the hearts and minds of consumers? With convenience and seamless integration into their normal lives and routines. Customers who shop for groceries once a week are familiar with their local store. They know what products are offered. They know how these are laid out. Unless you can offer them the identical products at the identical prices they're used to receiving, along with the convenience of shopping from home, you'll never gain their loyalty.

Tesco plc. is a U.K.-based global supermarket chain with annual revenues of £20 billion. An established presence with a huge bricks-and-mortar infrastructure, Tesco is also the world's most successful and profitable online grocer.

There are three reasons that others have failed and Tesco has succeeded:

1. Other companies have had to develop the food distribution infrastructure from scratch; Tesco leverages its existing store-based distribution processes.
2. Other companies have developed pick, pack, and delivery from separate warehouses, adding a layer of cost into the equation. Tesco's in-store pick and pack system avoids this duplication and ensures that customers will get exactly the same products with which they're familiar.
3. No other online grocer has seamlessly integrated customers' in-store shopping and their online shopping. Tesco keeps track of what each family has bought, both in the store and online. And it doesn't violate customers' privacy by sharing that information with suppliers.

As all of the large supermarket chains are battling for their share of families' stomachs, many are competing on price. Tesco is competing on customer loyalty and customer experience. Its prices are competitive in each local market so customers always get a fair deal. Equally important, Tesco knows who its customers are and deepens its relationships with them over time. There are over 14 million active Tesco cardholders.

Tesco's online business, Tesco.com, uses the same balanced score card "steering wheel" as its in-store counterpart. Tesco measures and monitors what matters to customers, including which items are close to out-of-stock, how quickly its delivery vans make it through traffic, and how it performs customers' shopping scenarios from different Internet service points across the country.

The Battle for Share of Customers' Stomachs

Most companies worry about what share of each customer's wallet they have. In the food and grocery sector, this is jokingly described as "share of stomach." But stomach share is no laughing matter to the players who are duking it out in increasingly global markets. By January 2000, Tesco was clearly in the lead in the U.K. market and about to begin its assault on the rest of Europe. In second place but hot on Tesco's heels was invader Wal-Mart Stores, which had acquired the ASDA chain. J. Sainsbury was running third. According to an annual survey done by retail consultancy, Verdict Research, Tesco was the "undisputed leader in the U.K. food and grocery sector."

Customer Loyalty Is Eroding in the Grocery Business

In its report, Verdict went on to explain that "across the U.K. grocery sector as a whole, loyalty has been eroded over the past twelve months—the inevitable result of a price war which helps to destabilize shoppers' perceptions and behaviour." The researchers measured a five-point decline in overall customer loyalty, as measured by the number of shoppers who say they would shop elsewhere if they could (from 75% in 1998 to 70% in 1999). Yet Tesco ranked at the top of the customer loyalty numbers.

By early 1999 Tesco was not only the U.K.'s largest grocer, it had become the world's largest *online* grocer, with £125 million revenues from 250,000 customers doing online shopping with profit margins of 12 percent. In the fall of '99, when we asked U.S. supermarket executives which business they thought was doing the best job in online shopping, Webvan Group, Peapod, or MyWebGrocer.com, they replied that Tesco had the business model that they admired most.

How did Tesco grab the lead in customer loyalty, profitability, and stomach share in the online grocery arena?

The Tesco Direct Experiment

In 1994 Tim Mason, Tesco's then marketing director, pitched the idea of direct shopping to Tesco's board. Tim wanted to set up a call center, mail order, and online operation geared toward increasing the non-food side of Tesco business. Customers could receive mailers promoting special items and call, fax, or email in their orders. The orders could be shipped out the next day. This strategy would also enable Tesco to market items not normally sold in their stores—gift items, toys, and other consumer products. The board approved the strategy.

Tim pulled together a small team, and they launched Tesco's original call center/mail order/e-commerce operation in Dundee. Then, Tim took a different job, and the small group carried on.

Moving the Experiment into the Real World

At that point, Gary Sargeant was tapped to head up Tesco Direct. Gary had risen through the ranks as a store manager. He decided to combine the call center/mail order operation with in-store fulfillment. Local customers could order any item carried in their local stores and receive same-day delivery. He piloted this concept in Osterley. And he expanded the call center operation to accept Internet email orders as well as phone and fax.

PILOTING WITH A TARGET CUSTOMER GROUP

Having figured out his game plan, Gary went looking for a target set of customers, first looking at homebound old-age pensioners.

He approached the local authority responsible for old-age pensioners in the Brimford neighborhood and got its blessing to offer this service to their clientele. "This was an easy market for us. Most of these folks relied on part-time helpers or neighbors who would do their shopping at a local convenience store. The prices and the selection offered were terrible. We could do much better for them," Gary explained.

EXPANDING THE PILOT

Once the kinks were out of the system, the Tesco Direct Team expanded the home shopping offer beyond the older, housebound, customer base. Then they added a second store and a third. Soon Tesco had a customer base between 300 and 400 home shopping customers per week. Most of these folks would call or fax in their orders. Only 6 percent of the orders came via the Internet. Yet Gary knew in his bones that online shopping was where the real growth opportunities lay. By 1997 consumer usage of the Internet was increasing exponentially. Dixon's Freeserve—"free Internet" (you still had to pay for the phone calls) service had captured the hearts and minds of thousands of British customers.

Gary decided to target busy, upscale professionals—the kinds of people who would most value the home shopping service and who would be more likely to want to shop online. He added another store—this time in a very affluent neighborhood—Hammersmith. "Our research showed that these households were more than four times as likely to shop online," Gary explained. The average income of these families was £55,000. They owned two cars. They were either two working parent families, wealthy households, or starter singles. Gary's team did a marketing blitz of the area, and 9,000 people expressed interest in Tesco's online shopping offer. "Yet the day we went live, we received a single online order," Gary moaned. Online shopping was obviously going to have a slow ramp up.

What Gary and his team learned from the slow start in Hammersmith is that, just because you offer online grocery shopping, customers won't necessarily use it. In hindsight he recognized that his team had done very little to prepare fertile ground. "We just did blanket marketing. We dropped leaflets everywhere. We should have realized that there's a distinct group of people we needed to reach: working women and people who had already outsourced a number of household tasks, like ironing, cleaning, and so on." By trial and error, the Tesco Direct team refined its marketing and began to lure customers online.

Moving from Pilot Project to Mainstream

How did Tesco's small pilot project move from an experiment to a vital part of Tesco's strategy? How did the Tesco Direct team figure out a business model for online shopping that would soon become the envy of every supermarket in the world?

By late 1997 Tesco Direct was still primarily a call-center–based operation, with a handful of participating stores offering Tesco's full line of groceries to customers in their shopping areas. Others might have given up at this stage, but Gary Sargeant was undaunted. Still convinced that online shopping was about to take off, he turned his attention to streamlining operations and tweaking the business model so that he could offer online shopping profitably to all of Tesco's customers. He was supported by John Browett, Tesco's business strategist.

Many online grocery services presume that it's more cost-effective to handle inventory and fulfillment operations from a distribution warehouse. But Gary continued to hone the in-store fulfillment model. He wanted each customer to be purchasing online from the store in which they would normally shop in person. Customers would receive the same price for each item online as the price in the store nearest their home. This would permit regional pricing variations to be maintained, boosting overall profits. (In the supermarket business, certain neighborhoods support higher prices than others.) Yet customers' online prices would always be competitive with the prices charged by local stores. By linking the online shopping application directly to each store's inventory systems, it was unlikely that customers would order a product that was not available, saving considerable time and effort for both customers and for Tesco. Moreover, customers are familiar with the selection of products available in their local stores. Finally, the servers in each store could save a history of each customer's favorite products, to ensure that these were always in stock.

Gary handpicked a team of logisticians to help design the optimal in-store pick and pack system. The new streamlined system works like this: The pickers use a specially equipped shopping cart with six trays and an online display. The display gives them their routes through the store and a list of the items to be picked as they go down each aisle. The store routes are optimized to avoid the peak in-store traffic areas. Items are scanned as they're dropped into each customer's tray, so they can't be mixed up. And if the item the customer ordered has gone out of stock in the few hours that have elapsed since the order was placed, the picking application proposes an alternate product from a list of items that customer has previously purchased, either in the store or when shopping online. Seventy-five percent of Tesco's online shoppers also shop at the store from time to time. And because most of them use Tesco's loyalty card, Tesco has a complete history of each customer's orders.

Once the shopping cart is filled, the trays are loaded directly into the delivery vans that are ready and waiting behind each store. Again, the routing is optimized so that produce doesn't sit for hours but is delivered immediately after being picked from the store. Deliveries are scheduled based on customers' preferences (within a two-hour delivery window to allow for traffic delays). Any items that have been substituted are carefully placed on the top of each order so they can be reviewed and accepted or rejected when the order is delivered.

Providing a Seamless, Efficient Customer Experience

Let's briefly recap the brilliance of Tesco's in-store pick and pack model. First, the company doesn't need to set up separate warehouse distribution centers to support its online shoppers. Companies that have tried to do this have had particular difficulty with the perishables in the warehouses; there isn't enough volume and turnover to keep the freshest produce fresh. With Tesco in-store pick and pack approach, the online business is leveraging the inventory and rapid turnover of the existing stores. Because the Tesco Direct team optimized the traffic patterns through the store, the regular shoppers aren't inconvenienced. Best of all, the customer gets the same products at the same prices whether she shops online or stops at the store on her way home from work.

Every purchase the household makes—online and offline—is captured. That information is used to improve the shopper's convenience and her customer experience with Tesco.

Honing a Profitable Business Model

Tesco charges customers £5 (about $7.50) per delivery. This fee covers 60 percent of the operational costs of actually performing the service. The rest of the costs are covered by the fact that online in-home shoppers order more profitable items than in-store–only shoppers.

Grocers measure customer profitability by shopping basket. Gary reports that the "basket mix" of Tesco's online shoppers is 2 to 3 percentage points more profitable than the average customer's in-store market basket. Why is that? I would speculate that, when a customer grocery shops online, it's easier to check off a list of items and add to that list than it is to lumber down supermarket aisles picking out each item by hand. And Tesco's online shopping site does a good job of cross-selling and up-selling. When you check off an item (like bread), other related items (such as marmalade or butter) pop up on the screen.

The total profit margins for Tesco's online shoppers, including all operational costs, run 10 to 12 percent. This is consistent with Tesco's overall profit margins.

Rolling out across the Country

Once the Tesco Direct team had refined the logistics and proved out its business model, they began to roll the operations out in a number of stores. By mid-1998 eleven stores were online. Perhaps more exciting to Gary and his team was the fact that 85 percent of the orders being placed were Internet orders. Internet-savvy customers had discovered how convenient it was to do their grocery shopping online.

In July 1998, Gary met with Terry Leahy, Chief Executive, Tim Mason, Chairman, and John Browett, who was then chief strategist. "We should stop promoting phone and fax ordering," Gary explained. "The cost of having customers enter their own orders is so much lower, even with the hand-holding that's required. Let's focus on doing a really good job with online ordering," Gary suggested. They all agreed that Tesco Direct should become an Internet-only operation. Of course, they kept the call center operation. Existing customers who didn't have Internet access could still call in their orders—about 300 of them still do—but all new customers would be Internet-only customers.

One lesson the Tesco Direct team learned was to set customers' expectations. "The first time you do your grocery shopping online, it's going to take you a good forty minutes to complete your order. We hadn't prepared people for that. Online shoppers were used to the experience of ordering a single book or a CD," Gary reported. The Tesco team also discovered that it needed to focus a lot of effort on encouraging customers to place their second and third orders after the shock of food shopping online for the first time. "After your third online order, you're hooked," he explained. But getting customers to that point takes hand-holding and follow-through.

Tesco Direct began life as an orphan. Under Gary Sargeant's stewardship, it grew to become a strategic weapon in Tesco's battle for stomach share. In the spring of 2000, Tesco.com became a separate subsidiary, under the leadership of John Browett, CEO, and Carolyn Bradley, COO. While it's still 100 percent owned by Tesco, the separate governance has allowed the dot-com unit to continue to move at

Internet speed. "We were beginning to get bogged down in the corporate business processes," Gary reports. "We needed the ability to move faster." Now John has a direct line to Tesco's board. And the subsidiary is able to create its own incentive structure that is more competitive. "All Tesco employees will benefit from our success," Gary reports, "but with our own stock options and pay structure, we can compete for talent."

Monitoring Customers' Experiences

Tesco has long been a practitioner of the balanced score card approach to management. At Tesco this is a Balanced Steering Wheel. It has four quadrants: Customers, People, Operations, and Finance. Each quadrant contains a set of objectives. Examples of specific metrics that appear in each quadrant include customer loyalty, employee turnover, percentage of out of stocks, and profit target. Each store has a large steering wheel posted where every employee sees it. The metrics are updated weekly. Each one has a traffic light next to it. Green means you're right on target. Red means you're not achieving it. Yellow means that you're in danger of missing your goal. What kind of "steering wheel" did the Tesco Direct team implement for its operations? They use the same metrics and add a few of their own. For example, they measure the customer's total time online, number of pages viewed, and size of each order, and correlate these in order to continuously streamline the ordering process. Gary and his team understand that customers don't want to hang out online. They want an efficient grocery shopping experience.

The Tesco Direct team takes the customer experience very seriously. They monitor on-time deliveries, accuracy of orders, and customer satisfaction. They also simulate customers' online shopping experiences to proactively monitor the state of the end-to-end customer experience. Gary's team runs shopping scenario robots using a variety of different browsers, Internet Service Providers (ISPs), and dial-in numbers. This constant monitoring of the conditions that customers are facing helps Tesco proactively sort out problems as they occur. For example, Gary reports that one well-intentioned ISP was caching the Tesco site (keeping a local copy in memory and serving it up to customers) so as to speed access. The problem was that it had cached the information including pricing and availability—from one of 200 stores. Since each online customer might be shopping at a different store, this approach aggravated rather than improved customers' experiences.

Gary's team uses simple sanity checks as well. By trial and error, Gary discovered that if any store's orders fall 15 percent below the orders for the same time period on the previous day, there may be a technical problem. He now has a simple alert set to go off whenever that condition occurs.

Sustaining Tesco's Customer Experience

A big part of Tesco's brand image is to be friendly and helpful. It's no wonder that the folks who deliver groceries to Tesco.com customers are often asked to lend a helping hand. Here are some of the most popular requests that Tesco's delivery personnel have received during the last year:

- Borrow your (Tesco) van to help move
- Request for a ride
- Help changing a tire
- Hold my ladder
- Put things in cupboard (for elderly customers)
- Change clock on video OR set video to record
- Help choose wallpaper
- Request for fashion opinion ("Does my bum look big in this?")
- Post a letter
- Change a light bulb
- Answer the phone and give messages
- Unblock a sink
- Take videos/library books back

Some of the more unusual requests made in the last year were:

- Feed a pet while its owners are on holiday
- Join customer for candlelit dinner (after customer was stood up)
- Offer marital advice
- Take a family photo/video
- Give a pregnant customer a lift to hospital (false alarm)
- Babysit
- Witness a will
- Drive customer to a wedding (hired car didn't turn up)

- Call in sick to customer's job
- Drop the kids off at school

Carolyn Bradley, Tesco.com's chief operations officer, commented: "At Tesco we pride ourselves on looking after our customers, but there are limits. We are advising our drivers to be as helpful as they can, but we have to strike a balance without inconveniencing other customers by being late."

From Groceries to One-Stop Shopping

Once a company is successful in building and sustaining customer loyalty through its customer experience—both in store and online—most companies begin to extend their product offerings. Tesco is no exception. Even before the advent of online grocery shopping, Tesco offered its loyalty card, the Tesco Card. Next the grocer offered a credit card. Soon other personal financial services followed. Today you can have a Tesco savings account and checking account with online banking. You can invest in an individual retirement account, locate a mortgage, and buy insurance for your house, car, pet, and your next trip.

In addition to selling groceries from its stores, Tesco Direct continued to offer a line of giftware and housewares both online and via catalog as well as apparel. Next it offered a baby store, with everything that busy moms might need including diapers, formula, baby clothes, and strollers. Then came the online book store, followed quickly by the online music and entertainment store and the consumer electronics store.

From Commerce to Community

Once it had established itself as the most widely used online weekly shopping site in the U.K., Tesco's customers—many of them women—began looking for the one missing ingredient in the Tesco online experience—community. Tesco.com management entered into a joint venture with iVillage, the popular American women's portal site. Together they formed iVillage.co.uk, which will be linked to Tesco.com. iVillage U.K. was set up to function as an independently managed entity to provide women in the U.K. and the Republic of Ireland with an interactive community. Tesco and iVillage plan to provide a combined total of approximately $70 million in marketing, branding, cash, intellectual property, and other resources in support of the venture through online and offline activities. Tesco will provide $18 million in cash over the next three years, online and offline promotional considerations, and expert knowledge of the deepest and broadest customer relationships in the U.K. iVillage will provide the i-village women's brand online, intellectual property, content, online community know-how, and deep understanding of what women want on the Web. iVillage.co.uk will also promote Tesco.com's retail business. Revenue will be derived primarily from advertising and sponsorship.

Results

By September 2000, Tesco.com had 750,000 registered customers and had blanketed 90 percent of the U.K. In other words, 90 percent of the grocery-shopping customers in Britain could avail themselves of Tesco.com. The order run rate had hit 60,000 orders per week with revenues of over £5 million per week. Also, by August 2000 Tesco had delivered its millionth order. There are 14 million active Tesco Clubcard holders. In 2000, Tesco reported record sales and earnings, with an overall increase in U.K. sales of 7.5 percent. Tesco's personal finance business had 1.7 million customers by August 2000 (more customers than Egg!).

Takeaways

Attention to the details of execution is what sets Tesco apart from the pack. From the careful design of the in-store pick and pack system to the careful monitoring of customers' online experiences, the Tesco Direct team keeps its eye on the ball.

It's also interesting to note that, when its e-business group began to gain traction, Tesco management decided to set it up as a separate, unencumbered business unit. Yet despite its relative independence, Tesco.com remains tightly integrated into the in-store operations.

Another important facet of the Tesco story is the fact that customer's order histories are maintained across touchpoints—online store and physical store. This integrated order history gives customers a much better all-around shopping experience. If an item is out of stock by the time the picker gets to the shelf, a more intelligent substitution will be made based on the customer's total purchase history.

Patty's Suggestions for Tesco

As Tesco.com begins to expand beyond the U.K. into other markets in Japan, Thailand, Western Europe, and Eastern Europe, the logistics team will have its work cut out for it. Will the in-store pick, pack, and delivery systems designed for the U.K. stores work in stores in other countries? Obviously, the system will need to be modified and perhaps tailored for other environments and cultures. It is not clear that the online grocery shopping experience will be as popular in other countries as it has become in the United States and the U.K.

We suggest that Tesco.com use the same approach to piloting and testing online sales in other countries that it used in the U.K.: start small with pilot stores and targeted customer sets. Get in-store managers to help in the design of the in-store systems. Link online inventory and pricing directly to the customer's local store. And above all, integrate the offline and online shopping experiences.

Beyond this, however, is the plain desire to make online shopping profitable for the company at the same time it is beneficial and convenient for the customer. Retail grocery is a thin-margin business, and there are only two proven ways to make money—at least in a sustainable manner—in this circumstance: keep costs low and keep volumes high. It turns out that Tesco approach is actually changing the equation slightly, in that it has discovered that higher margins are possible with its online customers. Still, the need to drive down costs is ever-present, and operational excellence is a good place to start. The in-store pick and pack operation is a clear improvement over the warehouse model that has bedeviled other online grocers. And the faster this operation is done, the better for both company and customer. But overall cycle time is also affected by road traffic. Delivery delay due to road traffic probably doesn't matter to most of Tesco customers, because they don't submit an order and then wait around for it, the way they would for pizza or Chinese food. But it matters a great deal to Tesco itself, because the longer a driver is tied up in traffic, the less time he will have to do other things. Consequently, drive and stop time are important metrics for Tesco, as would be fleet uptime and service turnaround.

In-store pick and pack is also affected by inventory. It is true that the picking application knows when and how to substitute an item. It is also true, however, that a substitute is exactly that; it is not the item of choice. It behooves Tesco, then, to work closely with its suppliers and distributors to make sure that its out-of-stock rate is kept as low as possible.

Finally, Tesco must always remember that customers are paying for the convenience of ordering online. That convenience goes away if online ordering becomes a difficult or time-wasting operation. *Server performance* is thus a critical measurement area, and one that the company must keep close tabs on, since it is also affected by traffic, albeit of a different kind. A Tesco Customer Flight Deck would therefore include all these factors, in addition to the Balanced Steering Wheel so central to the company's understanding of its performance.

A Sample Flight Deck for Tesco

	Navigation	Performance	Operations	Environment
Customer Numbers	Number of active Tesco cardholders Number of active online shoppers Number of known customers in each household	Change in number of customers ordering online Change in number of active Tesco cardholders Change in number of customers shopping each week: • online • offline • online and offline	Number of unique visitors to the Web site Percentage of Web visitors who purchased: • once • twice • three or more times Percentage of Tesco cardholders who shop online	Number of households in store area Number of households using online shopping
Customer Retention	Customer retention rate Household retention rate Account penetration	Retention rate by customer segment Customer loyalty rating	Percentage of customers who are active online shoppers Decline in customer activity online and in store	Competitors' offers Comparative retention rate Share of Stomache
Customer Experience	Satisfaction by customer segment Balanced steering Wheel metrics	Satisfaction with online ordering Percentage of items substituted On-time delivery ratio	Performance of end-to-end on-line shopping scenario In-stock percentage: • inventory replenishment rate Drive/stop time Fleet uptime In-store route time	In-store and online buyers' satisfaction Comparative customer satisfaction with other delivery services
Customer Spending	Average revenue per customer Average profitability per customer Customer lifetime value	Average order size Profit per order	Recency/frequency of purchase Cost to serve by touchpoint Customer acquisition cost Customer retention cost	Competitive Stomache share

TIMBUK2 DESIGNS: TAKING MASS CUSTOMIZATION TO THE 'NET

Today's customers want to roll their own. They want to put their personal stamp on the products and services they buy. They prefer products they can tailor to meet their own unique tastes and needs. The answer is mass-customization—produce each customer's product uniquely for that customer.

Timbuk2 Designs is a company that was designed from the ground up to offer mass-customized products. Over the last ten years, Timbuk2 has developed and refined the only mass customization manufacturing system in the U.S. sewn-goods industry. Its manufacturing technology lets the company produce a unique backpack—out of 7 billion possible custom configurations.

Timbuk2 has a fiercely loyal group of quality-conscious customers. These are the bicycle messengers and the urban-cool teenagers and young professionals around the world who use the company's bicycle messenger bags and backpacks. They love the ability to custom-design their own bags. But for the first nine years of its history, Timbuk2 couldn't convince retailers to offer the customization option.

Designing the Best Bag for the Job

In the '80s, Rob Honeycutt was a young man with a bicycling passion. He worked days as a bicycle messenger, and as soon as he saved up enough money he planned to set off on his bike across the country. He was, of course, particular about the loads he carried while bicycling, so he began experimenting with the design of over-the-shoulder bags. By 1989 he had designed and sewn a number of really great messenger bags. He began selling them to friends and colleagues. Soon he was selling through bicycle shops. That's how Timbuk2 Designs came into being.

By 1992 Rob's small business was growing. He was earning $50,000 per year designing and sewing his own bags. Demand was increasing. He knew he needed help. He placed an ad in his local paper in Berkeley, California, looking for some one who knew how to set up and run a small manufacturing company. Brennan Mulligan answered the ad.

Passion for Mass-Customized Manufacturing

Brennan was just finishing college at the University of California in Berkeley. He had a passion for "lean" manufacturing. Manufacturing had been changing since the '70s, when recessions and oil crises had thrown a wrench into mass production. And technology and process-orientation had also had heavy impact on demand for manufactured goods. Brennan was attracted to the Japanese methods of lean production of achieving lower costs at smaller volumes with higher quality. He found a guru in Joseph Pine, author of *Mass Customization—The New Frontier in Business Competition,* who first proposed what he called mass customization—production systems that are designed to produce a number of different, high-quality products via short production runs, low changeover times, and low work-in-process. Brennan Mulligan intended to do just that at Timbuk2.

Brennan learned how to sew messenger bags and studied their design and manufacture. "The critical element to success in the design of a mass customization system," Brennan explained, "is the single-piece flow." Historically in mass production of sewn goods, companies used a progressive bundle system. Each sewing station received a batch of 100 pieces, the seamstress would do the same procedure with each piece, and the completed bundle would be passed to the next workstation for the next step. In a single-piece continuous flow, a team of people makes a single product and then moves onto the next. Rob Honeycutt redesigned the product in 1994 so that it could be customized. Each bag contained three separate pieces that could be different colors, and there were four optional pieces (internal dividers, straps, etc.) and twelve different accessories that could be sewn on.

"Rob, Joanie, the first employee, and I sat in a circle with three sewing machines and a portable phone to take orders and communicate with retailers. For each order that came in, we'd pass the bags around, each one of us doing a piece of the work and then passing the batch onto the next person. We made the batches smaller and smaller—first working on twelve bags at a time, then six, and eventually we were able to do one bag at a time just as fast as we could do a dozen. It took us between '94 and the end of '96 to get single-piece flow and custom color combinations working smoothly. When we first started making the more complex bags, it took 144 minutes per bag. Now it's down to fifteen minutes per bag."

"The retailers loved the custom color combinations we were able to offer," Brennan continued, "Most backpacks were black, navy, and dark green. But bicycle messengers—our core customers—are individualists. We made our bags more fashionable by adding in lots of different color combinations. We also offered custom features and accessories. Each bag could be configured with at least four custom features and four custom accessories, like the ballistic nylon boot that will keep the contents dry even if you set your bag down in a pool of motor oil."

Optimizing the Mass-Customization Process

By 1996 Brennan and Rob had perfected the design of their bags and honed the design of their custom-manufacturing operation. They had set up operations in a 17,000-square-foot loft space in the Mission district of San Francisco. By 1999 there were two manufacturing cells (each with four sewers per shift), one subassembly cell (with four sewers), and a one-person cutting station.

Brennan instituted a "bump back" workflow. As soon as a sewer had completed a bag, she would bump back to the previous machine and take the place of that sewer, who would bump back to the previous station, and so on. Each team of sewers produces complete bags, and each sewer performs every step in the process, throughout the day. There's little boredom and lots of movement. With this set-up, Timbuk2 was able to produce 500 custom-made bags per day. And the manufacturing operation was easy to expand or replicate in another location. Timbuk2 was using American labor in an expensive American city. Its competitors were using offshore, mass-production techniques. (Timbuk2's competitors in the messenger bag market were three similarly sized companies: Manhattan Portage and Yak Pak in the United States, and Ortleib in Europe. The company also competed against much larger, traditional daypack manufacturers, such as Jansport and Eastpak.) Yet despite the real estate and labor costs, Timbuk2 was profitable, and it had very little inventory carrying costs.

Moving Mass-Customized Products through the Retail Channel

Timbuk2 sold its bags to retailers that served its target segments: bicycle, outdoor, travel, action sport, international and private label. These markets are served by large national chains as well as thousands of smaller specialty stores. For its international business, which makes up about 20 percent of revenues, Timbuk2 targets foreign-based bicycle-courier companies and other outlets selling bicycles, motorcycles, and accessories. Timbuk2's private label sales include logo-ed bags for the courier company Kozmo and for companies that use the bags as premiums for employees and customers, such as Powerbar, Motorola, and Birkenstock.

Between 1996 and 1999, Timbuk2's sales grew at 55 percent per year!

Trying to Sell Custom-Designed Products through Retail Channels

By 1999 privately-held Timbuk2 had become the market leader in the messenger bag business and was about to design and offer new product lines such as day packs, backpacks, laptop bags, and adventure travel luggage. But Brennan and Rob had one major problem to solve: They could custom-produce one-off bags, they just couldn't figure out how to sell them. "We tried to encourage retailers to take orders for custom-designed bags," Brennan explained, "We gave them displays and custom order forms, incentives and spiffs, we trained their employees, but the employee turnover in retail is so great, it was a losing battle."

From 1996 through 1999 Timbuk2 had stumbled upon a way to create a buzz around its custom-manufacturing capability. As Brennan described, "We would sign up for a retail trade show and take an entire manufacturing cell to the show. We would make and sell fully custom bags right there on the trade show floor. It was a way of educating the retail buyers about what we could do. They loved it! People would crowd around the booth, order their bag, and watch it being made. They were ecstatic about the experience. Some people actually cried! There's an emotional connection that happens when folks devote time and energy and creativity into making something for you and then you can start using it right away." At first this trade show strategy appeared to be paying off. It created a huge buzz and gave Timbuk2 a much stronger brand presence within the industry segments it served. "Our sales reps were fired up; the retailers were talking about us after the show." But Brennan realized that they weren't getting many orders for custom-designed bags. "We would spend $50,000 on the tradeshow, bring home $45,000 in cash from the sales we made at the show, and get a great buzz," Brennan reported, "But there was no follow-through in the retail stores." The strategy just wasn't working.

The Internet Epiphany Strikes

In August 1998 Brennan was on his way to an Outdoor Retailers' Trade Show in Salt Lake City. On the long hot drive from San Francisco to Salt Lake City he thought about his dilemma. He had spent five years perfecting his lean manufacturing operation so that he could cost-effectively produce a custom-designed backpack every fifteen minutes. His competitors had all moved their manufacturing operations offshore to cut costs. In other words, they were still engaged in mass production with traditional six-month product design cycles. He was beating his competitions' manufacturing costs, and he could deliver a brand new design in minutes. But the retailers couldn't train their employees to sell the custom-designed products. They kept ordering and selling the same "standard model" bags. That didn't allow Timbuk2 to differentiate itself in the market, to gain higher margins, or to establish relationships with end customers. Stewing about this seemingly intractable business predicament, Brennan had a thought: "What about the 'Net?" He grabbed his cell phone and called his friend, Dave, who worked for Excite. Dave told him about the dozens of companies that let customers custom-configure products on the Web. As they talked, Brennan became more and more excited. By the time he pulled into Salt Lake City, he was psyched about this new business direction. "We need to change how we're doing business and go direct to customers over the 'Net."

"I arrived at 8 A.M.," Brennan recalled. "Rob met me at the trade show. We began setting up our booth and our manufacturing cell in this huge tent. Then we went off to grab some lunch. When we got back to the truck it had started to hail like crazy. All of a sudden we realized, there's a tornado coming right toward us, and it's enormous! We dove under the truck and held onto the wheels."

Brennan remembers wrapping his arms around the truck's tires, girding himself for the force of the wind as he peered under the body of the truck. He watched the tornado cut through the tent and saw his industrial sewing machines circling above him in the sky. "What if the whole truck lifts off the ground and falls back on top of us," he wondered in an eerie moment of lucid thought. Suddenly, the force of the gale was upon them. The truck shuddered and rose about six inches, then it settled back on the ground.

As the tornado continued its destructive progress across the Utah landscape, Brennan and Rob climbed out from under the truck, hugged each other, and rushed off to see how the others had fared. The tent was gone and so were their exhibit booths. Brennan saw bits and pieces of his sewing machines and Timbuk2–logo-ed booth littering the field. "That tornado was the wake-up call I needed," Brennan reported. He remembers thinking, "Never again! No more retail trade shows! I can't convince retailers to sell our custom-designed backpacks in their stores anyway. They can't handle one-off products. We'll go direct to the customer and do it on the Internet. Customers can design their own backpacks, we'll ship them out the next day, and if the retailers want to participate, we'll set up shop on their Web sites, too!" The tornado was the near-death experience he needed to convince him he was on the right track.

Rob and Brennan wrote off the $150,000 worth of lost equipment, met the sewers at the airport, and drove everyone back home. That was the beginning of Timbuk2's "Build Your Own Bag" e-commerce strategy.

Letting Customers Design Their Own Bags

Timbuk2 had had a brochure-ware Web site since 1997. They'd only spent about $5,000 on it. When they returned from Salt Lake City, Brennan and Rob hired a local Web design team and began a phased approach to design and test an application that would let their customers custom-design their own bags. The first test drive was a simple picture of a Timbuk2 bag with a set of colors that you could select to see how the bag would look in different color combinations. There was no online ordering function; they did no advertising or promotion.

They just sat back and watched what happened, and this is what they found. Between April 1999 and October 1999, the number of unique visitors who found their way to the Timbuk2 Web site grew from 3,500 per month to 5,500 per month. About half of those visitors used the mock configurator. More than two-thirds of those clicked on the order page, where they were told that the company doesn't sell direct to consumers. Of course, many people emailed the company or called, complaining that they couldn't actually order online. Jordan Riess, Timbuk2's Vice President, had taken this cautious approach to test the waters for two reasons. First, he didn't want to build a full-blown e-commerce capability until he knew he had the money to build the site correctly. Second, he didn't want to alienate Timbuk2's retailers.

The second test—to let customers custom configure and order a bag—Timbuk2 chose to do at a non-affiliated site, in other words, one that its current retail channel partners were not likely to wander on to. Starting in January 1999, Timbuk2, working in conjunction with a small etailer, let customers configure a bag and order it online. It wasn't a completely automated process. Once the order was placed, it would be emailed to Timbuk2 to be manufactured and fulfilled. But it was a great way to test the waters. Again, this was a very basic configurator. It simply let customers select the bag size and the colors they wanted although without any visual representation of the product. But the orders grew by 350 percent from January 1999 to December 1999 without any promotion.

They also ran a test to see whether customers were simply interested in ordering the bags online or whether they valued the customization capability. For four months Timbuk2 ran a parallel test pilot with several other online Web sites. But this time it didn't offer the customization capability, just the ability to order the bag online. They found that, although the other Web sites had higher overall traffic, there were 75 percent fewer orders placed. And on the site that let customers customize their bags, the average price that customers were willing to pay was 20 percent higher.

It was clearly time to move ahead.

In May 2000, Timbuk2 Designs quietly launched its "Build Your Own Bag" (BYOB) configurator. This was still a beta-version of the configurator, but you could use it to design, buy, and receive a bag. Customers interested in trying out the early BYOB configuration had to apply for and wait to receive a password via email. They also had to have Shockwave running on their PC or be willing to download it. Once a prospective customer had jumped those hurdles, he could select all the options and, through animation, see the bag come to life before his eyes! Customers flocked to the site. They told their friends. Here are some of their comments:

> "Just wanted to let you know how happy I am with my new Timbuk2 bag and the whole buying experience. You guys made it so easy and your bag builder software rocks! . . . All my friends are digging my new bag and are planning on ordering their own."

> "Not to knock any retailer, but do you know how much of a pain it is to find the bag you want in the colors and size you're looking for? And (being a child spoiled by the Internet), who the heck wants to fill out actual paper to special-order anything these days?"

> "I thought it would be cool to create a bag to my specs and not be forced to buy something someone else determined I needed. Thank you for providing a quality product at a reasonable price."

Evolving the Functionality

In mid-October Timbuk2 launched the production version of its BYOB application. There were two versions—one with Shockwave animation and another simpler one without dynamic animation features. Those customers who didn't want to bother loading Shockwave or who didn't need to see the color combinations and accessories built in front of them could use the simpler, drop-down menu version.

This version also included complete e-commerce functionality, including the ability for customers to track the progress of their bag through manufacturing, packing, shipping, and delivery.

Building Relationships with Customers

From the time they began piloting the Build Your Own Bag module, the Timbuk2 team were gratified by the intense interactions they suddenly had with customers. "Before, we rarely received direct customer feedback," Jordan Reiss exclaimed. "All of a sudden we began getting comments on our products and the online shopping experience as well as suggestions for new products. It was great! In the past, the retailer had always been a buffer between us and our customers."

By mid-2000, Timbuk2 had the beginnings of its first customer relationship management system—customer profiles for 15,000 customers, order histories, and email interactions and feedback.

Keeping Retailers Happy

How did Timbuk2's retailers react? Were they concerned about channel conflict? "We had very little pushback," Jordan recalled. "We were surprised." The owner of one small chain of bicycle shops complained. Customers began coming into his store, checking out the bags, and then saying that they were going to go home and order their own custom-made bags online. Jordan reminded him that Timbuk2 was not pricing below retail and that if his customers wanted to special-order custom-designed bags, he could do that in his store and keep the sale.

In fact, Timbuk2 experimented with online sales in the store. A retailer in Santa Cruz brought a laptop into his store and let customers design their own bags. His orders increased threefold! Jordan began explaining to retailers that if they'd put a computer in their stores and let customers custom-configure their bags, they would increase sales dramatically. At the same time, he was working on the design of in-store kiosks that Timbuk2 could offer to its retailers.

Online retailers quickly arranged to link Timbuk2's site to theirs. Jordan was kept busy doing referral and commission deals with all these etailers. Clicks-and-bricks retailers were also enthusiastic. For example, one of Timbuk2's biggest retailers was happy to put a "Build Your Own Bag" button in the Timbuk2 section of its e-commerce site. When its customers clicked on the button, a co-branded window would open up. The customer could configure her bag, special-ordering it direct from Timbuk2, and then return to filling her shopping cart at the retailer's site. The retailer received a percentage of all of these referral sales.

Results

During the beta-testing phase, Timbuk2 was receiving orders at a rate of ten bags per day. Once the full function version of the configurator went live on the site, orders shot to forty bags per day within the first week, 10 percent of its then manufacturing capacity. As the year 2000 drew to a close, there were more than a dozen e-tailers offering Timbuk2's Build Your Own Bag module from their Web sites. Twenty percent of Timbuk2's orders were for one-off bags, and that percentage was on the rise as the company's total order volume continued to grow. The company had found a way to let customers take advantage of its custom manufacturing capability.

Takeaways

To offer true custom-manufacturing you need to design a manufacturing operation that's built from scratch to enable the production of lots of different items. That's exactly what Brennan Mulligan did at Timbuk2. Yet when he realized that customers couldn't take advantage of the mass-customization efficiencies, Brennan didn't give up. He held onto his vision and persevered.

Notice how slowly and carefully Timbuk2 rolled out its strategy. Part of that speed had to do with the fact that the company was funding its e-commerce initiative out of operating profits rather than venture capital money. It wasn't until the fall 2000 that Timbuk2 succeeded in gaining the investment capital that allowed the company to accelerate the development of its e-commerce capability.

Timbuk2 probably trod more cautiously than it needed to in dealing with retailers. Online retailers were delighted to be able to snap Timbuk2's custom-ordering and design module directly into their Web stores. Manufacturers that offer customers and retailers special capabilities like custom-designed products are unlikely to meet resistance from their distribution partners. After all, they're offering a capability that customers value.

Patty's Suggestions for Timbuk2

I'd like to see Timbuk2 take a more aggressive stance in selling its custom-designed bags on other retailers' Web sites. The company also needs to develop the tools required for its orders to link seamlessly into those of its online retailers. Customers won't be happy placing two separate orders with two separate bill-to/ship-to transactions and two separate ways to track their orders. This needs to be tightly integrated into the retailers' systems so that customers can configure their bag in the Timbuk2 virtual aisle of the retailer's Web site but place a single order with the retailer and be able to track the progress of the manufacturing and shipment process through the retailer. This is the seamless, integrated process that Timbuk2 and its online retailing partners are planning for. But it wasn't possible to get it finished and integrated before the 2000 holiday shopping season.

Second, for the in-store experience Timbuk2 needs to work with its retailers to offer them a complete package of robust in-store Web kiosks they can use to place their Timbuk2 orders. Some retailers may want to use the same kiosk for customers ordering other products they don't happen to have in stock. Other retailers may be content to make this a Timbuk2-only kiosk. The development, roll-out, and maintenance of these kiosks will be expensive and tricky. I recommend that Timbuk2 also pursue the less-elaborate route that it has already been piloting: suggest that retailers keep a laptop in the store that customers can use to custom-configure their own bags. The retailers can use the laptop for other purposes. And it wouldn't be something that Timbuk2 would need to get involved in maintaining. For many of the smaller retailers that Timbuk2 sells through, this low-tech approach would be ideal.

Finally, I am looking forward to the next product line—laptop bags and general-purpose day packs and backpacks. I want to be able to configure my own stylish laptop carrying case or backpack with my own colors and pocket preferences. I'd also like to be able to put my own company or personal logo on the bag instead of the Timbuk2 logo. The customer scenario I'd like Timbuk2 to support is to let me start my bag configuration session by selecting the make and model of my laptop from a drop-down list and having Timbuk2 automatically fill in the dimensions required for that particular laptop.

Naturally, all of this requires Timbuk2 to focus ever more closely on something it's proved it knows how to do: drive down the manufacture time and cost of each bag. In fact, its ability to do this is one reason it has been able to succeed in an area—mass customization—where so many others have failed.

The company therefore needs to watch its manufacturing process: *time, steps, error rate,* and the like. All of these can rise, perhaps dramatically, for each new configuration variable introduced.

A Sample Flight Deck for Timbuk2 Designs

	Navigation	Performance	Operations	Environment
Customer Numbers	Number of active known customers Number of online customers Number of referred customers Number of customers who referred others	Number of new registered Web site users Number of customers who placed Web orders Number of known customers from each retailer	Number of unique visitors to the Web site Percentage of Web visitors who configured a bag Percentage of people that configured a bag who bought a bag	Number of bicycle messengers per region Number of "urban cool" prospects and students in region Total number of bags sold by type (messenger, laptop, day pack)
Customer Retention	Customer retention rate Rate of repeat orders	Retention rate by customer segment Rate of repeat orders by customer segment	Number of bags owned per customer Number of bags bought per customer per year	Competitors' offers Comparative retention rate Share of backpacks
Customer Experience	Satisfaction by customer segment Customer perception of value Return rates	Availability of custom-configuration capability Satisfaction with online configuration and ordering On-time delivery ratios Number of customer support requests per channel and touchpoint Return rates by channel and touchpoint	Performance of end-to-end online configuration scenario Number of configuration variables Percentage of returns due to customer configuration error Percentage of returns due to manufacturing error	Comparative customer satisfaction Comparative manufacturing time Comparative defect rate
Customer Spending	Revenue per end-customer Profit per end-customer Total sales of custom bags	Average order size Profit per order Sales through online channel partners Sales through in-store retailers Profit per order by channel Size of order by channel	Recency/frequency of purchase by end-customers Cost to serve by channel partner and touchpoint	Competitive backpack share

HONE OPERATIONAL EXCELLENCE: OBSERVATIONS ABOUT THE CASE STUDIES

I was truly amazed when Gary Sargeant walked me through Tesco's in-store pick and pack system. The attention to detail was astounding. Not only was the process nicely automated, with the pick lists organized for the most efficient routing through the store, but the additional attention to operational details impressed me. The in-store routing is optimized to avoid high-traffic areas. The timing of the pick and pack operation is designed to keep groceries from sitting; they're loaded right into the vans and delivered within an hour or two. And the fact that substitutions are made based on a customer's past buying behaviors is impressive. Some industry pundits believe that the business model of picking and packing in the stores will break down, in part because in-store customers will be annoyed by the pickers in their way. We see it differently. Each time you're in the store shopping, you see the Tesco.com crew and you wonder why you're wasting your own precious time when for £5 someone else could be doing this more efficiently and quickly than you could. It's a great example of using operational excellence to promote the branded experience. Notice too, that Tesco's operational efficiency doesn't have a sterile, robotic feel to it. These are real people who make selections for you and real people who deliver your groceries and point out any substitutions they've made; real people that customers often rely on to help with other day-to-day tasks, from changing a light bulb to holding a baby still on the changing table!

Tesco is a great example of a company that has seamlessly integrated its physical and its online operations, taking advantage of the strengths of each. The key to Tesco's excellence in execution is both its attention to the details that matter to customers and its corporate culture and passionate commitment to measure and monitor everything that impacts customers.

Timbuk2's operational excellence comes from a similar passion, in this case Rob Honeycutt's and Brennan Mulligan's passion to hone the custom manufacturing process. To take advantage of its custom manufacturing capability, Rob has redesigned his products to be optimally configurable and manufacturable. This is something we hear over and over again as more companies begin to let customers custom-configure their own products. For this to work, not only does the manufacturing process have to be designed to support it, the products need to be designed so that customers can't make a mistake.

Issues to Master for Operational Excellence

In summary, here are some of the issues you'll want to be sure that you're tracking and executing on:

1. Design your back-end processes first.
2. Ensure that there are no black holes, that is, no points in the process you can't see into and make changes.
3. Instrument and proactively monitor performance of all key services.
4. Take responsibility for the end-to-end experience from the customer's home, office, or other touchpoint through the entire supply/value chain.
5. Monitor and manage every element that impacts customers, shortens cycle time, and improves your costs to serve.

14

THE SIXTH STEP: VALUE CUSTOMERS' TIME

DESIGN AND REFINE CUSTOMER SCENARIOS

What frustrates customers the most? When you waste their time! Although most businesses are well-intentioned when it comes to valuing their customers' time, they're not fanatically focused on it. That's the difference between a company that will thrive in the customer economy and one that's just getting by or losing ground.

There are a number of elements that companies that are serious about their customers' time focus on. They are:

- Streamline decision-making
- Offer ubiquitous, convenient access
- Design using customer scenarios

The first two are reasonably well-understood. The third remains a mystery to most. We'll focus most of our discussion and examples on customer scenarios. But first a word about customer decision-making.

Streamline Decision-Making

Most businesses now offer customers a lot of information about their products and services. Very few companies organize that information in such a way that it's really easy for customers to make decisions. Here are some of the basic requirements that most companies neglect.

- Offer multiple types of searching (by key words, by specifications, by categories, by function).
- Offer decision-making tools (which of these will solve my problem?).
- Offer side-by-side product comparisons.
- Offer photographs or illustrations.
- Specify price, availability, and arrival time (when will it reach the destination?).
- Provide access to trouble-shooting and installation information before the sale (so the customer can find out what issues others have had).

Offer Convenient, Ubiquitous Access

We live in a world of mobile devices and mobile people. Don't waste customers' time by offering them only one or two modes of interaction. Make sure that they can get the information they need and transact business with you twenty-four hours a day from virtually any device they choose to use.

DESIGN USING CUSTOMER SCENARIOS

As we've watched companies struggle to streamline their customer-facing business processes, we've found that the biggest impediment to success is that most design teams don't know how to put themselves in their customers' shoes. They think about the workflows they offer customers as ways to "help the customer buy something" or "make appropriate offers" or "personalize their experiences." Customers may prefer the personal touch, but what they really require are streamlined processes that are designed to help them accomplish the tasks they need to get done. We call these "customer scenarios."

What's a Customer Scenario and Why Is It Important?

A customer scenario is comprised of a set of tasks that a customer wants to or is willing to do to achieve a desired outcome. A customer scenario starts with a customer's need, includes an interaction with your business, and ends with the customer's goal achieved. The better you understand the scenario, the better the customer experience will be.

Examples of consumer customer scenarios are paying the household bills, replacing a worn-out refrigerator, selecting and buying a car, and applying for and getting a mortgage.

Examples of business customer scenarios are booking travel for a business trip, researching and procuring a new phone system for your business, locating and procuring the parts for a new product you're about to manufacture, and designing the electrical system for a new building. Each involves a very different set of tasks, information, and results.

Within these scenarios are steps, or tasks, that bring the customer to you. "Replacing my refrigerator" is a scenario that drives me to BestBuy to look at appliances. Knowing about the latest appliances is not a basic need; keeping my ice cream frozen is the need. For BestBuy, there is a world of difference between a customer buying appliances for a new house that is under construction and a customer whose frozen desserts are turning to mush. One customer is a candidate for a truckload of gadgets sometime next month, and the other needs whatever's available right now. Many customer scenarios don't involve selecting and buying a product but rather some other business need, such as getting advice, checking on the status of a delivery, or coordinating a project. Your goal is to understand who these end customers are and what they're trying to do and to help them do their jobs.

Even the most basic customer scenarios can get pretty complicated. The companies that excel in providing a great total customer experience are those that excel in understanding and focusing on customer scenarios. What are the tasks that customers are trying to perform? What steps do they need to take? How can we move them quickly and painlessly through each of the required steps?

Let's take a look at a concrete example of a company that has been using customer scenarios successfully for several years: National Semiconductor.

NATIONAL SEMICONDUCTOR: USING CUSTOMER SCENARIOS TO SAVE CUSTOMERS' TIME AND CEMENT LOYALTY

National Semiconductor is a relatively conservative high tech company. With $2.4 billion in revenues and 10,500 employees, it does not have the sex appeal or the high P/E multiples of Intel. Yet in its own quiet way, National Semiconductor has been leading a revolution—a revolution for the hearts and minds of its customers and a revolution from PCs to information appliances and mobile wireless devices. National made its reputation as the world's leader in analog chips. It is the industry leader in the amplifiers, regulators, and wireless components that are embedded in virtually every one of the world's mobile phones. It also has a growing share of the market for DVD players and set-top boxes as well as digital cameras. Think sound and image, and you'll be on the right track.

National Semiconductor is also becoming known for its innovative e-business initiatives, all of which are designed to save customers' time. Starting in 1994, Phil Gibson, National's Vice President of Web Business, launched a Web site targeting design engineers, the key influencers in the decision about which integrated circuits to use in the design of a mass-produced device like a mobile phone. Over time Phil and his team extended the capabilities of the site to offer tools for National's distributors, purchasing agents at customers' sites, and National's direct sales execs and their key accounts.

National Semiconductor has built deep customer relationships with three distinct sets of target customers: those who influence the purchase of its products (e.g., design engineers); those who actually do the purchasing, (e.g., purchasing agents); and the distributors through whom purchasers procure not just National parts but the complete bills of materials they need for each product they're going to manufacture. The most valuable part of National's customer franchise, in our opinion, is the deep relationships that National has built, primarily through its Web-based tools, with the design engineers at the front end of the product selection process.

Today half of the world's design engineers visit National's Web site at least once a month. Fifty-eight percent of the traffic on the site is international. Customers download 400,000 data sheets per month, place

21,000 orders per month, use seven different search tools, interact in ten different languages, and (42,000 of them) subscribe to semi-weekly technical newsletters. In addition, National's distributors receive 48,000 Web referrals per month from customers who are not only qualified but have already selected the products they want to buy.

Pioneering with Customer Scenarios

Phil Gibson's team at National Semiconductor was one of the first to use a customer-scenario methodology for strategic advantage. These scenarios focused on making it easy for customers to decide which chips to test, to download data sheets, to run software simulations, and to order samples. In 1999, National launched its first truly ambitious customer scenario: a series of tools that enabled engineers to design power supplies for the products they were building. Version 1.0 of National's WEBENCH design tool was the centerpiece of a new purpose-built Web site targeted at design engineers who needed to get a power supply designed but were not, themselves, one of the rare breed of power supply design experts. They are designers of mobile devices, and the last piece of the design that they need to finish (and the part they care least about) is the power supply module. The outcome they want is a completed design that works for a particular application (e.g., a battery monitoring application) in a particular context (e.g., a mobile phone).

These designers are typically pressed for time and are not particularly interested in running expensive software on expensive and difficult-to-maintain technical systems in their own shops. Yet to do this kind of design without software simulation takes three months. They usually only have three days to get the simulation done.

The First Power Design Scenario: WEBENCH 1.0

Early on in this project, Phil created a SWAT team to drive the power supply design scenario. This team, made up of specialists in marketing, applications, and software design met with customers and learned which tasks they needed to do to design a power supply. Richard Levin, Phil's manager of community applications development, captured the tasks that engineers said they needed to do:

1. Select a part.
2. Create a design.
3. Analyze the design using powerful simulation tools.
4. Build the design (into a prototype for testing).

Therefore that was exactly the way that Phil's team built the online power design scenario, providing all the necessary tools on National's Web site so customers wouldn't need to run any special software or buy special systems.

Here's how it works: The engineer walks through the steps of the design scenario, in which he or she is prompted to specify parameters and to identify the key components necessary. A list of appropriate products is generated along with complete technical specifications, pricing, and a cost/benefit analysis for the various suggested parts.

The designer can then select from among a number of proposed sample designs, which he can manipulate to his satisfaction.

When he's satisfied with the design, he can run a real-time simulation. This part of the process takes highly specialized software. National's power product line found the best of breed tool that engineers preferred—a software application from Transim. National licensed the application and Rich's developers ported it to run as an application service from National's Web site. An engineer can run and save multiple simulations. He can even email links to his colleagues to try them out. All of the designs and simulations he has ever created on National's site are saved for him in his own private designs portfolio.

When the National Semi team first rolled out this Web-based simulation tool, they knew that it would be popular among engineers because it would save them so much time. The company decided to charge engineers for the use of the tool as a way to recoup the costs of licensing the software from Transim. Phil's marketing specialist on the team, Jeff Perry, discovered almost immediately that engineers came to the Web site and got as far into the process as the point at which they'd need to enter their credit card numbers to use the tool, then backed out. Based on that observation, Phil and management switched gears and made the simulation tool available for free. Immediately engineers began using it. What's more, they placed orders! Instead of nickel and diming his customers on the use of the design simulator, Phil opted to hold out for the larger rewards down the line: design wins for National parts.

Once an engineer has a design she likes, she needs a bill of materials. The application provides a complete bill of materials including National Semiconductor parts and parts from other manufacturers as well as the links to the distributors who carry each part and the distributor's current price for each part. Further, because National's Web site is already linked directly to the inventory and list prices for each of the distributors who stocks parts for the small quantity orders that are needed for these design prototypes, the application provides one-button ordering direct from the distributors.

Customers' Reactions

National's customers loved this scenario. They used it to design more than 20,000 power supplies in the first year. One customer iterated his design 250 times! Others averaged five to ten iterations and simulations. Customers are able to accomplish in a few hours what it would have taken months to do before. And they now have time to explore alternatives—time they would never have taken before. As one customer, Martin Volk from Motorola's Cellular Systems Division, said, "Using these tools, I can go from an idea to a working prototype in a few clicks. National has thought of everything I need—from a huge catalog of parts to fast simulations."

Upping the Ante with Customer Scenarios

Of course, with this kind of customer reaction, Phil's team couldn't just sit on their laurels. They asked customers what they wanted next. They heard two different answers.

THERMAL SIMULATION

The first thing that customers wanted was to be able to do thermal simulations of the complete design. When you design a cell phone with a lot of circuits in it, for example, it's important to know how hot the device will become as these circuits interact with one another. Today's testing method is typically the "thumb test." If you can hold your thumb on the prototype for five seconds without getting burned, you know you have a pretty good design. A more sophisticated method is to build the prototype and take a digital image of it using special heat-sensing film. This will give you an approximate idea of where the "hot spots" in the design are. There are also thermal software simulations that run on very large, number-crunching computers. However, most companies don't have access to these in-house.

Again, Phil Gibson and team went looking. They asked their customers which company had the best thermal simulation software in the business. The answer was U.K.-based Flomerics Corporation, a leader in the field of virtual prototyping. This time, Jeff Perry successfully arranged to license Flomerics' thermal simulation software and loaded its database with lots of National Semiconductor proprietary data. Now engineers can use the new tool, called WebTHERM, from National's Web site. This is a sophisticated process that lets design engineers adjust airflow parameters while optimizing heat dissipation and electrical performance—capabilities that have never been possible before online. Unlike the simpler power-supply simulation, this one consists of 5 million calculations and takes a while to run. But you can launch it from the Web site and continue working on something else while it runs your simulation. The result that WebTHERM produces is a very accurate thermal picture a minute or two later. In fact, the thermal simulation is proving to be more accurate than engineers can get by building a prototype and taking a thermal photograph of the running board to see which areas are heating up.

DESIGN A WIRELESS PHONE

Why only enable design of the power management system for a wireless device, customers asked. Now that many of the components of a wireless phone are becoming more standardized, why not let customers design more of the phone's circuitry online?

This request resulted in a new Web site with its own scenarios for engineers who design wireless devices. This scenario works in much the same way as the power supply design. It begins when the designer selects one of the most basic components in any wireless phone—parts that National Semiconductor supplies for 90 percent of the world's cell phones: Phase Lock Loops and Voltage Controlled Oscillators. The engineer proceeds to select from a series of proposed designs, which he can then alter. He can simulate the resulting design, test its thermal properties using the WebTHERM simulation, and get a bill of materials or order a reference design—a prototype built for him by National Semiconductor or its distribution partners.

Measuring the Right Stuff

Phil Gibson has been zealous about measuring what matters to customers since he began his group's efforts in 1994. He began by watching the click-stream traffic on the site and analyzing the patterns. As soon as he could tell what customers were trying to do (e.g., select a product and download data sheets), he would concentrate on eliminating all unnecessary clicks. Within six months, engineers who used to need five clicks to accomplish their outcomes were down to two clicks.

Phil has continued to measure and monitor what matters to his customers. Every morning, he gets a list of the top 200 search terms used by customers the day before and what results were yielded. He looks through the list carefully to see what changes need to be made to the site that day to make it easier for customers to find what they're seeking. He's also gained an additional bonus from this practice. As soon as customers start searching his site for a competitor's part (often looking for a National Semiconductor equivalent), he catches it on the first day. He always knows what's on his customers' radar.

National Semiconductor is one of many companies that monitors the end-to-end performance on the customer scenarios it offers, using Keynote third-party services to monitor performance of its Web tools from locations around the globe.

As for customer value, Phil's team measures and monitors the number of design simulations customers do. Phil calls these "buying signals." By being involved at the front end of the design process, National is better able to predict which devices it will need to manufacture in quantity.

Results

National Semiconductor has very tangible results to report from its Web-based design efforts to date. First let's look at National's customer franchise. Fifty-five percent of National's business is direct sales to 1,000 large accounts. National has 16,000 profiled individuals at these accounts (about 16 people per company). The remaining 45 percent of the business goes through National's worldwide distribution channel. This consists of 100,000 companies, for which National has 213,000 profiled customers (2.1 per account). What's even more important than the fact that this product-centric company actually knows who its 101,000 accounts and 229,000 individual customers are is the fact that it has built pretty deep relationships with most of them. In addition, there are 521,000 additional anonymous visitors per month who use National's Web site on a regular basis. This is out of a total world population of 1.2 million design engineers.

National's business is currently growing 30 percent a year in revenues with 25 percent profits before taxes. This trend is likely to continue given the company's brand leadership, mindshare, and marketshare in the wireless market. National gets early design wins from the key players: Motorola, Nokia, and Ericsson. And its value add is increasing from $2 per phone to $20 per phone as the circuitry for these devices becomes more and more integrated.

This is the importance of the customer scenarios and design tools that National offers on the Web. If customers, using these tools, commit to National's circuitry early in their design cycle, it is highly unlikely that they'll take the time to switch suppliers in mid-design.

And the tangible results that National delivers to its customers? Based on more than eighteen months of experience to date, National knows that it has saved its customers an average of forty-three hours per design for an average savings of $2,580. In the first year these tools were offered, customers did 20,800 designs for a total customer savings of more than $53 million. More important than the dollars saved, of course, were the time savings and the design efficiencies for customers. Customers are now able to do hundreds of iterations of each design in the time it used to take for them to finalize a single design.

By fall 2000 when National rolled out its WebTHERM and Wireless Phone design tools, National's Web site was seeing 31,000 unique visitors per day with 3,000 orders (for sample parts or referrals to distributors for parts) per day. While this may translate to small dollars per day of actual sample parts orders on the site (a big day would be $26,000 worth of sample parts), each early design win will translate into millions of dollars. As Phil points out, "one integrated socket win with Nokia translates into 40 million units for us of at least $3 each."

Takeaways

Whenever we try to explain the concept of customer scenarios to people, we find ourselves using Phil Gibson's work at National Semiconductor. What Phil and his team have done is to put themselves in their customers' shoes and figure out how they can save them time in the most valuable parts of their jobs. This of course begins to make National an indispensable partner for its customers. They make suggestions for the next set of innovations they'd like to see, and Phil's team implements them. The customers feel invested. They definitely have a strong connection with the branded experience National wants them to have.

Notice too, that these customer scenarios are getting more elaborate. What started as a set of relatively simple tools to help customers accomplish the tasks en route to their outcomes morphed into a more elaborate and complex set of tools. National has become an application services provider, offering Web-hosted applications to its customers for free.

In the past we've talked about stickiness and lock-ins, but we now know that, in the throes of the customer revolution, we don't get to lock customers in anymore. National uses a different technique: seduction. By seducing its customers into designing their products on its Web site, National saves them time and makes it highly unlikely that they'll squander the time they saved by going elsewhere to check out alternatives.

Patty's Suggestions for National Semiconductor

I'd like to see Phil do a better job of correlating the design wins and design seduction that takes place on National's Web site with the eventual revenues and profits the company gains. Right now there's no easy way to close the loop. The design engineers who do the preliminary designs don't place the production orders. In fact, these orders are increasingly placed by third-party outsourced manufacturers such as Solectron. If Solectron is manufacturing mobile phones for Nokia, National Semiconductor probably won't know that. A Nokia engineer does some design work on the Web site in June, and an order for 20 million components may arrive from Solectron in October. Since there's no direct connection, it's hard for the Phil's team to see the extent to which they're influencing the bottom line.

But given Phil's passion for measurement, I suspect he can figure out a way to begin to close the loop so that National's product-driven management and culture will appreciate the pay-offs the company is reaping from its e-business design efforts. As a start, I'd like to suggest a few things he can include in the National's Customer Flight Deck.

First would be an analysis of the importance of a given scenario to a user's job function or project, which the user can indicate with a simple check box or radio button right at the beginning of a simulation. The hard part would be determining just how good the scenario-based design tool was. That goodness can be measured by how much money the user saved by taking advantage of National's Web tools. This could be real savings, because the tool is free, whereas other simulation mechanisms cost money. And it could include the cost of the engineer's (and everyone else's) time, both during the simulation and in the design and build processes that follow.

Down the road, there are also savings of time and money thanks to optimized designs and reduced time-to-market. Thus, National's Flight Deck could begin with something like you'll find on page 292.

Observations from the National Semiconductor Case Study

Notice that Phil Gibson's team constantly takes its cues from its target customers. What are the things that design engineers need to do in their jobs that involve National's core competencies? Note too, that customers have been very involved in specifying these detailed design scenarios and in testing them out. Also notice that Phil's team offers every step the customer needs to do, including the cost/benefit analysis, run the design simulation, prepare a bill of materials, order the parts, and test the design. And what's most impressive—if the customer needs access to non-National parts, not only does National provide that information, it links the customer directly to the distributors that have those parts in stock.

A Sample Flight Deck for National Semiconductor

	Navigation	Performance	Operations	Environment
Customer Numbers	Number of active known customers in each customer segment Number of Web site subscribers in each customer segment Number of online customers using simulations in each segment	Number of profiled customers in each account Number of new registered Web site users Number of online customers saving simulations Number of completed designs from simulations Number of shared designs	Number of unique visitors to the Web site Number of online customers not completing simulations Number of monthly data sheet downloads per customer Number of monthly sample parts ordered per customer	Total number of design engineers Number of customers using other simulation tools
Customer Retention	Customer retention (by individual and account) • Rate of repeat simulations • Rate of repeat orders	Increase in number of completed scenarios by account and by customer Increase in number of designs by account and by customer Number of visits to the community	Percentage of returning customers using new scenarios Percentage of customers using multiple scenarios	Competitors' offers Comparative customer retention Win/loss ratios
Customer Experience	Customer satisfaction by segment, design community, and distributor Number of scenarios available	Increase in number of completed scenarios by account and by customer Increase in number of designs by account and by customer Importance of scenarios Satisfaction with: • samples • simulations • ordering process • delivery	Number of clicks to complete each task or scenario Percentage of "back" clicks during search Percentage of input terms not matching search engine keywords Accuracy of search returns Performance of end-to-end scenarios	Comparative customer satisfaction
Customer Spending	Revenue and profit per end-customer Revenue and profit per account Downstream value of design wins	Average design wins per use of simulation Average revenue and profit per design win by customer segment	Actual orders placed linked to simulations Repeat orders linked to simulations and design wins	Designs won by competitors Comparative average value of design wins

Customer Scenario Design Is a Business Function

Customer scenario design is a critical skill that your business team needs to learn if you're going to be successful in the customer economy. Customer scenario design is a business function. You want to ensure that you make it as easy as possible for customers to transact business with you. Don't leave this critical design function up to the developers or the user interface specialists. They won't get it right. Only the customers themselves, and the subject-matter experts who can walk in your customers' shoes, really understand how customers think about achieving their outcomes.

How to Do Customer Scenario Design

We've been doing customer scenario design for ten years now, before e-business came into vogue. While others were doing business process design, we were designing from the end customer's point of view. As businesses evolved into e-businesses and back again into multi-touchpoint, multi-channel businesses, we've refined this technique.

How can your team get really good at designing customer scenarios? We recommend that you start by doing a few scenarios, then get your customers to do their own scenarios, and then refine your designs based on the customer input and priorities. From those scenarios you can quickly derive prototypes, workflows, and IT architecture. We've been leading our clients through Customer Scenario℠ mapping sessions for ten years. Like most powerful ideas, it's elegantly simple. The art form lies with the subtleties and, of course, the execution.

Here are the basic steps:

- Select a target customer set. Be as explicit as possible (e.g., working mom with preschool kids, business traveler with a corporate travel agent, building contractor who builds housing developments).

- Select an end-to-end scenario that the customer needs to perform (e.g., plan meals for the week, get the shopping done and the items put away; change travel itineraries in the middle of a trip; provide a customizable bill of materials from which end customers can pick and choose, such as plumbing fixtures, lighting fixtures, carpeting, or appliances).

- Decide on a context (e.g., harried mom at the end of a busy day, business traveler staying in a hotel overnight, contractor wanting one-stop pick-up of supplies).

- Determine a start point and an end point. The end point represents what the customer considers to be successful achievement of her goal.

- Map out each scenario with all of the what-ifs you can think of. Walk through each step.

- Capture the customer profile information needed to perform the scenario (and at the times when it makes sense to gather it, from the customer's point of view), key business events (tasks), key business objects (orders, items, shopping cart, configurator), and key business rules (*if* this is a new customer, *then* send a welcome package).

- Do this for each key target audience, each scenario, and each context. After a while you'll get pretty fast. By doing multiple scenarios, you'll surface all the key reusable elements you need to have within your applications. This is what your information technology people need to design from.

- Give these detailed scenarios to whomever is going to prototype your applications (ideally, these folks should be in the room when you're doing this exercise).

In designing each target customer's ideal scenario, you'll want to make use of the Internet, use mobile wireless devices, and/or let the customer interact by phone or face-to-face. The customer you select may want to deal directly with your company, go through distributors or retailers, or both. Today's business strategies shouldn't be limited to the Web. They need to be true clicks-and-bricks implementations with blended channel strategies.

Once you've designed or captured end customers' scenarios, you can figure out what your company can do to make more relevant offers or make it easier for these customers to get the help they need through your distribution partners. As you create your own scenarios, don't start with the products you sell or with the distributors, channel partners, or retailers who make your products available. Instead, begin by focusing on the customers who will select and buy your products to use. Then add in the partners, products, services, and offerings that make sense from the end customer's point of view.

After your team has designed each scenario, think about any organizational, policy, business, or technology issues that need to be addressed to be able to implement this scenario.

We recommend that you do between three and six customer scenarios for each target customer set. Then look at the organizational and business process issues that arise. This will tell you what policies, processes, and organizational structures need to be changed first.

Next, have your information technology partners map out the IT infrastructure and services that will be required to support each scenario. What you'll find, of course, is that there are many shared services. You can then prioritize which infrastructure elements to tackle first based on the priorities of the target customers and their key scenarios.

We've discovered that having customers design their own scenarios shaves six months off design cycles, since your customers will design your business processes to reflect the ways they want to interact with you from the outset.

15

THE SEVENTH STEP: PLACE CUSTOMERS' "DNA" AT THE CORE

BUILD E-MARKETS AND CUSTOMER SCENARIO NETS AROUND CUSTOMERS' PROFILES, PORTFOLIOS, PROJECTS, AND POSSESSIONS

What's the best way to win customer loyalty? Save customers' time and streamline customer scenarios. There's an additional dimension that's important. You can help customers simplify their lives by managing the things that are important to them. Customers are increasingly willing to use electronic services to manage portions of their lives for them. Some examples in the consumer world are: financial portfolios, medical records, photo collections, car repair and maintenance, bill payment. Some examples in the business world are: bills of materials, building construction and facilities management, computer and network inventory and configuration, insurance and risk management, office supply replenishment, and supply chain management.

We refer to this broad category of customer- and project- or task-specific information as customers' "DNA" because it triggers the actions that need to take place and informs all the interactions among participating players. Much more than a simple customer profile, a customer's DNA incorporates living, breathing, dynamically changing states and conditions—the inventory that needs replenishment, the car whose sensors indicate it needs a tune-up, the financial portfolio that suddenly needs re-allocation of assets.

By placing customers' DNA at the core of a web of cooperating and/or competing services suppliers, customers get the benefit of one-stop-shopping, customized services, and time-saving project management.

We are convinced that the e-markets that will succeed in the long run are those that are organized around customers' DNA. Why? Because they will be offering more than an efficient way to buy and sell things. They'll be saving customers' time on projects and issues that matter to them.

Not a Customer "Lock In" Strategy

While it's true that managing customers' important stuff is more likely to keep customers loyal, don't think of this as a way to lock customers in. Remember, customers are in control. They will insist on having completely portable information. They won't invest their time in entering and/or maintaining information if they believe that they're being held hostage. Financial services firms have already learned this tough lesson. While each firm is vying with the rest to manage our investments, each also has to offer us easy ways to move our accounts and our information or we won't entrust the firm with our information.

Customers will insist that any information we hold for them be held in trust and that it adheres to completely open standards. Time is too precious to invest with one partner without being sure that we have an easy migration strategy for our critical information.

Customer DNA Acts as a Magnet

Just as biological DNA orchestrates the body's processes, customer DNA attracts and orchestrates the right services, in the right context, at the right time. If your car needs service, an appointment time may be offered and scheduled. If your inventory needs replenishment, your approved suppliers and logistics partners will spring into action. If you've completed a design and generated a bill of materials, a set of players will propose to supply the parts you need along with pricing and availability. The proposed offers and actions on the part of any potential or existing partner or supplier are summoned by the state of the projects or processes being managed.

DNA Means "Do Not Annoy"

Having customer DNA at the core of your offering does not give you permission to bombard customers with advertising or offers in which they haven't indicated any interest. Most customers will be receptive to offers that are germane to the task at hand, particularly those that are customized to their specific needs—"your muffler needs replacing; we have a high quality, reconditioned muffler for your model car in stock at half the price." But other customers will find such offers invasive. Remember that the customer "owns" both his or her information and the ability to control which parties know about it and what actions they are permitted to take.

Customer DNA and Viral Marketing

There's a very interesting side effect to organizing a collection of services, suppliers, and partners around customers' DNA. In most cases, you're able to create a viral marketing effect. Here's how it works. Each customer's core information acts as a magnet for a variety of suppliers and partners. As customers' needs are met, they tend to tell others. This customer referral mechanism has an exponential effect, because each new customer begets a new ecosystem of suppliers and partners. Each new participant brings a network of new players. The network effect takes over. The more participants there are in the network, the more valuable the entire network is for all players.

The Power of Customer Scenario Nets

There are many forms of exponential or viral marketing that take advantage of the network effect. Auctions and exchanges have viral properties. The more buyers there are, the more sellers they attract, and vice versa. That's why eBay has become such a powerhouse and why it has exhibited such staggering growth.

A Customer Scenario Net goes one step beyond the multiple buyers/multiple sellers model. It starts with a partnership: e.g., a doctor and a patient, or an architect and a contractor. But because the two parties are trying to accomplish something together beyond a simple one-time transaction, they tend to attract additional participants and players. The customer scenario in the patient's case is "improve and maintain my health and that of my family members." To accomplish that requires repeated visits and interactions, diagnostic tests, procedures, medication, nutrition, exercise, monitoring, payment, and so on. The customer scenario in the architect's case is "bring this building project to completion while respecting my design criteria." The players include the contractor, subcontractors, project owner, financial backer, suppliers, regulators, and so on. As each player becomes involved in one customer's Scenario Net, he experiences the power of dynamic real-time and near-real-time collaboration to accomplish an outcome. If the experience is a good one, he's likely to recommend this way of managing customers' scenarios to other customers and partners. Customer Scenario Nets offer compounded growth possibilities. Each customer's DNA combined with each customer scenario spawn a network effect of their own. We are not suggesting that Customer Scenario Nets will grow more quickly than other forms of viral communities. We are suggesting that they may have more staying power, since they are not organized around one-time transactions or fads, but around customers' core projects and issues.

Let's take a closer look at two examples: Medscape and Buzzsaw. Medscape is the result of a merger between a supplier of electronic patient records' software (Medicalogic) and a prestigious medical information site (Medscape/Medline) serving the professional physicians' community. What we like about Medscape's model is that it starts with the end customer—the patient—by giving patients' access to their own secure electronic medical records. And it revolves around the care-giver—the physician—and the patient/doctor relationship, by making it much easier for patients and doctors to collaborate on their mutual outcome: keeping the patient healthy.

Buzzsaw is an electronic marketplace and project management site for the construction industry. Spun out of AutoDesk in 1999, Buzzsaw quickly bolted to a leadership position in the landgrab for e-markets in the building construction industry. What we like about Buzzsaw's approach is that it helps the key players—architects, engineers, contractors, subcontractors, owners—manage their building projects.

Both of these Customer Scenario Nets are also e-markets. They attract partners, suppliers, advertisers, sponsors and service providers. But in each case, the customers' scenarios form the core organizing principle around the marketplace. Customers' DNA is at the core. And customers' scenarios form the focal point.

BUZZSAW.COM, INC.: EVOLVING AN E-MARKET WITH CUSTOMERS' BUILDING PROJECTS AT THE HUB

The building construction industry was one of the first in which B2B e-markets sprang into being and have begun to flourish. Customers—designers, owners, and builders—wanted more control over what is a very complex and messy process to manage. Every building project has hundreds of steps, dozens of players, and thousands of supplies to be procured and decisions to be made. Moving these projects into the digital world is a seductive opportunity for customers and suppliers alike.

AutoDesk didn't intend to spawn an e-market. The California-based software company was doing just fine as the world's leading supplier of computer-aided design (CAD) tools. AutoDesk's AutoCAD software had become the *de facto* standard design package used by architects and engineers. (AutoCAD is now used by 4 million design professionals around the world).

Architects, contractors, subcontractors, and building owners have collaborated on building projects for centuries. But today there's something different. They do much of the design work—including blueprints, 3D models, and engineering stress tests—electronically. Therefore they expect and demand to be able to share work in progress in electronic form. They don't want to just email files back and forth. They want to be able to manage projects electronically and to do their work in a concurrent, efficient fashion.

In late 1996 Anne Bonaparte was in AutoDesk's sales organization. As she was gathering input from customers about how they used the company's tools and what they wanted in future releases, she got a surprising answer. "Don't give us more functionality," customers said. "We need help getting these construction projects completed. There are too many places where things slip through the cracks." One customer told her about a problem he had had completing a chip manufacturing facility for Intel. He said he sent the drawings in electronic form, but they didn't make it through the client's Internet firewall. He lost a day on the project. "When you lose a day in building an Intel fabrication plant, you're losing $1 million!" he exclaimed.

That story and others got Anne's creative juices flowing. Why not create a better way for engineers, architects, contractors, and subcontractors to share their drawings electronically and manage their projects from end-to-end? When she tested this idea out with customers, they were enthusiastic, but they added a few caveats: 1) "Don't foist a particular project management approach or application on us," they warned. Anne discovered that each participant in a building construction project typically has his own preferred project management method. And it's unusual for the same group of people to work together on more than one project. Each project brings together a unique collection of fiercely independent participants. 2) "Don't require us to use your software," they added. Although AutoCAD was the industry-leading package, many companies used multiple applications and needed to interchange electronic documents with professionals using other suppliers' software.

Organizing a New Venture

Anne put together a project plan for a collaborative project management workspace and pitched it to AutoDesk's CEO, Carol Bartz, and the company's board in January 1997. The board liked the idea and suggested that Anne set up a small team as a skunkworks project. But Anne resisted that approach and instead suggested that, while the team could be handled on AutoDesk's books as a separate, start-up venture (under AutoDesk Ventures), it should be incubated within the company's existing software development organization. She believed that it was crucial to have senior AutoDesk engineers working on the project, and that some of the customers' requirements (like the ability to interchange electronic files with competitors' file formats) would influence the design of AutoDesk's core software offerings.

Carl Bass, AutoDesk's Chief Technology Officer, who ran a big part of the AutoCAD software development group, was enthusiastic about creating a team within his group to develop this new offering. Anne and Carl built a team of about thirty people, with technologists from the AutoCAD software development team and subject-matter experts—architects who understood how their peers actually did their jobs. "This integrated approach worked really well," Anne said. "We were able to share what we were doing with the broader AutoCAD development group. Even though we were solving a different problem, the engineers were open to sharing ideas. And because we created this bridge between the AutoCAD team and our team, they were more open to making changes in AutoCAD." The project got its nickname from one of the team members, joking one day about a colleague's ability to cut right to the heart of any issue. "You're such a buzzsaw," he said. Thus, Buzzsaw was born.

Gathering Customer Input and Piloting the Offer

How did the team gather customer requirements for this collaborative project management/file-sharing initiative? "We did a lot of customer research," Anne recalled. "We ran fax surveys; we ran email surveys. We interviewed people who weren't AutoDesk customers. We didn't want to bias the results by only talking to our customer base. We asked architects to tell us what it meant to them to communicate with others on a project. What tools did they currently use—FedEx, fax, email attachments?" As the team continued to refine the customer requirements, it recruited an advisory board of six customers. "These were our gunslingers." They were professionals with a job to do. "We would bring them in and let them bang on each prototype we came up with. Their input was instrumental in shaping the product."

Anne added, "We also needed users who were outside of the AutoDesk community. We asked them, 'Is this really a software-neutral platform?' We wanted to be sure that customers could view and manipulate any file format, from MS Word and Excel to their own favorite packages. Anything that could be viewed through a Web browser worked fine." Non-AutoCAD customers seemed comfortable with the generic file viewing and manipulation capability. AutoCAD customers expected a different set of capabilities. They wanted to be able to search for particular design elements—(e.g., windows, doors, electrical fixtures)—within AutoCAD drawings that were managed in the shared project folders. "We spent about a year and a half solving a bunch of customer problems around the exchange and collaboration of design and construction information," Carl Bass recalls.

By March 1999, AutoDesk quietly piloted its first alpha release of Buzzsaw's project folders with a handful of AutoCAD customers. By

June 1999, both existing AutoCAD customers and non-AutoCAD customers were using the beta version of the software to manage real live building projects, coordinating and managing them on the Buzzsaw project folders from the AutoDesk Web site.

The most interesting and surprising feedback from customers impacted Buzzsaw's eventual business model. The Buzzsaw team discovered that customers had very different ideas about what constituted a project. Some teams, such as Disney's Disneyland–Hong Kong team, set up entire multi-year, multi-building construction programs as a single project. Other teams considered each floor of a building to be a project. For others, each building on a campus was a project. "We had some projects with literally gigabytes of data and others with only six drawings." Still other teams divided projects into phases, such as the design phase, the construction phase, and the documentation phase. Anne realized that Buzzsaw shouldn't set its pricing model around projects, even though the competitive online construction management sites were using this model. Instead, Buzzsaw decided to charge the project owner based on the amount of disk storage used by the project team. The project owner—usually the building owner or contractor but sometimes the architect—would be the paying customer. The other members of each project team would simply register and use the site and its tools for free. This business model turned out to be one that customers understood and appreciated.

Spinning Buzzsaw.com out of AutoDesk

By spring 1999 Anne determined, for a number of reasons, that Buzzsaw was ready to leave the incubator and strike out on its own as a separate business venture.

First, the B2B e-market space was heating up. Although Buzzsaw had started life as a tool to help customers manage their projects and exchange documents, it was clear that this was simply the first step in the design of a much more comprehensive electronic marketplace. Customers had already indicated that they wanted to be able to find subcontractors and building supplies online. They wanted to submit requests for bids. They would probably be happy to purchase many building supplies and services online. In short, if customers were managing their projects online, it made sense to offer them everything they needed to handle their design and construction projects. But there were already a number of competitors in that space—companies like Citadon (formerly Bidcom), BuildNet, and a dozen others. After all, the construction industry is a $4 trillion global industry with a lot of inefficiencies waiting to be driven out of its core business-to-business processes.

Second, the Buzzsaw team wanted to acquire some technology—and possibly companies—that would flesh out its offerings. "The acquisitions we wanted to make would be off-target for the core AutoDesk business. And our competitors were all pure-play B2B dot-coms that were playing by a different set of rules. They could make deals quickly. They could fund them with their own stock. I thought we needed to spin ourselves out."

This spawned some heated discussions with the board, Anne recalled. "We were a pretty hot area within AutoDesk. We had a different business model. Money was going to start flowing in from a different set of customers (building-supplies companies that would be able to sell their wares online). The idea of spinning Buzzsaw off was an emotional one for all of us." In the end it was decided that Anne would look for a venture capital partner that had experience in B2B and would be willing to invest. AutoDesk wanted to retain controlling interest, at least for the time being. But the board realized that attracting outside investors would also be a good way to get validation from the venture capital community.

They didn't need to look far. John Mumford at Crosspoint Venture Partners had been investing in B2B plays for about three years. He quickly became a believer. And John brought management talent to the team. He introduced Anne to Larry Wares. Larry, who had founded and sold off a company called BidFax in the early '90s, had more than twenty years' experience in the construction industry. He had submitted a business plan to Crosspoint describing a way to use the Internet to improve communications between general contractors and subcontractors. Larry estimated that the inefficiencies in this communication process consumed about 10 percent of the resources on every construction project. "We hit it off immediately," Anne recalls. "After a few dinners we were completely in synch. We agreed that we were talking about solving the same collaboration problem. We knew we wanted simplicity and speed, and we agreed on what mattered and what didn't matter." By June 1999 Anne pitched the new deal to the board. Crosspoint Venture would invest $15 million. Larry would join the Buzzsaw team as head of strategic development. Carl Bass would be president and CEO. And Anne would continue to head up business development. Buzzsaw.com became a separate company in October 1999, and the production version of the site was officially launched in November 1999. There were sixty-six people in the fledgling company and twenty active customers running hundreds of construction projects.

Evolving Buzzsaw's Functionality

PLANNING AND DESIGN

The first release of Buzzsaw.com was a planning and design project hosting system that provided a central workspace where design and construction professionals could work together online. All building plans, schedules, contracts, and procurement documents are accessible online. Team discussions, management decisions, and document revisions are automatically tracked. And online meeting tools let team members collaborate on revising drawings online in real time.

CONSTRUCTION MANAGEMENT

Next Buzzsaw added a flexible workflow system that let customers define rules for routing documents among team members and for sending alerts to team members. Each team member can specify whether he prefers to be alerted by email, phone, fax, or pager.

BIDDING

In the fall of 2000, Buzzsaw added a bidding module so that general contractors could quickly broadcast Request for Proposals (RFPs) and gather detailed information (bids, proposed schedules, and references) from a variety of specialty subcontractors. Subcontractors could register their specialities and receive RFPs at no charge.

DIRECTORIES AND SPECIFICATIONS

From the outset, Buzzsaw included lots of resources for design and construction professionals. Over time this evolved to include product literature, specifications, technical data, graphics, and reference material on thousands of building supplies.

BUYING AND SELLING

Buzzsaw partnered with Ariba in March 2000 to develop a building materials and equipment exchange. By combining forces with one of the largest providers of trading exchange platforms, Buzzsaw gained both the functionality of Ariba's Trade-Ex exchange software as well as access to the hundreds of suppliers that had already begun making their wares available using that platform. This was a smart move. That meant that a supplier like Owens Corning didn't need to provide separate product information, inventory availability, and fulfillment and logistics support to multiple players. Instead, it could focus on integrating tightly into the Buzzsaw/Ariba combined offering.

Customer Uptake

"Our goals for the first few months were pretty conservative," Anne recalls. "We just wanted to launch the company, get through the Y2K period, and deliver a great customer experience. We weren't trying to acquire new customers. We didn't want to drive more customers to our site until we had more experience under our belts." The marketing push began in the first quarter of 2000. By then Buzzsaw had attracted about 230 customers, many of whom were running multiple projects on the site. These included large corporate customers such as DuPont and the Walt Disney Company, large architecture and engineering firms such as Ellerbe Becket and Skidmore Owings and Merrill, as well as small one- or two-person architecture firms.

In March 2000, Bank of America came to call. BofA is the largest provider of commercial loans in the United States. "They were looking for a way to improve the construction loan process," Anne reported. General contractors submit drawings to the bank at each stage of a construction project in order to get progress payments. The bank's loan department receives a letter or a fax and a set of drawings from the contractor stating that he's 30 percent done and wants to get paid. "At the bank they call this the 'envelope process,' " Anne explains. "They stuff a project's drawings in an envelope and pass it around for different people to approve it." When the bank's loan officers saw how easy it was to log onto Buzzsaw.com, check on the progress of a project, access the drawings electronically, and interact with the contractor online, "They got very excited! They realized that they could improve the efficiency of the construction loan draw-down process and reduce their risks at the same time." Bank of America decided to standardize on Buzzsaw.com to manage the construction loan process.

New construction loan holders would be required to submit their progress reports on Buzzsaw.com. Of course, if you were using Buzzsaw.com to get paid, you might as well use it to manage more of the job.

Real estate developers have also become early adopters of Buzzsaw.com, Anne reports. "They're the fastest decision-makers. We always talked about starting at the very beginning of a project and handling the full life cycle, but we weren't sure how to get upstream of the architect. What we've discovered is that real estate developers move very quickly from hearing about Buzzsaw.com to getting a demo to deciding to use the tool to manage their next project."

Viral Marketing

The real secret to Buzzsaw's burgeoning success is the way customers recruit each other. You start with a pilot project and involve a couple of people. That goes well. For the next project, you get the whole team to register and use Buzzsaw. Then someone on that team starts working on another construction project. He suggests the use of Buzzsaw to that project team. And so it goes. In the first seven months of operation, Buzzsaw was growing at a rate of seventy new projects per day. Some projects have six to ten members. After nine months, the number had increased to 130 new projects (or 500 new project users) per day.

By summer 2000, Buzzsaw's customer base had grown to 90,000 users running a total of 17,400 projects. And by November 1, a year after it officially opened its cyberdoors, Buzzsaw was hosting 20,000 projects with more than 100,000 active users.

Financing Growth: Competing for Capital

Although 2000 was a banner year for B2B investments, once the dot-com crash occurred in April 2000, even B2B companies had a difficult time raising capital. Buzzsaw was fortunate in securing $75 million in financing in early April 2000. Morgan Stanley led this second round, which included a strategic investment from its real estate fund. Bank of America participated in the financing, as did its early investors AutoDesk and Crosspoint Venture Partner. This brought the company's total investment capital to $90 million.

Evolving the Business Model

As mentioned above, Buzzsaw charges its customers a subscription fee to manage their set of projects based on the amount of disk storage used. Typically architects and project managers are the paying customers. They're paying for the storage and the project management service. In its first year of operation, most of Buzzsaw's revenues came from the subscription fees. By its second year, Buzzsaw was gaining revenues from sponsorship and advertising. (Although standard directory listings are free, many specialty contractors pay extra to add their logos and extra information.) Building materials and services suppliers pay to sponsor relevant content or to place ads. By mid-2001 Buzzsaw expects approximately one-third of its revenues to come from transactions that occur through the site.

Results

By November 2000, a year after its official launch, Buzzsaw had 20,000 projects underway with an average of 7.5 users per project for an estimated total of 150,000 active users. Fifteen percent of the customers were located outside of the United States, and several U.S.-based customers were using Buzzsaw.com to manage projects remotely in countries around the world.

Takeaways

What I like about the Buzzsaw story is that it starts with the customer's project. Customers flock to the Buzzsaw site because it lets them do something they really need to do: manage and coordinate complex projects involving lots of partners and players. But notice that Buzzsaw didn't take a top-down, project management–heavy approach to the problem. Having been warned by its customers that each player had his own project management methodology that he had been using for a decade or two, Buzzsaw offered an easy-to-use workflow management approach. This allowed customers to continue to use their project management software of choice and even to post that software on the Web site. Users could also set up simple tracking, routing, approval, and alert workflows among the players from a variety of different organizations—including the bank managing the construction loan, the contractor overseeing the construction, the architect signing off on design changes, and the project manager or building owner approving change orders.

Next, notice the natural viral marketing approach that leads to exponential growth. Customers sell each other. They refer their colleagues to Buzzsaw. And each successful project is likely to spawn five more projects, each with a new set of players.

On the technology front, Buzzsaw has used best-of-breed software wherever possible instead of building its own. WebEx Communications provides the online collaboration facilities, Wiznet the product catalogs, Ariba the exchange platform, and so on.

Finally, notice that Buzzsaw has been scrupulous in its pursuit of providing an open environment that everyone can participate in. You can use any design software, any project management software, and link to a variety of partners, from reprographics shops that will print your blueprints on their large format printers to software firms that will turn your blueprints into a bill of materials.

Patty's Suggestions for Buzzsaw

Buzzsaw is off to a great start. But the competition is fierce. There are more than 170 companies competing in the online construction space, according to Carl Bass. To continue building momentum, Buzzsaw may need another influx of capital. It's imperative that Buzzsaw continue to focus on its customer experience and to keep pace with competitive offerings in terms of functionality. The AutoCAD heritage should give Buzzsaw an advantage. It gives the company the ability to gain marketshare from existing AutoCAD customers. And it allows Buzzsaw to move forward rapidly toward providing more complete integration. For example, suppliers' catalogs will begin to contain not just text, images, and some parameters but the actual software objects that designers can drag and drop into their electronic drawings. Buzzsaw's customers will be well positioned to move toward a more all-digital design process—which includes design, simulation, ordering, construction, and maintenance—in much the same way that Boeing can now design its planes electronically.

Finally, we think that Buzzsaw should begin educating investors about the value of its customer franchise. The real value of Buzzsaw's proposition to investors lies in the loyalty of its customers—the number of active users there are, the number of active projects each is involved in, and the depth and breadth of those project management activities.

A Sample Flight Deck for Buzzsaw

	Navigation	Performance	Operations	Environment
Customer Numbers	Number of active customers (project owners) Number of active users (project members) Number of active projects Number of active suppliers	Number of new active customers by referral Number of new active users by referral Number of new projects	Growth in number of repeat projects per user Growth in size of average projects Growth in number of suppliers	Number of construction-related firms: architecture, contracting, subcontracting, etc. Number of large construction projects underway Number of competing online construction sites
Customer Retention	Retention rate per customer Retention rate per user Retention rate per project	Percentage of users returning with another project Relevance, accuracy, and availability of subcontractors and supplies offered on the site	Percentage of team members using site Number of RFPs generated from the site Number of construction loan officers requiring submissions	Ease of use of competitive offerings Ease of data transfer to competitive offerings (required)
Customer Experience	User satisfaction with collaboration tools and resources User satisfaction with project efficiency User satisfaction with purchasing opportunites	Time to receive progress payments Compatibility ratio of software and applications End-to-end performance of key customer scenarios	Speed of desired functionality improvements Network uptime Network transfer rate	Ease of use of competitive offerings Customer scenario performance of competitive offerings
Customer Spending	Revenues and profits per project Revenues and profits per customer Revenues and profits per user	Average project fee Average transaction size Average number of transactions per project Revenues from project spending (subscription fees) Revenues from transactions Revenues from advertising and sponsorships	Average project disk storage Average days saved per project Average cost saved per project	Total construction spending Total design spending

MEDSCAPE, INC.: MAKING PATIENTS' DIGITAL MEDICAL RECORDS THE HUB OF CARE

Just a few short years ago, the relationship between doctor and patient was a paternalistic one. Doctors knew all. Patients had to rely solely on their doctors for information and care. Today's patients have much more power. Thanks to the plethora of detailed medical and healthcare information available to us, we can arm ourselves with information before we visit or contact our doctors. We can research symptoms, deduce causes, and research alternative remedies. Yet, today's global healthcare ecosystem is still archaic. Mired in paper and bureaucracy, patients, doctors, clinics, hospitals, and health insurers are struggling to modernize the delivery of healthcare. Thankfully, as you'll see from this case study, this industry transformation is just beginning. We think that the most powerful catalyst will be the emergence and adoption of digital medical records.

Mark Leavitt set out to create a revolution in primary healthcare. Maybe it was Mark's technical background that made him impatient with the status quo in healthcare. He began his career as an electronic engineer in the '70s but switched to medicine and became an internist in the late '70s. As a practicing physician, Mark was frustrated by the "appalling information infrastructure" that existed in healthcare. In the early '80s, he began to develop his own homegrown software to manage his workload and keep track of his patients' medical histories electronically. "The core relationship in healthcare is the patient-physician relationship, and it's stored in a manila folder," Mark complained.

Soon other doctors were asking Mark if they could use his electronic patient management application. He realized that he was sliding from the practice of medicine into the software business, so he capitulated. He founded a software company in 1985 to develop and sell digital medical records software to practicing physicians. The company was called Medicalogic.

By mid-1999, Medicalogic's digital medical records application, called Logician, was in use by 10,000 physicians and caregivers in 340 sites for a combined total of 7 million electronic patient records. But this was a drop in the bucket. And Mark Leavitt knew it. The biggest transformation was yet to come—giving patients access to their own medical records and letting doctors and patients share access to these records. And the Internet had arrived.

Issue: How to Share Medical Information

In many countries basic healthcare is paid for by the government, and the keeping and sharing of medical records is more advanced than it is in the United States. In the United States, with its largely private healthcare infrastructure, the industry is very fragmented. Doctors still keep patients' records on paper, photocopying and faxing them to other physicians or healthcare providers as necessary. Claims for payments and reimbursements by insurers and the government's Medicare and Medicaid programs are increasingly submitted electronically. Patients have a difficult time keeping track of the status of their medical records, the results of their diagnostic tests, and their medications.

SECURITY AND PRIVACY

Many people think that the healthcare industry will be the last one to be transformed because of the issues surrounding the security and privacy of medical records. Yet the U.S. government has enacted a series of legislative measures that are laying the groundwork for the secure sharing of digital medical records. And the transformation of the U.S. healthcare industry is picking up steam.

In 1996 the U.S. Congress enacted the Health Insurance Portability and Accountability Act (HIPAA). This calls for the standardized, electronic transmission of administrative and financial transactions in the healthcare industry. Healthcare providers were given five years to comply with the legislation. By 2001 providers will be expected to be able to transmit all their health-insurance records using the new standards. Although the HIPAA legislation doesn't explicitly require patient records to be maintained in a standardized electronic form, it does require insurance and claims-related information to be submitted electronically. The Health Care Financing Administration (HCFA) of Medicaid also provides for the use of standardized medical terminology on all claims being submitted to that agency. And the HCFA sets standards for the encryption and transmission of medical information over the Internet.

In July 1999 the U.S. Senate passed the Patients' Bill of Rights Act. After the usual bipartisan revisions and endorsement by the American Medical Association, the Act was passed in the U.S. House of Representatives in October 1999. It safeguards patient privacy but requires physicians to maintain records in a timely and accurate manner and assure "reasonably quick" patient access to records and information. Digital-signature legislation followed, enabling digital signatures to be legally binding. In short, during 1999 and 2000 most of the legal infrastructure was put into place to enable patients' records to be securely stored in digital form and transmitted across the Internet with appropriate safeguards and recourse.

Ensuring Patient Privacy and Access

Perhaps the most revolutionary part of these various legislative efforts has been the unified acknowledgment that patients have the right to access and control their own medical records. Yet doctors have rights, too. As a physician, Mark Leavitt wanted to know which patients were accessing their records, to control access to the parts of the record that contained his personal notes and those that contained the "official" information, and to ensure that the information patients were seeing was accurate and up-to-date.

Providing a Secure Infrastructure

The first requirement was a safe, secure environment that doctors could use to store medical records and to post them for access by their patients and by other physicians who were authorized to view them. The Medicalogic team set about creating a secure data center, with digital certificates used for authentication. The physical data center is carefully monitored. "We use biometric authentication for people who enter the room where the electronic charts are stored, and we require two authorized people to be present anytime they enter the room where the digital certificates are kept," Mark Leavitt explained.

Enabling Internet-Based Digital Medical Records Collection and Sharing

The second requirement was digital medical records software that could be accessed and used over the Internet without requiring physicians to install the Logician software in their offices. Medicalogic began this software redesign project in 1999 and by March 2000 had rolled out Logician Internet, a Java-based application that physicians and their clinics could use via the Internet without having to install software and systems in their offices.

Of course, no one is logged onto the 'Net all the time, particularly a doctor on the go between his office, hospital, and clinic. The application was designed to enable doctors to log on in the morning and download patient records into their laptops for the day. They could create new patient records offline and even add updates to patient records they didn't have handy, synchronizing the new with the old when they dialed in later in the day.

Doctors who already had laptop computers could purchase the application for a flat fee of $99 per month regardless of the number of medical records they created and stored online. Medicalogic also offered a complete bundled "Go Kit," which included a Dell laptop with the Internet software, a voice-recognition software application so that doctors could dictate into their computers, and the other accessories needed. All of this was available at a cost of $199 per month for three years.

Giving Patients' Online Access to Their Medical Records

The third requirement was to design a Web-based user interface that would allow patients to view their digital medical records and to enter and update their own patient histories. The Medicalogic team launched a separate Web site that was linked to the digital medical records that had been created by the physicians using its software. Called Aboutmyhealth.net, this became a pilot Web site where physicians could invite their patients to access and view their own medical records. Each patient was provided an ID by his physician that would enable him to download a digital certificate and gain secure access to his patient records. Medicalogic piloted this application with four groups of physicians and their patients in spring 2000 and discovered that the patients loved two aspects to the online access. First, they liked the fact that they could easily get a transcript of their records and their interactions with their doctor. Second, they liked the ability to update the rest of their medical histories and keep all their information in one place.

As they were piloting the Aboutmyhealth.net online patient access, the Medicalogic team realized that it had stumbled onto a pent-up consumer need: a secure, easy-to-use environment in which to manage their own medical records. Medicalogic launched a consumer website called 98point6.com. The idea behind this management site was to make the patient's personal health record the core of a set of services—prescription ordering, health research, and (eventually) scheduling appointments and accessing secure medical records from participating physicians. 98point6.com used the same underlying digital medical records infrastructure and format as the Logician Internet software. Consumers who wanted to take control of their own health records could then seek out healthcare practitioners who were willing and able to share their records electronically.

Building the Team to Tackle the Healthcare Industry

By spring 1999 Mark Leavitt and his executive team realized that it was time to take the company public. "We knew that we were going to need close to $100 million to realize our dream of revolutionizing the healthcare industry by providing physicians and patients shared access to medical records," Mark explained. Medicalogic raised just over $100 million in its public offering in December 1999. Donaldson, Lufkin, and Jenrette (DLJ) underwrote the offering, but the underwriters had an even bigger play in mind.

Planning the Medscape/Medicalogic Merger

In the early fall of 1999 DLJ had taken another company public—Medscape. Medscape had been one of the earliest healthcare portals, providing healthcare information since 1995. Medscape had a very targeted and loyal audience of physicians and healthcare professionals. By making physicians' favorite information resource—Medline—available online, Medscape had built a loyal following among healthcare professionals. Medline lets you search for information across hundreds of medical journals. Most doctors who use the Internet log onto Medscape several times a week, looking for the latest information on new drugs, new treatments, or other timely information. At the time of its IPO in September 1999, Medscape had 1.2 million registered users, 300,000 of them doctors and 500,000 of them other healthcare professionals. Medscape also had a presence in the consumer market. Just before its IPO, Medscape had signed deals with CBS and with America Online. Medscape agreed to provide the medical content for the CBS Healthwatch Web site in exchange for advertising on the site and a $150 million investment by CBS in Medscape.

It wasn't surprising that DLJ got the two executive teams talking. The two groups realized that, by combining forces and offering both the top health information site for medical professionals and the leading digital medical records offering, the combined company would be well positioned to serve healthcare professionals with all the tools they needed to do their jobs. Through the CBS Healthwatch consumer presence, they would begin drawing healthcare consumers in larger numbers—consumers who would be able to inform themselves and interact with their physicians online as well as get their prescriptions refilled and proactively manage their families' health.

Building Critical Mass and Consolidating the Brand

By early 2000 the merger talks were underway, and the two companies began experimenting with synergies. Medicalogic began offering free downloads of its Logician Internet medical records software on the Medscape home page. Sure enough, through Medscape, Medicalogic gained 7,600 physicians as customers in three months—a 60 percent gain in its customer base.

At the same time that Medicalogic and Medscape merged, Medicalogic acquired another privately held company that offered an important piece of functionality for its ambulatory physician customer base. Total eMed is an online transcription services company. Doctors dictate their patient notes over the phone. These voice files are captured electronically and routed via the Internet to medical transcriptionists around the country. The resulting file is submitted to the doctor for review and attached to the patient's digital medical record. The result is faster medical transcriptions and the ability for doctors who prefer dictation to create digital medical records without changing their habits.

The three-way merger was finalized in May 2000, and the combined company, now renamed Medscape, continued to focus on its core target market: physicians and healthcare professionals. Although there were many other Web portals targeting the same community, Medscape had two advantages it needed to hold onto: a customer base of frequent repeat visitors and a customer-centric online application (digital medical records) that was designed to meet the needs of most ambulatory care physicians. Medscape became both the company's name and its brand identity. To physicians Medscape meant trusted information. "We deliver healthcare information that matters to both physicians and consumers," became the mantra of the combined companies.

Growing the Customer Franchise

By September 2000 the new Medscape had more than 33,000 physicians using its electronic patient record software. Of this total, two-thirds were using the company's Internet and hand-held (wireless) products, and 30 percent of these users were paying subscribers. The total number of patient records in all of the company's systems was 15.6 million as of September 30, 2000.

The number of registered physician users on the Medscape site exceeded 480,000. The number of non-physician clinician users reached 1.3 million. Consumer membership exceeded one million.

What's the value of Medscape's customer franchise? Mark Leavitt is excited about the subscription model. So far doctors are happy to pay the $100 per month charge for the use of the electronic patient records software. Assuming an eventual 50 percent profit margin on that revenue stream, Medscape can expect to earn $600 per year per physician. Of course the company also expects profits from the other services it provides, from transcription services to referral fees from pharmacies, fees for the continuing medical education courses it offers to physicians, as well as other e-commerce-related revenues (lab fees, etc.). The profits per physician from services and fees could easily climb to $1,000 per year. If we assume that the physician continues to be a customer for ten years, he will bring in $10,000 in total direct profits.

Of course, Medscape has other revenue streams, the most prominent one of which is advertising. "Each doctor controls $1 to 2 million of healthcare expenditures simply by using his pen," Mark Leavitt explains. That's why the pharmaceutical companies will pay high rates to advertise on Medscape, to sponsor a conference, or to provide continuing medical education (CME) in a specific area.

Neither of these counts the value of Medscape's end customer franchise—the patients and consumers who will use Medscape's services for free, either by accessing their patient records or by looking up information. The more end consumers use the service—and in particular, the more who access their medical records online—the greater the value of Medscape's customer franchise will be.

Making the Numbers Work

This ambitious merger was expensive. The total purchase price for Medscape and Total eMed was more than $1 billion. It left Medscape with a total of approximately $924 million of goodwill that will be amortized at an aggressive rate of $90 million per quarter. It will take two and a half years for Medscape to amortize all of that goodwill. There's no real prospect of profitability before then.

As of September 2000, the combined company had a starting deficit of $268 million. The revenues of the combined companies were $14.8 million in the quarter ending September 2000. The net loss before all the restructuring, amortization, and depreciation charges was $25.6 million in the same quarter. In other words, there's quite a gap to close before Medscape can become profitable. Nevertheless the company's current plan is to become cash-flow positive in 2001 and profitable by the fourth quarter of 2001.

Honing the Medscape Customer Experience

Medscape has been building its brand recognition among physicians since 1995. Many doctors typically spend thirty to forty-five minutes on the Medscape site each week scanning medical journals. The company has now moved from just providing information to providing services for the physician. For example, doctors have to accumulate a certain amount of Continuing Medical Education each year in order to retain their certification. Medscape has become the leading online publisher of CME, delivering over 24,000 hours of education per quarter as of the fall of 2000. "Continuing Medical Education is growing faster than any area in our company," Mark explained. "The doctor reads the material online, is tested online, and gets a CME certificate online. Before the Web, doctors would travel to conferences. These were nice tax-deductible vacations, but they're becoming impractical as everyone is more squeezed for time. An interesting aspect of online CME is that we can deliver it right when the doctor and patient need it—when they're about to make a decision. The doctor can actually click on the patient's problem in the electronic record, it brings up the latest articles, and she learns just what he needs in a very real-world situation which should produce the best learning retention, too, I believe. I think of it as 'just-in-time education.' " Who pays for development of the CME service? Most of the content is sponsored by the pharmaceutical companies, according to Mark. "But there's an editorial wall that prevents them from controlling the content."

What do Medscape's physician customers think about using online medical records? "I am in so many places—a different office on Monday, Wednesday, and Friday plus hospital procedures on the other days—that records management becomes a key issue," reported gastroenterologist Dr. Larry Kosinski. "I may know who is scheduled to come in but not who will call that day. But with my patient records on the Internet, no matter where I am I have the patient's chart with me."

At first he would take his notes by hand during the exam, then enter them into Logician Internet later. "Finally, I plunked a laptop down in the exam room one day and asked the patient if he would mind if I used it to record my findings. He not only didn't object, he was intrigued with the whole idea. Now I use it with patients all the time," he says. According to Dr. Kosinski, the best thing about working this way is that when the exam is complete, his chart notes are completed as well. "I don't have to spend more time dictating or typing in notes in my office. It's a terrific timesaver," he says.

"In my practice I may see a patient and schedule a procedure that will take place weeks later. At the time the procedure occurs, I may need to know if this patient has a heart valve or hip replacement—so that I should place him on prophylactic antibiotics. With a digital medical record, the chart is readily accessible all the time and I don't have to ask the patient for the same data over and over again. It improves the quality of the patient care that I provide."

Many of Medscape's digital medical records customers offer similar testimonials. However, note that most of them are individual practitioners who work in a small practice. Doctors who are connected to hospitals or other larger practice groups tend to have their own internal medical record software. It's unlikely that Medscape's digital medical records will be adopted by their firms.

Medscape continues to invest in leading technology solutions that make physicians' lives easier. In addition to its online dictation services and electronic diagnostics, the company introduced a mobile version of its medical records application in September 2000; 10,000 physicians signed up for the Mobile Medscape product in the first nine days!

Will patients take to viewing their medical records online? The early tests are very positive. The doctors who have made patients' records available to them via the Internet are getting rave reviews from busy moms, harried dads, and concerned seniors.

Takeaways

Note that Mark Leavitt has kept an unwavering focus on the core relationship—between the patient and the physician. His goal has been to improve this working relationship by saving time for doctors, giving patients more control over their medical records, and improving the quality of the information available to both parties. Mark's vision has been to improve the quality of healthcare by starting with the most critical information at the core—the patient's medical records.

Medicalogic began life as the provider of a software application for doctors' offices. The company could have followed the natural course of evolution from client/server software to an Internet-based application software provider, allowing customers to use its application without installing and maintaining software in their offices. But Mark had a bigger vision. Like many others, he wanted to transform the healthcare industry and he realized that he needed a big brand and a big presence to gain critical mass.

The Medicalogic/Medscape story is a great example of focusing on key customers and their outcomes while at the same time building momentum and marketshare by leveraging the branded experience that physicians already trusted. Medicalogic's metamorphosis also provides a good example of how a software company can evolve from selling software packages to providing the core value proposition for an e-market.

And the Medscape example clearly shows us how the customer's core information (medical records) and the customer's key scenario—

becoming and staying healthy—forms the hub around which all the other activities revolve. Patients, doctors, and partners can easily coordinate tasks like getting tests done, prescribing medications, tracking results, and getting educated about new possibilities and procedures.

Patty's Suggestions for Medscape

Medscape's challenges are focus, execution, and, of course, achieving profitability. Keeping its systems scaling, its content current and state-of-the-art, and its various Web sites humming is not inexpensive. Continuing to evolve the software and tools physicians need and use will also require additional R&D spending. Luckily, the pharmaceutical companies that provide 50 percent of Medscape's current revenue (in terms of advertising and sponsorship) are not likely to walk away from the information source that many doctors spend hours on each week. The other 50 percent of its revenues currently come from software licenses and fees. We expect that number to increase as more and more physicians begin to manage their patient records electronically. Over the next few years, Medscape expects to receive about a third of its revenues and profits from e-commerce (payments received for transmitting lab results and prescriptions to partners) and from digital healthcare partnerships (using the healthcare data it has to reduce costs and inefficiencies). Will Medscape hit a plateau in customer acquisition once it has many of the early adopter/technology friendly doctors? That's certainly possible.

We'd like to see Medscape provide even more Medscape-branded services to patients—by providing them even more tools to manage their own healthcare, while keeping them in connection to their physicians. Patients and their families will appreciate the ability to both organize and better manage their health. Today, Medscape provides most of its consumer-related services and information through the CBS-sponsored HealthWatch Web site and programming. While that's a great way to acquire new consumers as customers and to keep consumers informed about health-related issues, CBS isn't a trusted brand when it comes to managing my medical records and information—Medscape is.

A Sample Flight Deck for Medscape

	Navigation	Performance	Operations	Environment
Customer Numbers	Number of active physician customers Number of active clinician users Number of active patient users Number of stored active patient medical records	Number of doctor-to-doctor referrals Number of patient-to-doctor referrals Number of patients referred from HealthWatch site Number of consumers who have entered their own medical records	Number of unique visitors to the Medscape and HealthWatch Web sites Number of physicians and clinicians who reference Medscape articles each week	Growth in use of online health and medical sites Competing digital medical record providers Number of healthcare providers and physician networks using alternative digital medical record software
Customer Retention	Customer retention rate (by physician) for Medscape free services Customer renewal rate (by physician) for medical records software license renewal Percentage of physicians obtaining CMEs online	Frequency and number of patient use of services Frequency and number of services used by physicians Percentage of physicians and clinicians who access medical records every day Percentage of consumers who access medical records three times/year	Growth in use of partners' services (e.g., diagnostic services, dictation, Rx fulfillment) Growth in number of digital medical records per physician Number of times digital records are shared with referring physicians (with patient's permission)	
Customer Experience	Physician satisfaction Patient satisfaction with health management services Scores on customer "trust" survey	Physician satisfaction with record accuracy and security Physician satisfaction with record download and upload time Patient satisfaction with site security	Network uptime Network average transfer rate Transcription turnaround time and accuracy Performance on end-to-end customer scenarios	Comparative customer satisfaction with healthcare providers and services
Customer Spending	Revenue and profit per physician Revenue and profit per patient	Revenues from subscription fees Revenues from transaction fees Revenues from sponsorships	Software upgrade costs and infrastructure costs Costs of providing content and services Customer support costs	Alternative providers of cost-effective total healthcare solutions

PLACE CUSTOMERS' DNA AT THE CORE: OBSERVATIONS ABOUT THE CASE STUDIES

When we discussed the emergence of Customer Scenario Nets in chapter four (Surviving the E-Market Revolution), we defined a Customer Scenario Net as a customer- and project-specific set of interrelated tasks that can be managed via the Internet to accomplish a specific outcome. And we said that we felt that Customer Scenario Nets would be one of the most viable forms of e-market, precisely because they are so customer-driven.

Notice that both of these Customer Scenario Nets were spawned by software companies. This is not at all unusual. If you look carefully at many of the digital markets that have emerged over the past two years, particularly in the B2B arena, you'll discover that many of them began life as some form of software. And that the underlying software application was typically used to manage an end-to-end process. For example, there are e-markets that have been formed by makers of procurement software (like Ariba). There are e-markets that have been launched by suppliers of software for auto parts inventory management. There are e-markets that have been spawned by suppliers of software for managing insurance claims. Therefore it's not surprising that Medicalogic's electronic patient record software and AutoDesk's computer-aided design software found their way into the fabric of these two typical Customer Scenario Nets.

Notice, too, that these initiatives are being led by people with deep subject matter expertise. Doctors design tools for doctors. Architects design tools for architects. Sure, you need business managers and technology managers, but without a very strong core of subject matter experts, you'll never gain traction in these increasingly special-purpose electronic offerings.

Not Just Content, Community, and Commerce

For years, industry pundits proclaimed the virtues of building electronic portals and e-marketplaces around the three "C's." We were always skeptical. First, because we know that community is very difficult to build online. (In general, people don't come to "hang out," they want to get something done.) Second, there's the "if we build it, will they come" problem. (Lots of players tried to build portals for communities of practice, from doctors to lawyers to gardeners; the majority of them have failed to gain traction.) Third, there's the compelling need problem. (If I don't have a compelling and recurring need that brings me to this business or Web site, then you don't have a strong enough value proposition for me.) And fourth, there's the product decision-making problem (it's not enough to provide prospects with a directory of products or a set of online catalog pages; you have to actually help customers make product selection decisions—that takes hard work and objectivity).

Customer scenarios and Customer DNA provide a compelling foundation for dynamic e-markets. Once you have Customer DNA at the core and you're actually helping customers handle their scenarios, you can wrap context-sensitive content, supportive community, and task- or scenario-specific commerce around these core customer scenarios.

16

THE EIGHTH STEP: DESIGN TO MORPH

"Expect to change your business model four times a year," *is* the advice we give our clients. Those who have been in the e-business game for a while nod with recognition. The newbies blanch. But everyone recognizes that there's something fundamentally different about running a successful business in this new customer economy. That's why the airplane analogy (running an Internet-enabled business is like flying a plane while you're changing the engine in mid-flight) seems so apt. Today's businesses need to be highly adaptable. They try one business model and if that doesn't work, they try another. Even if it does work, they add another.

But how do you change your business on the fly? And under what circumstances does it make sense to do so? The "how" is actually the easy part. The why and when are a bit trickier.

WHEN SHOULD YOU CHANGE YOUR BUSINESS MODEL OR SPAWN A NEW ONE?

1. When It Feels Right. First and foremost, trust your intuition. There's no business logic or market research that can rival human intuition. When Richard Duvall walked into Mike Harris's office at Prudential Direct and said, "I'm the MIS director for a bank that's failing," he was responding to a strong intuitive nudge. At the time, of course, Prudential Direct was doing fine. In fact, it still is. But what Richard was reacting to were the alarms that were going off in his brain. At first he didn't realize what was triggering them. Once he thought about it, he realized that what had set his instinctive radar beeping was the local supermarket. The fact that many of his friends had begun doing their weekly grocery shopping online had gotten his attention. Add to that the fact that this same supermarket chain was offering credit cards and deposit accounts with interest rates, and he began to see a pattern forming. The Huns were at the gates! Prudential spawned Egg Bank as a way to compete for the hearts and minds of this new breed of time-pressed but tech-savvy customers.

2. When Your Customers Give You Cues. Send.com's core customers were busy professional men who need help in remembering, selecting, and sending the perfect gifts for the important people in their lives. (Of course, Send.com had female customers as well, but its target customer was the male gift-giver; it turns out that men have different gift-giving needs than women.) A few of these customers began asking if Send.com would offer a discount for bulk orders. It turned out they wanted to send between 20 and 100 gifts at a time to business clients. And they didn't want to type in the names one by one. Instead, they faxed a list or emailed a rolodex, indicating a price range and type of gift they wanted for each. What started out as a wine-selling Web site for consumers wound up being a business-to-business site for gift-giving by professional people to their clients. (Unfortunately, Send.com's investors weren't willing to wait for this B2B strategy to pay off. The company was shut down in January 2001.)

Schwab discovered that the most active of its active traders were beginning to put new sources of funds into competing online trading offerings. These active traders were looking for capabilities that Schwab was slow in providing: access to IPOs, lower prices for frequent trades, and access to Electronic Communication Networks (ECNs) so they could bypass the market-makers. So, Schwab joined with a group of competing brokerages to form an ECN, REDIBook. And, Schwab acquired CyBerCorp—a firm that caters to active traders.

Sometimes you have to look pretty carefully. It wasn't until Schwab's customer experience group sent people out to customers' homes to sit and watch the way they used the Internet for their financial planning that they discovered that sad truth. Many Schwab customers keep their investment portfolios on Yahoo!, Quicken, and other free portal sites instead of at Schwab.com, where they actually make their investments. So, in January 2001, Schwab partnered with Yodlee to offer an account aggregation service—"My Accounts"—that lets Schwab customers aggregate their accounts from all financial institutions in one secure location.

3. When Would-Be-Customers Give You Cues. How many avid amateur mechanics do you think have driven by or run up to a Snap-on van to get the dealer's attention? And how many years did it take before Snap-on finally figured out a way to let consumers buy direct? Once Snap-on embarked on a self-service site for its high-end business customers and implemented its dealer extranet, it was a simple matter to expand the project to consumers.

As you'll see in the Grainger case study that follows, Grainger didn't target hardware store chains or competing e-markets when it designed FindMRO.com. Grainger was simply trying to make its parts brokerage service available to its customers more cost-effectively. Somehow Ace Hardware discovered the FindMRO brokering service and wanted to offer it electronically to its 5,000 store managers so they could locate and procure the hard-to-find parts their customers were seeking. The folks at ENI-Net—an emarket for the environmental industry—discovered FindMRO too. Soon dozens of e-market makers wanted Grainger to make the service available to them for their customers.

4. When Existing Partners Want You to Provide a Service for Them. Send.com had hundreds of small businesses as partners and suppliers around the country. They began asking Send.com for customer management systems, workflow applications, inventory management systems, and gift certificate management services—a slew of capabilities that Send.com could easily provide to its business partners for a fee.

5. When Would-Be Partners Want You to Provide a Service for Them. Most of the marketing executives we've spoken to have a surfeit of partnering opportunities. American Airlines and Hertz, for example, receive hundreds of partnering requests every week. How do you decide which ones to heed and which ones to ignore? Most of these companies have developed a focused triage process, and they typically have one or two people whose job it is to sort through the clutter looking for the partners with the right fit.

It's a win-win situation when you have a branded service you can provide to a would-be partner that will, in turn, prove valuable to its customers. When Egg approached Boots about partnering on a health-care portal, Boots was much more interested in leveraging Egg's online credit card services and offering a jointly branded Egg/Boots loyalty and credit card. Boots valued the credit card processing services that Egg had in place, but it also valued the quality of the branded experience that Egg was capable of delivering.

When Toys "R" Us approached Amazon.com, it was because the bricks-and-mortar retailer valued Amazon's ability to run an e-commerce operation, including its ability to handle large-scale direct-to-consumer fulfillment. Toys "R" Us was happy to offer a co-branded solution to mutual customers—the Toys "R" Us toy selection and value with the Amazon.com e-commerce and fulfillment.

6. When You Know You're Onto Something, But You Haven't Quite Nailed It. Sometimes you know you're sitting on top of a core competency that's valuable to a much broader market than the one you're currently serving, yet you haven't managed to tap into that larger market. That's when you may need to try the "throw the spaghetti against the wall" strategy we describe in the (upcoming) Grainger and Okobank case studies. You spawn a few parallel efforts and see which one(s) get traction. As long as you have the deep pockets and management bandwidth to handle several parallel initiatives, it's probably the fastest way to find the right model. As you'll see from reading the Grainger example, you also need to know when to cut your losses, the way Grainger did with its OrderZone initiative.

7. When the Market Begins to Shift Away from Your Business Model. Sometimes, the market shifts in a direction that doesn't appeal to you. That's what was happening to Finland's Okobank. Its board and its member banks were enthusiastic about the proposition of a complete vertically integrated suite of Oko-branded financial services offerings as part of an online portal play. When it became apparent that, to participate in the leading online portal, Okobank would need to shed its own brand identity for its core offerings and vie with best-of-breed competitors in the highly competitive investment, insurance, and loans businesses, Okobank's executives thought twice. But it didn't deter them. Brand or no brand, they realized they needed to be in relationship with the young self-service customers the online portal was attracting—consumers who might never think of doing business with a conventional bank.

8. When Your Business Model Is Still Taking Shape. In Brazil, Superbid.com.br was founded by Veronica Allende Serra, an entrepreneur, and brothers Rodrigo and Ronaldo Sodre Santoro, auctioneers at one of Brazil's leading auction houses. Superbid.com.br began life as a way for multinational and Brazilian suppliers to sell excess inventory of expensive, high-margin consumer products such as DVD players, washing machines, computers, and carpeting. The auction site caught on quickly. Buyers could bid, do reverse auctions, and participate in group auctions. The deals were great!

But within a month, the executive team noticed something important. Most of the site's sales were to small businesses, not consumers. Most of these small-business customers used the site to buy computers and electronic gear. The team realized that the B2B market in Brazil was ready to take off, with tens of thousands of small businesses as a ready market. At the same time its suppliers—a variety of multinationals (Apple, Canon, and Maytag) and large Brazilian companies (Conibra, Brazil's equivalent of Home Depot and Casa Fortaleza, a carpet and rug supplier)—began asking to purchase goods from their own suppliers via the 'Net. The team realized they had stumbled on two very different market needs: small businesses and consumers wanting to buy computers and electronics, and large companies wanting to buy industrial supplies.

Based on this customer and supplier feedback, the founders quickly realized that they had the makings of a series of e-markets. They formed a new umbrella company called SuperVertical, headed by Veronica. Superbid.com became one of a series of vertical e-markets under a new umbrella company, SuperVertical.com.br. Veronica repositioned Superbid as an e-market for computers and electronics and launched an industrial equipment B2B vertical market, Supernei.com.br, in partnership with Brazil's largest industrial equipment supplier, Noticiario de Equipamentos Industriais (NEI).

HOW TO CHANGE YOUR BUSINESS ON THE FLY

Morphing is the best way to describe what seems to happen with these businesses. Often they begin life as one kind of business and soon they have spawned two or three parallel business models, each with a life and logic of its own, but all leveraging the same core competencies. Egg is an excellent example. Egg first found its legs as an Internet savings bank and credit card issuer with a distinctive, hip, branded experience. Next the company created a branded online shopping mall so its Egg cardholders would have a place to shop online. Then Egg became an aggregator of others' investment products. Then it became an aggregator of best-of-breed insurance products (including those from its parent company, Prudential). And in midstream, Egg became the co-branded online credit card services provider for Boots pharmacies' customers. All of this activity took place in twenty-four months. And Egg still has more transformations ahead of it.

Notice that Egg, Grainger, Okobank Group, Amazon.com, and many of the other companies mentioned above have some important characteristics in common. These are the all-important how-to's you need to master if you're going to morph with the best of them.

1. Leverage Your Branded Experience. Whenever possible, keep your branded experience in customers' faces. Egg's deal with Boots and Amazon's deal with Toys "R" Us are both good examples. In each case, both partners' branded experiences are strong and complementary. Customers can easily perceive the value in the additive combination.

When Timbuk2's virtual aisle turns up inside a major sporting goods retailer's online store, the customer who enters that virtual aisle and custom-configures her backpack is having a "Timbuk2" experience. When a business customer visits an e-market and enters the Snap-on department to select the right tool for the job, he's having a "Snap-on" experience.

Even when it's not possible to keep your brand in customers' faces, it still makes sense to leverage your branded experience. Of course, it's best if you can use the "Intel Inside" style branding so that customers who are buying a Compaq computer know that they're getting genuine Intel parts. But as you'll see as you read the Okobank case study, the Finnish portal, Sonera Plaza, didn't want its customers to know that their electronic and mobile banking services were being "brought to them by Okobank." Given the bank's somewhat stodgy brand image, it would be a turn-off. Besides, it would have alienated Sonera Plaza's other financial services providers. Sonera wanted to offer all players an even playing field. Should Okobank have walked away from the deal because it couldn't brand its core offerings? Not at all. Customers will still be having the same customer experience. If it's a good one, they'll grow to appreciate it. Okobank Group will still be in relationship with these customers. They'll simply be doing it through a different brand entity. What counts most is the depth of the connection you have with your customers and the quality of the experience they receive.

Every customer experience has a unique "feel" to it. That's even more the case when you're interacting online, because you're using a common set of underlying services, decision-making tools, and navigation. Customers will feel more comfortable when they're dealing with the same cognitive experience. That gives you a subtle leg up, even if customers don't see your brand.

2. Invest in Core Infrastructure and Operational Excellence. Your customer experience is based on a set of core infrastructure services. These include everything from your call center operations to your fulfillment and delivery processes. They include your Web-based search engine and the data attributes you use to describe the characteristics of your products. They include your cross-selling and upselling (merchandising) expertise. They include the cross-touchpoint services you've deployed to make it easy for customers to interact using wireless data or touch-tone phones. And they certainly include your customer database and customer relationship management processes and systems.

In the Okobank Group case study that follows, you'll see how Okobank has focused on providing electronic banking and mobile banking services to the Finnish market. Once these e-services were in place, Oko was able to leverage them across its core banking business and use them to enter new markets.

3. Leverage Your Core Services as an Asset. This brings us to the next point. What's the one thing that makes morphing your e-business on the fly actually feasible? The fact that you are leveraging a set of common core services each time.

What's Amazon.com offering to Toys "R" Us besides the trust that consumers will receive their toys in time? It's offering a set of highly refined and tested e-commerce services, from its patented 1-Click®[9] ordering to its highly automated picking, gift-wrapping, and shipping services. What's Egg offering to Boots' customers, besides the cachet that comes with being an Egg cardholder? It's offering a set of tried and tested online credit card application, credit-checking, authorization, processing, and billing services along with a world-class customer care center.

What were the services that made it possible for Superbid.com to move from consumer auctions to B2B vertical markets? The company had invested heavily in four critical aspects of its platform. First, it needed to guarantee that Internet payments would be secure and that sellers wouldn't receive payment until the goods had arrived in good order and been accepted by the buyer. Second, it needed to be able to track deliveries from each supplier to the customers. Third, it needed to offer complete auction services that would allow customers to bid and track auctions in progress. Fourth, it needed to have a dispute resolution process in place to handle any issues that might arise. Once these core services were in place, it was a relatively simple matter to extend into new business models to handle purchase orders and other forms of payment, for example.

4. Start with Trusted Leadership. What won't work is to turn your e-business experimentation over to someone you bring in from the outside. To carry off this "morph your e-business on the fly" way of doing business, you need a seasoned executive who has already earned the trust of your board, colleagues, and investors. Of course this person will be a renegade. Otherwise she wouldn't be leading your e-business initiatives. But she needs to be a renegade with strong track record of delivering on promises. Take Don Bielinski at Grainger, for example. Don is a veteran who knows the core business well. He has proven himself in a variety of posts in the twenty-seven years he's been with the company. Grainger's executives trust Don to know when to spawn a new business and when to cut his losses. Don, in turn, recruits the new blood required to lead each of his experimental businesses.

[9] 1-Click is a Registered Trademark of Amazon.com.

5. Have Supportive and Patient Executives and Investors. Superbid.com's first round of financial backing came from the founders and from its business partner, Unibanco. When the Superbid executive team realized that they needed to change their business model, their backers were just as excited about the promise of the new, larger vision as they had been with the company's original game plan.

Okobank Group's funding comes primarily from its hundreds of member banks. Several of the ventures Okobank is undertaking challenge the company's traditional way of doing business (i.e., the branch banking franchise). Yet these member banks have been supportive and the Group has been able to move quickly to seize opportunities in the face of extreme competitive pressure.

Grainger's board and investors have been patient with the company as it has invested heavily in its electronic commerce initiatives. They are proud of the company's track record in forging new ground and supportive of the incubator approach that has given rise to Grainger's digital businesses.

The key ingredients in these cases are education and full disclosure along with trust and vision. In each case, the business leader is someone who inspires trust, who has gained respect within the business, and who is constantly elucidating decision-makers on what he sees happening in the market. The decision-makers and investors, in turn, need to be risk-takers and willing to experiment.

OKOBANK GROUP: MOVING FROM A TRADITIONAL BRANCH BANKING MODEL TO PIONEERING IN M-COMMERCE AND INTERNET PORTALS

The popularity and ubiquity of mobile phones and wireless hand-held devices has spawned a revolution in customer convenience around the world. As soon as it became possible for mobile phone users to use their phones to send and receive short email messages, customers began to think of other services they'd like to be able to do conveniently from their cell phones. Why wait in a call center queue so you can ask a simple question? Why not perform simple tasks like checking your bank balance, booking a ticket, or checking on the status of an order by simply letting your mobile phone or personal organizer directly contact the computer system that has the information you need?

The mobile/wireless revolution is just beginning. Okobank is one of the revolutionaries that is leading the charge in Scandinavia. By responding quickly to its customers' needs, Okobank has consistently remained on the front lines of the customer revolution. And by designing a reusable, flexible infrastructure to support its customers' needs, Okobank has been able to experiment with a number of new business models simultaneously.

How should a bank change its strategy as its customers' and prospective customers' needs evolve? Finland is a great place to gain some insights. The customer population is among the most aggressive in its adoption of both Internet and mobile technologies. Yet customers' needs are varied. In cosmopolitan Helsinki, many customers are self-directed and on the move. In the rural parts of the country, many customers prefer the human touch and they're eager for guidance.

Let's take a look at how an old-line organization run by its member cooperative banks—each of which has a great deal of independence and autonomy—has become a profitable and nimble player in the customer economy. In the last five years, Okobank has led the pack in its deployment of e-commerce and m-commerce solutions. Okobank is a good example of a company that has a number of different e-business models in play simultaneously. All of them leverage the same core customer experience and operational efficiencies.

Okobank is the second largest bank in Finland and the largest native Finnish bank. (MeritaNordbanken, a Scandinavian bank—serving Sweden, Denmark, and Norway, as well as Finland—has the largest marketshare in Finland.) In a country with a population of just over 5 million people, 2.1 million of them are Okobank's customers, including 100,000 Finnish businesses. Unlike some other players in Scandinavia, Okobank does not have a goal to "go global" or even European. It simply wants to be the best financial services provider serving the Finnish market. With €20 billion of deposits and assets under management, Okobank was the most profitable retail bank in Scandinavia in 2000. It has to be doing something right!

WHAT'S A COOPERATIVE BANK?

There's a strong tradition of cooperative banking in Europe. Small local banks join together to combine the best of both worlds—economies of scale along with local knowledge and the kind of deep customer relationships that come from centuries of being part of the neighborhood. These cooperative banks—France's Credit Agricole, Hollands' Rabobank, Germany's DG Bank, etc.—have their own back-scratching network; they're all members of Unico Banking Group, an association formed by the nine leading cooperative banks in Europe. Okobank, like its brethren, is owned jointly by its member banks and by the public.

Finland's Okobank Group currently comprises 244 member banks. Since their beginning as providers of government-sponsored loans to farmers, these member banks' community roots have continued to deepen.

Okobank's Tradition of Customer Care

What's the brand image of Okobank in Finland? It's not considered the most modern or most aggressive bank. In fact, in high tech Helsinki, Okobank has only a 16 percent marketshare. But when you ask Finns about the company, the image that comes to mind is the "people's bank"—the bank that cares the most about the common man. Ten years ago, there was a banking and credit crisis in northern Europe. Times were tough. Still, Okobank member banks worked hard to stick by their customers, willing to find flexible solutions to problems whenever possible. Today, in more prosperous, ebullient times, Okobank's loan officers find they often have to practice "tough love," refusing loans to customers who would become overextended. "We look out for the customer, in good times and bad. We won't let our customers get in trouble. And if they do, we'll stand by them. They know that about us," explains Jarkko Anttiroiko, business development manager for Okobank's central banking group and Okobank Group's e-business leader.

Meeting the Customer Challenge

Self-directed customers are a growing, but still small, segment of the overall financial services market in Finland. Most people want some hand-holding and advice when they make important financial decisions. Okobank believes that its strong branch network and personal service give customers the comfort they need. Yet while Okobank has a healthy percentage of the Finnish population as its customers, there are several customer-related challenges confronting this old-line company:

1. Customer Perception of the Okobank Brand. Stodginess and reliability don't go very far in creating fanatical customer loyalty. Even though Okobank does a great job with personalized customer service—both for its business customers and its consumer customers—the brand image is pretty staid. In hip Helsinki, in particular, Okobank is not even on most customers' radars.

2. Share of Wallet. While 2.1 million customers have a relationship with Okobank, only 1.5 million of them are solely Okobank customers. Almost a third of its customers also bank with competitors.

3. Luring Younger Customers. When a baby is born in Finland, parents usually open a bank account for the child. When the child begins to need a bank account and access to an ATM machine, usually she begins using that same account. However, just because a young person takes money out of a cash machine, doesn't mean she has a relationship with the bank, particularly since the ATMs are all generic "OTTO" cash machines that give all Finns access to funds from any bank in Finland's ATM network. When that same person needs a credit card or a loan or wants to begin saving or investing money, it may not occur to her to start with the bank she's already doing business with. Okobank is currently not attracting these younger urban customers. In fact, the company's brand image probably works against luring the younger set.

4. Satisfying Self-Directed Customers. Through its aggressive deployment of Web-based and m-banking services, Okobank does a great job of serving the self-directed set. However, many of these customers are also drawn to companies with a stronger Internet brand—such as eQ Online, the E*Trade equivalent in Finland. Okobank's online trading offers equivalent access to equities, functionality, and pricing. Yet many of its customers still have separate online brokerage and mutual fund accounts.

5. Offering One-Stop Shopping. Like most banks, Okobank is striving to offer customers the convenience of one-stop shopping for all their financial needs (including banking, investments, credit, insurance, and pension funds management). Okobank has been offering mutual funds for ten years, yet the company hasn't marketed them aggressively until the last couple of years. Its portion of customers' mindshare is low. Many of the company's recent moves are about offering customers—both self-directed ones and those who need guidance—a comprehensive set of best-in-class financial services.

Offering Customers a Seamless Multi-Touchpoint Experience

Today, Okobank Group has 695 branch offices scattered throughout the towns and countryside of rural Finland and seventeen in downtown Helsinki. The Group also has 669 bill payment ATM machines and 374 Internet customer terminals. This is in addition to the ubiquitous OTTO ATM cash machines. There's a one hundred–person call center in Helsinki that serves all Okobank customers. "Call centers were relatively slow to take off in Finland," Jarkko explained. "We Finns are modest people. We don't want to bother other people. We're hesitant to ask for help. And we always believe that our own issues aren't so important." Yet the call center has become an important building block for Okobank's multi-touchpoint strategy. Customers are able to get help on technical issues as well as receive guidance on financial matters.

This multi-touchpoint strategy is a critical foundation for Okobank's future success.

Organizational Structure

Okobank's member banks jointly fund a set of shared group-level services based in Helsinki. These include the information technology infrastructure for all the member banks and the shared call center. There is also a small amount set aside each year to fund innovative projects. Jarkko and his boss, Executive Director Matti Korkeela, are typically the ones who scan the horizon, spot new opportunities, and present them to the bank's member board for approval.

There is no one at Okobank who owns the customer experience. There are five coordinating teams at the corporate level that are responsible for defining and implementing Oko's "customer-oriented service model." These teams aren't designed around customer segments or products but rather around customer needs such as housing, building wealth, and everyday banking needs.

There is a mechanism for sharing information between the call center and the member bank that currently "owns" each customer. However, as of 2000, there was no central customer relationship management system in place to make all customer information and interactions available to all member banks. Jarkko sees this current organizational structure as a problem in moving forward. "In the future, when the customer relationship is more clearly established and maintained through multiple touchpoints, stronger corporate-level control is clearly needed."

Seizing the Internet Opportunity

As you're no doubt aware, Finland is an extremely wired country. Internet penetration is very high, with over 2 million Finns regularly using the Internet. Okobank's most popular early electronic banking application turned out to be online bill payment. Before the Web, you would receive your bills by mail and then take them to your bank branch or to a bill-paying ATM machine. Each bill had a bar code. By passing a wand over the bar code for each bill, you could authorize the payment from your bank account. Moving this function to the Internet meant that Finns could pay bills conveniently from home, and could receive and review the bills electronically. Internet-based bill payment took off! By the fall of 1999, 400,000 Okobank customers, or 20 percent, were paying their bills online. (Based on the rapid adoption rate, Jarkko predicts that 50% of the bank's customers will be using online bill payment by 2002.) Customers could also handle their other banking functions—transferring money from one account to another, reviewing credit card transactions, investing in mutual funds, trading stock online, investing in mutual funds, and applying for or checking on the status of a loan—all via the Web.

Timo Ritakallio, a member of Okobank's executive board and the head of corporate banking and debt capital markets, watched these early consumer Internet successes carefully, and listened to what his business customers were requesting. He quickly realized that business customers were going to be equally aggressive in wanting to be able to transact online. He put corporate banking initiatives into the e-commerce team's list of priorities. Between 1998 and 2000, the company delivered secure extranet linkages for its corporate customers, including bank guarantees with pre-negotiated limits, bond issues, foreign exchange, money market trading, and electronic billing. Web-based cash management services were offered in early 2001.

Pioneering in Mobile Commerce

In 1996 Okobank became the first bank in the world to let customers use their mobile phones to do banking via wireless data services. The wireless digital media team used the basic Short Messaging Services (SMS) available on most of Europe's GSM-standard mobile phones to let customers check their account balances, look at their credit card transactions, or pay their bills. Despite the limitations of the small device, customers liked the convenience of being able to control their money from anywhere at any time. Within three years, more than 200,000 Okobank customers were banking online via their cellular phones. Soon, customers were able to perform a wide range of wireless data transactions, including checking stock quotes, getting alerts on stock prices, and executing buy or sell transactions when stock prices reached the threshold they had set.

In 1998 Nokia introduced the Communicator 911. This was a combination mobile phone and organizer that became extremely popular in Finland among business executives. Most companies purchased these appliances for their employees. As soon as he previewed the new device, it was clear to Jarrko that customers would want to take advantage of the larger screen and keyboard to manage their finances wirelessly. The Okobank team was able to take advantage of the increased memory in the Nokia Communicator to download a small application, offering a much friendlier user interface with self-explanatory menus and less need to enter cryptic codes. Customers could pre-load most of their account numbers and profile information to expedite commonly performed functions. Yet it is impossible for someone to steal your phone and transfer funds. Each time you execute a transaction involving the transfer of funds, you are re-authenticated. (You are challenged to enter a PIN number and given a unique code for each transaction). By the end of 1999, tens of thousands of customers were doing their banking from their mobile Communicators.

In early 2000, as the Wireless Application Protocol (WAP) became popular, the team, under the direction of Erkki Ervasti, also implemented a WAP version of Okobank's m-banking applications. This proved a bit less popular because of the lack of availability of WAP devices, the high cost of use, and inconvenient service activation. (To use WAP services you had to make an additional, separate phone call!) Still, Okobank had proved to its customers that no matter what the latest and greatest offering in m-commerce, Okobank would be the first to offer it. This commitment began to change Okobank's reputation from stodgy, conservative player to innovator.

Getting the Member Banks' Support for New E-Business Models

These Internet and mobile commerce initiatives originated from Okobank Group's central IT group in Helsinki. But of course, all such initiatives had to be approved by the member banks that are the majority owners of the Group. At first, these pilots were encouraged as a way to reach out to customers and to cement relationships. Customers seemed to take to the Internet and to wireless data services.

By early 2000, however, the member banks were getting nervous. If customers began to bank via the Web and over their phones, would the Okobank Group decide that local branches were no longer necessary? What would become of the personal relationships that had been so painstakingly established? Would the bank begin to close down branches, making it inconvenient for customers to do business face-to-face? Okobank's existing customers clearly favored the multi-channel/multi-touchpoint approach to banking. Customers wanted the convenience of banking online, in the branch, by phoning the call center, or by serving themselves using wireless data. Closing down branches and other points of presence wouldn't make sense for the majority of customers who still needed occasional guidance. But for the more self-directed customers, and for the next generation of prospective customers who were self-directed, the Okobank strategists felt that Oko should experiment with different approaches.

Strategy formulation in Okobank Group is a process through which Group Central and member banks jointly discuss the issues and define the future course of action. Matti Korkeela headed the subcommittee that planned the e-banking strategy for this decision-making process. This subcommittee suggested that the Group run a number of different parallel projects:

1. Launch a portal site that would include Oko's banking services in the context of the activities customers needed to perform, e.g., buy a car, finance a home, or relocate. (This project was already underway.)
2. Partner with an Internet Service Provider and existing portal player to provide banking and credit card services under a different brand name to the young, hip crowd who wouldn't ordinarily think of coming to Okobank.
3. Form an alliance with insurance and pension fund management companies that would offer customers one-stop shopping for a broader range of services, and take advantage of Okobank's existing multi-channel, multi-touchpoint infrastructure to service those customers.

The presentation was compelling. The member banks' executives realized that, if Okobank were to gain marketshare within Finland, the Group had to become even more aggressive in reaching out to new markets. That meant luring new customers with different brands and different customer experiences. "What we did for the first five years was an online extension of our vertically integrated banking model," Jarkko explained. "That's not what today's customers want. They're telling us they want to pick the best-of-breed solutions for their one-stop financial services needs. We're going to have to offer both approaches—vertically integrated solutions and mix-and-match solutions—in order to compete."

Sponsor a Consumer Portal

Okobank embarked on two parallel consumer portal strategies. Both carry different brand names. Jarkko describes the first as a "defensive portal strategy." It's designed to offer broader services to Okobank's existing banking customers, while attracting a new, younger clientele to the new brand. Here's how it came about.

In late 1998, Okobank's executives, like many other executives around the world, became intrigued by the idea of sponsoring an online portal. The board approved funding for a joint venture between the Okobank Group, an insurance company, Pohjola, and one of Finland's largest magazine publishers, A-Lehdet. Okobank group and the insurance company partner put in 95 percent of the funding, and the portal venture was set up as a separate entity. Olli Latola, an energetic lawyer with eighteen years of experience in banking and insurance, was appointed managing director, and Sallamaari Muhonen, a creative young woman with a background in television production, was appointed producer.

The idea was to develop and launch a newly branded, consumer-oriented portal that would assist the average Finn in handling all the life events he needed to cope with—moving, buying a car, going to university, starting a family, building a nest egg. They correctly perceived that consumers would be drawn to the site not to "do their banking" or to "go shopping," but to conduct research and get help with various issues and scenarios. By partnering with a magazine publisher, the portal would have all the necessary content they'd need to provide timely information on a variety of issues, like which car to buy. And of course, Okobank Group and Pohjola would be able to provide car loans, home loans, and other financial services as welcome offerings in the course of the customers' scenarios.

The plan is to launch this site, code-named "Virtual Finland," in early 2001, initially targeting young families. The portal site is expected to have four separate "channels"—one for the home, one for the family, one for travel, and one for economic and legal matters. Why did Okobank opt to create a new brand identity for this portal? Jarkko explains, "Our bank brand is fine for banking. We are seen as reliable, familiar and customer oriented. Our banking site is on the top ten list of Finnish Web sites. But a bank is surely not the place to relax and spend time in. We want to offer our consumer customers a broader set of useful services and entertainment. We can use our heavily trafficked Okobank site to drive traffic to this new, broader portal site. And by building a consumer-needs–oriented portal with rich content, we believe we can also create a better marketplace for our merchant customers than we can by just simply pulling together buyers and sellers on our Web site." Jarkko believes that bank-operated shopping malls haven't been a great success because they're not organized around key consumer scenarios.

Partnering with Sonera

Okobank's executives knew that many non-banks were going to become the new players as financial services intermediaries. Consumers, particularly younger consumers, don't feel the need to deal with a bank in order to avail themselves of financial services. Concurrent with the work on "Virtual Finland," Okobank also started exploring opportunities of a joint venture with Sonera, the leading Finnish portal/Internet Service Provider (ISP). Launched in 1994 as an Internet Service Provider, Sonera had become the number one portal in Finland, with 840,000 unique visitors per month and 300,000 ISP accounts. A typical horizontal portal with content, commerce, and community, Sonera was largely an advertising-based site. Very little commerce was actually being conducted online. Sonera had decided to beef up its commerce offerings in the form of a new commerce initiative, "Sonera Plaza," and was planning to link up with Leonia Bank, the third largest bank in Finland, to provide the credit card, debit card, and other financial services needed. Sonera and Leonia were both majority owned by the Finnish government.

MOBILIZING FOR ACTION

Jarkko had recognized the potential threat from ISPs since late 1998 and had identified Sonera as a potential player in that field. Even though it seemed that rival Leonia Bank would have the upper hand in potential partnerships (Harri Hollmen, the new Managing Director of the Sonera Plaza initiative, was former CEO of Leonia), Oko's opportunity came in the summer of 2000. Thanks to Jarkko's lobbying and the recently approved strategic initiatives, one of Okobank Group's executives approached Harri to see if he'd be willing to let Okobank, rather than Leonia, play the role of "behind the scenes" banker for the financial services section of the Sonera Plaza portal. Harri agreed. He was impressed with the e-commerce and m-commerce capabilities Oko already had in place. He knew that it would be a simple matter and a safe bet to slide Oko's e-banking and m-banking services under his new venture.

AGILE PARTNERING

The deal that Okobank Group struck with Sonera Plaza was an innovative one. They formed a new joint venture to build the financial services section of Sonera Plaza. Sonera Plaza would have 80 percent ownership and Okobank would have 20 percent. They would split the expenses and the profits accordingly. Okobank invested 40 million Finnish marks in cash and would provide all of the underlying banking and credit card services, including support for m-commerce transactions. Jarkko estimated that Okobank had already invested an additional 40 million Finnish marks in building the multi-touchpoint infrastructure that would support the core services. Okobank's branding would be invisible in the core online banking section of the financial services portal. Instead the banking, credit card, and debit card services—the core basic services—would carry the Sonera Plaza brand.

But, Okobank's *branded* offerings would be available to Sonera Plaza customers in the investments, loans, and insurance sections of the financial services portal. There, Okobank's offerings would compete with those of competitors in each category. Sonera Plaza customers would be able to mix and match their own best-of-breed offerings from a series of competitive suppliers. Sonera Plaza would manage the customer relationships and the customer experience across the brands. And as a 20 percent owner in the financial services portal, Okobank would gain 20 percent of any profits, whether or not they came from the Okobank offerings.

What we like about this business structure is that it allows Okobank to be in relationship with every single Sonera Plaza customer by being the exclusive provider of the basic financial services he'll most likely want and need. True, the customer doesn't know he's being serviced by Okobank. But since this is a new target market—mostly young people who don't value the Okobank brand—it's not a liability. Only time will tell whether Sonera Plaza's financial services portal becomes profitable.

A One-Stop Financial Services Alliance for Customers Who Want Guidance

With two very different Internet portal plays under their belt, Oko's executives weren't finished yet. These two portal initiatives were targeted at the technology-savvy, self-directed investor. That was still only 20 percent of the Finnish market. What about the majority of the customers who needed a bit of hand-holding from time to time and who valued the face-to-face experience? For this customer segment, Oko came up with another e-business strategy that leveraged its existing infrastructure investments. Through a set of complicated buy-outs and investments, Oko managed to put together a very strong alliance with all of the top insurance and pension providers in Finland—

Pohjola Insurance, Suomi Mutual Life Assurance, Ilmarinen Mutual Pension Insurance company, and a couple of smaller players. The game plan is to provide an alliance, much like the Star or One World alliances among the major airlines. Customers will be able to walk into any of the alliance partners' offices and branches and transact any business—insurance or banking—from any combination of partners. And of course, the Alliance Partners will join to offer a shared online financial services portal. Whether customers interact via the Web, by wireless data phones, or by walking into any branch bank or insurance office, they will have access to all of the partners' services and access to a shared customer relationship management system.

Takeaways

Notice that the Okobank story starts with an aggressive adoption of leading-edge technologies to let customers serve themselves. Okobank began with online bill payment and Internet banking services, and continued to innovate with each wave of mobile wireless technology. At the same time, the bank stayed focused on its core mission: caring about customers and their outcomes. Instead of building a fragmented set of services for each new online initiative, the bank's central technology group was able to leverage its 40 million Finnish mark investment to address a number of very different markets and needs.

Oko has shown itself to be a risk-taker in launching several parallel e-business projects, with aggressive partnering required for each one. Each of these initiatives has been set up as a separate, independent business venture, with its own management and autonomy, but all are built to leverage the shared core e-banking and m-banking services. The result is a portfolio-approach to business evolution. Some ventures may fare better than others, but Okobank is clearly hedging its bets.

Finally, Okobank's e-commerce strategy has one other very interesting characteristic. Okobank is experimenting with both a vertically integrated approach and with disintegrated, mix-and-match approaches. It is using the Okobank branded experience, and yet it is also hiding its customer experience behind other brands that are more likely to appeal to a new customer segment.

Patty's Suggestions for Okobank

What appears to me to be missing in Okobank's current strategy is enough emphasis on branding. Okobank needs to beef up the core brand, reinforce the customer-centric values of the Okobank brand, and modernize its brand—to shed its stodgy, conservative image. Okobank's new, separately branded ventures need to be given edgier brand personalities to break out of the pack and give customers an opportunity to identify with them.

My bets are on Sonera Plaza over the Virtual Finland portal. Sonera already has the market awareness and momentum. And the small Finnish market probably doesn't have room for two major consumer portals. I suggest that Okobank cut its losses now on the Virtual Finland project and go full steam ahead on two fronts, instead of three: the Sonera Plaza venture and its bricks-and-clicks Alliance venture. Both are much more likely to appeal to customers. They presume that customers are in control and will want to mix and match financial services from among the best-of-breed players. On the other hand, what I like about the Virtual Finland project is its focus on customer scenarios and the fact that Okobank's small business customers could offer their services to consumers in the context of scenarios they're trying to accomplish. Perhaps there's another partnering deal in the making—Virtual Finland could become an integral part of the Sonera Plaza offerings. Either way, Okobank wins.

A Sample Flight Deck for Okobank

	Navigation	Performance	Operations	Environment
Customer Numbers	Number of consumers with active accounts by customer segment Number of active accounts per household Number of online consumers Share of wallet/portfolio per consumer Number of business customers and business accounts Share of wallet/portfolio per business account	Number of new consumer accounts in the 18–34 age group Percentage of customers who are self-directed Percentage of customers with multiple products Growth of assets per consumer and household Growth of assets in business accounts	Percentage of customers using online bill pay Percentage of customers using mobile access Percentage of customers using other online/mobile services Percentage of customers shifting all accounts to Okobank Number of new business accounts	Finnish customers using online financial services Growth rate of the 18–34 age group Number of EU banks marketing within Finland Number of nonbanks offering financial services in Finland
Customer Retention	Retention rate per customer segment Share of wallet per customer segment Customer loyalty ratings per customer segment	Increase/decrease in retention rate per customer segment Increase/decrease in share of wallet per customer segment Change in use of weekly/monthly services (e.g., bill pay) per segment	Recency of customer interactions by customer segment Frequency of customer interactions by customer segment	Competitors' retention rates Competitors' share of wallet Competitors' share of weekly/monthly services
Customer Experience	Customer satisfaction by customer segment Customer satisfaction by touchpoint: • In-branchl • Online • Call center • Mobile/wireless	Satisfaction with banking, brokerage, etc., tasks Satisfaction with cycle time (lines, Web response, etc.) Satisfaction with service quality and interactions	End-to-end performance of key customer scenarios Server response time Server uptime	Ease of use of competitive offerings Customer scenario performance of competitive offerings
Customer Spending	Revenues and profits per customer Revenues and profits per household or business account Total assets held by customer	New deposits per customer Loan income Fee income Average account balance Share of wallet	Costs to serve per customer Costs to serve per touchpoint	Competitors' profits per customer Competitors' costs-to-serve

W. W. GRAINGER, INC.: FROM INDUSTRIAL SUPPLIES MIDDLEMAN TO E-MARKET MAKER AND E-UTILITIES PROVIDER

The e-market revolution is upon us! Business customers are now demanding convenient, one-stop sourcing, with price and product comparisons for many of the products and supplies they use. Grainger was one of the catalysts of the e-market revolution. As a long-time B2B catalog supplier, Grainger had been offering one-stop shopping to business customers who needed industrial supplies to run their operations. Then, when Grainger took its catalog onto the Internet, that e-catalog became one of the first e-markets, letting buyers compare and source products from thousands of suppliers.

This is a story about an industrial supplies middleman that has been in the forefront of the B2B e-market revolution. What steps did W. W. Grainger, Inc., take to become one of the key players in a variety of B2B markets?

Grainger focused first on its customer experience: making it easy for customers to locate and buy hard-to-find tools and supplies using a multi-touchpoint business model. Organizing product information for easy decision-making became one of Grainger's core competencies. Then the company experimented with a variety of e-business models and ventures, all leveraging the company's deep understanding of industrial supplies buyers and their decision-making needs. Grainger has designed itself to morph—in whatever direction customers take these e-markets.

One-Stop Shopping for Hard-to-Find Industrial Supplies

W. W. Grainger, Inc., was founded in 1927 by William W. Grainger as a wholesaler of industrial electric motors. The company's original, eight-page MotorBook catalog quickly became the preferred resource for purchasing agents and maintenance managers needing to locate replacement motors. Within six years, Grainger's sales had grown to $250,000 and the company had begun to expand beyond electric motors to include a broad array of industrial products. By its fiftieth birthday, Grainger had 141 branch stores and 424 sales representatives serving businesses in forty states. MotorBook had grown to 756 pages. By 1984 Grainger had surpassed $1 billion per year in sales and had renamed its catalog to reflect the much broader diversity of products being sold. In 1992 Grainger acquired Lab Safety Supply, a direct-marketing company focused on industrial safety products. And in 1996 Grainger acquired Acklands, Ltd., the leading maintenance, repair, and operations (MRO) supplier in Canada. In the United States, there are approximately 150,000 distributors selling industrial supplies to about 10 million businesses. Industrial supplies—MRO to industry insiders—is a $250 billion U.S. market. Chicago-based W. W. Grainger, Inc., with 1999 revenues of $4.5 billion, is the world's largest player. Grainger's sales are currently concentrated in the United States, Canada, and Mexico.

The "Red Book," as Grainger's catalog came to be called, became a common fixture in corporate purchasing offices. If you needed industrial supplies, you'd look there first. Grainger's Supply division mails out 2 million copies of its red catalog each year, featuring more than 86,000 brand name items ranging from A-coils to Zip screws. The company stocks around 220,000 discrete products for maintenance, repair, HVAC, testing, and construction. These products are available for same-day delivery or pickup from any of Grainger's 385 branches across the United States and 190 branches in Canada and Mexico. That means that more than 70 percent of U.S. businesses are within 20 minutes of a Grainger branch. Each branch carries an average of $1 to 2 million worth of inventory. Grainger's Parts division offers an additional 285,000 repair and replacement parts from 550 different manufacturers. These are available twenty-four hours a day, seven days a week, and are shipped worldwide from Grainger's Parts distribution center in Northbrook, Illinois.

How did customers deal with Grainger pre-Web? They could consult the paper catalog, which contained the stocked subset of the available items, along with the list prices. They could call the nearest branch to locate a part and get their customer specific price and availability. Accounts could also access a CD-ROM catalog, which would have their company-specific prices. Or, they could contact one of Grainger's 1,500 direct sales representatives to discuss their needs and then place the order.

The Grainger Brand

Grainger has high brand recognition among North American business customers and manufacturers alike. Most think of Grainger today as a broad line distributor of industrial parts and supplies. Customers associate Grainger with excellent, knowledgeable, friendly service and fast fulfillment. You go to Grainger first when you need something quickly or when you don't know where else to find it. Grainger is the place to turn for spot buys of a wide variety of products and parts. Grainger doesn't compete on price. It competes on speed and convenience.

Core Values

Grainger's corporate culture is extremely customer-centric and surprisingly agile for an older, established company. Agility and learning are two core values, as are employee empowerment, accountability, teamwork, and having fun. The company's "no excuses" guarantee for the products and services it offers gives employees a lot of leeway. They're encouraged to do what it takes to satisfy customers. This customer-centric culture is reinforced by stories, in which Grainger's branch managers or sales reps tend to be the heroes and heroines who will open up a branch at 2 A.M. to get the part a customer needs to get his assembly line running again.

The Internet Came Knocking on Grainger's Door

LISTENING TO THE CUSTOMER

Hewlett-Packard is one of Grainger's largest customers and HP's Mike Johnson collared Martha Frey, Grainger's enthusiastic Director of Catalog Marketing, when she was visiting HP in Palo Alto in early 1995. He told her that he had begun ordering office supplies over the Internet and would love to order industrial supplies the same way. Martha was intrigued. She and Paris Devine, Grainger's district sales manager, went to Mike's office and watched him select and order office supplies from an online catalog on HP's intranet site. As Martha recalls, "The light went on for me at that moment. I could visualize everyone from janitors to maintenance professionals buying tools and motors over the 'Net from Grainger."

Martha returned to Grainger's Chicago headquarters and looked for people who knew something about the Internet. She recruited Jeff Brandon from Grainger's Emerging Technology department and Jamie O'Neil, from Grainger's Planning department. After brainstorming the possibilities, Jeff, Jamie, and Martha wrote a memo describing their vision for a Grainger.com e-commerce site and requested $75,000 in funding to get started. That memo landed on Don Bielinski's desk.

LISTENING TO THE MARKET

In the meantime, the Internet had also come knocking on Don Bielinski's door. Don had spent twenty-seven years at Grainger—"I was born here," the lean, energetic fifty-year old chuckles. Don began his career in finance, rising to become Grainger's CFO. He also spent time leading strategy and development. By the time these Internet opportunities came calling, Don was Senior Vice President of Sales and Marketing for the portfolio of Grainger's businesses that accounted for the bulk of the company's revenues and profits.

Two companies—a large telco and a large cable company—had the same proposal: to take Grainger's industrial supplies catalog onto the Web. Each group gave a similar pitch: "Instead of mailing out catalogs and taking orders over the phone, be an anchor tenant in our online mall(s), and you'll expand your reach to the millions of businesses that will soon be shopping online." In early '95, of course, very few companies were doing business on the Internet. Most other ex-CFOs would have dismissed such proposals as a waste of money and sent the suitors packing. But Don was quick to realize that the Internet was a tornado on Grainger's horizon.

Don brought the e-commerce proposal to Richard Keyser, the Chairman and CEO, and they established an executive steering committee for the project.

Pioneering an Integrated Clicks-and-Bricks Strategy

How could Grainger use the Internet and the Web to make life even more convenient for its customers, the e-commerce team wondered. Here's what they come up with. Grainger.com could:

- Give customers access to all the products Grainger makes available (over 220,000), not just the 86,500 that could be presented in the paper catalog.
- Give customers much better tools for searching, locating, and selecting the product that best suits their needs.
- Deliver products the same day from the branch closest to the customer who placed the order, or ship them from one of Grainger's five regional distribution centers and have them delivered the next day.

Establishing an Internet Commerce Unit

The strategy team decided to create a separate, new Internet Commerce unit to develop and deploy Grainger's e-commerce initiatives. According to Richard Keyser, "We did a couple of things right. Very, very early on, we set up a separate unit for our Internet initiative. We put it in a separate location. It developed its own culture, and it was able to act a lot like a dot-com. I don't know if we were brilliant or lucky, but that has worked out really well."[10]

Tackling the Complexity of B2B

Looking back on it, Don describes Grainger's initial vision as "quite profound." As the team was creating its vision in 1995, the best example of online commerce was Amazon.com's early B2C site. Nobody had really articulated a strong vision for B2B e-commerce at the time. Don realized that Grainger.com would need to offer:

- **Customized Pricing.** "In the B2B world, there's no 'one price fits all.' We knew we had to have custom-tailored pricing for each business customer." (Grainger offers 65 million different price points!) The Web site would need to honor each business account's unique prices.
- **B2B Payment Methods.** Business customers generally don't use credit cards; they establish an open account. This involves checking the business customer's credit, verifying that the particular person you're dealing with is authorized to conduct business on that com-

---

[10] From an interview in *BusinessWeek Online,* "Grainger's Richard Keyser: Cranking an Old-Line Company to Net Speed."

pany's behalf, and establishing the purchasing guidelines (spending limits, quantity discounts, and so on).

- **Real-Time Inventory and Availability.** "In B2B, product availability isn't a nice feature to have; it's an imperative. If my assembly line is down, I can't wait six days to get the item I need. If my plant is in the Chicago area, I need to know that the Arlington Heights branch has the part in stock."

Key Customer Scenario: Locating the Right Product for the Job at Hand

Deep subject matter expertise about industrial products—how customers think about them and what attributes customers care about—remains the foundation that Grainger has built on as it has expanded from the original Grainger.com site into e-markets. Grainger's e-commerce team focused on making it easy for customers to find the products they really needed. In the industrial parts business, return rates are high. "If you want to select the right electric motor among the 4,000 we carry, how are you going to find the right one?" Don explained. "We knew that we had to make it really easy for customers to find the right product for their application." The design team started thinking about how they could let customers enter known parameters about each category of product to narrow their searches. By February 1997, the team had evolved parametric searching into a more complete application, a specific customer scenario (e.g., "I need to find the motor that will work in my situation"). Called "MotorMatch," this product selection tool makes it comparatively easy for a customer to find a motor for a specific type of machinery or context (e.g., 12-volt power supply) or to select a replacement motor that will work as well as the original model.

Creating a Consistent, Cross-Touchpoint Experience

Despite the fact that Grainger.com was initially set up in its own Internet Commerce division, Grainger's management team never thought of Grainger.com as a separate entity. The e-commerce site was always thought of as an adjunct to the Grainger experience and a logical extension to the Grainger branch network. Here's how the original system worked. As customers placed their orders online, they would be automatically acknowledged. The orders themselves would be automatically faxed to the branch closest to the customer, where they would be rekeyed into Grainger's branch order entry systems. Although Grainger.com used a semi-automated order entry process at the outset, the actual process was relatively seamless from the customer's point of view. Orders were immediately acknowledged and typically entered into the "real" systems within a few minutes rather than hours. From that point on, Grainger's existing systems and processes could track the orders through to fulfillment.

Coopting the Sales Force

One very smart decision the strategy team made was to compensate its direct sales people for any orders their customers placed on the Web site. Incentives were added to strengthen the bond of the sales reps to the Internet channel. Web orders quickly became the most profitable since the cost to process them is lower. In addition, the Grainger.com team discovered that customers who place orders on the Web tend to up-sell and cross-sell themselves, thanks to the efficient organization and compelling merchandising of the online experience. The size of Web orders averaged twice that of off-line orders.

Evolution of Grainger.com

Grainger spent $6.7 million on developing Grainger.com during the eighteen months it took for the Web site to reach full functionality. But the company kept going. What impressed Don and the other executives the most was the fact that customers who did business online placed much larger orders than those who shopped using the catalog and the phone or stopping in at a branch location. Of course, Grainger has made continuous improvements to the Grainger.com site between 1997 and the present.

In addition to the customized pricing that its business customers already receive, Grainger.com now also supports buying communities. The first was the U.S. Federal Government whose buyers see a government-only product catalog. They use their purchasing card numbers and receive the pre-negotiated pricing.

Grainger.com remains one of the world's preeminent multi-supplier, multi-product e-marketplaces. What distinguishes Grainger.com from other e-market offerings is the tight integration with Grainger's physical branch and phone support network.

Results

In 1999 Grainger spent more than $20 million for the combined development, marketing, and customer service to support Grainger.com. The site generated $100 million worth of orders during that same period. In the first half of 2000, Grainger.com generated $120 million of revenues from 100,000 business accounts. The size of the average order placed through Grainger.com was $250, compared with $140 for branch and phone orders.

Experimenting with New Business Models: *Throwing Spaghetti Against the Wall*

Many companies would have been content to evolve their e-business strategy through continuous innovation of their initial offering. But having been bitten by the Internet bug, Grainger realized that the company couldn't content itself with "Webifying" its current product line and offerings. So in 1999 and 2000, Grainger's Internet Commerce Group launched four different e-commerce initiatives, each with its own compelling business logic. What they had in common was an appreciation for the complexity of B2B purchasing and an understanding of the requirement for completeness, easy searchability, and side-by-side comparisons of product descriptions.

Once Grainger.com had become an integrated capability of the Grainger Industrial Supply business—and while OrderZone.com (the first e-market experiment) was still proving itself and evolving—the Grainger management team did something very interesting. Instead of slowing the pace of innovation, they picked it up! As new customer needs and patterns emerged, Don Bielinski would appoint a president for each new e-business venture, give him or her the seed money needed to get going, and look for early results—at least in terms of customer feedback and traction. Looking over Don's shoulder reminded me of watching my first husband cook spaghetti. When Jim thought it was close to ready, he would take a few strands out of the pot and throw them onto the kitchen wall. If they stuck, the spaghetti was ready to eat. Don has mastered the process of cooking digital businesses. You listen carefully to customers, watch the market, and throw new ideas out into the marketplace to see what sticks!

FIRST INITIATIVE: ORDERZONE

Grainger's management team surmised that customers would soon want products that the company didn't offer—products like office supplies and furniture, uniforms, laboratory equipment, and electronic components. Customers were increasingly looking for one-stop shopping for everything they needed. But this posed a strategic problem for Grainger: should the company extend its product line and its brand beyond the traditional industrial supplies market?

An Early E-Market Experiment

The next business model Don and the management team decided to try was one of the first multi-distributor e-marketplaces. (Grainger.com was a single-distributor e-market.) The idea was to provide small and mid-sized business customers with the convenience of one-stop shopping across multiple suppliers' and distributors' products. Since Grainger currently owned only 2 percent of the fragmented MRO market in the United States and had 1.5 million active business accounts (of a potential 10 million), one logical strategy was to aggregate many of these distributors into an online market that would attract the millions of smaller businesses that weren't currently doing business with Grainger. Other large distributors had the same needs. Their largest customers would do business with them directly, but to reach the broader market of smaller companies they needed to band together.

The Grainger vision of a true e-market wasn't like a shopping mall or a product showcase, in which customers go from store to store to make their purchases and transact business with each store separately. Grainger's execs had already learned that customers valued aggregation and convenience. They realized that business customers wanted to be able to search quickly and easily across suppliers' product lines. Customers wanted to establish a single business relationship for credit approval and open order processing. They wanted to be able to purchase goods from these multiple suppliers on a single order and keep track of their shipments and deliveries in one place. And of course, customers would still expect to receive the customized pricing they were used to getting with each supplier.

Partnered with Multiple, Non-Competing Suppliers

Don began sounding out the suppliers of complementary products. Since the venture was Grainger's idea, and because much of its presumed success would be based on Grainger's experience in evolving Grainger.com, Grainger's executive team decided to launch this new venture as a Grainger-owned business. However they believed they'd have more luck recruiting other distributors if they came up with an identity separate and apart from the Grainger brand. Eventually they settled on "OrderZone by Grainger."

Daniel Hamburger joined Don's team in late 1998 to head up the OrderZone project. Don was able to recruit Cintas (suppliers of uniforms and work clothes); Corporate Express (for office and computer supplies); Lab Safety Supply, a Grainger subsidiary (for safety supplies); Marshall Industries (for electronic and production components); and VWR Scientific Products (for laboratory supplies).

Outsourced Everything

Having gained experience designing and implementing one Web business internally, Don decided this time to outsource everything—including Web site development, call center support, and credit checking. To build the site Grainger selected Perot Systems' TimeZero subsidiary. This was an experienced group of B2B e-market developers who had cut their teeth on an early, but failed, B2B marketplace called Nets, Inc. Don figured that the combined learning of his Grainger.com team and the ex-Nets team would yield good results for this ambitious project.

First-to-Market with a New Business Model

OrderZone broke new ground in several areas. It was an initial e-market in which multiple suppliers' inventories, availabilities, and customized pricing systems were combined. It was one of the first e-markets in which customer information was shared between the retailer and each of its suppliers. And it was in the first wave of e-markets to attempt to create a set of standardized business processes that would flow directly into suppliers' systems.

Easy-to-Search Product Information at the Core

As they began to design OrderZone's multi-supplier catalog, the Grainger/TimeZero team tried to leverage as much of the learning as they could from the Grainger.com team. For example, Grainger.com's content management team had spent a lot of time developing a dictionary of product categories and subcategories as well as a set of parameters that customers wanted to search on. In developing its metacatalog infrastructure for OrderZone, the TimeZero team began with the Grainger.com dictionary. They evolved an even more sophisticated product categorization framework. The tricky and time-consuming part, of course, was pouring all of Grainger.com's product information, and that of each of the other partners, into the new framework. Next the product catalogs had to be linked to each distributor's dynamic pricing rules and into their real-time inventory systems. OrderZone became one of the world's first integrated, real-time aggregators.

OrderZone Gave Grainger a Head Start in Complex E-Markets

OrderZone by Grainger was announced in February 1999, while it was still in beta mode. Then it went live in May 1999. The initial implementation had some gaps in terms of giving customers the completely seamless experience they wanted, so it was probably good that Grainger hadn't led with the Grainger brand.

Here's how it worked. Once a business customer had registered with OrderZone and received credit approval,[11] the buyer could select his preferred suppliers. Any pre-negotiated price lists and related

---

[11] The credit-checking was one process Grainger kept in-house; they couldn't find a third party that could do real-time credit checks as efficiently as Grainger's own systems did.

terms and conditions that the customer already had with these suppliers would be loaded into his OrderZone profile. The customer could search across product catalogs by keyword or by using the supplier's product number, but there was no parametric search available at the outset, nor was there a way to compare and contrast multiple products from multiple suppliers. It was easy to order from multiple suppliers, however, and easy to pay your account with a single corporate check each month.

A single customer service number was available to help customers with questions about the various companies' products or the OrderZone purchasing process. What customers missed most in the initial offering was an integrated delivery tracking application. Since these products were shipped from a number of suppliers, each using different shipment methods, it became difficult for the OrderZone service reps or the customers to track all the items in each order.

According to Don, it took about eighteen months for OrderZone to attain the full set of features and functions that customers expected. Grainger spent $8 million on the development of OrderZone in 1998 and another $21 million in 1999 for development, operations, and marketing. Revenues from OrderZone in 1999 totaled approximately $500,000, for a net loss in 1999 of $20 million.

Finding a Home for OrderZone

By mid-May 2000, Don knew that Grainger alone didn't have the wherewithal to make OrderZone successful. "We came to the conclusion that OrderZone needed a fair degree of independence," Don recalled. "And we wanted to get some risk diversification." Grainger had already been in conversation with a venture-capital–funded start-up, Works.com, which was providing a full service Web-based procurement solution to small and medium-sized businesses. It was a good fit. Don characterized it as a "marriage between the carpet and the concrete." By merging the two entities, Works.com gained immediate access to a huge set of industrial supplies it could add to the office supplies it already offered. The merger was consummated on August 1, 2000. Grainger transferred all of the assets and operations of OrderZone and invested an additional $21 million in the new merged company. Grainger received a 40 percent equity stake in this promising start-up and a more direct online channel to the small and medium-sized business market for its core products, plus it no longer had the burden of funding and operating this complex, multiplayer e-market.

SECOND CONCURRENT INITIATIVE: FINDMRO

What do you do when there's a customer need you can't fill cost-effectively? Here's how Grainger met the challenge.

Six months after OrderZone was launched, Don and his Internet strategy team were at it again. What triggered their next Internet venture was a business dilemma. For years Grainger had had a side business. When a customer needed a product that Grainger didn't supply, it would locate the product and procure it for the customer. Customers who needed these products in a hurry were happy to pay a premium to have Grainger track the goods down. However, this business wasn't a very profitable one for Grainger. Grainger wanted to capitalize on the business, not walk away from the information asset it had built up over the years—a database of more than five million products that Grainger didn't supply. And Grainger executives knew that customers would value the ability to easily locate hard-to-find products. The solution: take it online.

The Birth of FindMRO.com

Don tapped Ron Paulson to head up this new initiative. Ron's goal was to build an online e-market/portal in six months. And he did. There were several reasons that it took less time to launch this new e-business than the previous two. First, Grainger didn't need to convince suppliers to participate in this new marketplace. Since Grainger had traditionally been taking orders for their products and passing those orders on, there was no change in the business model. Second, the core database of 5 million products across 100,000 brands from 12,000 suppliers already existed, as did the business processes for keeping that database up-to-date. Third, FindMRO could leverage many of the applications that had already been developed for Grainger.com and OrderZone. Although Grainger didn't test, source, or guarantee these products, it was equipped to locate them, order them, take title to them, handle credit-checking, and open account-ordering. The products were shipped direct from the suppliers.

Great Idea: Early Uptake

FindMRO.com was launched in November 1999 with little fanfare. This was now Grainger's third online MRO venture, and the business press and potential customers were beginning to be confused about Grainger's direction. Don and his team didn't want to exacerbate that confusion with a major advertising campaign, at least until they knew if they had a winner. After its first four months of operation, FindMRO had booked $6 million worth of orders. This exceeded the executive team's expectations.

Shift in Business Model to a Syndicated Service

E-business projects often shift business models in mid-stream. FindMRO began life as an attempt to create another one-stop shopping opportunity for businesses that wanted to save time in locating hard-to-find products, to salvage a key Grainger asset, and to make the MRO brokerage business a more profitable one. Within two months of opening its online doors, a different business model came knocking. A number of companies that catered to the industrial market immediately spotted FindMRO as a valuable service they could offer *their* customers. Commerce One, the platform supplier for B2B e-marketplaces, began talking about incorporating FindMRO into its e-market offerings. And other suitors came calling. Ron realized that his team had created a syndicatable asset—an information resource and a service—that would generate revenues for Grainger as well as new leads for Grainger's customer database.

The first two companies to syndicate the FindMRO service and link it to their own offerings were Ace Hardware and ENI-Net.com (an e-market for the environmental industry).

Ace Hardware signed a multimillion-dollar sourcing contract with FindMRO in mid-January 2000. By the second quarter 2000, Ace had linked FindMRO to its ACENET 2000 Intranet site and demonstrated the use of the service to its 5,000 store managers. Ace's motto is: "If you need it, we can get it." FindMRO gave Ace's retailers an efficient way to make good on that promise. As Paul Ingevaldson, Senior Vice President of International and Technology at Ace Hardware, explained, "This online connection to FindMRO is packed with benefits for the Ace retailer and Ace Hardware Corporation. It gives our retailers the opportunity to use and leverage our ACENET 2000 Intranet system to lower their procurement cost on this category of product while enhancing service to their customers."

ENI-Net became the first emarket to incorporate FindMRO as a service to its registered users. ENI-Net is a B2B emarketplace for environmental products and services used by industrial, environmental, and related construction industry organizations worldwide. Adding FindMRO to its burgeoning emarket gave ENI-Net immediate scale in the volume of products it could offer its members as well as the added convenience of one-stop shopping. FindMRO is now hosted within the ENI-Net portal.

In fall 2000, FindMRO signed several more syndication deals:

- eFiltration, a global eHub for filtration products and services.
- GPS Marine Supply, a provider of supply chain solutions for the global shipping market.
- Smart Electrical, a provider of services for small to medium-sized electrical contractors.

These were all co-branded arrangements. Customers shopping in these e-markets can use FindMRO's search and procurement services.

Emphasis on Product Information, Availability, and Logistics

The underlying services that made FindMRO so valuable for the thousands of companies and e-markets that began to use its service were based on the core competencies Grainger was learning to leverage. As Ron explained, "Content is king. We like to get 15 to 20 product attributes in the database for each product. Then we add more attributes as we go. It's important to be able to get a supplier up and running quickly." He also explained that FindMRO's database and integrated ERP systems "put a big emphasis on product availability. Buyers will pay more for immediate access to products." And he said, "buyers like our fulfillment strategy. We take title to the goods, and we have them drop-shipped direct from the supplier. We bill the customer directly."

By mid 2000, seven months after its initial launch, FindMRO had 25,000 customer accounts with a revenue run rate of $70 million for its first year of operation.

THIRD PARALLEL INITIATIVE: GRAINGER AUCTION (MROverstocks)

By the fall of 1999, e-market momentum had begun to build. In particular, there was an increasing buzz around the idea of using B2B auctions to dispose of surplus inventory. Don Bielinski consulted with several of Grainger's largest suppliers and discovered that they were, indeed, interested in finding a way to participate in online auctions. But they worried about the sleaze factor that was rampant in consumer-to-consumer auctions. In the B2B world, buyers would need to have a high level of trust in the quality of the goods being provided and in the logistics surrounding payment and delivery of those goods. Don realized that the Grainger brand would engender the trust that business customers were seeking, and in November 1999 Grainger Auction was launched within the Grainger site. Once the auction site gained traction within the Grainger community, it was renamed MROverstocks in September 2000. This new name is more accurate (since the products on offer come from a variety of suppliers and buyers). It also will make it easier for Grainger to syndicate the service into others' offerings.

As with FindMRO, it took less than six months to bring this new business proposition online. MROverstocks also has something else in common with its sister venture. Although it has its own distinct Web site, MROverstocks is also a resource that can be imbedded into other B2B sites. In May 2000, Don described MROverstocks as "embryonic." The difficulty with auctions, he explained, is building critical mass. Some auction sites take off. Others stagnate. Building buzz and attracting buyers and sellers is an art form that takes time to learn, particularly if you don't have a background in the auction business. But Grainger has stuck with its auction business, waiting to see if it will grow to critical mass or simply provide an ancillary service for Grainger's suppliers needing to move surplus inventory.

FOURTH PARALLEL INITIATIVE: TOTAL MRO

Provide MRO Sourcing across All Industry E-Markets

In 1999 Don's e-commerce strategy team looked out over the B2B landscape and saw a need that Grainger had the core competencies to fulfill. As more and more large companies installed electronic procurement applications, Grainger could provide an e-commerce utility that would provide real-time product information and availability from thousands of suppliers. Grainger could provide a supplier-neutral, real-time, networked MRO catalog with decision-making and matchmaking applications and tools to a variety of e-markets and hence be accessible from companies' internal procurement applications.

The experiences Grainger had with OrderZone and with FindMRO were both instrumental in leading the company to this epiphany. OrderZone had proved that it was possible for Grainger to create a supplier-neutral e-marketplace that would be attractive to other distributors. And with FindMRO, Grainger had learned that the best way to extract the value from Grainger's former brokering services was to offer it as an electronic service that could be syndicated.

But OrderZone—now Works—had been designed with the needs of small to medium businesses in mind. It didn't offer the features that mattered to large companies.

E-procurement companies and e-market makers like Ariba and Commerce One looked at FindMRO and found it interesting but didn't want to offer. They didn't want to only offer a matchmaking service for 5 million products from 12,000 suppliers. Instead they needed to offer current and accurate product information, real-time inventory, location, availability, and rules-based pricing for 10 million products from thousands of manufacturers and distributors. This was a job for Grainger's digital business unit.

In October 1999, Don Bielinski appointed Liz Olig president of a new division whose mission was to develop an MRO utility that could be syndicated to a large number of e-procurement vendors and e-markets. Liz's goal was to recruit a large number of distributors and to quickly create the total MRO utility, which could then be plugged into the emarkets that were catering to large companies, hence the name "TotalMRO."

The services that TotalMRO offers to its participating distributors are:

- To cleanse their product data and put it into a single database.
- To display up-to-date pricing for all participating distributors and their customers.

- To display up-to-date product availability (inventory and location) for participating distributors.

Launched in March 2000, TotalMRO was first offered through Ariba. A few months later, it rolled out to other e-procurement providers, including SAP. Grainger believes TotalMRO to be well on its way to becoming a *de facto* standard in the B2B world.

Results

Grainger has invested aggressively in its Internet commerce initiatives. In the first six months of 2000, Grainger.com had $120 million of revenues. These were counted as part of the overall Grainger catalog business, which had revenues of $2.2 billion and total operating earnings of $175.2 million. (Grainger doesn't separate out the profits for its Grainger.com entity.) In the same six months, the combined digital businesses—OrderZone, FindMRO, TotalMRO, and MROverstocks—brought in $20 million in revenues but lost $27 million. Grainger expects to spend $120 million on its Internet businesses (including Grainger.com) in 2000 to produce and support $350 million in revenues. Grainger.com and FindMRO.com are close to being profitable. MROverstocks should achieve profitability in the coming years. TotalMRO needs more time before it reaches profitability.

Notice that Grainger's Internet team has tried out a variety of business models to anticipate and meet business customers' hard-to-define expectations. They've built a premier one-stop shopping e-marketplace for industrial supplies (Grainger.com). They've offered business customers the convenience of clicks-and-bricks ordering and fulfillment. They've provided e-businesses with a complete industrial supplies brokerage service that they can insert directly into their own e-business offerings (FindMRO.com). They've responded to customers' and suppliers' desires for trusted online auctions in the industrial supplies space. And they're pioneering with an e-utility offering that will give large corporate buyers real-time, dynamic access to hundreds of thousands of products from tens of thousands of suppliers.

The Grainger executive team has proved that it's willing to experiment and invest strategically. The investments Grainger has made to date and the learnings from those initiatives should keep it in the forefront of the B2B emarket world. Without these investments, learning, and flexibility, the company probably wouldn't have been able to become one of the key players in shaping the future of a customer-driven B2B ecosystem.

Takeaways

What fascinates us about Grainger's forays into e-business is how aggressive the company has been and how many parallel business ventures it has spawned. One thing to notice is that, just because a company is close to a hundred years old doesn't mean it can't "get it" and be willing to invest aggressively in experimenting with Internet-based business models. Grainger is determined to remain in a leadership position in its industry as that industry is transformed by technology and by customers' constantly changing requirements.

What's at the heart of all of these e-businesses is a priceless core knowledge-base. Grainger now has an ever-evolving product attribute data schema. For every product it offers in every category—from screws to office supplies—Grainger's merchandisers have had to figure out the dozen or more attributes and parameters that customers need to know about when making a buying decision. Customers care about price and availability. But before they worry about those two things they need to find the products that suit their needs and to be able to compare their characteristics in factors as varied as heat tolerance to viscosity. Over the five years it has been experimenting with building e-businesses, including huge product catalogs and a variety of search engines, Grainger's team has amassed world-class knowledge about how to describe and categorize products so that business customers can find what they need.

Because of the relative autonomy of these different business units and the different technical approaches each team has taken, there's no single database that is being leveraged over and over again. But there is clearly a core competency that keeps improving. And it's one that Grainger's competitors will be hard-pressed to emulate. They'll probably just give up and hand Grainger their product information to manage, which is, of course, what the company had in mind!

Patty's Suggestions for Grainger

I'd like to see Grainger do a better job of pulling together the core infrastructure and product databases and reusable services across all of these disparate businesses. I suspect they are in the process of doing just that. Rapid experimentation is great. But it's much easier to morph quickly and cost-effectively into different business models if you're working from a single core set of infrastructure, applications, databases, and data models.

I also believe that Grainger has delivered a consistent branded experience across all of these ventures. All of them have the inimitable Grainger stamp: make it easy for the business customer to find and procure the many hard-to-find products needed to run any large firm.

My biggest concern, however, lies with Grainger's seeming inattention to customer information and customer relationships. Despite its customer-centric culture, Grainger hasn't done enough to understand the needs of each individual customer. Grainger and its sister entities still think in terms of business accounts and customers' Web sites. They haven't yet done enough to build the kind of seamless customer relationship management system that's required to serve individuals who want to do business across touchpoints and channels.

Grainger also needs to give a lot more time and attention to understand more than just the buying scenario and begin streamlining other key customer scenarios—including plant design, facilities management, and replenishment. And each of these key customer scenarios should be instrumented so that Grainger can monitor the quality of customers' experiences as they interact with these various touchpoints and channels to achieve their outcomes.

A Sample Flight Deck for Grainger

	Navigation	Performance	Operations	Environment
Customer Numbers	Number of individual active end-customers Number of active business accounts Number of active end-customers per account Number of end-customers using online services	Percentage of end-customers who transact business online Growth in number of active business accounts Growth in number of end-users per account Growth in number of end-customers using online services	Percentage of business conducted online per customer Number of accounts acquired through Grainger e-utilities other than Grainger.com (e.g., FindMRO)	Number of total MRO customers Percentage of customers using other MRO sites
Customer Retention	Retention rate per end-customer Retention rate per business account Share of MRO-spend per customer/account Customer loyalty ratings per customer segment	Increase/decrease in retention rate per customer and account Increase/decrease in share of MRO-spend per customer and account	Recency of customer interactions by customer and account Frequency of customer interactions by customer and account	Competitors' retention rates Competitors' share of MRO-spend
Customer Experience	Customer satisfaction with Grainger products and services, by touchpoint Customer satisfaction by customer segment	Satisfaction with key customer scenarios Satisfaction with product availability Satisfaction with product information Satisfaction with decision-making tools Satisfaction with delivery Satisfaction with customer service	End-to-end performance of key customer scenarios Number of relevant attributes per product Success rates for locating and comparing desired products Average time and clicks for customer to complete Web order	Ease of use of competitive offerings Customer scenario performance of competitive offerings
Customer Spending	Revenues and profits per end-customer Revenues and profits per business account	Average revenue per order Change in customer spending by touchpoint Percentage of revenues derived from Web sales	Costs to serve per customer and account Costs to serve per touchpoint Average cost to process and fulfill orders (Web and non-Web)	Total MRO revenues Competitors' profits per customer Competitors' costs-to-serve

DESIGN TO MORPH: OBSERVATIONS ABOUT THE CASE STUDIES

These two stories are quite different. Okobank Group and W. W. Grainger are in different industries and countries. What they have in common is that they are both "old line" companies, yet they exhibit the characteristics of agile e-businesses. In both cases, the strategies are being led by long-time executives in each firm, executives who have proven track records. The boards of the two companies seem to be remarkably open to new ways of doing things and willing to take some risks by experimenting with several business models in parallel. There's a sense of urgency afoot. Notice that these two companies have taken similar approaches to branding yet different approaches to infrastructure.

Grainger and Okobank have both created a series of new brands for their new ventures. I believe they did this in part because their existing brands had too much perceived "baggage" for the new ventures they wanted to create. In my opinion, this may be a mistake. I would have recommended revitalizing the core brand and extending it and its associated branded experience as far as the brand could comfortably reach. In both cases the brand identities generate a lot of trust and customer loyalty. Yet Grainger opted for new branding because it was trying to attract competing suppliers as partners. It realized that these suppliers probably didn't want to be subsumed under the Grainger brand. In Oko's case, the core brand identity isn't valued by its new target market, so Oko is going with a brand name that young Finns know and appreciate: Sonera.

On the infrastructure front, Okobank Group has invested in and leveraged a single set of core electronic banking, mobile banking, and call center services along with the transactional systems that sit behind them. Grainger, on the other hand, has experimented with different e-commerce platforms, different product database architectures, and different search technologies with each of its ventures. What Grainger has leveraged, however, is the core knowledge its merchandisers have. Because Grainger has subject matter experts who understand industrial supplies, they know what factors are critical for customers making decisions. No matter what technology they employ, Grainger's e-businesses all make sure that customers see pictures of the items being sold; that they can locate them by category, function, part number, and brand; and that customers can enter key parameters to find the products that meet certain characteristics.

Yet both companies have followed a similar pattern in setting up each new business venture as a separately funded and semi-autonomous business unit. Okobank has taken the joint venture approach. Grainger has maintained ownership but done aggressive partnering. And when Grainger spun off its first ebaby (OrderZone) by merging it into Works.com, the company maintained a stake and, in fact, invested further.

The Ingredients Required to Change Your Business on the Fly

In summary, what are the secret ingredients for successfully transforming your business model(s) on the fly? There seem to be at least seven steps that are fundamental:

1. Start with an executive team that has vision, flexibility, and deep subject matter expertise as well as investors and backers who are willing to support that team.
2. Develop a core branded experience that customers love and appreciate; one that saves customers' time.
3. Invest heavily at the outset in a set of well thought out, robust, scalable, and fully functional infrastructure and business processes. Design this infrastructure to deliver your customer experience.
4. Listen deeply and carefully to the customers and suppliers who are in relationship with you. They will tell you exactly where your business needs to go. Take your cues from your end customers. Listen to your suppliers. Watch the market.
5. Spawn new e-businesses to meet emerging customer, market, and partner needs, always leveraging, evolving and reinforcing your core set of assets and services.
6. Educate your investors and board members as you go. Get them excited about designing the business on the fly.
7. Be prepared to cut your losses and walk away from models that don't work by closing them down or spinning them off. Harvest the education and experience from each one.

17

CONCLUSION: FLIGHT PLANS FOR THE CUSTOMER ECONOMY

The bad news is that today's demanding business and consumer customers can shoot your company down faster than ever before. Armed with information, access, and power, today's customers can dictate new practices and policies faster than your firm is likely to be able to implement them. Thanks to the Internet and to today's global media, customers will learn about and embrace new trends quickly. They'll also band together and complain vociferously about companies that ignore their interests and needs.

The good news is that your firm now has the wherewithal to compete aggressively for the hearts and minds of customers. Now for the first time in the history of business, you can actually monitor, in near-real time, many of the things that matter most to your customers. You have the opportunity to build, sustain, and instrument a great customer experience that will keep your customers coming back for more and recommending your firm to their friends and colleagues. You can provide your branded experience to customers in a whole slew of ways: face-to-face, over the phone, on the Web, using self-service kiosks, and via wireless devices. You can deliver your branded experience to customers by selling and servicing customers directly. You can offer your products and services through retailers or through dealers, resellers, or distributors. Or you can offer your products, services, and branded experience through a variety of e-markets and e-channels.

What's different today is that your customers will choose how and where you offer your products and services. And they'll expect to receive a consistent branded experience no matter which touchpoint or channel they use. The good news is that it's becoming increasingly easy to measure and monitor what matters to customers across channels and touchpoints.

QUICK REVIEW OF THE BASICS

Let's recap a few core concepts you'll need to keep uppermost in your mind as you prepare to embark on your next flight into the customer economy. Then we'll outline the key organizational and technology concepts you'll want to include in your flight plans. Finally, we'll provide some tips on how you can develop and refine your own instrumentation framework—your Customer Flight Deck. You'll find more detailed guidance and pre-flight checklists on our Web site, www.customerrevolution.net.

CUSTOMERS' DEMANDS WILL RESHAPE YOUR BUSINESS AND YOUR INDUSTRY

Remember the "digital dozen" customer demands that are currently in play (see Chapter 3). Don't try to ignore or refute these forces. Instead, embrace these new rhythms and improvise on them. Watch the early-adopter customers and the renegades both in your industry and in other, nonrelated industries. Devote a section in your regular management meetings to sharing customer patterns you've observed and discussing the moves you should be making to dance with your customers.

INVESTORS WILL WANT TO KNOW YOUR CUSTOMER NUMBERS

Don't expect to be able to raise money, sell your company, or keep investors happy without being prepared to share detailed information about your current customer capital, projected customer momentum, and total customer franchise. In the customer economy, the strength and value of your customer relationships count. When you project revenues and profits, tie those projections to the customer numbers that underlie those projections.

MANAGE YOUR COMPANY BY AND FOR CUSTOMER VALUE

Even if you don't agree with the notion that outsiders should have access to your customer numbers, you definitely need to be managing your company by and for customer value as soon as possible. You don't want to be flying blind through the customer economy. Set goals and measure how you're doing with:

- Growth in number of active customers
- Growth in customers' commitments to you
- Customer retention
- Customers' propensity to defect
- Customer referrals
- Customer acquisition costs
- Share of customers' wallets

Track these metrics in your Customer Flight Deck. Expose the Flight Deck to all your employees and partners, not just your top management team. Ensure that your employees and partners see these metrics and are committed to the importance of improving them for the profitability of your business.

DELIVER A GREAT TOTAL CUSTOMER EXPERIENCE

Of course, most of this book has been devoted to the "how to's" involved in delivering a total customer experience. You've read about the importance of creating and sustaining a branded experience, not just a brand. And you've read about how a variety of companies have approached some or all of the eight steps required to deliver a great experience. Here are some additional takeaways that may not have registered on your radar on the first read through:

- **Invest in Content Management and Leverage that Investment across Channels and Touchpoints.** For prospects and customers to have a great experience with your brand and your products, they'll need complete, actionable information. You'll need to go beyond providing marketing descriptions and technical support information. The quality and completeness of the information that surrounds your products pre-sales and post-sales is vitally important.

Today's customers want and need every bit of information at their fingertips, including accurate pricing, real-time inventory, product samples and trial versions, and vast competitive-product databases that they can search based on their own selection criteria.

All the information about your company, your products, and your services will need to be XML[12]-tagged and encoded with searchable attributes so that people and software programs can selectively retrieve only the most relevant and useful information and products for their purpose. This is merchandising taken to a whole new level for the digital age. And it will require a significant commitment in focus, people, and skill.

The good news is that, once you've made the investment in surrounding each of your products and services with actionable information, you can leverage that investment. By making the same actionable information and product attributes available to your retailers, your distributors, and in e-markets and e-catalogs, you'll have control over the branded experience your end customers and decision-makers have with your products across channels.

- **Design Your Customer-Facing Solutions Using Customer Scenarios.** For each of your key target customer segments, identify (with customers' help) the half-dozen or so key customer scenarios that really make a difference in the quality of their experience in doing business with you and your channel partners. Make sure that these customer scenarios work across the various interaction touchpoints and distribution channels your customers are likely to want to use.

- **Instrument Your Customer Scenarios.** For each customer scenario that you've explicitly designed or discovered (because customers began to do something a certain way), find out what steps

[12]XML stands for eXtensible Mark-Up Language—a standard encoding scheme for flagging searchable or important attributes or parameters in text. Items like the product description, price, weight, dimensions, ingredients, components, and so on, need to be tagged and identified in order for people and programs to be able to quickly and easily retrieve the items that meet customers' criteria.

and outcomes matter the most to the customers in each segment. Determine what that set of customers considers to be a satisfactory or delightful result for each task. Measure how well you and/or your partners are doing in executing that task according to customers' expressed priorities. This is how you "measure what matters to customers." These are the key metrics that you'll want to include in your Customer Flight Deck. Each set of employees may have a slightly different set of metrics they will monitor (i.e., the ones their team can control).

Pre-Flight Check: Organizational Readiness

How will you know if your business is likely to be able to thrive in the customer economy? Obviously there are no guarantees. But here are some of the things we suggest you take into account as you survey the worthiness of your craft:

- **Do You Have a Top Executive Who Owns the Total Customer Experience (TCE)?** This may be single person who has purview over all customers, or a group of cooperating executives, each of whom owns the customer experience for a customer segment. This is a full-time job. This is not an honorary title you give to someone who already has a full-time job. And this is not a lip-service position. Your entire staff, including the other executives, must be willing to accept directives and to meet objectives set by your TCE executive.
- **Do You Have an Operationally Efficient Engine?** How efficiently can your business deliver value to customers? How fast can you respond to customer demand? How quickly can you scale back? How well are you managing your profit margins so that you can compete in the customer economy? The winners in the customer economy are lean, mean, customer-focused companies that have the operating cash flow to invest in continuously improving the customer experience and in innovations that will keep them ahead of the competition. They manage their bottom lines carefully, yet they invest in the areas of the business that impact customers the most as well as in R&D.

- **Do You Have a Customer-Focused Culture?** How vital is it? Does your top executive live and breathe customer-centric values? Are these values kept alive and inculcated in old and new employees alike through stories? Is there agreement throughout the organization about who your end customers are and what matters to them? Is your compensation linked to customer loyalty and satisfaction metrics?

Pre-Flight Check: Technology Readiness

What are the main areas of technology investment you're going to need to make in order to thrive in the customer economy? Again, this will vary by company size and by industry, but here are some hints:

- **Do You Have a Strategic Technology Architect in Charge of Your Infrastructure?** Like your Total Customer Experience executive, this should be someone who has been with your firm for a long time. You're looking for the person who understands your existing systems deeply but who has imagination, robust design experience, a detailed knowledge of the latest technologies, and a passionate commitment to end customers. Many companies are fortunate to have a team of senior architects. Most companies are lucky if they have a single architect. This is typically not your CIO or your MIS director but someone who has been more directly involved in actual system design and implementation for a number of years. She should have experience designing using object-oriented techniques and using distributed computing approaches. She should be very Internet-savvy and tuned into mobile wireless technologies.

  While you may be able to outsource or buy many of your technology underpinnings and applications, you'll need a strong architect to design and oversee the development of a flexible, scalable architecture that will allow you to morph your business on the fly.

- **Do You Have a Customer Relationship Management Strategy and Architecture in Place?** To thrive in the customer economy, you'll need to provide your customers with a seamless way to manage their relationships with your company. Don't design your

CRM systems from the inside out to serve your employees. Design them from the outside in to serve your customers. Implement Internet-based CRM systems for your customers to use over the Web, via hand-held devices, or by phone. Then give that same information and assistance to the employees who serve your customers, whether they are in call centers, in stores, or at your dealer locations. Once you've provided customers and customer-facing employees with the information and streamlined processes that customers care about, you can add functionality that may be of value to your direct sales organization or to your marketing department.

- **Have You Provided Your Channel Partners with the Tools They Need to Co-Manage Your Customer Experience?** Don't make your agents, dealers, or retailers pay for systems that will streamline relationships with your customers and your firm. We think that the manufacturer or supplier of products should take responsibility for the branded experience, including providing channel partners with the tools they need to deliver that branded experience and to gather and share customer information with the manufacturer (with the customer's permission, of course).
- **Will Your Information Architecture Support Mobile Wireless Devices and Other Interaction Touchpoints?** Today's customers demand that you let them use a variety of devices and technologies to interact with your firm and its partners. That means that your information and technology architectures need to be ready to support whatever the next new thing is that customers adopt. And customers won't interact via only one type of device. They're very likely to begin a transaction via the phone, continue it using email, and complete it on their hand-held wireless personal digital assistants. Plan now to incorporate location-based services into your infrastructure. The world's wireless infrastructures are evolving rapidly to include global positioning services (GPS) as part of their core services. Today's Asian customers already have the ability to let service providers know where they're standing or riding when they initiate a request. Responses can be tailored to the context in which the customer finds him or herself (e.g., the nearest ATM machine, subway stop, or retailer with product in inventory). Tomorrow, location-based services will roll out in Europe. In a few

years, they'll be available in the United States (which currently lags the rest of the world in wireless infrastructure).

- **Is Your Architecture Making Full Use of XML, Business Events, Objects, and E-Services?** Flexibility is the name of the game in the customer economy. Today's senior technology architects now have at least a decade of experience designing and evolving distributed computing infrastructures that are robust, scalable, and dynamically flexible. They use business objects and business rules to create manageable yet dynamic systems. These objects spring into action triggered by business events according to a set of easy-to-change business rules. What's wonderful about this architectural approach is that it's well suited to a completely networked world. The objects in one company's system can make requests of objects in another company's system. The resulting services (e.g., query inventory, configure a product, process a transaction, debit or credit an account) are well understood and well protected. Yet there's no real limit to the scale to which these dynamic and flexible inter-business systems can scale. Today, the XML coding convention is used to tag the properties of objects, so that applications can discover and take advantage of one another's services and attributes over the 'Net. If your architect and designers aren't implementing using these kinds of principles, you may need to invest in people with more experience in distributed computing architectures.

- **Are You Able to Monitor the Quality of Your Customers' Experiences across Systems, Applications, and Organizational Boundaries?** Customers will be won or lost based on the quality of the end-to-end experience they have with your brand. It's time for you to put the probes in place to be able to monitor, at a very granular level, the things that matter the most to customers. You'll need to monitor end-to-end performance of customer scenarios that span multiple companies' systems. You'll need to monitor the ease with which customers are able to perform the tasks they need to do to accomplish the outcomes they care about (pay their bills, replenish their inventory, source new products, and so on). To do this, you'll need to instrument your applications and those of your partners so that you'll be able to monitor the timing and the performance and the outcomes of key business events. Which business events you need to monitor will change over time as you learn more about what customers want and need and how to continuously improve the quality of their experience. Monitoring what matters to customers is not a one-time investment or exercise. It's going to be a continuous learning virtual cycle. The more you can monitor and improve in the things that matter to customers, the more you'll discover what else matters and what else you need to monitor.

Where will you store all the information you gather about customers' experiences? We recommend that customer experience information and measures be added to your customer intelligence systems. In the past, companies have used customer intelligence to improve their marketing efforts. By analyzing customers' behaviors and demographics, companies' marketeers have been able to be more precise in targeting new offers and in finding new profitable customers. But instead of simply using customer intelligence to manipulate customers into buying more from you, think instead of using the power of customer intelligence to improve customers' experiences and strengthen their relationships with your firm and its brand.

Design a Customer Flight Deck Framework for Your Firm

If you want your company to be one of the beneficiaries of the customer revolution, if you want your company to foster fierce loyalty, *if you want your company to thrive in the customer economy,* we think you should embark on a strategy of giving your customers a great total customer experience, building on the eight steps we've described in this book. Each of the companies in the case studies is doing at least one of those steps very well. Imagine the company that fires on all eight cylinders!

But that's the trick, isn't it? It's one thing to look at each of these eight steps in isolation, and quite another to integrate them into a unified organism that can then master the three principles of the customer revolution. That's why we included sample Customer Flight Decks for the companies we wrote about. We wanted to make the point that each step to delivering a great total customer experience requires the company to evaluate very carefully what it's doing; after all, the Customer Flight Deck is a measurement and evaluation tool.

But as you read those case studies and looked through our sample Customer Flight Decks, you might have noticed that some metrics kept appearing from time to time. You might have noticed that one or more of the Flight Decks could have been a useful illustration for several of the case studies. You might have then concluded that a great total customer experience could be measured and evaluated with an overall Customer Flight Deck.

Well, we made one, using the individual Flight Decks from the case studies. We collected all the metrics into one framework, deleted the duplicates, and came up with a composite Flight Deck that still ran to more than five pages. That is emphatically not what a Flight Deck is supposed to do! If you monitor everything, you'll wallow in information overload.

But we also noticed that there were commonalities even among seemingly disparate metrics, commonalities that might lead to the development of "meta-metrics" that describe the kind of metrics they are. Back in the 1980s, for example, when Motorola was developing the six-sigma concept that has recently caught fire, their Total Quality Management (TQM) strategy rested on twin goals of six-sigma performance for *defect rate* and *cycle time.* In effect, they concluded that all internal metrics could ultimately be reduced to those two metrics, all others deriving in one way or another from them.

Without going to quite that extreme, we were able to "compress" the Flight Deck metrics into several classes of high-level meta-metrics. Visit our website (www.customerrevolution.net) to download a full description and explanation of the "Meta" Customer Flight Deck.

Time to Take Off into the Customer Economy

We hope you've found the operational framework and guidelines in these pages useful. We know there's a lot to digest here. The main ideas are simple. Manage your company by and for customer value. Measure and monitor what matters to customers. That's the basis of the Customer Flight Deck approach we're recommending.

Over the next two years, companies around the world will begin to pay a lot more attention to the quality of their customer relationships.

And because it's both desirable and possible, these firms will be putting into place the kind of operational framework we're recommending. They'll be monitoring customer value and customer experience in near-real time. Employees and business partners will have better, more timely information that will enable them to take actions to continuously improve both the customer experience and the efficiencies with which a great branded experience can be delivered. We hope you'll choose to be one of the companies that thrives in the customer economy.

Index

Note: Page numbers in **boldface** type refer to illustrations.

E

F

G

H

I

O

P

About the Author

Patricia B. Seybold is the founder and CEO of the Boston-based The Patricia Seybold Group (www.psgroup.com), which specializes in helping companies with their e-business strategies, best practices, and technology architecture decisions. Founded in 1978 and based in Boston, Massachusetts, the firm offers customized consulting services, an online strategic research service, executive workshops, and in-depth research reports. Patricia Seybold is also the author of the international bestseller *Customers.com*.